MOSES MAIMONIDES

MOSES MAIMONIDES
Physician, Scientist, and Philosopher

edited by
Fred Rosner, M.D.,
and
Samuel S. Kottek, M.D.

JASON ARONSON INC.
Northvale, New Jersey
London

This book was set in 10 pt. Schneidler by Lind Graphics of Upper Saddle River, New Jersey, and printed by Haddon Craftsmen in Scranton, Pennsylvania.

Copyright © 1993 by Fred Rosner and Samuel S. Kottek

10 9 8 7 6 5 4 3 2 1

All rights reserved. Printed in the United States of America. No part of this book may be used or reproduced in any manner whatsoever without written permission from Jason Aronson Inc. except in the case of brief quotations in reviews for inclusion in a magazine, newspaper, or broadcast.

Library of Congress Cataloging-in-Publication Data

Moses Maimonides : physician, scientist, and philosopher / edited by
   Fred Rosner and Samuel S. Kottek.
     p. cm.
   A collection of many of the papers presented at the symposium
"Maimonides as a physician, scientist and philosopher" held in
Jerusalem, Oct. 29–31, 1990–Pref.
   Includes bibliographical references and index.
   ISBN 0-87668-470-3
   1. Maimonides, Moses, 1135–1204–Congresses. 2. Medicine in
rabbinical literature–Congresses. 3. Medicine, Medieval–
Congresses. I. Rosner, Fred. II. Kottek, Samuel S.
R135.5.M58 1993
610–dc20   92-41882

Manufactured in the United States of America. Jason Aronson Inc. offers books and cassettes. For information and catalog write to Jason Aronson Inc., 230 Livingston Street, Northvale, New Jersey 07647.

Contents

Contributors ... ix

Preface ... xiii

President's Address ... xvii
    Joshua O. Leibowitz

I MAIMONIDES THE PHYSICIAN

1 Moses Maimonides the Physician ... 3
    Fred Rosner

2 The Medical Works of Maimonides: A Reappraisal ... 13
    Elinor Lieber

3 Maimonides on the Perfect Physician ... 25
    Samuel S. Kottek

4 Sex and Health in Maimonides ... 33
    W. Zev Harvey

5 An Encounter with Maimonides ... 41
    Haskell D. Isaacs

6 Maimonides' Concept of Mental Illness and Mental Health   49
   Harvey N. Kranzler

7 The Art of Cure: A Medical Text by Maimonides   59
   Uriel S. Barzel

II MAIMONIDES THE SCIENTIST

8 Maimonides and the Makings of Modern Science   67
   Nachum L. Rabinovitch

9 Maimonides' Stance on Astrology in Context: Cosmology,
   Physics, Medicine, and Providence   77
   Gad Freudenthal

10 Maimonides and Gersonides on Astronomy and Metaphysics   91
   Menachem Kellner

11 The Sciences as "Maidservants of the Torah" in
   Maimonides' Writings   97
   Yehudah Levi

12 Maimonides on the Distinction between Science and
   Pseudoscience   105
   J. David Bleich

III MAIMONIDES THE PHILOSOPHER

13 Medical Categories in Maimonidean Ethics   119
   Alexander Broadie

14 Well-Being of the Body or Welfare of the Soul:
   The Maimonidean Explanation of the Dietary Laws   127
   Hannah Kasher

15 Psychological Formulations in the Works of Maimonides   135
   Reuven P. Bulka

16 Maimonides' Philosophic Medicine   145
   David J. Eisenman

17 The Cosmology of Maimonides and His Critique of the
   Inconsistencies and the Insufficiency of the Aristotelian Physics 151
   Hubert Dethier

18 Some Insights into Maimonides' Approach to Mental Health Issues *Mordechai Reich*	167

IV ON AND AROUND MAIMONIDES

19 Remarks on Eight Pseudo-Maimonidean Treatises *Fred Rosner*	175
20 The State of Maimonidean Scholarship Today and Prospects for the Future *Jacob I. Dienstag*	185
21 Maimonides and the Cure-All Book *Yehudah Gellman*	189
22 Maimonides' Approach to Jewish Bioethics in the Areas of the Treatment of the Critically Ill and Abortion *Daniel B. Sinclair*	197
23 Maimonides, an Enemy of Authoritarianism *Alfred Soffer*	207
24 The State of Arabic Medicine at the Time of Maimonides According to Ibn Gumay's *Treatise on the Revival of the Art of Medicine* *Paul B. Fenton*	215
Notes	231
Index	273

Contributors

Uriel S. Barzel, M.D.
Professor of Medicine, Albert Einstein College of Medicine of Yeshiva University, Bronx, New York

Rabbi J. David Bleich
Rosh Yeshiva and Rosh Kollel le-Hora'ah, Rabbi Isaac Elchanan Theological Seminary, Yeshiva University; Professor of Law, Cardozo School of Law; and Herbert and Florence Tenzer Professor of Jewish Law and Ethics, Yeshiva University

Alexander Broadie, Ph.D.
Professor of Philosophy, University of Glasgow, Glasgow, Scotland

Rabbi Dr. Reuven P. Bulka
Rabbi, Congregation Machzikei Hadas, Ottowa, Ontario, Canada; Founder and Editor, *Journal of Psychology and Judaism*

Hubert Dethier, Ph.D.
Professor of Philosophy, University of Brussels, Brussels, Belgium

Professor Jacob I. Dienstag
Professor of Bibliography and Chief of the Judaica Division, Yeshiva University Library, New York (retired)

David J. Eisenman, M.D.
Resident Physician in Otolaryngology/Head and Neck Surgery, Yale University Medical Center, New Haven, Connecticut

Paul B. Fenton, Ph.D.
Professor of Jewish Literature, Department of Hebrew and Jewish Studies, University of Strasbourg, Strasbourg, France

Gad Freudenthal, Ph.D.
Research Fellow, *Centre National de la Recherche Scientifique (C.N.R.S.)*, Institut d'Histoire des Sciences, Paris, France

Yehudah Gellman, Ph.D.
Associate Professor, Department of Philosophy; Norbert Blechner Chair of Jewish Values, Ben Gurion University of the Negev, Beer Sheba, Israel

W. Zev Harvey, Ph.D.
Associate Professor, Department of Jewish Thought, Hebrew University of Jerusalem, Jerusalem, Israel

Haskell D. Isaacs, M.D., Ph.D.
Retired general physician; Research Associate, Cambridge University Library; Member of the Faculty of Oriental Studies and Supervisor in Arabic Studies, Cambridge, United Kingdom

Hannah Kasher, Ph.D.
Senior Lecturer, Department of Philosophy, Bar Ilan University, Ramat Gan, Israel

Menachem Kellner, Ph.D.
Wolfson Chair of Jewish Thought, University of Haifa, Haifa, Israel

Samuel S. Kottek, M.D.
Harry Friedenwald Chair of the History of Medicine, Hebrew University-Hadassah Medical School, Jerusalem, Israel

Harvey N. Kranzler, M.D.

Clinical Director, Bronx Children's Psychiatric Center, Bronx, New York; Associate Clinical Professor of Psychiatry, Albert Einstein College of Medicine of Yeshiva University, Bronx, New York

Joshua O. Leibowitz, M.D.

Emeritus Professor of the History of Medicine, Hebrew University-Hadassah Medical School, Jerusalem, Israel

Yehudah (Leo) Levi, Ph.D.

Professor of Physics/Electro-Optics and Rector Emeritus, Jerusalem College of Technology, Jerusalem, Israel

Elinor Lieber, M.B., Ch.B., D.P.H. (London)

University of Oxford Center for Postgraduate Hebrew Studies, Oxford, England (Correspondence to 2 Benson Place, Oxford OX2 6QH)

Rabbi Nachum L. Rabinovitch, Ph.D.

Dean, Yeshivat Birkat Moshe, Maaleh Adumim, Israel

Mordechai Reich, Ph.D.

Director, Beit Schemesh School Psychological Service, Jerusalem, Israel

Fred Rosner, M.D.

Director, Department of Medicine, Mount Sinai Services at Queens Hospital Center, Jamaica, New York; Professor of Medicine, Mount Sinai School of Medicine of the City University of New York, New York, New York

Daniel B. Sinclair, LLB, LLM, Dr. Juris

Lecturer in Jewish Law, Tel Aviv University; Associate Research Fellow, Institute for Research in Jewish Law, The Hebrew University of Jerusalem, Jerusalem, Israel

Alfred Soffer, M.D.

Editor-in-Chief, *Chest*; Professor of Medicine, Chicago Medical School, Chicago, Illinois

Preface

A three-day symposium entitled "Maimonides as a Physician, Scientist, and Philosopher" was held in Jerusalem on October 29–31, 1990. The symposium was cosponsored by the Ministry of Religious Affairs of the Israeli government, the Hebrew University of Jerusalem, and the Ben-Zvi Institute of Jerusalem for the Study of Jewish Communities in the East. The symposium was organized by ISAS International Seminars, based in Jerusalem, and originally included a tour of Spain, Morocco, Egypt, and Israel to trace the footsteps of Maimonides from his birthplace to the site of his grave in Tiberias. The tour had to be canceled because of the tense atmosphere in the Middle East immediately preceding the Gulf War against Iraq.

This book is a collection of many of the scholarly and erudite papers presented at the symposium. Presentations portrayed the contributions of Maimonides to the medical, scientific, and philosophic knowledge of his day and the relevance of his work to modern medicine, science, and philosophy. The lecturers presented a fresh look at Maimonides' work in light of newly discovered sources and a reevaluation of his relationship to the work of other philosophers, scientists, and physicians. The distinguished faculty whose contributions are contained in this volume are cited in the list of contributors.

The attendees at the symposium—scholars, physicians, and lay people alike—increased their knowledge and appreciation of Maimonides in their areas of interest. They also achieved a deeper understanding of Jewish attitudes toward issues of medical and scientific practice, philosophy, and ethics.

I am deeply indebted to my co-editor, Professor Samuel Kottek, a renowned medical historian, for all his help and guidance in bringing this volume to publication. I also thank the very professional and expert staff of Jason Aronson, Inc., who worked hard and meticulously to insure the outstanding quality of the finished product. Finally, I appreciate the vision and foresight of Arthur Kurzweil, Vice-President of Jason Aronson, Inc., in seeking to bring to the public high quality works of Maimonidean scholarship and the Maimonidean controversy.

Fred Rosner, M.D., F.A.C.P.

In his essay on "Moses Maimonides the Physician," Harry Friedenwald – a noted Baltimore ophthalmologist and faithful supporter of Jerusalem's Hebrew University at its very beginning – wrote: "Maimonides appeared at the time of the glorious evening glow of Arabic culture. The sun was soon to set on its science, philosophy and medicine. Maimonides imbibed its learning and scholarship wholly. . . ."[1]

Both Jews and Arabs consider Maimonides (Moses ben Maimon) among their most illustrious scholars. All ten authentic medical works authored by Maimonides were written in Arabic. Most of them were addressed to Arabic rulers or dignitaries. Although it may be argued that the foremost considerations of Rabbi Moses ben Maimon were directed toward theology and philosophy, and that only family and financial reasons induced him to practice medicine, his substantiality suffers no dichotomy. Maimonides was indeed an exemplary personification of the accomplished medieval scholar. He added to his high degree of learning an unusual – though not unheard of – bent to criticism toward the sources he used and perused. "Not pretending to be original, Maimonides manifested his own view and approach by his discriminating choice of the material handed down from antiquity."[2]

In his introduction to his *Pirké Moshe (Moses' Aphorisms),* Maimonides explains the propaedeutic value of his work, as well as the rationale for his choice of citations from the works of previous authors:

> I have selected the following aphorisms for myself to facilitate remembering them. Similarly, anyone who is at my level of learning, or he who is less knowledgeable than I, can benefit from them. I have not selected and explained them for the use of someone at the level of Galen or close to it. . . . Where I believe that I removed some doubts, be it in substantiating the correctness of a subject matter or in clarifying a concept, others may have had no doubts whatsoever [in these matters] owing to their degree of perfection in the Art.[3]

This modest epistemological statement may be considered relevant to the whole work of Maimonides, with the exception of his theological writings. The latter imply a selection as well, but he there chooses and decides from a position of authority. There might be – and there were – differences of opinion, but the approach was definitely normative in essence.

In his scientific and philosophical writings, Maimonides forwards the "state of the art" to the best of his vast knowledge. This means much more than thorough learning; it means also thoughtful selection, careful clarification, concise and precise exposition, and confrontation with his personal experience.

These qualities were commended and eulogized in a number of papers that were read at the Symposium on "Maimonides as a Physician, Scientist, and Philosopher" that was convened in Jerusalem October 29–31, 1990. In the troubled weeks and months that preceded the Gulf War, these three busy days were experienced by most participants like living in an oasis of peace and learning. The meeting was evidently multidisciplinary; the lecturers came from several universities in Israel and from the United States, Canada, England, France, and Belgium. The presidency was quite naturally held by the veteran of medical historical and Maimonidean research, Professor Joshua O. Leibowitz. Three chairmen took their share in the preparation of the meeting: Dr. Menachem Ben-Sasson, a specialist of medieval Egyptian Jewry; Professor Fred Rosner, the well-known translator and editor of Maimonides' medical works; and myself. This symposium was the fourth of a series initiated in 1981, the former meetings being devoted to various aspects of medicine in the Bible and Talmud.

I would like to thank particularly Dr. Ben-Sasson and the Ben-Zvi Institute for the Study of Jewish Communities in the East for their dedicated help and participation in planning and organizing this conference and, last but not least, Professor Fred Rosner, who accomplished most of the editorial work on this book in his usual quick and efficient way.

The main acknowledgments, however, go to the contributors who have made this volume more than just another entry in the bulky Maimonidean bibliography.

Samuel S. Kottek, M.D.

President's Address

Joshua O. Leibowitz
President, Symposium, "Maimonides as a Physician, Scientist, and Philosopher"

Although Maimonides has been the subject of much research and writing ever since his death, it is only in the last hundred years that there has been a definitive assessment of his medical literary achievements and ideas. The labor goes on to this day, when new material is being discovered, more texts are being edited in scholarly fashion, and the integration of facts and ideas into ever-expanding medical historical research is in process. Apart from historical facts about his person and his works, the Jews regard Maimonides as the ideal figure of a physician. The longing both of the public and of the professional world to create such an image was partly realized in his personality. Our generation, with all its technological advances, is undergoing a spiritual crisis and has greater need than ever for a guiding figure to look up to. In medicine, as in other spheres of human civilization, we can find inspiration and guidance in a physician of the past, broadminded, striving for accomplishment, scholar and humanist.

I

Maimonides the Physician

1

Moses Maimonides the Physician

Fred Rosner

Moses, son of Maimon (acronym RaMBaM in Hebrew, Abu Imran Musa Ibn Maimun in Arabic, and Maimonides in Greek)[1] was born in Cordova, Spain, on March 30, 1135 (or 1138 according to several recent essays) corresponding to Passover eve of the Hebrew year 4895. His mother died in childbirth and consequently his father *Dayan* (judge) Maimon raised him. Persecution by the Almohades, a fanatical group from North Africa, forced the Maimon family to flee Cordova in the year 1148. The family wandered through southern Spain and northern Africa for the next ten years and finally settled in Fez, Morocco.

Little is known of Maimonides' early life and medical education. There are no sources indicating that Maimonides had any formal medical education. In his *Medical Aphorims* (see below), he mentions "the elders before whom I have read"; this is the only allusion to some semiprivate study of medicine. A few times he mentions the son of Ibn Zuhr, from whom he heard teachings of the latter's illustrious father (the great physician Abu Merwan Ibn Zuhr) whom Maimonides held in great esteem.

Maimonides must have been an avid reader, since his medical writings show a profound knowledge of ancient Greek authors in Arabic translations and Moslem medical works. Hippocrates, Galen, and Aristotle were some of his Greek medical inspirations, and Rhazes of Persia, Al Farabi, and Ibn Zuhr, the Spanish-Arabic physician, are Moslem authors frequently quoted by Maimonides.

The Maimon family left Morocco in 1165, traveled to Palestine, landing in Acco, and from there to Egypt, where they settled in Fostat (old Cairo). Maimonides turned to medicine as a livelihood only after the death of his father in 1166 and the death of his brother in a shipwreck shortly thereafter. Maimonides was left with his brother's wife and child to support and, after a year's illness following his brother's death, entered into the practice of medicine. He was appointed Court Physician to Vizier Al-Fadhil, Regent of Egypt during the absence of the Sultan, Saladin the Great, who was fighting in the Crusades in Palestine. It was at this time that Richard the Lion-Hearted, also fighting in the Crusades, is reported to have invited Maimonides to become his personal physician, an offer which Maimonides declined. His reputation as a physician grew in Egypt and neighboring countries, and his fame as theologian and philosopher became worldwide.

In 1193, Saladin died and his eldest son, Al Afdal Nur ad Din Ali, a playboy, succeeded him. As a result, Maimonides' medical duties became even heavier, as described in the famous letter he wrote to his friend, disciple, and translator, Rabbi Samuel Ibn Tibbon, in the year 1199:

> I live in Fostat and the Sultan resides in Cairo; these two places are two Sabbath limits [marked-off areas around a town within which it is permitted to move on the Sabbath; approximately one and one-half miles] distant from each other. My duties to the Sultan are very heavy. I am obliged to visit him every day, early in the morning, and when he or any of his children or concubines are indisposed, I cannot leave Cairo but must stay during most of the day in the palace. It also frequently happens that one or two of the officers fall sick and I must attend to their healing. Hence, as a rule, every day, early in the morning, I go to Cairo and, even if nothing unusual happens there, I do not return to Fostat until the afternoon. Then I am famished but I find the antechambers filled with people, both Jews and Gentiles, nobles and common people, Judges and policemen, friends and enemies – a mixed multitude who await the time of my return.
>
> I dismount from my animal, wash my hands, go forth to my patients, and entreat them to bear with me while I partake of some light refreshment, the only meal I eat in twenty-four hours. Then I go to attend to my patients and write prescriptions and directions for their ailments. Patients go in and out until nightfall, and sometimes, even as the Torah is my faith, until two hours and more into the night. I converse with them and prescribe for them even while lying down from sheer fatigue. When night falls, I am so exhausted, that I can hardly speak.
>
> In consequence of this, no Israelite can converse with me or befriend me [on religious or community matters] except on the Sabbath. On that day, the whole congregation, or at least, the majority, comes to me after the morning service, when I instruct them as to their proceedings during the whole week. We study together a little until noon, when they depart. Some of them return and read with me after the afternoon services until evening prayer. In this manner, I

spend the days. I have here related to you only a part of what you would see if you were to visit me.

Maimonides was also the spiritual leader of the Jewish community of Egypt. At age 33, in the year 1168, shortly after settling in Fostat, he completed his first major work, the *Commentary on the Mishnah*. In 1178, ten years later, his *magnum opus,* the *Mishneh Torah,* was finished. This monumental work is a fourteen-book compilation of all biblical and talmudic law and remains a classic to this day. In 1190, Maimonides' great philosophical masterpiece, the *Guide for the Perplexed,* was completed.

Maimonides died on December 13, 1204 (*Tebet* 20, 4965, in the Hebrew calendar), and was allegedly buried in Tiberias. Legend relates that Maimonides' body was placed upon a donkey and the animal set loose. The donkey wandered and wandered and finally stopped in Tiberias. That is the site where the great Maimonides was buried.

Maimonides was a prolific writer. We have already mentioned his famous trilogy, the *Commentary on the Mishnah,* the *Mishneh Torah,* and the *Guide for the Perplexed.* Each of these works alone would have indelibly recorded Maimonides' name for posterity. However, in addition to these, he also wrote a *Book on Logic (Maamar ha-Higayon),* a *Book of Commandments (Sefer ha-Mitzvot),* an *Epistle to Yemen (Iggeret Teman),* a *Treatise on Resurrection (Maamar Tehiyat ha-Metim),* commentaries on several tractates of the Talmud, and over 600 responsa. Several additional works, including the so-called *Prayer of Maimonides,*[2] are attributed to him but are, in fact, spurious, the prayer having been written in 1783.

Over and above all the books we have just enumerated, Maimonides also wrote ten medical works.[3] The following is a brief examination and analysis of these medical writings. The first is called *Extracts from Galen* or *The Art of Cure.* Galen's medical writings consist of over 100 books and required two volumes just to catalogue and index them all. Maimonides therefore extracted what he considered the most important of Galen's pronouncements and compiled them verbatim in a small work intended primarily for the use of students of medicine. This work, as all of Maimonides' medical books, was originally written in Arabic. At least two Arabic manuscripts exist today, one in Hebrew and one in Arabic letters. This work has heretofore never been published in any language, but brief excerpts therefrom in both English and Hebrew appeared in a Hebrew periodical.[4] The complete English and Hebrew translations by Uri Barzel are in press.

The second of Maimonides' medical writings is the *Commentary on the Aphorisms of Hippocrates.* The famous aphorisms of Hippocrates were translated from the Greek into Arabic by Hunain Ibn Ishaq in the ninth century. Maimonides wrote his commentary on this translation. Two incomplete Arabic manuscripts exist. A good medieval translation into Hebrew was made by Moses ben Samuel Ibn Tibbon. In this work, Maimonides occasionally criticizes both Hippocrates and Galen where either of these Greeks differs from his own views. For example, in chapter five, Hippocrates is quoted as having said, "a boy is born from the right ovary, a girl from the left," to which Maimonides remarks: "A man should be either prophet or genius to know this." The introduction to this work was edited in the original Arabic, with two Hebrew and one German translation, by Steinschneider in 1894.[5] The entire work was published by Hasida in 1935[6] and again in a definitive edition by Muntner in 1961.[7] Bar Sela and Hoff published Maimonides' interpretation of the first aphorism of Hippocrates.[8] This is the famous aphorism which has been called the motto or credo of the art of medicine: "Life is short, and the art long, the occasion fleeting, experience fallacious and judgment difficult. The physician must not only be prepared to do what is right himself, but must also make the patient, the attendants and the externals cooperate." I published Maimonides' *Introduction* to this work[9] as well as the entire work[10] in English.

The third of Maimonides' medical works, the most voluminous of all, is the *Medical Aphorisms of Moses (Pirké Moshe)*. This book is comprised of fifteen hundred aphorisms based mainly on Greco-Latin medical writers. There are twenty-five chapters, each dealing with a different area of medicine, including anatomy, physiology, pathology, symptomatology and diagnosis, etiology of disease and therapeutics, fevers, bloodletting, laxatives and emetics, surgery, gynecology, hygiene, exercise, bathing, diet, drugs, and medical curiosities. A complete Arabic original manuscript exists in the Gotha library in Germany. A Hebrew translation was made in the thirteenth century and published in Lemberg, Poland, in 1834 and again in Vilna in 1888.[11] The definitive Hebrew edition is that of Muntner, dated 1959.[12] Maimonides' Aphorisms[13] were also translated into Latin in the thirteenth century and appeared as an incunabulum in Bologne in 1489 and again in Venice in 1497, followed by several printed Latin editions.[14] Only small fragments of this work appeared in a Western language[15] until the complete English version by myself and Muntner was published in two volumes[16] and reprinted.[17]

A few excerpts from this most important work will give the reader the flavor of Maimonidean medical thinking. Maimonides speaks of cerebrovascular disease: "one can prognosticate regarding a stroke, called apoplexy. If the attack is severe, he will certainly die but if it is minor, then cure is possible, though difficult . . . the worst situation that can occur following a stroke is the complete irreversible suppression of respiration."

Maimonides explains that diabetes mellitus was seldom seen in cold Europe, whereas it was frequently encountered in warm Africa. He also reports this disease to be associated with the imbibition of suave water of the Nile (Maimonides lived in Fostat, or old Cairo). There follows the

English translation of this most important aphorism no. 69 from the eighth chapter:

> Moses says: I, too, have not seen it in the West [Spain, where Maimonides was born, or Morocco, where he fled from the persecution of the Almohades] nor did any one of my teachers under whom I studied mention that they had seen it [diabetes]. However, here in Egypt, in the course of approximately ten years, I have seen more than twenty people who suffered from this illness. This brings one to the conclusion that this illness occurs mostly in warm countries. Perhaps the waters of the Nile, because of their suaveness, may play a role in this.

A very accurate description of obstructive emphysema is provided during a lengthy discussion of respiratory disease: "... reason [for respiratory embarrassment] is narrowing of the organs of respiration, then the breast is seen to greatly expand. This expansion produces rapid and cut off [respirations]."

Clubbing of the fingers associated with pulmonary disease, already described by Hippocrates, is beautifully depicted: "With an illness affecting the lungs called *hasal,* namely, phthisis, there develops rounding of the nail as a rainbow." The signs and symptoms of pneumonia are remarkably accurately described: "The basic symptoms which occur in pneumonia and which are never lacking are as follows: acute fever, sticking [pleuritic] pain in the side, short rapid breaths, serrated pulse and cough, mostly [associated] with sputum." Hepatitis is just as beautifully described: "The signs of liver inflammation are eight in number as follows: high fever, thirst, complete anorexia, a tongue which is initially red and then turns black, biliary vomitus, initially yellow egg yolk in color which later turns dark green, pain on the right side which ascends up to the clavicle... Occasionally a mild cough may occur and a sensation of heaviness which is first felt on the right side and then spreads widely."

So much for the *Medical Aphorisms of Moses.*[18]

The fourth of Maimonides' medical writings is his *Treatise on Hemorrhoids.* This work was written for a nobleman, as Maimonides says in the introduction – probably a member of the sultan's family. There are seven chapters dealing with normal digestion, foods harmful to patients with hemorrhoids, beneficial foods, general and local therapeutic measures such as sitz baths, oils, and fumigations. Maimonides disapproves of bloodletting or surgery for hemorrhoids except in very severe cases. Maimonides' whole approach to the problem seems to bespeak a modern medical trend. The *Treatise on Hemorrhoids* was first published by Kroner in 1911 in Arabic, Hebrew, and German.[19] A general description of the work in English appeared in 1927 by Bragman.[20] The definitive Hebrew edition is that of Muntner, dated 1965,[21] and an English translation of the entire work was published by myself and

Muntner.[22] An improved, more fully annotated English translation was recently published.[23]

In the introduction to this work, Maimonides describes the reason for writing it:

> There was a youth, [descended] from knowledgeable, intelligent and comprehending forebears, from a prominent and renowned family, distinguished and charitable and of great means, in whom the affliction of hemorrhoids occurred at the mouth of the rectum, that interested me in his problem and placed the task [of healing them] upon me. These irritated him on some occasions and he treated them in the customary therapeutic manner until the pain subsided and the protruding hemorrhoids became reduced and returned to the interior of the body so that his [bodily] functions returned to normal. Because this [illness] recurred many times, he considered having them extirpated in order to uproot this malady from its source so that it not return again. I informed him of the danger inherent in this, in that it is not clear if these hemorrhoids are of the variety which should be excised or not, since there are people in whom they have once been [surgically] extirpated and in whom other hemorroids develop. This is because the causes which gave rise to the original ones remained and, therefore, new ones develop.

Here Maimonides provides an insight into the etiology of disease in general, in that he regards operative excision of hemorrhoids with skepticism, because surgery does not remove the underlying causes that produced the hemorrhoids in the first place.

The fifth work is Maimonides' *Treatise on Sexual Intercourse,* written for the nephew of Saladin, the Sultan al Muzaffar Omar Ibn Nur Ad-Din. The sultan indulged heavily in sexual activities and asked Maimonides, his physician, to aid him in increasing his sexual potential. The work consists mainly of recipes of foods and drugs which are either aphrodisiac or anti-aphrodisiac in their actions. Maimonides advises moderation in sexual intercourse and describes the physiology of sexual temperaments. There are two versions to this book, a short authentic and a longer spurious version. Both were first edited and published by Kroner in 1906 in Hebrew and German.[24] Ten years later, Kroner published the true short version from the original Arabic manuscript in Granada.[25] An Italian edition appeared in 1906,[26] and English[27] and Spanish[28] translations were published in 1961. The definitive Hebrew edition of both authentic[29] and spurious[30] versions of Maimonides' books on sex is that of Muntner, dated 1965. A new English translation of the true work by myself was published[31] and reprinted.[32]

The sixth medical book of Moses Maimonides is his *Treatise on Asthma.* The patient for whom this book was written suffered from violent headaches which prevented him from wearing a turban. The patient's symptoms began with a common cold, especially in the rainy season, forcing him to gasp for air until phlegm was expelled. The patient asked whether a change of climate might be beneficial. Maimonides, in thirteen chapters, explained the rules of diet and climate in general and those rules specifically suited for asthmatics. He outlined the recipes of food and drugs and described the various climates of the Middle East. He stated that the dry Egyptian climate is efficacious for sufferers from this disease and warned against the use of very powerful remedies. The first critical edition of this work appeared in Hebrew in 1940, edited by Muntner.[33] Additional manuscripts became available after World War II and a corrected, improved, and revised second Hebrew edition appeared in 1963.[34] Only three hundred copies of this edition were printed and thus a third edition was published by Muntner in 1965.[35] An English version of Maimonides' book on asthma was published in 1963[36] and a French translation in 1965.[37] I have commented extensively on this work elsewhere.[38]

The last chapter of this work deals with concise admonitions and aphorisms which Maimonides considered "useful to any man desirous of preserving his health and administering to the sick." The chapter begins as follows: "The first thing to consider . . . is the provision of fresh air, clean water and a healthy diet." Fresh air is described in some detail: "City air is stagnant, turbid and thick, the natural result of its big buildings, narrow streets, the refuse of its inhabitants . . . one should at least choose for a residence a wide-open site . . . living quarters are best located on an upper floor . . . and ample sunshine. . . . Toilets should be located as far as possible from living rooms. The air should be kept dry at all times by sweet scents, fumigation and drying agents. The concern for clean air is the foremost rule in preserving the health of one's body and soul." Let our air-pollution-control programmers take cognizance of Maimonides' prophetic statements nearly 800 years ago.

The seventh medical work of Maimonides is his *Treatise on Poisons and Their Antidotes.* It is one of the most interesting and popular works because it is very scientific and modern in its approach and was, therefore, used as a textbook of toxicology throughout the Middle Ages. The book was written at the request of Maimonides' noble protector, the Grand Vizier and Supreme Judge Al Fadhil, who asked Maimonides to write a treatise on poisons for the layman by which to be guided before the arrival of a physician. In the introduction, Maimonides praises Al Fadhil and his feats in war and peace. He mentions Al Fadhil's orders to import from distant lands ingredients lacking in Egypt but necessary for the preparation of two antidotes against poisonings, the "great theriac" and the "electuary of Mithridates."

The first section of the book deals with snake and dog bites and with scorpion, bee, wasp, and spider stings. The first chapter concerns the conduct of the victim in general. Thus Maimonides states as follows:

> When someone is bitten, immediate care should be taken to tie the spot above the wound as fast as possible to prevent the poison from spreading throughout

the body; in the meantime, another person should make cuts with a lancet directly above the wound, suck vigorously with his mouth and spit out. Before doing that, it is advisable to disinfect the mouth with olive oil, or with spirit in oil.... Care should be taken that the sucking person has no wound in his mouth, or rotten teeth ... should there be no man available to do the sucking, cupping-glasses should be applied, with or without fire; the heated ones have a much better effect because they combine the advantages of sucking and cauterizing at the same time.... Then apply the great theriac.... Apply to the wound some medicine which should draw the poison out of the body.

In his book on poisons, Maimonides also describes the long incubation period for rabies (up to forty days). Numerous Arabic, Hebrew, and Latin manuscripts are extant.[39] A German translation was published in 1873 by Steinschneider.[40] A French translation appeared in 1865 by Rabbinowicz and was reprinted in 1935.[41] An English translation of Steinschneider's German version is that of Bragman in 1926.[42] The definitive Hebrew edition of Muntner appeared in 1942,[43] and Muntner's English version was published in 1966.[44] I commented on this work[45] and published a fully annotated new English translation with commentary and bibliography.[46]

The eighth book is the *Regimen of Health (Regimen Sanitatis),* which Maimonides wrote in 1198 during the first year of the reign of Sultan Al Malik Al Afdal, eldest son of Saladin the Great. The sultan was a frivolous and pleasure-seeking man of thirty, subject to fits of melancholy or depression due to his excessive indulgences in wine and women and his warlike adventures against his own relatives and in the Crusades. He complained to his physician of constipation, dejection, bad thoughts, and indigestion. Maimonides answered his royal patient in four chapters. The first chapter is a brief abstract on diet taken mostly from Hippocrates and Galen. The second chapter deals with advice on hygiene, diet, and drugs in the absence of a physician. The third extremely important chapter contains Maimonides' concept of "a healthy mind in a healthy body," one of the earliest descriptions of psychosomatic medicine. He indicates that the physical well-being of a person is dependent on his mental well-being and vice versa. The final chapter summarizes his prescriptions relating to climate, domicile, occupation, bathing, sex, wine drinking, diet, and respiratory infections.

The whole treatise on the *Regimen of Health* is short and concise but to the point. This is the reason for its great success and popularity throughout the years. It is extant in numerous manuscripts. A Hebrew translation from the original Arabic was made by Moses ben Samuel Ibn Tibbon in 1244, and this version was reprinted several times in the nineteenth century (Prague 1838, Jerusalem 1885, Warsaw 1886). Two Latin translations were made in the thirteenth century. Several fifteenth-century incunabula and sixteenth-century editions of these Latin versions exist. One of the first Hebrew editions is that of Bloch in 1838.[47] An annotated German translation by Winternitz was published in 1843;[48] and Russian[49] and Spanish[50] translations in 1930 and 1961, respectively. The Arabic text with German and Hebrew translations was published by Kroner in 1925,[51] although he had already published the all-important chapter three dealing with psychosomatic medicine eleven years earlier in 1914.[52]

English translations of chapter three have been published by Bragman,[53] Savitz,[54] and Butterworth[55] and of the first two chapters by Skoss.[56] The definitive Hebrew edition is that of Muntner dated 1957,[57] although the Maimonidean bibliographer Dienstag[58] cites several additional Hebrew editions. Two English translations of the entire work were published: in 1958 by Gordon[59] and in 1964 by Bar Sela, Hoff and Faris.[60] Another German translation by Muntner appeared in 1966.[61] These numerous editions in many languages attest to the importance and popularity of Maimonides' *Regimen of Health*.

The ninth medical writing of Maimonides is the *Discourse on the Explanation of Fits*. This work has been called Maimonides' swan song, as it was thought to be the last of his medical works, having been written in the year 1200, four years before his death. It was also written for the Sultan Al Malik Al Afdal and is sometimes considered to represent chapter five of the *Regimen of Health*. The sultan persisted in his overindulgences and wrote to Maimonides, who was himself ill, asking advice about his health. Maimonides confirms most of the prescriptions of the sultan's other physicians regarding wine, laxatives, bathing, exercise, and the like and, near the end, gives a very detailed hour-by-hour regimen for the daily life of the sultan. The original Arabic was edited and published with Hebrew and German translations by Kroner in 1928.[62] English editions by Bar Sela, Hoff and Faris in 1964[63] and myself and Muntner in 1969,[64] another German version by Muntner in 1966,[65] and another Hebrew edition by Muntner in 1969[66] are available. The most recent and best edition is that by Leibowitz and Marcus, entitled "On the Causes of Symptoms,"[67] in which the text is presented in four languages (Arabic, Hebrew, Latin, and English) and is accompanied by a running commentary, explanatory essays, and a comprehensive catalog of drugs.

The final authentic medical book of Maimonides is the *Glossary of Drug Names*. This work was discovered by Max Meyerhof, an ophthalmologist in Egypt, in the Aya Sofia library in Istanbul, Turkey, as Arabic manuscript no. 3711.[68] Dr. Meyerhof edited the original Arabic and provided a French translation with a detailed commentary, which he published in 1940 in Cairo.[69] A Hebrew edition by Muntner appeared in 1969,[70] and my English translation was published in 1979.[71] The work is essentially a pharmacopoeia and consists of 405 short paragraphs containing names of drugs in Arabic, Greek, Syrian, Persian, Berber, and Spanish.

In summary, Maimonides' medical writings are varied, comprising extracts from Greek medicine, a series of monographs on health in general and several diseases in particular, and a more recently discovered pharmacopoeia demonstrating Maimonides' extensive knowledge of Arabic medical literature and his familiarity with several languages. Some people feel that Maimonides' medical writings are not as original as his theological and philosophical writings. However, his medical works demonstrate the same lucidity, conciseness, and formidable powers of systematization and organization so characteristic of all his writings. The *Book on Poisons,* the *Regimen of Health,* and the *Medical Aphorisms of Maimonides* became classics in their fields in medieval times.

I would like to conclude by citing a paragraph from my first paper on Maimonides:[72]

Maimonides died on December 13, 1204 [*Tebet* 20, 4965 in the Hebrew calendar] and was buried in Tiberias, Palestine. The Christian, Moslem and Jewish worlds mourned him. His literary ability was incredible and his knowledge encyclopedic. He mastered nearly everything known in the fields of theology, mathematics, law, philosophy, astronomy, ethics, and, of course, medicine. As a physician, he treated disease by the scientific [as opposed to empiric and/or popular] method, not by guesswork, superstition, or rule of thumb. His attitude towards the practice of medicine came from his deep religious background, which made the preservation of health and life a divine commandment. His inspiration lives on through the years and his position as one of the medical giants of history is indelibly recorded. He was physician to Sultans and Princes, and as Sir William Osler said, "He was Prince of Physicians." The heritage of his great medical writings is being more and more appreciated. To the Jewish people he symbolized the highest spiritual and intellectual achievement of man on this earth; as so aptly stated, "From Moses to Moses there never arose a man like Moses," and none has since.

2

The Medical Works of Maimonides: A Reappraisal

Elinor Lieber

There exist few scholarly appraisals—let alone reappraisals—of the medical works of Maimonides, taken as a whole, but much uncritical prejudice. The need for a reappraisal was brought home to me not long ago, in connection with a program of evening lectures on Maimonides that the Jewish students at Oxford University organized recently as part of the presently fashionable search for our cultural "roots." The series was to cover all aspects of his life and works, with one exception: his medical writings. On inquiring the reason for this, to me, surprising deficiency, I was informed by the organizers—intelligent young men with a wide knowledge of Judaism—that the medical works of Maimonides "contained nothing original" and were of little interest today.

I did not pursue the matter further, since these students were apparently unaware that no medieval scholar—Jewish, Muslim, or Christian—laid claim to "originality" in any branch of knowledge. This applied equally to Maimonides, not only in his medical writings, but also in his theological and philosophical works.

Although his very early theological treatise, the *Commentary on the Mishnah*, has still not been translated into any European language, there has of course been no cessation of interest in his other major contribution to the subject: his *Mishneh Torah* or *Code of Jewish Law*, while his philosophical *Guide for the Perplexed* has always influenced Jews, Muslims, and Christians alike. Like earlier Muslim philosophers, such as Avicenna, Maimonides attempted in his

Guide to reconcile, as far as was possible, the pagan philosophy of Aristotle with the tenets of his own religion. In Avicenna's case, not only his philosophical writings but also his medical encyclopedia, the *Canon,* were always held in the highest esteem, and the latter continues to be lauded today in both East and West, despite the fact that it does not exist in any modern tongue except Russian. Like practically all other medical works of the medieval Islamic world, it was essentially based on the writings of Galen. From the late thirteenth century onward, many of these Arabic works, including the *Canon,* began to be translated into Latin for readers in the West.

The importance of these works to Renaissance Europe lay in their very lack of "originality," for initially they served as the main vehicles of transmission of ancient Greek medicine to the West, and particularly of the writings of Galen above all – to the West. Unfortunately it soon became clear to many European scholars that such encyclopedias could not be considered as a satisfactory summary of these works. They consisted essentially of paraphrased excerpts, mainly from Galen's writings, although rarely providing any reference to the source. To this travesty of Galen's ideas, the compilers then added clinical and therapeutic observations of their own, or of their time, in order to bring them "up to date." Avicenna in particular also tried wherever possible to correlate Galen's views with Aristotle's biological ideas. Moreover, any original misunderstandings of Galen's writings were compounded by the numerous errors of the translators. Despite these failings, the Latin versions of these works acquired such general popularity that certain scholars in Europe called for the "liberation" of Greek medicine from the hands of the "barbarians," who were perverting Galen's text. The sixteenth century thus saw a proliferation of new translations of Galen's works into Latin, directly from the original Greek.

Yet four centuries earlier Maimonides had, quite exceptionally, been fully aware of the distorted picture of Greek medicine hitherto presented by most Arabic works on the subject, and had consciously dedicated his own writings to the faithful transmission of Galen's ideas. In order to understand how he came to adopt this highly individual attitude in the context of his time, one must, however, first approach his works as part of the continuous sweep of medicine – Jewish and non-Jewish – from a very early period up to his day.

Ancient Jewish medicine includes the medicine of the Bible, the medicine of the rabbis, as found largely in the Talmud, and the physical healing undertaken by Jesus and his disciples. Little is known about any of these aspects, which seem to have been based on local folklore or on Egyptian or Babylonian practice. By the talmudic era, however, there also existed literate Jewish *professional* physicians, who wrote in Greek and practiced Greek medicine. Among them was Rufus of Samaria in Palestine, who lived in the second century C.E. According to Galen, his pagan Greek contemporary, he had written commentaries in Greek on Hippocratic works, drawn from the commentaries of others before him.[1] Yet even Galen's own writings, though including numerous original contributions on all aspects of the medicine of his time, were based largely on the works of his Greek predecessors, particularly the so-called Hippocratic corpus, as he himself constantly acknowledged. He was also a great admirer of Aristotle's ideas, which he transferred to the medical plane. Moreover, since he very often indulged in lengthy polemics with others, dead or alive, his writings, despite some inevitable bias, present a wide panorama of Greek culture, including many works of which today there remains no other trace. Thus Galen's output soon came to be universally considered as a distillation of all of Greek medicine up to his time, including the Hippocratic corpus; and in this lay his significance, not only up to the Renaissance but even far beyond. Hence, in the sixth century Syrian Christian monks began to translate his works into Syriac, together with those of Aristotle. From the middle of the eighth century, wealthy Christian and Muslim patrons commissioned the translation of Galen's works into Syriac or into Arabic (often via the Syriac), mainly from the school of Nestorian Christian translators in Bagdad under Ḥunain ibn Isḥāq. By the tenth century all Galen's medical treatises existed in Arabic, including some that are still lost in the original Greek.[2] From then on literate Jewish physicians of the medieval Islamic world, like their Muslim and Christian colleagues, were to base their ideas essentially on the writings of Galen and, through them, on the Hippocratic corpus—that is, on pagan Greek concepts. And the same held for the medicine of Christian Byzantium.

This international, or rather interfaith, unity of medicine was made possible by the fact that it was essentially untouched by theological considerations. Only very rarely do pagan Greek or Roman medical writings make any reference to their own or any other religion. Similarly, apart from such exceptional works as the *Book of Medicines* attributed to Asaf the Sage,[3] the Bible or Talmud are hardly ever invoked in medieval Jewish medical writings; just as the Koran makes little intrusion into the mainstream of Islamic medicine.

As a physician, Maimonides was consulted by some of the highest members of Muslim society, including the Sultan al-Afḍāl, Saladin's son, and probably by Saladin himself. He seems to have devoted himself seriously to the actual practice of medicine only in the later years of his life, but once he had completed his theological and philosophical works, he wrote solely on medical topics until his death in 1204.[4]

While Aristotle greatly influenced his philosophical writings, Galen was the template for his medicine. However, he also quotes "Hippocrates" and other Greek medical writers—mainly through the medium of Galen's works—and occasionally refers to Muslim physicians, particularly with reference to treatment.

The bulk of his medical treatises consists of lengthy written "reports," commissioned by patients and patrons. In a tradition reaching back to ancient Greece and Rome, the educated layman took an amateur interest in medicine on his own account and as paterfamilias. Maimonides insists that even laymen "should learn by heart many of the *Aphorisms* [of Hippocrates], as a child learns from his teacher."[5] In the medieval Islamic world, as later in Renaissance Europe, medicine – including its practical aspects – was considered part of general knowledge.

Around 1195 Maimonides wrote the report now known as the *Regimen of Health*. This was in answer to a letter from the dissipated Sultan al-Afḍāl, who requested his medical opinion on the basis of the symptoms and signs which the sultan there describes. The reply includes instructions for a regimen, or way of life, to be followed by the sultan in accordance with his case. It also contains details of a further regimen which, according to Maimonides, was only to be adopted if "a physician is not to be found, or when the physician available is deficient and his knowledge is not to be trusted."[6] Both are largely based on Galen's celebrated work on regimen: *De sanitate tuenda* (VI, 1–452′K.).

Some time later the sultan wrote again to Maimonides, describing new symptoms. He reported the diagnoses and treatments proposed by various physicians who had already been called in to his case, and asked Maimonides to mediate between their conflicting opinions. In his reply, now generally known as *The Treatise on Accidents* (from the title of its medieval Latin translation), Maimonides criticizes the suggested prescriptions and offers still another regimen of his own.[7]

Here, quite exceptionally, Maimonides introduces the subject of religion: although only in order to dismiss it from consideration in purely medical matters, for Maimonides prescribes wine and song to improve the sultan's mood, despite the fact that both were normally forbidden to Muslims under Islamic law. While admitting that the precepts of religious Law – both Jewish and Muslim – must be absolutely obeyed, he claims that when sick, a person is allowed to take advantage of any treatment offered to him by his doctor, even if it contravenes that law. "The physician," he maintains, "because he is a physician, must give information on the conduct of a beneficial regimen, be it unlawful or permissible, and the sick have the option to act or not to act."[8] The motive behind this declaration has been widely debated for years, without any consensus of opinion. It has been suggested that Maimonides, being a Jew and thus allowed to drink alcohol, was wisely protecting himself against the opposition of orthodox Muslims in the sultan's entourage.[9] Others have maintained that Maimonides was here safeguarding the freedom of choice of the patient and respecting his conscience.[10] Yet it has rightly been noted that he was normally dogmatic regarding the compliance of his patients with any treatment he recommended, even elsewhere in this very same work.[11] Perhaps the real question to be asked is why he should put himself at risk in this way. As far as Jews are concerned, measures to save human life normally take precedence over any religious ruling, but there is no evidence here that the sultan was mortally ill. Moreover, although Maimonides certainly believed in the therapeutic efficacy of wine and song, particularly in a case of this kind, there is nothing in his discussion of their medicinal properties, here and in other works, to indicate that he considered them as totally irreplaceable remedies. It is possible that Maimonides was simply aware that the sultan would have been only too happy to drink wine and hear songs, had they not been forbidden to him on religious grounds. When he was sick, Maimonides could thus "dare" to advise such treatments in the form of a *medical* prescription, backed up by some rather doubtful philosophy, and so allow the sultan to accept them.

In this same period other laymen commissioned Maimonides to provide similar reports on their particular medical problems, including sexual difficulties, hemorrhoids, and asthma.[12] Maimonides was also interested in the adaptation of remedies prescribed by ancient Greek writers such as Dioscorides and Galen to the *materia medica* available in the Islamic world at his time, and to this end wrote his *Explanation of the Names of Drugs*.[13] Snake and scorpion bites have always been a major problem in hot lands, and Maimonides helped the Qāḍī al-Fāḍil (the chief judge at the time) to set up stores of local versions of the Great Theriac and the Electuary of Mithridates: extremely complex and expensive mixtures which had been the traditional remedies for poisoning since very ancient times. At the Qāḍī's command he then prepared a short treatise, *On Poisons,* telling the public what to do if they were far away from such stores, or what alternative remedies could be taken in the case of less dangerous bites.[14]

These reports to laymen were almost entirely based on Galen's ideas. According to tradition, however, they aimed to transmit no more than the essence of Galenic concepts, adapted to particular topics, and to some extent brought up to date, especially as regards treatment. Thus, they simply added to the numerous examples of this type of work which, as has been seen, already existed in Arabic. Since Maimonides, however, appended some moralizing of his own, leavened by much practical good sense, and in view of his great reputation as a philosopher, in earlier times most of these works achieved a wide popularity among physicians and laymen alike, in Arabic, Hebrew, and Latin.

Yet, if only because of his own near obsession with Galen, Maimonides himself was perfectly aware that this type of literature was inadequate for the literate practitioner. One of the most important medical developments over the millennium that had elapsed between the death of Galen and his time, was the evolution of a literate class of *professional* physicians. In the ancient Greek and Roman worlds skilled, literate practitioners, such as the Hippocratic doctors or Galen, had been few and far between. According to Aristotle some knowledge of medicine was required by the "philosopher," but only as part of the general study of "nature" (*De sensu* 436 a–b). The actual care of patients was often delegated to slaves, and Aristotle considered even the professional physicians as craftsmen, like illiterate carpenters or weavers (*Politics* 1337b; VIII 2). Although practicing physicians largely continued to be classed in this way for almost two thousand years, some upgrading of the more learned among them gradually took place in both the Greco-Roman and Islamic worlds. This occurred in parallel with the establishment of hospitals and other appropriate facilities for the care of the sick and the training of doctors, and particularly with the ever-increasing number of literate practitioners.

By the later Middle Ages, the time of Maimonides, the distinction between philosopher and practitioner was already becoming blurred. In the East it was now customary for the philosopher who had obtained some understanding of medicine in the course of his philosophical studies to put this knowledge to professional use at some stage in his career – for example, to finance his travels. Certainly, Greek medical literature was now abundantly available in Arabic for study or for professional use. According to Ḥunain ibn Isḥāq, 129 Galenic items were translated into Arabic by his school alone. Some of these comprised more than one treatise, of which many were fair sized and a few were lengthy indeed. Among them were many Galenic commentaries on Hippocratic works, which, in their complete form, included the original lemmata to the commentary of Galen, so that the Arabic reader was simultaneously provided with much or all of the corresponding Hippocratic treatise.[15]

Maimonides himself had probably read a large part of this extraordinary output, including Galen's lesser-known ethical and philosophical treatises in the complete translated versions. Even so, some of the numerous quotations and paraphrases found in his writings may have been indirectly reproduced, without acknowledgment, from other medieval Arabic works, and from those of Rhazes in particular. In any case, such a choice of Galen's writings could scarcely have been available to the average reader, let alone mastered by him. It is for this reason that a relatively short Greek "Canon," or list of Galen's writings, selected as being suitable for the study of medicine, had already been drawn up, probably before the sixth century C.E., in Byzantine Alexandria, then a renowned center of medical instruction. It seems to have originally included only works dealing with the *theory* of medical practice, including Galen's own elementary treatises on anatomy and the functions of the body. However, although its core remained constant over the centuries, it continually underwent modification and expansion, mainly with the aim of increasing its practical content. In the Islamic world the list became known as the "Sixteen Books of Galen," as it then comprised around sixteen Galenic items. Not all of these were individual treatises, and some works were to be read only in part. To these a small number of Galen's more practical works were usually added to taste, particularly those dealing with treatment by diet or drugs.[16]

Yet Galen's writings are essentially polemical in nature. They are also excessively prolix, as we are constantly being reminded by Islamic writers, although, according to Maimonides, Galen was by no means the worst. "I used to think," Maimonides wrote, "that Galen was one of those who spun out his comments the longest, in most of his works." However, after reading Galen's own criticism of the useless verbosity of another Greek commentator on a Hippocratic work, he realized "that Galen wrote them very briefly indeed, compared with the works of the men of those times."[17] The physicians also complained that such volumes were far too unwieldy to be carried around on their travels. Hence, in their original form many of Galen's writings were of little use to the practicing physician, particularly for his day-to-day activities.

It is thus not surprising that by the time of Maimonides there existed an abundance, or superabundance, of commentaries on the writings of Galen, particularly the canonical items, and to this must be added a host of paraphrases, abridgments, and summaries, which were intended to be shorter, simpler, and easier to understand than the original version. However, the authors tended to encumber them with so many additions of their own that they were often longer than Galen's own work, while his meaning was even further obscured.

This trend was accentuated by the fact that Arabic writers tended to follow the ancient Greek and oriental tradition of producing encyclopedias in different fields of knowledge: attempting to encompass all aspects of the chosen subject within a single work. In fact the most famous Arabic medical writings, dating mainly from the ninth and tenth centuries C.E., are of this type. They include the vast collection of notes by Rhazes, known as *al-Hāwī* (in Latin, the *Continens*), as well as works such as *al-Kitāb al-Malikī (The Kingly Work)* of 'Ali ibn al-'Abbas al-Majūsī (Haly Abbas) and the *Canon* of Avicenna. All of these, though indeed shorter than Galen's entire medical output, are still enormous both in size and in scope.

In his later years Maimonides spoke out, in true Galenic fashion, against the Aristotelian view that a medical practitioner was no more than a craftsman. "It is not true," he wrote, "that a person can become an expert [in medicine] by watching and observing how things are done and have no theoretical knowledge. For medicine is not a craft, like carpentry and weaving, the knowledge of which can be acquired [solely] by practice."[18] He therefore produced a number of works intended to equip the average literate physician with the knowledge, drawn from Galen's works, which he required for his practice. This information was provided in terms of what Galen actually wrote, often in Galen's own words.

The first of these was *al-Mukhtaṣarāt,* a collection of Arabic abridgments of Galen's works, only some of which have so far been found, in whole or in part. The items chosen are essentially those on the list of "Sixteen Books" but, in the Arabic tradition of this "canon," with the addition of five extra, more practical treatises dealing with drugs and diet. However, while previous Arabic and Hebrew works of this kind were paraphrased summaries, these, as Maimonides himself notes, are extracts, entirely in Galen's own words. Maimonides simply removed all Galen's polemics, anecdotes, and philosophical asides – anything in fact which was not strictly concerned with the theory of practice alone – so that the average *Abridgment* was probably around one-third of the original length. Any additions by Maimonides himself were kept to the absolute minimum.[19] This was a wholly humanistic endeavor, and although the same intention was frequently expressed by other medical writers, it was never so successfully achieved. Yet, being consecrated to the humanistic ideal, it essentially looked back to the past. Unlike the summaries and abridgments of others, little attempt was made to adapt Galen's ideas to the conditions of the time and the place. Moreover, while Maimonides aimed at transmitting the essence of Galen within a compass that could be comprehended by a student and also could conveniently be carried around, in practice these *Abridgments* were obviously too long and complex to be consulted by the physician in his everyday work, let alone for the use of the layman.

These failings may account for the fact that the *Abridgments* were never even translated into Hebrew. Perhaps their drawbacks were realized by Maimonides himself, for the subsequent compilation of his *Aphorisms* seems to represent a compromise solution. Though by far the longest of his medical treatises, it is short enough to be portable. This was to become his most popular work, and it was repeatedly printed in Hebrew, as well as in two different Latin translations, the first time in Bologna in 1489.[20] Again his primary aim was to transmit Galen's ideas, but here, as he states in his Introduction to the work, he used the format of aphorisms in order to present them in a manner that could be clearly comprehended and yet could be memorized with ease. He also stresses the fact that, apart from a few aphorisms of his own, the vast majority were not "composed" by him, but that he "selected" and "gathered" them from "all of Galen's writings," although he reproduced them only partly in Galen's own words.[21] These sources include the commentaries on Hippocratic works and some of Galen's lesser-known ethical and philosophical tracts, as well as a number of treatises that are no longer extant. A few aphorisms are also drawn from the writings of physicians of the Islamic world, such as Rhazes and Ibn Zuhr. Apart from the last chapter of the work, Maimonides only occasionally adds a brief comment of his own, but he does provide exact references to his sources. This extremely valuable feature, although also found in the *Aphorisms* of Rhazes, is otherwise rare in the medical literature of the time. It was probably meant to stimulate the reader to consult the actual treatise from which a particular aphorism was drawn.

Today the main interest of the work lies in its long twenty-fifth chapter, which is lauded for the fact that it is devoted to "doubts" regarding various utterances of Galen, the very existence of which is held to be evidence of his independence of received wisdom. In fact this criticism deals mainly with various inconsistencies found in Galen's works or with minor differences of clinical judgment, rather than with matters of principle. However, the chapter also includes a polemic against one of Galen's few "religious" interpolations, which occurs in his treatise on functional anatomy, *On the Use of the Parts*.[22] Here Galen opposes his own Greek pagan view of the creation of the universe to the biblical account as presented by "Moses."

In Maimonides' philosophical work, the *Guide for the Perplexed*, Maimonides devotes a large section (part 2, chapters 13-29) to refuting Aristotle's views on the physical basis of the creation. In his *Aphorisms* he deals mainly with the biological aspects as expounded by Galen along the same Aristotelian lines. At first sight both works by Maimonides present the impression—doubtless intentionally—of outright opposition to these ancient Greek views. Yet in fact Maimonides believed, just like Aristotle and Galen, in a teleological basis of creation, and deeper consideration of these two polemics thus reveals that, with remarkable courage, he tries as far as possible to vindicate Galen.

Maimonides claims that, according to "Moses," the universe was created out of nothing, at a specific moment of time; contrasting this with the Aristotelian belief that the universe is eternal. He first pays genuine homage to Galen the physician, maintaining that he is "the leader [*Imām*] in this science [medicine] and has to be followed in it."[23] Then, with heavy sarcasm, he scoffs at Galen's presumption in believing that he is as accomplished a philosopher as he is a physician. It was Galen's "confusion" in philosophical matters which led him to misinterpret much of the biblical account of creation, apart from its teleological aspects. Yet, according to Maimonides, Galen expressed doubts as to the eternity of the world[24] and also revealed his "perplexity" regarding the nature of time.[25] Maimonides consequently seems to imply that, were it not for his weakness in logic, Galen might have totally accepted the biblical view, for as a physician he would surely have concurred with Maimonides that: "God . . . caused His book to open with an Account of the Beginning which, as we have made clear is natural science."[26] Maimonides does not deny Galen's assertion that "Moses" believed in miracles, and admits that they might possibly occur. However, he essentially agrees with Aristotle and Galen that miracles were not concerned in the creation of the universe, which was accomplished by the Creator according to natural laws. Thus, even this one major "criticism" of Galen serves partly as an apologia for Galen's views.

Since Maimonides was forced to discuss such controversial matters with extreme circumspection, as he already hints in his *Eight Chapters* "a very early ethical tract that forms part of his *Commentary on the Mishnah*,"[27] many of his arguments are of an ambiguous or ambivalent nature. Hence from the beginning his views on the creation have been interpreted in many different ways, and this triumph of reason is often denied, even today. On the other hand, already in his time, and certainly soon after his death, his *Guide* and some of his ethico-religious tracts evoked vociferous opposition by both Jews and Christians, motivated by mysticism or blind faith.[28]

Like most other medical writers up to very recent times, Maimonides lays no claim to originality in any of these works. He believed that Galen's works epitomized the accumulated medical knowledge of past ages, as well as much of ancient wisdom in other fields. Such genuine – and fully deserved – reverence for Galen by his successors, up to the Renaissance and beyond, was in no way mitigated by the fact that they might attempt to assert their individuality by "criticism." This was a common feature of even the most pro-Galenic medical writing in the medieval Islamic world[29] and for centuries later in Europe and, as has been noted, by no means always represented true independence, let alone originality, of thought. However, the fact that Maimonides could introduce such highly charged "scientific" questions into a theological polemic, even in his philosophical writings, can indeed be considered as evidence of his intellectual independence, and it is this, rather than assertions of his "originality," which should be lauded today, and from which lessons are still to be learned.

On the other hand, while up to the Renaissance and beyond such criticism generally concerned relatively minor matters, based on the writer's own experience, some of the greatest original medical discoveries of the premodern age were to be announced in such terms. They included the description of the pulmonary transit of the blood by the thirteenth-century Muslim physician Ibn an-Nafīs and the discovery of its circulation by William Harvey in the early seventeenth century. Yet the fact that at the same time such innovators could proclaim their indebtedness to Galen should not solely be explained as a sop to the traditionalists: in part it was undoubtedly genuine.

Subsequently Maimonides produced a *Commentary on the Aphorisms of Hippocrates* since, as he maintains in his Introduction to this work, "these are aphorisms which every physician should know by heart." He stresses that the commentary consists essentially of a selection of extracts from Galen's *Commentary* on the subject (XVIIB, 345–887; XVIII A, 1–195 K.), although only partly in Galen's own words. For the sake of brevity any "explanation" of his own is restricted to a very few aphorisms, for otherwise he agrees with the comments provided by Galen.[30]

However, the first Aphorism of Hippocrates, beginning: "Life is short, the art is long," receives exceptional treatment, for here Maimonides adds a lengthy commentary of his own which, quite unusually, owes little or nothing to Galen. This aphorism is not limited to the customary citation as above, but goes on to speak of the role of the physician, who must also deal with any "external matters" concerning the patient. Maimonides interprets this cryptic expression as "any outside matter which may oppress the patient." He then provides an example that seems quite startling in its humanity, even today, for he insists that if the patient is poor, the physician is personally responsible for providing him with food, medicines, or anything else needed to restore him to health.[31] Nothing like this remarkable injunction appears in the Galenic *Commentary* on this aphorism, nor, as far as I know, in any of the other numerous commentaries on this subject that were produced over the centuries in Greek, Latin, Arabic, and Hebrew.[32] However, in a totally different kind of work, his relatively little-known ethical treatise *On the Diagnosis and Cure of the Diseases of the Soul,* Galen gives expression to his own humanity in a somewhat similar vein. Here he claims that at all times he shares his own clothing with some of his slaves and arranges nourishment and nursing for others.[33] Yet this only forms part of his personal ethics: unlike the little Hippocratic work on medical etiquette known as *Precepts* (Sect. 6), he does not maintain that it is a specific task of the physician. Whether or not Maimonides was here influenced by Galen, his own wording seems to show that he based himself directly on the Hippocratic work, which was well known in Arabic. This latter, together with other small Hippocratic tracts on the subject—*Law, Decorum, The Physician,* and the probably pseudepigraphic *Testament,*[34]—seem to have been considered by Islamic physicians as a kind of commentary on that universal paradigm of medical ethics and etiquette: the Hippocratic Oath. Hence they played a major part in the medical aspects of the *Adāb,* or ethical literature that was such an important feature of Islamic culture at this period. It is thus not surprising that a very similar precept to the above is enjoined on physicians—without mentioning the ancient Greek source—by Sā'id ibn al-Ḥasan, an eleventh-century Christian physician of Iraq, in his treatise on medical ethics,[35] and corresponding sentiments may well have been expressed in other works of this kind, which were possibly known to Maimonides.

It has been seen that the medical works of Maimonides are unusual for his time in remaining extraordinarily true to their roots. They thus played an important part in transmitting to the medieval Islamic world the essence of ancient Greek medicine and in keeping its spirit alive up to the Renaissance and beyond. Though this pioneering effort is of great historical importance, it has not been sufficiently recognized. It is generally considered, moreover, that his medical works were but an offshoot of his medical practice, which he undertook largely to earn his bread,[36] and that the significance of his writings lay essentially in the theological and philosophical spheres.

The extensive ancient Greek influence on Jewish postbiblical culture, in both East and West, has of course been acknowledged (not always with grace) since the earliest times, while Greek medical concepts—and those of Galen in particular—are openly displayed in Jewish medical works, and above all in those of Maimonides. However, it does not yet seem to be appreciated that, since many other Jewish theologians and philosophers of the medieval period were also physicians, Greek medical concepts and, above all, Galenic ideas, played a role throughout Jewish thought, and not only where purely medical matters were concerned. As Maimonides himself asserts, the province of the mind is not restricted to theology and philosophy but also includes medical theory.[37] Since a fertile intelligence cannot in reality be compartmentalized, he in fact considered every problem from all three aspects, although in a written judgment one aspect might predominate. Hence, while in deference to the susceptibilities of the time he largely kept theology out of medicine, he was unable to resist the introduction of Galenic concepts into his theological writings, albeit in a Judaized guise.[38]

Thus the medical works of Maimonides express an extreme type of humanism in a thoroughly Judaized form, and yet are in no way scholastic. Tempered as they are by the human touch and pervaded by humanity, for those who seek the Jewish past they remain of great interest today.

3

Maimonides on the Perfect Physician

Samuel S. Kottek

In Greek, the notion of being perfect, accomplished, complete, is rendered by the adjective *téleios*. In *Metaphysics,* Aristotle gives a twofold definition of the concept of perfection.[1] First, it designates something outside of which it is impossible to find even a single part. Second, it designates something which cannot be surpassed with respect to excellence. Aristotle chooses two professions to illustrate his discourse. "A doctor," he says, "and a musician [i.e., a flute player] are accomplished when they show no deficiency with respect to the form of their peculiar excellence."[2] The term *aristos,* meaning "excellent" or "superior," is thus confronted with *téleios* in a way that remains unclear concerning the case of the physician.

The pseudo-Galenic work *Definitiones Medicae* tries to differentiate between both terms applied to the physician. We read: "The perfect [*téleios*] physician is one who has completed the whole cycle of theoretical and practical studies."[3] The next passage reads: "The excellent [Greek *aristos,* Latin *optimus*] physician is one who practices medicine according to the right doctrine [*orthòn lógon*]."[4] Both Aristotle and the author of the *Definitions* consider perfection as wholeness in knowledge and practical experience, whereas excellence seems – at least in *Definitions* – directed at the results achieved by the physician who has chosen the right cure.

25

HUMAN PERFECTION

The Hebrew term *shalem* used by Maimonides—at least by the translators from the Arabic—includes seemingly both Greek terms,[5] although its etymology brings it closer to *téleios*. In the Bible, *shalem* is used some twenty-five times, of which the majority (some fifteen times) are linked with "heart," with the meaning of full agreement, of being perfectly attuned to someone else.[6] Another frequent use is with weights and measures (cf. Deuteronomy 25:15). While elaborating on the biblical verse Genesis 33:18, the Midrash describes several kinds of perfection attained by the patriarch Jacob. He was accomplished in his body, in his progeny, in his resources, and in his learning.[7]

In the *Guide of the Perplexed* (3:54), Maimonides differentiates four categories of human accomplishment *(shelemut)*.[8] First, perfection in resources, in property, including money, clothes, utensils, servants, real estate, and so forth. From such wealth, one can derive a certain amount of satisfaction, but there is nothing substantial in such enjoyments. Second, physical perfection, that is, being in optimal bodily condition. This is certainly enjoyable but should not be considered as a goal in itself. Third, ethical perfection, which aims at achieving all moral qualities to the highest degree possible. This type of perfection refers to optimal social life. Only the fourth type can really be called human perfection, that is, intellectual excellence,[9] with an emphasis, in this context, on theological knowledge. Wealth, health, morals, and knowledge are four categories in which the physician, as any other human being, should be able to attain perfection, the stress being put on intellectual excellence.

PERFECTION IN MEDICAL KNOWLEDGE

Is perfection in medical knowledge actually achievable? In his commentary on Hippocrates' *Aphorisms*, Maimonides quotes Galen,[10] who asserted that man cannot achieve perfection in the knowledge of the medical art. Maimonides strongly opposes this statement, for—he contends—whoever does not attain perfection in that art will do more harm than good. It is much better not to seek any medical advice than to follow the recommendation of a physician who commits errors.[11] Maimonides stresses here the time factor, following Hippocrates' admonition ("life is short . . . time is pressing"). There is often no time to try several schemes of treatment with the aim of choosing the most convenient for the patient. For Maimonides, perfection is here the aptitude of making a decision with the least possible percentage of error. The controversy between Maimonides and Galen is in this case more pedagogical than fundamental. Both obviously agree on the incompleteness of the medical art. Maimonides, however, wishes his ideal physician to constantly invest his whole energy at getting as close as possible to perfection, and considers

Galen's statement as dangerous inasmuch as it might deter physicians from doing so.

For Maimonides, the perfect physician *(ha-rofe ha-shalem)* is a physician to which the patient "is ready to entrust in his hands both his soul and body, and follow all his directions."[12] Do we infer from this statement that, for Maimonides, blind trust in a practitioner is what makes him an ideal physician? Obviously the patient's trust is a consequence of the physician's excellence – not a cause or a definition. This statement on the treatment of body and soul is, however, central in a comparative approach to professional excellence in Galen's and Maimonides' views.

MAIMONIDES VS. GALEN

When Galen wrote (if ever) his brief dissertation entitled *De Optimo Medico Cognoscendo*,[13] he was not writing for his peers but rather for "anyone who wishes to distinguish between the best and the worst physicians" (9:22). On the other hand, he seemingly addresses physicians when he points out that they should be philosophers.[14] He states, however not in a very convincing way, that physicians should study logics, natural sciences, and physics.

To this educational program should be added the dimension of ethics. "Science will give him [i.e., the physician] an understanding of nature and disease. Ethics will give him the attitude he needs to be a student of nature, and a guide for men whom he is to treat by diet, i.e., by regulating their way of life."[15] Psychology is however excluded from Galen's definition of philosophy.

Maimonides was first of all Rabbi Moses ben Maimon, the Rabbi Moysi of medieval Latin manuscripts. Being a theologian, but also a philosopher, he could not overlook the welfare of the soul. The often-quoted poem written by Al-Said Almulk[16] and mentioned in Ibn Abi Usaibi'a's appraisal of Maimonides should not be wrongly interpreted. When the poet states that "Galen's medicine is only for the body, that of Abu 'Imran [Maimonides] is for both body and soul," this does not mean that Galen had nothing to say about diseases of the soul. Galen was perfectly aware of this category of ailments. He was also aware of psychosomatic influences on health. Humoral physiology and pathology included imbalance due to the "motions of the soul" (i.e., emotions). As a consequence, the therapeutic value of music, a pleasant and refreshing environment, games and exercise, on psychic affections, was mentioned by Galen, who was Maimonides' source for his statement in *Pirké Moshe (The Aphorisms of Moses)*.[17] Therefore, Almulk's encomium does not mean that Galen was only prepared to treat physical or somatic diseases. Rather, it stresses the fact that Maimonides considered and treated *each patient in toto*, body and soul, whereas Galen only treated the soul when it was diseased.

TREATING BOTH BODY AND SOUL

The mutual influences of soul and body is a topic that has been dealt with repeatedly.[18] Regarding the practice of medicine, Maimonides stresses in his *Regimen Sanitatis* (2:13) that the patients' "movements of the soul" should be considered with absolute priority and put straight. This is true not only in case of disease but also in a state of health. Maimonides cites quite a number of these aphorismatic formulas. "The physician should remember that any sick individual has a contracted heart [i.e., is anxious],[19] whereas a healthy one's soul is roomy." Thus, by the mere driving away of those "motions of the soul" that lead to anxiety (*kotzer ruah*), one extends and protracts the health of the healthy and should initiate the treatment of the sick. Maimonides is not discussing psychic diseases in particular, but diseases in general. A seemingly capital exhortation by Maimonides is his delineating of the perfect physician.[20] A physician may be tempted to dismiss psychological considerations insofar as they do not really pertain to the medical art. Maimonides readily acknowledges that psychology is closer to philosophy and to what he calls biblical ethics.[21] Both philosophers and ethicists offer pedagogic training with the aim of acquiring that foremost quality called *aequanimitas*, extolled many centuries later by the illustrious William Osler as a prominent virtue for physicians.[22] Common people (*peshutei ha-am*) do not master their emotions, which may cause or aggravate a number of illnesses. Therefore the physician has to constantly take into account these "motions of the soul."[23] This merging of philosophy (here, rather, psychology) with medicine, although briefly advocated by Galen, was best expressed by Aristotle: "Hence one may say that most natural philosophers, and those physicians who take a scientific interest in their art, have this in common: the former end by studying medicine, and the latter base their medical theories on the principles of natural science."[24]

THE WAY OF PERFECTION

"Man is not endowed with perfection from the beginning, but at first possesses perfection *in potentia*, not in fact."[25] "Not many are those who become sages" (Job 32:9), and there are numerous obstacles on the way to perfection. The preliminary, or preparatory, studies are long and exhausting—but absolutely necessary in order to achieve excellence.[26] In his commentary on the first aphorism of Hippocrates, Maimonides quotes Al-Farabi, who divides the study of theoretical and practical medicine into seven parts.[27] Even, writes Maimonides, if one would memorize all this enormous literature, which would necessitate many years (cf. "The Art is long"), one would not yet be called an accomplished physician. He first has to come in close contact with individuals, sane and sick, and become familiar with signs and symptoms and how they are portrayed by the patients. He has to learn how to determine the general and particular constitution (cf. *mezeg,* i.e., *krasis*) of each individual.

For Galen,[28] "Anyone who wishes to distinguish between the best and the worst physicians must first inquire what are the activities to which the candidate has devoted most of his time. Are these the reading of books and the treatment of patients?" Then he is worth being examined, both on his theoretical and practical knowledge. Galen also introduces ethical considerations: "The really accomplished physician should not abandon the treatment of patients who suffer from severe illness [here the case of hemoptysis], as long as there is some hope of recovery."[29] For Hippocrates, excellence in medical practice is mainly related to the ability of establishing accurate prognosis. "A physician . . . who can inform the sick, not only of their present state, but of what preceded it and of what might be expected . . . will readily be esteemed as being *perfectly* acquainted with their disease, and they will therefore with confidence commit themselves to his care."[30] Maimonides, particularly in his *Treatise on Asthma,* recommends the personalization of medical care, with emphasis on the patient's environment.[31] The attendants should be instructed in detail about the diet, the treatment, and all other "external factors" that have to be cared for, in behalf of the particular patient, writes Maimonides. He further states that, in medicine, reflection and deliberation precede any action. Every patient requires a renewed reflection; one should never say "This disease is similar to that one." Then comes a statement that is extremely modern, but for too long has been overlooked: "The physician does not cure a disease, he cures a diseased person." For Maimonides, an accomplished physician first acquires knowledge, then practical experience,[32] always taking into consideration the constitution *(mezeg)* of the patient and his psychology – in one word, his individuality.

ON PRETENDING TO BE PERFECT

There is one disease, writes Maimonides toward the end of his medical magnum opus *Pirké Moshe,*[33] that very few are capable of avoiding. This disease, he says, is a disease of the soul in which an individual considers himself more accomplished than he really is. These individuals are convinced that they are able to answer any question, without even reflecting or searching at all. This happens particularly to scholars who are genuine experts in a certain domain, but readily answer questions pertaining to some other field in which they know nothing or very little. Alternatively, they dismiss the question as being of no value or interest. Maimonides then cites Galen, an unequaled expert in medical matters, as having suffered from this disease, for having dabbled in logic and philosophy, of which he had little, or at least insufficient knowledge. Later in the same chapter [25:69], Maimonides delineates his own views on scientific epistemology. If somebody who seems straight and reliable develops a theory that he has himself experienced, one should listen to him carefully and think it over thoroughly; then one should experiment again oneself, without taking into account his own results. The same method should be applied even if the information has been forwarded by a number of scholars. With such high standards, Maimonides really attains excellence. On the one side, he says, do not accept any scientific theory that one has not previously scrutinized and verified, and on the other hand, do not offer advice in a matter with which one is not perfectly familiar.

MAIMONIDES' SELF-APPRAISAL

Having expounded in the *Treatise on Asthma* the characteristics of the accomplished physician, Maimonides remarks:[34] "Do not infer from what I just stated, that I am the one [i.e., the physician] to whom it is legitimate to entrust your body and soul and follow his directions. I call Heaven to testify that I am among those who are incomplete in this art . . . and, no doubt, I know myself better than anybody else . . . Again I call Heaven to testify that I do not state this out of humility, neither out of saintship [*hasidut*] . . . I state things as they really are." Maimonides' aim was not, while speaking of the perfect physician, to advertise his own perfection. On the contrary, he considered himself as being among those who need to complete themselves.

If we take for granted that Maimonides did not express this sentiment out of humility or saintship (which may of course be questioned), why did he intentionally make this statement? We can only surmise that he thought that a perfect physician does not exist: he is constantly in a dynamic state of accomplishment. His excellence being based on knowledge which is itself mainly based on memory, the process is in constant need of being refreshed.[35]

Moreover, humility has, for Maimonides, an outstanding place among moral qualities. In his *Eight Chapters*[36] he considers it as being equidistant from pride on the one side and self-abasement on the other. Maimonides has a much more stringent attitude in his *Mishneh Torah* (*Hilkhot Deot* 2:3), where he writes that it is not adequate to choose the middle way; one should always seek extreme humility. "The best of the physicians to Gehenna," says a sage of the Mishnah.[37] This strange statement has been accurately interpreted as meaning: He who holds that he is the best of physicians will meet his punishment. Maimonides wished that all physicians be of excellence, but he would not consider himself as "the best of physicians."

Toward the end of the *Treatise on Asthma,* Maimonides introduces another factor that might help incomplete physicians attain some degree of perfection in the medical art. This factor is the joint consultation[38] between several physicians *(consilium)*. One fills the gaps of the other, and perfection results from their joint endeavor. For this reason, princes and high officials usually appoint several physicians at their service.[39] Maimonides himself was one of such a group of physicians appointed at the Egyptian court. He was obviously cautious not to give the impression that he considered himself more accomplished than his colleagues.

CONCLUSION

Maimonides wrote ten medical treatises and dissertations, none of them dedicated to medical education. We lack even fragmentary information on his own medical curriculum. For him, healthy diet and life-style are of such importance that he included these rules, together with others of ethical content, in his legalistic work *Mishneh Torah*.[40] However, as we have shown earlier in this paper, bodily perfection is not an ultimate goal. It only permits, together with material means and ethical values, the attainment of perfection in knowledge. Unlike Hippocratic authors, Maimonides feels that a physician's training should include the study of philosophy and ethics. It should include not only the knowledge of human nature (constitution), but also a thorough awareness of psychological traits. The physician should shun routines, but consider every patient to require renewed reflection.

At the top of his career as a physician, in the year 1190, Maimonides wrote a letter to his pupil Ibn Aqnin, in which he complained of not being able to pursue his medical studies, for sheer lack of time and strength. "For you know how long and difficult this art is for a strict and scrupulous man who refrains from affirming anything that he cannot support by argument and who does not remember where it has been stated and how it may be demonstrated."[41]

Learned and experienced, strict and scrupulous, open-minded though critical, considering ethics and psychology not less crucial than diet and drugs, Maimonides was no doubt, at least in the eyes of his fellow men, an accomplished physician. If he was not perfect in his own eyes, it may well be that he considered himself an everlasting student, just as a learned theologian always remains a *talmid hakham,* (a student sage) to his last breath.

SELECTED BIBLIOGRAPHY

Aristotle. *The Metaphysics.* Books 1–4. Trans. H. Tredennick. London: W. Heinemann Ltd., 1947.

Feldman, W. M. "Maimonides as Physician and Scientist." In I. Epstein, ed., *Moses Maimonides, Anglo-Jewish Papers in Connection with the 8th Centenary of His Birth.* London: Soncino Press, 1935.

Galen. *Opera Omnia*. C. G. Kuhn, ed. 20 vols. in 22. Hildesheim, 1964-65.

Gourevitch, D. "Un Therapeute Accompli; note sur l'adjectif *teleios*." *Revue de Philologie* 61:1(1987):95-99.

Hippocrates. With an English translation by W. H. S. Jones. 4 vols. London: W. Heinemann Ltd., 1948-1959.

Iskandar, Alb. Z. *Galen On Examinations by which the Best Physicians Are Recognized* [Corp. Medic. Graec. Suppl. Orient. IV]. Berlin: Akademie Verlag, 1988.

Kottek, S. "Maimonides on the Treatment of Body and Soul." *Bulletin of the Israel Academic Center in Cairo* 12(1989):24-28.

Leibowitz, J. O. "Maimonides as Physician and Medical Author." *Frankfurter Israelitisches Gemeindeblatt* 13(1935):300-1 [German].

──── . "Maimonides on Medical Practice." *Bulletin of the History of Medicine* 31(1957):309-17.

──── . "Maimonides, the Man and His Work. Different Kinds of Wisdom." *Ariel* 41(1976):37-52.

Muntner, S. "Die Psychosomatologie in der Medizin des Maimonides." *Medizinische Klinik* 59. Jahrgg., Nr. 37 (1964):1482-85.

Temkin, O. "Greek Medicine as Science and Craft." *Isis* 44(3), no. 137 (1953):213-25.

See also: *750 years anniversary of Maimonides' death*. Series of papers by D. A. Friedmann, S. Muntner, J. O. Leibowitz, A. Brand-Auraban. *Harefuah* 47(9) [1954]: 181-99. Hebrew, English summaries.

N.B. We do not include in this bibliography the medical works of Maimonides edited by S. Muntner (Hebrew) and F. Rosner (English), nor do we refer to the nonmedical works taken into account in our essay.

4

Sex and Health in Maimonides

W. Zev Harvey

Sex was an important subject for Maimonides.[1] In one of his medical treatises, he complained: "No physician of antiquity included in his general health regimen the regulation of coitus. ... To my mind, regulation of coitus should be included."[2] Elsewhere, he similarly remarked: "The performance of sexual intercourse is something which is part of the regimen of health."[3] When he wrote his own *Regimen of Health,* he did not neglect to include a discussion of sex.[4] He also composed at least one manual *On Sexual Intercourse.*[5] Indeed, it has been accurately observed that "Maimonides discusses the rules of sexual intercourse in almost all his [medical] compositions."[6] Moreover, sex holds a prominent place in his halakhic and philosophic works as well.[7] My following remarks are not intended to exposit Maimonides' entire thinking on sex and health, but only to provide a framework for understanding his views on the subject.

Maimonides treats sex just as he treats all other biological needs: sleep, drink, food, and so forth. One is to fulfill them to the extent that they are truly *needs;* that is, in accordance with the requirements of health, no more and no less.

This approach of Maimonides' is summed up in the *Mishneh Torah,* Book of Knowledge, *Hilkhot Deot* 3:2:

> When one eats, drinks, or has sexual intercourse, he should not intend to do these things only in order to have pleasure, such that he would eat and drink

only that which is sweet to the palate, and have sexual intercourse in order to have pleasure, but he should intend to eat and drink *only in order to make healthy his body and his limbs*. Thus, he will not eat everything for which his palate lusts, like a dog or an ass, but will eat things beneficial to the body, whether bitter or sweet. . . . He will thus eat and drink *by way of medicine alone* [*derekh refuah bilevad*] in order that he be healthy and sound of body, since it is impossible for a human being to live except by eating and drinking. So too when he has sexual intercourse, he should not have sexual intercourse except to make his body healthy, or to maintain the species. Thus he will not have sexual intercourse whensoever he should lust, but whenever he knows he has a need to emit sperm, as by way of medicine [*derekh refuah*] or to maintain the species.

In this passage, sexual intercourse, together with eating and drinking, is treated as a biological need. Biological needs, Maimonides teaches, must be satisfied if the individual is to be healthy, and should be strictly regulated "by way of medicine." Sex, however, is somewhat different from eating and drinking, for while the latter are justified by way of medicine alone, sex has an additional justification, the propagation of the species. Nonetheless, Maimonides' opinion is clear. As one should not eat and drink whatever one desires, so one should not have sexual intercourse whenever one desires. The satisfaction of biological needs is not to be regulated in accordance with subjective desire, but objective biological need.

Maimonides is more explicit concerning sex and health in the following passage from *Hilkhot Deot* 4:19:

> Semen is the power of the body, its life, and the light of the eyes. When emitted in excess, the body degenerates. . . . Anyone who overindulges in sex, old age leaps upon him; his power fails; his eyes become dim; a bad odor exudes from his mouth and armpits; the hair of his head, eyebrows, and eyelids fall out; the hair of his beard, armpits, and legs increase; his teeth drop out; and many other pains befall him. Therefore, a man must be careful in this matter, if he wants to live well. He should not have sexual intercourse unless he finds his body healthy and very strong; and he frequently has involuntary erections, and though he divert his mind to something else, his erection persists; and he feels a heaviness from his loins down, as if his testicular cords were being stretched; and his flesh is hot. This person *needs* to have sexual intercourse, and it is *medicinal* for him to have sexual intercourse [*u-refuah lo she-yival*].

The text from *Deot* 3:2 indicated that insufficient satisfaction of true sexual needs is detrimental to health. Now this text from *Deot* 4:19 makes emphatically clear that too much sex is exceedingly detrimental to health. This text from *Deot* 4:19 also clarifies in vivid language what had been meant in *Deot* 3:2 by the statement that one should have sexual intercourse "by way of medicine." Acute physical discomfort is the sign that sexual intercourse is required "by way of medicine."

The two texts I have quoted from Maimonides' *Hilkhot Deot* are marked by a pronounced medical attitude, unmitigated by either romanticism or moralism. They are also colored by a glaring androcentrism.[8] In the following text from *Hilkhot Deot* 5:4, the medicalism and the androcentrism are still very much present; however, they are mitigated in an important way:

> Although a man's wife is always permitted to him, a scholar should conduct himself with sanctity, and should not be frequently with his wife, like a rooster [cf. *Berakhot* 22a]; but on Sabbath nights [*Ketubot* 62b], if he has power. When he converses with her, he should not do so at the beginning of the night, when he is sated and his belly full, nor at the end of the night, when he is hungry, but in the middle of the night [cf. *Nedarim* 20b], when the food is digested in his intestines. And he should not be exceedingly lightheaded; nor should he profane his mouth with vulgar talk, even if only between him and her . . . The two may not be drunk, lethargic, or sad; nor may even one of them be so. She must not be asleep. And he may not force her, if she is not willing. Rather, it must be *in accord with the will of the two of them, and in their joy* [*bi-retzon sheneihem u-ve-simhatam*]. He should converse and play with her a little, so that she be content, and should have sexual intercourse modestly, without impudence, and withdraw immediately.[9]

In this third text from *Hilkhot Deot,* Maimonides remains concerned about sex and physical health (e.g., one should have sex only "when the food is digested in his intestines"); and he continues to discuss sex from the standpoint of the male (e.g., "a scholar . . . should not be frequently with his wife"). However, he is now also concerned about sex and *psychic* health (e.g., one must not be "lightheaded" or "profane his mouth"); and he now is also concerned about the sensibilities and desires of the female (e.g., she must be willing, and should be contented). Moreover, the proposition asserted here by Maimonides that sex must be "in accord with the will of the two of them and in their joy" *(bi-retzon sheneihem u-ve-simhatam),* strikes me as being of particular importance in his general thinking about sex. In the remaining sections, I will return to this proposition more than once, and hope to clarify its significance.

Maimonides' views on sex and health must be understood in the light of his zealously teleological ethics. According to this ethics, human beings should have only one ultimate *telos:* the intellectual knowledge of God, which (since God cannot be known) amounts to the intellectual knowledge of His creation, that is, nature.[10] This means that *everything* one might do should be done if and only if it leads one to that *telos*. As Maimonides phrases it in *Hilkhot Deot* 3:2: "A person must direct his heart and all his deeds to know God, may He be blessed, alone; and his sitting down, his rising up, and his speech should all aim at this" (cf. Deuteronomy 6:7). One should not sit down, rise up, or speak, unless it is a means to the knowledge of God.

The Maimonidean individual knows that human beings are not disembodied intellects, able to cognize God continuously and exclusively, but they are animals with material bodies, and as such have needs: biological, psychological, political, and so on. These animal needs must be satisfied as a necessary means to the attainment of the one true human goal, the knowledge of God; and they must be satisfied in due measure, neither in deficiency nor in excess. In a sense, for Maimonides, the same one regimen (Arabic: *tadbīr;* Hebrew: *hanhagah*) may be said to apply to health, morals, politics, and to everything else: it is to follow zealously the direct path to the knowledge of God.

In Maimonides' understanding, a human being who rationally satisfies his true animal needs, not for their own sakes, but for the sake of attaining the knowledge of God, is in so doing *serving God*. Not only does the political leader, prophet, or judge serve God when he acts to establish a community of peace *in order* that human beings may have a suitable environment for pursuing the knowledge of God (cf. *Guide for the Perplexed* 1:54; 3:54), but so does the individual who satisfies his biological needs not for their own sakes but *in order* to be physically fit to pursue the knowledge of God. Thus, Maimonides writes explicitly in *Hilkhot Deot* 3:3: "He who walks in this path all his days [i.e., directs all his deeds toward the knowledge of God] serves God always, even when he is conducting business negotiations, and *even when he is having sexual intercourse* . . . and even when he sleeps."

In short, the Maimonidean individual does not value his animality qua animality, and certainly does not relish sex for sex's sake. Indeed, no less than four times in the *Guide for the Perplexed* (2:36, 40; 3:8, 49), Maimonides alludes sympathetically to a remark of Aristotle's in the *Nicomachean Ethics* (III, 10, 1182b) to the effect that the sense of touch is a disgrace to us, since we have it as animals, not humans.[11] In his *Regimen of Health,* he advises: "Whoever wishes to remain healthy should chase the idea of sexual intercourse from his mind as much as he can."[12] Furthermore, in the *Mishneh Torah,* Book of Women, *Hilkhot Ishut* 15:3, he goes so far as to justify halakhically a scholar who does not marry because his "soul lusts for the Torah," provided the scholar is not disturbed by the sexual urge.[13] To be sure, such intense scholars are an anomaly, to say the least, and the Maimonidean individual recognizes that sex is a true biological need that must be satisfied if one is to be healthy and to know God.

In the *Guide for the Perplexed* (1:2) and elsewhere, the biblical Garden of Eden story serves Maimonides as a state-of-nature parable.[14] More precisely, it illustrates for him the difference between a purely rational society and the kinds of societies we have in the real world. Before eating of the fruit of the Tree of Knowledge of Good and Evil, Adam and Eve were purely rational: they lived in accordance with their intellects, not their imaginations; they had perfect objective knowledge of true and false, but no inkling of the subjective notions of good and bad; they perceived only the necessary, not the excessive or the deficient; and they were thoroughly healthy in body and mind.

What was their sex life like, and how was it affected by their eating the fruit of the Tree of Knowledge of Good and Evil? Maimonides nowhere answers these questions explicitly; however, the answers may be inferred without great difficulty.

Living the purely rational life, Adam and Eve would have satisfied their biological needs in due measure, that is, "by way of medicine" (*derekh refuah*): they would have slept in accordance with their bodily needs, no more and no less; they would have eaten and drunk in accordance with their nutritional needs, neither excessively nor deficiently; and they would have regulated their sexual activity precisely in accordance with their true aggregate physical and psychic needs, not in accordance with their individual imaginations. In the Garden of Eden, sex – like sleeping, eating, and drinking – would have been purely rational; but sex is in a crucial sense unlike the other biological needs; for sex concerns *two* people. Sex must be "in accord with the will of *the two* of them, and in *their* joy." Sex, in other words, is the beginning of society. Sexual communion (Arabic: *jimāʿ*), Maimonides might have punned, is the beginning of community (*jamʿ*).

The sexual relationship between Adam and Eve illustrates for Maimonides the origin of the political problem. When living purely rationally before eating the forbidden fruit, they would have regulated their sex *in accord with the will of the two of them, and in their joy*. Adam would not have been able even to imagine raping Eve, and so there would have been no need of laws or customs designed to protect the weak from the strong: Adam and Eve were free to be nude. They were free from the coercion of laws and norms, free from heteronomy. Their Garden of Eden was a Garden of Anarchy and Freedom, not only a Garden of Pure Reason.

Adam and Eve ate the forbidden fruit of the Tree of Knowledge of Good and Evil; that is, they abandoned the rational life and strayed after their subjective, egocentric fantasies; for such, according to Maimonides, is inevitably the human condition. No longer living rationally, Adam and Eve now had to don fig leaves. Eve had to be protected from Adam, who might now force himself upon her against her will and contrary to her happiness. In addition, the fig leaves would protect Adam and Eve from their own imaginations and aid them to live less irrational lives. From now on, sex – like everything else – would be regulated by laws and customs. With the victory of imagination over reason, the political problem had arisen.

I wish to pose just one question. Did Maimonides' Adam and Eve have more erotic pleasure when they were living rationally or after they began to live irrationally? That is, did they have more erotic pleasure before they ate the forbidden fruit or after they ate it?

It might be argued, in the spirit of Maimonideanism as I understand it, that rationality is not the enemy of erotic pleasure, but on the contrary, makes true erotic pleasure possible. Rationality frees the lovers from the blinding egocentrism of their imaginations, enabling them to appreciate each other's needs, and only when each lover appreciates the needs of the other is it possible for their sexual intercourse to be "in accord with the will of the two of them, and in their joy." In the Garden of Eden, before their sin of irrationality, Maimonides' Adam and Eve enjoyed a sexual relationship that was always wholly voluntary and joyful. After their sin, they fervidly and feverishly sought after erotic pleasure but would not have been able to attain anything approximating the erotic pleasure they had previously enjoyed as perfectly rational beings.

There is a paradox here: one can only attain true erotic pleasure if one does not seek it. You grab for the forbidden fruit in order to increase your carnal delight, but in actuality the fruit decreases it.

Yet the Maimonidean position I have sketched here is not at all counterintuitive. It would not be surprising, should it turn out that the person who eats only nutritious food enjoys what he eats more than does the junk-food glutton. Nor should we be amazed if it turns out that those who conduct sex for the sake of the service of God derive more erotic pleasure from the act than do those who indulge in it for its own sake.

The Maimonidean view, which I have just called a paradox, might be prosaically explained in one sentence. Although considerations of health may at first seem to contradict those of pleasure (cf. *Hilkhot Deot* 3:2, the sweet vs. the beneficent), health is in fact a necessary condition of pleasure.

The question of erotic love in Maimonides may be raised in a different context. Does the love of God leave room for erotic love?

The love of God, for Maimonides, is the lust to know Him (see *Mishneh Torah*, Book of Knowledge, *Yesodei ha-Torah* 2:2; 4:12), and it should be all-consuming. This overpowering passion is described in *Mishneh Torah*, Book of Knowledge, *Teshuvah* 10:3:

> How is the proper love [of God]? It is that one love God with a very mighty, exceedingly great love, such that one's soul is bound up in the love of God, and one is ravished with it always [*shogeh . . . tamid;* cf. Proverbs 5:19, "With her love be thou ravished always *(tishgeh tamid)*"], as if he were love-sick, his mind never free of the love of that woman, and he is ravished with it always [*shogeh . . . tamid*], whether he sits down, or rises up, or whether he is eating or drinking. Greater than this shall be the love of God in the heart of his lovers, who are ravished with it always [*shogim . . . tamid*].[15]

The biblical commandment to love God (Deuteronomy 6:5) is followed by the exhortation: "thou shalt talk of [these words] when thou sittest in thy house, and when thou walkest by the way, and when thou liest down, and when thou risest up" (6:7). This exhortation was already alluded to in a text from *Hilkhot Deot* 3:2 (quoted above), according to which all one's deeds ("his sitting down, his rising up, and his speech") should be directed toward the knowledge of God. Here in *Hilkhot Teshuvah* 10:3, the love of God is described as the ravishing passion that drives one to direct all his deeds toward that knowledge.

It follows, I think, that just as the act of sexual intercourse is part of those deeds that advance one toward the knowledge of God, so the erotic love attendant on sexual intercourse (when performed for the sake of the knowledge of God) is part of the all-consuming love of God.

If this is so, then the erotic love of the Maimonidean lover will be decidedly greater than that of the lover who pursues sex for its own sake, for it is part of the "very mighty, exceedingly great love" of God, which ravishes the truly rational human being with an all-consuming passion.

5

An Encounter with Maimonides

Haskell D. Isaacs

For centuries orations have been delivered, and much has been written, on the life and works of Maimonides, with the result that much has been revealed about his personality, character, and achievements.[1] What we have then, is nothing short of a full-scale well-documented study of the man himself as a learned rabbi, a great philosopher, and accomplished physician. The high quality of such work makes it difficult for a new contributor to introduce a relevant topic not already handled.

Most of the information at hand is based upon traditional sources. In his letters to his pupil Ibn 'Aqnīn[2] and his translator Samuel ben Tibbon,[3] Maimonides tells us how he saw and treated his patients, both Jews and non-Jews. But here in this short paper, I believe it is the first time we have a description of an encounter by a patient who sought advice from Maimonides. Paul Fenton describes a casual meeting with Maimonides, extracted from an unsigned letter written in Judeo-Arabic – but the meeting was purely social.[4]

The document in question is one of the many fragments in the Taylor-Schechter Genizah Collection preserved in the Cambridge University Library. Classified as T-S NS 321.34, it is written in Judeo-Arabic on both sides of a piece of paper. It measures 24.2 cm × 10.4 cm, and on one side there are 35 lines and on the other 38 lines. The paper is frayed and stained, and the ink has faded in some places. It seems to have formed part of a letter by an author who was apparently known to Maimonides, though the two had not previously met each other.

The style of the letter is simple and the language semi-colloquial. It follows popular Jewish practice in Egypt of that period, but with an admixture of grammatically correct Arabic. It is interesting to note that the writer confuses his pronouns as, in fact, Arab writers often did. Thus we see him alternating the singular with the plural, referring to himself sometimes as "we," and on other occasions as "I."[5] After reading the text, one may conclude that the recto should in fact follow the verso; for despite the loss or illegibility of words in the first four lines of the verso, it can be detected that here we have the beginning of a letter.[6] In this connection it should also be noted that at the beginning of the recto the word קאל ("he said") naturally follows on from the additional line found in the margin of the verso.

Most of the letter is concerned with news, business requests, and other personal matters relating to different persons, some of whom can be identified as, for example, Rabbenu Yitzhak (recto, line 8)[7] – a famous judge and member of a Jewish religious court. Those who are unidentifiable are Ibn Hilāl and Dāwūd, al-Faqīh, and the merchant by the name of Abū al-Qāsim Ibn ʿAlī. Nevertheless, the most important of the people who figure in this letter are Maimonides himself and members of his family: his nephew Abū al-Riḍā, his sister Umm Abū al-Riḍā, his brother-in-law Abū al-Maʿālī, and a physician colleague of Maimonides whose name is al-Muwaffaq. According to the late S. D. Goitein, Abū al-Riḍā was chief physician.[8] As for Abū al-Maʿālī, al-Qifṭī (d. 646/1248) states that this man, who was then secretary to the mother of Nūr al-Dīn,[9] married Maimonides' sister, one of whose children was Abū al-Riḍā – "a serene, wise physician who became employed by Qilij Arslan in the lands of the Rūm."[10]

In the history of medicine we have many case histories written by doctors, but in the present instance it is the patient himself who recounts for us his encounters with his physicians. Whether such encounters were prearranged appointments we do not know. Be that as it may, it appears that at his first meeting with Maimonides the author writes (verso, line 8) that he was awed by his (Maimonides') handsomeness (אלחסן).[11] On his second visit, the writer was inquisitive enough to ask Maimonides' advice about reading[12] some medicine (לנקרא שי מן אלטב) whereupon Maimonides replied, "I shall speak on your behalf with al-Muwaffaq,[13] who will take you for one session a day." It would seem that Maimonides was a very busy man with numerous commitments, as has already been discovered from his letters, that he could spare no time for taking on students or apprentices. We learn also that laity explored the fringes of medicine and our inquisitive man, the author of the letter, was one of them. We understand later from his letter that he was fixed with al-Muwaffaq and was also well received by the other "students" who were happy to meet him (ופרחו כלהם ביא כתיר).

As far as the clinical examination is concerned, and the doctor who conducted it, there is here uncertainty, but in all likelihood it was al-Muwaffaq. For, if we accept that the recto of the fragment follows on from the verso, we find that our author, the patient, added in the margin of the so-called verso that, feeling excessively hot, he went to al-Shaykh al-Muwaffaq to tell him of his complaint, whereupon he was told to raise his urinary flask (קארורה) and al-Muwaffaq then proceeded to examine the urine.

What follows is irrelevant to identification, but it is interesting from the point of view of diagnosis and treatment. Having inspected the urine, the doctor next made his pronouncement, "You have no fever." He then felt his patient's pulse and told him: "You have nothing but dryness in your body; go and take barley gruel [כשך אלשעיר]." Being nonresident in the town, he was invited by Maimonides' sister, Umm Abū al-Riḍā, to lodge in her house. Upon her insistence and on the recommendation of one of his acquaintances, Rabbenu Yitzhak, he decided to stay with her until he finished his four-day course of treatment with barley gruel as prescribed by the doctor. He felt much better; he no longer felt thirst, and he regained his previous healthy complexion.

From this short clinical history we can see that inspection of urine and the feeling of the pulse were the two important procedures without which no "accurate" diagnosis could be established and no appropriate regimen prescribed. Jewish physicians, like their Arab colleagues in the Middle Ages, although needing "aids to diagnosis," were skilled observers and proceeded in clinical method along the same lines as their Greek predecessors, to whom they were undoubtedly indebted.[14] Uroscopy was an essential part of what at that time constituted medical examination of the patient. It remained one of the most favored techniques of diagnosis and prognosis. It achieved the dignity of a supposed science, and its devotees referred to Hippocrates as its founder. Urine was collected in a flask (qārūra) which was to become as symbolic of the medieval Arab physician as the stethoscope is of the present-day doctor. It was held by the physician, or the patient himself as in our case, for urine inspection was supposed to reveal the bad humor of the body, i.e., the offending agent. Isaac Israeli's book *Sefer ha-Sheten (De Urinis)* proved to be one of the classic works which influenced the later medieval writers. For years the urine lore loomed large in all diagnoses and the pictures of physicians show them almost invariably holding up a urinal for inspection.[15] What al-Muwaffaq, or any other contemporary physician, observed in his patient's urine was its color, consistency, froth, and the copious or scanty quantity, the different kinds of clouds and the sediments,[16] if any, all of which assisted the examiner to draw most important and far-reaching conclusions. Here, the examining physician was looking for substances which he believed were removed from the body by way of the urinary tract.[17]

Another clinical method which the physician of that period generally used during his clinical examination was the feeling of the pulse. The importance of the practice was already recognized by the Greek physicians, and, before them, their Egyptian colleagues.[18] The Arabs, compared with their predecessors, the Greeks, were just as keen to describe the pulse fully, and several treatises were written by men like Rhazes (al-Rāzī, 865–925) and Avicenna (Ibn Sīnā, 980–1037). On the whole, their general views appear to be almost identical, but Avicenna's account of the pulse is characterized by extreme verbal subtlety.[19] The doctor who felt the pulse must have been trying to assess certain characteristics such as its rhythm, rate, expansion and prolongation, size and strength. Maimonides, in his *Aphorisms*, describes the pulse in detail and uses its characteristics in assessing the causes of fevers and the diagnosis and prognosis of the disease.[20] Like Rhazes, he differentiates between the regularly irregular and the irregularly irregular.

After having gone through such clinical examination our physician, al-Shaykh al Muwaffaq as we believe him to be, came to the conclusion that his patient, the writer of this letter, had no fever. He diagnosed the complaint as dryness of the body *(yabs)*,[21] probably being a concomitant of thirst—an aggravating symptom which the author claims ceased to exist after the strict regime of an appropriate treatment with barley gruel.[22] Maimonides favors the use of barley water as a gastric remedy, in the tradition of Hippocrates, who prescribed it repeatedly.[23]

Finally, I have tried, and I hope satisfactorily, to study the medical aspect of this document, and also what concerns the encounter with Maimonides, who was then held in such exalted status and revered reputation. The clinical examination, methods of diagnosis, and treatment fit well within the humoral doctrines with no evidence of modification through experience. We also learn that the methods of imparting knowledge were through holding study sessions (seminars) which were open to medical students and those members of the laity interested in acquiring medical knowledge. The interesting feature of this letter is that the patient himself relates the information to us.

The other items concerning personal matters and business dealings are, in this case, of secondary importance. But, considered from the linguistic side, this fragment is in a purely Judeo-Arabic world, the vocabulary of which is almost entirely in Arabic, lending a variety in the usage of grammar and syntax which makes possible greater affective expression. It is a pity that in most of such Genizah fragments, where lacunae exist as a result of faded ink, illegibility, or paper destruction, transcription becomes difficult and translation poor. Nevertheless, I have tried my best to extract and translate as much as possible the material concerning the clinical aspect of this fragment, and left the other material available to those who may venture further study and research.

TEXT

T-S NS 321.34 (verso)

1) ... פי קלבי נאר ....
.... וצאקת עלי ....
מנך ולעל .... גריב ....
... מנך אלדעא .... פי שי סודה
5) והקבה ינגמע שמלי בך עלי כיר ועאפיה
... אני דכלת לענד רבינו משה ולקית
מנ[ה] מן [אל]הסן כמא אבצרתה פי אלנום
וקאל לי [ר]בינו יצחק ישכרך עמ[לך] [כ]תיר
ואנ[ת]מעת ברבינו יצחק וברצי אלדולה
10) ופרחו ביא כתיר גדא ... ואסתנגמעת
ברבינו משה וקאל לי כיף טלעת קלת לה
מא טלעת אלא לנקרא שי מן אלטב קאל מא
הו אלא צואב אנא אתחדת לך מע אלשיך
אלמופק יכון יקר[י]ך נובה כל יום וקאל לי
15) אלדיאן ... אבן ... רצי אלדולה ואכו אלשיך
אבו אלמחאסן צהר
.... יקראו עליה
תכון .... ופרחו כלהם ביא כתיר
.... נבתדי אלא אני משגול מע
20) אכי חתי מא יסאפר וכנת מע כאלתי תוקלב
פי אלנהאר עדת טהר וטלעת אלקאהרה חתי
נאכד להם כתאב אן יטלקוהם מן דמיאט אבאן
יטלקו נסא ואכר אלחאל הם מעולין פי אלבר ואמא
חדית אלשיך אבו אלמנצור ואלשיך אבו אלחסין
25) פאן עליהם אליום מאיה ועשרין דינאר דין
ואלדיאן לה ענדהם מנהא עשרין דינאר ורצי
אלדולה לה ענדהם אלאכר כמסין דינאר מא
קדרו יאכדו מנהם ולא כרובה ואכר אלחאל
קאלת לי אם אבו רצי אן אבנה ברכאת נמע
30) ענדהן גאליתה מא וצלת אידיהם יופהא לה
אלא בקא מסתכבי פי אלבית לס[א]עה חתי דפעו לה
בעצהא ובקי ענדהם בעצהא לס[א]עה ו[י]כפאך
דא ואמאני נפסהם ינו לסכנדריה עסי יחצל
להם מן אבן הלאל ודאוד שי ואנא בעלמך
35) מא כרנת ומעי ולא כרובה ולולא מוסי יון עלי חק

added from the margin:

פי מא נר... כנת נשכו מן דיך אלחראה ונא מציח אלי ענד
אלשיך אלמופק ושכית לה אלחאל קאל

1.34 (recto)

(1) קאל לי ארפע לי מאך פרפעת לה אלקארורה
קאל מא ענדך חמא ואבצר נפצי קאל מא בך
אלא יבם פי בדנך אסתעמל כשך אלשעיר
ולמא סמעת ביא אם אבו אלרצי ערצא נאת

(5) וחלפת עליא אני מא ננזל אלא ענדהא קאלת
פ(אנא) קאעדה וחדי ואבן אכתי מעי צגיר מרית אל[י]
ענדהא קעדת סאעה ומצית אלי ענד רבינו
יצחק קאל תכן ענדהא ותקצי חאגתך
מ ... קלת לה מא נעמל אלם[א]עה שי חתי יסאפר

(10) אכי ויטמאן קלבי מן נהתה ועמלת לי אלכשך
ושרבתה ארבעה איאם קטע עני שרב אלמא
וצלח לוני וקאל לי אסתנגמה קבל אלעיד פלו
בקית עלי דאך אלתדביר כאנו יברדו מעדתי
ונרגע נחמיהא ומא כנת אלא מתדארג ללמר[ץ]

(15) ללמרץ אלאול וכל מן ילקאני יוהמני פלו אני מא
טלעת אלא לדא [כדא?] פכיף אכון אן שא אללה מא ננחדר
אלא בפצאיל כתיר פי חיאתך פמא נחב מנך אלא
אלדעוה ומא כאן יתהיא לי נקול אלכדב אני טלעת
נסלם עלי אכי א[ל][ס][א]עה עסי תנפדו לי אלעמאמה

(20) ואלשקה ואלכצר ו[אל]כתפיה אלדהך תדפעוה ללפקיה
ירסלה הו ואלשקה ואלעמאמה אן כאן אוצא בה
וצו אלמצפי עליהא באן יסקיהא אלניר חתי תביץ
ויכרג אלטבוע אלדי פיהא וערפו אלפקיה אן
לי פי אלדהב דינאר ואן כאן רבינו אלעזר אחד

(25) אלעשרין דרהם אלדי כאן ענה ירסלהא ערפוני
וקד ארסלת ... מתאע אלכמר מע (נלאם אלוכול) והוא אלענבר מע
אלמכארי והו מערפה ואחד תאגר אסמה אבו
אלקאסם בן עלי אלקבארי וע[ר]פו אלפקיה אן קד
וצלני אלדינאר אלדי ארסל וקד אתחדרתה מע אלשיך

(30) אבו אלמעאלי צהר רבינו משה קלת לה אדא כאן מע
ואחד עשרין דינאר נציב רגל תקה בחית
תכון מנה אלוצול מחפוטה קאל לע הונא צבו[ה]
דין עטימה ארא דפעת לה שי כאנת אלאצול
מחפוצה ומא תערם פאידה פאן

(35) .... פצה כתיר קאל לי ואן לם ...
תכון ארא וקעת .... רכיצה נש ...
לך ונפדוהא מע אלמ ... ה מא ...
....

N.B. [ ] = reconstruction by the editor.
( ) = added from the margin.

TRANSLATION

(verso)

1) ... Fire in my heart ...
... Oppression overwhelmed me ...
From you ... probably ... strange ...
... from you invocation of God ... in matter, black (melancholy?)
5) And may the Holy One blessed be He (God) reunite us in excellence and health.
... I called on Rabbenu Moshe and was met with such handsomeness (*ḥusn*–"beauty") just as I have dreamed of him.
Rabbenu Yitzhak (Isaac) said to me: "He thanks you profusely for what you have done."
I met Rabbenu Yitzhak together with Riḍā al-Dawla
10) and they were very pleased to see me. I also came to be with Rabbenu Moshe who asked me why (lit. how) I came out, and I said to him:
"I only came out to read some medicine." "This is nothing but correct," he said, "I shall speak on your behalf with al-Shaykh al-Muwaffaq and he will make you read one session a day."
15) The judge (dayyan) ... son ... Riḍā al-Dawla and the brother of al-Shaykh Abū al-Maḥāsin (brother-in-law or son-in-law) ...
... study under him you will be ... they all were very happy to meet me.
... we were to start but I was busy with
20) my brother until he left. I was with my aunt *Tuqlub* during the day. I returned at noon and went to Cairo to take a letter to them so they will be allowed to leave Dimyāṭ, whereupon they let their women go. Finally, they were determined to leave by road. As for the matter concerning al-Shaykh Abū al-Manṣūr and al-Shaykh
25) Abū al-Ḥusayn, they are today in debt of one hundred and twenty dinars, the judge has twenty dinars from this debt and Riḍā al-Dawla's share is fifty dinars. (These two) could not get out of them even one *kharrūba*. Finally, Abū al-Riḍā's mother told me that his (Abū al-Riḍā's) son Barakāt
30) had collected the poll-tax which is what they could afford to pay him, but he remained hidden until now in the house until they paid him some of it and the rest of it remained with them. This, (I hope) will satisfy you, but I trust they themselves will go to Alexandria where they may get something from Ibn Hilāl and Dāwūd. You (must) know
35) that I did not leave with even one *kharrūba*.

added from the margin:
I was complaining of that heat, and it happened that I went to al-Shaykh al-Muwaffaq and described my complaint to him and he spoke.

(recto)

1) He said to me: "Hold up your water for me [to see]." So I raised the (urinary) flask.
   He said: "You have no fever." He then felt my pulse and said: "You have nothing but dryness in your body, use barley gruel."
   When the mother of Abū al-Riḍā heard about me quite by chance, she came

5) and made me solemnly promise to stay with no one but herself, and said:
   "I am all on my own, and my sister's son who is with me, is young." So I went to her and stayed for a while, and then I went to (the house of) Rabbenu Yitzhak. "Stay with her," he said, "and do what you need to do."
   ... I said to him: "I shan't do anything just yet, [I shall wait] till my brother sets off

10) and one can be sure that all is well with him." She made me the barley gruel which I drank over a period of four days, as a result of which I stopped drinking water and my complexion was thus restored. He (Rabbenu Yitzhak) said to me: "Take full advantage of it [i.e., the regimen] before the festival." For, had I remained on that (previous) regime it would have chilled my stomach and I would have kept on warming it again, and all I was doing was slipping back into the illness,

15) the illness I had had at the beginning. Every one who met me could not imagine it was me. I wonder what would have happened to me had I not come out (to seek) such (treatment)!
   If God wills, we shall leave only with many kindnesses in your life time. We only wish you well and it was not possible for me to tell lies. I came out to greet my brother just now. Perhaps you will send me the turban,

20) the robe, the neck-band and the shoulder-band. You hand over the gold to the *Faqīh,* who will send it to me together with the robe and the turban if he so recommends.
   Bid the bleacher to soak (sponge) it with lime until it is bleached and (all of) the stains which are in it, are removed. Tell the *Faqīh* that I have a share in the gold, worth a dinar. If Rabbenu Elazar had taken the twenty dirhems

25) which he had to send them, let me know.
   I have sent ... wine utensils with the agent's servant and the medicine of amber with the muleteer, an acquaintance of a merchant whose name is Abū al-Qāsim Ibn 'Alī al-Qabārī. Tell the *Faqīh* that I received the dinar which he had sent me. I have spoken to al-Shaykh Abū

30) al-Ma'ālī, Rabbenu Moshe's brother-in-law ...

6

Maimonides' Concept of Mental Illness and Mental Health

Harvey N. Kranzler

Maimonides' approach to mental illness and mental health provides insight into the influence his knowledge of medicine and experience as a physician had on his development as a jurist, theologian, and philosopher.

HISTORICAL PERSPECTIVE

We have evidence of Maimonides' treatment of patients with mental illness only by implication in his medical writings, such as in his *Treatise on Asthma*, which clearly depicts asthma as a psychosomatic illness amenable not only to correct diet but also to spiritual treatment.[1] More specifically, in *Regimen of Health (Regimen Sanitatis)*[2] and *Treatise on the Causes of Symptoms*,[3] both of which were written for the Vizier Al-Malik al Fadil—who suffered from depression—Maimonides provides prescriptions of diet, physical exercise, proper breathing, sexual moderation, music, and walks in pleasant surroundings, as well as the study of prophets and philosophers to enhance calmness, moderation, and virtues for the maintenance of physical and mental health. In *Treatise on the Causes of Symptoms,* Maimonides notes that in addition to treating the vizier for his depression, he has treated others, probably of royal rank, with depression and mania.[4] One may assume, therefore, that during his study and practice of medicine, he had contact with and treated the mentally ill.

There is evidence from a letter Maimonides wrote in Hebrew in 1185 to R. Yephet ha-Dayyan[5] that he himself had suffered a reactive depression, or at least a sustained period of intense mourning. This occurred as a result of the death of his beloved younger brother, David, whose commercial endeavors in the family business had left Maimonides free to pursue his religious and scholarly activities. He describes movingly his reaction upon learning that his brother had been lost at sea in the Indian Ocean while traveling on business. With him was lost most of the family's financial assets. "I remained for almost a year, from the time I heard the terrible news, bedridden, with boils, fever, confusion and I was on the verge of destruction." Even eight years after this tragedy, at the time he was writing this letter, he described being strongly affected whenever he came across his brother's handwriting or books. Maimonides manifested symptoms very suggestive of significant depression or pathological mourning: remaining in bed for a lengthy period of time, psychosomatic symptoms, confusion, feelings of hopelessness, distress about his brother's death and his financial ruin. There is perhaps a hint at a wish to no longer live in his words: "I was on the verge of destruction." After this year of immobilization, Maimonides was impelled to leave the purely scholarly life and begin the practice of medicine in order to support himself and his family.

This letter to R. Yephet ha-Dayyan provides an insight into the human side of Maimonides in the aftermath of his personal tragedy. The contrast between this letter and the following statement in the *Mishneh Torah,* the Code of Law, *Hilkhot Evel* (Laws of Mourning) 13:11 is striking: "One should not mourn too much . . . for [death] is part of the natural order and a person who pains himself overmuch over the natural order of the world is a fool." The tension between the ideal as written in the Code of Law and his own intense reaction to loss as depicted in the letter may indicate a productive tension between Maimonides' ideal of philosophical serenity and the empathic physician who understands the human condition from his own struggle and experience. Despite the exacting standards of the code, he is able to understand the imperfections of man, as exemplified by this letter and by his caring for patients such as the Vizier Al-Malik al Fadil, a somewhat dissolute and depressed potentate.

HALAKHIC PERSPECTIVE

Maimonides' medical expertise and experience with patients manifesting symptoms of mental illness may have influenced his legal definition of insanity in the *Mishneh Torah,* the Code of Law, in *Hilkhot Edut* (Laws of Witnesses) 9:9–10:

> The insane person [*shoteh*] is unacceptable as a witness by biblical law, because he is not subject to the commandments. By *shoteh* is to be understood not only

one who walks around naked, breaks things and throws stones, but anyone whose mind has become disturbed so that his thinking is consistently confused in some domain. Although with respect to other matters he speaks to the point and asks pertinent questions, his evidence is nevertheless inadmissible and he is included among the insane.

In case of the epileptic, during a fit he is unacceptable; when he is free [of seizures] he is acceptable. This is the case whether the paroxysm occurs periodically or at irregular intervals, provided that he is not mentally disordered all of the time, for there are epileptics who are disturbed even when free of seizures. The testimony of epileptics requires very careful [judicial] deliberation.

The intellectually deficient who cannot recognize contradictions and are unable to comprehend things as ordinary people do and those who are extremely agitated and frantic are classed with the insane. Discretionary power is vested in the judge in this matter, as it is impossible to lay down detailed rules on this subject.

This definition of mental illness is based on Maimonides' interpretation of the Babylonian Talmud in *Hagigah* 3b, in which the symptoms of insanity are presented as follows: "Who is an insane person [*shoteh*]? One who goes out alone at night; one who spends the night in a cemetery and one who rends his garments. . . ."

The Talmud then presents two differing opinions as to the definition of insanity. R. Huna states that a person must manifest all three symptoms delineated to be considered a *shoteh* (legally insane), since any one of the actions may have a logical explanation and does not therefore constitute insanity. R. Yohanan claims that even if a person performs only one of the actions listed in the Talmud, he may be considered insane as long as it occurs in a deranged manner. The Jerusalem Talmud (*Terumot* 1:1) adds that the *shoteh* is one who destroys all that is given to him.

Maimonides interprets the symptoms noted in the Talmud to be merely examples of mental illness. He broadens the legal definition of insanity from very limited, narrow criteria so that it includes any symptoms that indicate confusion or psychosis, whether the etiology is mental illness, mental retardation, or a physical illness.[6] Maimonides gives discretionary power to the judge to make individual decisions in each particular case, implying also the possibility that the judge may request expert testimony of a medical nature to help determine the particular state of the person being judged competent or incompetent. This is a very modern concept, and Maimonides interprets the talmudic source in this manner, in marked contrast to the very narrow definitions of other halakhic (legal) authorities of his time, such as Rabbenu Simhah of Speyer and Rabbenu Avigdor ha-Cohen, who limit the definitions of mental illness to the examples given in the Talmud.[7]

Maimonides chose to place his definition of insanity in the Laws of Witnesses, where it is incorporated into the effort of defining competence and understanding of events, actions, and ideas. This perspective was influenced not only by Maimonides' interpretation of the talmudic sources, but also by his experience as a physician. He recognized that there are many biological conditions, as well as psychological states, that can influence the functioning of the mind. Each case should be adjudicated individually within broad guidelines that allow for differential diagnoses as well as a specific mental-status examination. The complexities of mental illness were understood by Maimonides the physician from his own clinical experience, and he reached the halakhic conclusion that to attempt to define mental illness legally by specifying only the particular symptoms listed in the Talmud was too limiting. This has serious legal ramification, such as in the Laws of Divorce, since granting a divorce requires full understanding and competence and is more difficult to accomplish if symptoms other that those enumerated in the Talmud are evident. Rabbenu Simhah of Speyer and Rabbenu Avigdor ha-Cohen limit the definition of mental illness for this reason. For Maimonides, however, the talmudic definition did not fit his clinical experience, and he could not limit his definition of legal competence, despite this motivation to do so.

NOSOLOGICAL PERSPECTIVE

Maimonides differentiates psychotic and confusional states from affective disorders and depression. In his commentary on the Mishnah (*Shabbat* 2:5), Maimonides takes the biblical term describing King Saul's madness (1Samuel 16:14), *ruah raah*[8] to be melancholia, an illness in which the person isolates himself from other people and avoids light, preferring to remain alone in the dark due to fears and sadness. Maimonides' clinical understanding of depression is further evident in the Code of Law, *Hilkhot Sanhedrin* 18:6:

> It is a scriptural decree that the court shall not put a man to death or flog him on his own admission [of guilt].... For it is possible that he is mentally disturbed in this matter. Perhaps he is one of those who are in misery, bitter in soul, who long for death, thrust the sword in their bellies or cast themselves down from the roof. Perhaps in the same way he comes to confess to a crime he has not committed, in order that he might be put to death....

Maimonides' knowledge of the symptomatology of depression is clearly evident, and rather than simply state the well-known talmudic principle (*Sanhedrin* 9b) "No man may incriminate himself," he provides a reasoning for the law which is based on his clinical understanding of the power of suicidal ideation. He uses this rare possibility of a despondent accused wishing to incriminate himself into the death penalty to explain the fundamental law preventing self-incrimination.[9]

In his letter *Iggeret Teiman*, sent to the Jews of Yemen in 1173 to inspire hope and courage in a community severely stressed by forced conversion to Islam, Maimonides also addresses the issue of mental illness. A member of the community claimed that he was the Messiah, and Maimonides describes this man as "mentally ill, without a doubt."[10] Further on in the *Iggeret Teiman*, Maimonides advises the Jews of Yemen to save themselves from the ire of the ruler of Yemen by showing that they considered the person claiming to be the Messiah mentally ill and placing him in custody. The ruler would thereby not persecute the entire community because of his activities.[11] In the *Letter on Astrology*, written in 1195 and sent to the Jews of southern France, Maimonides also described the situation in Yemen and reiterated that the false Messiah there was mad. He proved it by recounting that when this man was taken captive, he attempted to prove to the ruler of Yemen that he was the actual Messiah by stating that his head could be cut off and he would then be resurrected. When the ruler accommodated and decapitated him, he did not resurrect, definitively proving Maimonides' diagnosis concerning the false Messiah in the *Iggeret Teiman*.[12]

ETHICAL AND PHILOSOPHICAL PERSPECTIVE

In contrast to his legal definitions of insanity and his obvious familiarity with the spectrum of symptomatology of mental illness, Maimonides presents a different perspective on mental health and illness in his ethical and philosophical writings, in which he is concerned with the soul, the inner essence of man, and the development of character. For Maimonides, character is the observable external manifestation of the soul in the form of man's psychological state and his actions. In *Shemonah Perakim* (Eight Chapters), his Introduction to the *Mishnah Avot*, and in *Hilkhot Deot* (Laws of Ethics or Psychological Characteristics), Maimonides presents a schema incorporating Aristotelian ethics as well as traditional Judaic sources, in which mental health is defined as the balanced middle way between the extremes of any emotion or character trait, the golden mean. Illness of the soul and character is defined as any deviation from the balanced middle way. Maimonides applies the concepts of illness and health, the terminology of the physician, even in his philosophical thinking. This is stated as follows in *Shemonah Perakim*, chapter 3:

> The ancients maintained that the soul, like the body is subject to good health and illness. The soul's healthful state is due to its condition and that of its faculties, by which it constantly does what is right and performs what is proper, while the illness of the soul is occasioned by its condition, and that of its

faculties, which result from its constantly doing wrong, and performing actions that are improper. . . . Those whose soul becomes ill should consult the sages, the moral physicians, who will advise them. . . .

In *Shemonah Perakim,* chapter 4, he continues:

> Good deeds are such as are equibalanced, between two equally bad extremes, the too much and the too little. Virtues are psychic conditions and dispositions which are midway between two reprehensible extremes. . . . acts may incline toward either extreme . . . in which case his soul becomes diseased. . . . By the words of our prophets and sages of our Law, we see that they were bent upon moderation and the care of one's soul and bodies. . . . If a man always carefully discriminates as regards his actions, directing them to the medium course, he will reach the highest perfection possible to a human being, thereby approaching God, and sharing in his happiness.

In *Shemonah Perakim,* deviation from the golden mean is appropriate only for the especially pious man who uses extremes of behaviors such as renouncing particular foods, wine, or sexual intercourse as a means of restoring the health of his more sensitive soul to a state of balance. Withdrawal from society is acceptable only as a means of protecting the saintly from an immoral society. These behaviors were strongly proscribed for the common man, for whom moderation and the golden mean is the only appropriate path and for whom ascetic or extreme actions detrimentally affect the balance and health of the soul. Maimonides, in *Shemonah Perakim,* seems to be overtly attacking the form of Sufi asceticism and renunciation of the world that was attracting Jewish adherents at that time.[13]

In *Hilkhot Deot,* chapter 1, Maimonides repeats that the middle path is the correct one. For example, temperance is the healthy emotion or moral quality between the extremes of lechery and insensibility. Patience is considered the healthy balance between irascibility and impassivity, and modesty is the golden mean between haughtiness and meekness. The man who maintains the perfect balance of the middle way is characterized as a wise man *(hakham),* and the man who deviates toward the more positive extreme because he is especially careful and introspective is called a pious or saintly man *(hasid).*

> We are bidden to walk in the middle paths which are right and proper ways, as it is said, "And thou shalt walk in his ways" (Deut. 29:9). . . . How shall a man train himself in these dispositions so that they become ingrained? Let him practice again and again the actions prompted by those dispositions which are the mean between the extremes and repeat them continually until they become easy and are no longer irksome to him and so the corresponding dispositions will become a fixed part of his character. . . . Whoever walks in this way secures for himself happiness and blessing . . ." *(Hilkhot Deot* 1:5, 7).

Maimonides, however, appears to reverse himself in chapter 2 of *Hilkhot Deot* and states that there are two ethical or psychological characteristics—self-esteem and anger—in which one should not attempt to achieve the middle way but should rather make efforts to inculcate in oneself the extreme character. He advises not modesty in contrast to haughtiness but rather extreme meekness. He completely rejects the emotion of anger, even in a situation in which anger may be appropriate, and suggests that one may only simulate anger for educational purposes when this is the only method of teaching a child or community to improve. This espousal of the extreme appears on the surface to be in contradiction to his position in *Shemonah Perakim*, where deviation from the golden mean is accepted merely as a therapeutic technique for achieving the middle balanced way, even for the pious and spiritually sensitive. Maimonides seems to be shifting in tone, if not in actual substance, away from his overt espousal of the middle way in the first chapter of *Hilkhot Deot*, beyond even his differentiation between the wise man who follows the balanced middle way and the saintly man who deviates toward an extreme because of his religious or ethical sensitivity.

In the *Moreh Nevukhim (Guide for the Perplexed)*,[14] written approximately ten years after the Code of Law, Maimonides presents a very different picture in which balance, moderation, and the middle way are clearly of diminished importance. In the *Guide for the Perplexed* 3:48, Maimonides no longer condemns the Nazirite and the person who takes upon himself extra vows of abstention or restriction, as he does in *Shemonah Perakim*, chapter 4, and *Hilkhot Deot*, chapter 3. In the *Guide for the Perplexed* 3:54, the importance of moral, ethical, psychological balance is relegated to a level below his highest ideal, the fourth perfection, which is the intellectual knowledge of God. Has Maimonides given up the middle way in favor of an extreme, ascetic, purely rational, intellectual ideal? There have been numerous efforts to address this question.[15] A developmental approach may provide a further perspective.

DEVELOPMENTAL PERSPECTIVE

Modern psychology or psychiatry has mental health as its primary goal. For Maimonides, mental health, as defined by the healthy soul, is merely the means or a stepping-stone toward achieving the ultimate goal, which is the intellectual knowledge of God. In *Shemonah Perakim* and *Hilkhot Deot*, Maimonides' goal is to enhance the development of the self, with the ability to moderate passions, drives, and needs in the service of God. In the *Guide for the Perplexed*, the ideal is not the development of a healthy soul but rather the subordination of self, both body and soul, in the service of the highest perfection—the intellectual knowledge of God—to the point where all action and thought is dispassionate and derives directly from a transcendent closeness with God, not from one's own moral character, ethical standards, and psychological health. In other words, real mental health for Maimonides is achieved when man is no longer concerned with mental health or the self at all. To achieve this level, however, one must first have attained a healthy inner character, a sense of self that is able to provide a sound basis for further development. In normal development, both biological and psychological, each new stage of development is predicated upon the previous stage having been achieved. In Maimonidean terms, the healthy body and soul are essential prerequisites for the ultimate goal of being able to transcend them in the pursuit of the highest perfection. The healthy soul of the wise man (*hakham*) described in *Shemonah Perakim* and in *Hilkhot Deot*, with its emphasis on moderation and the balance of the middle way, is a necessary precursor and stepping-stone for man to achieve the level of the pious or saintly man (*hasid*) described in *Hilkhot Deot*, who moves off center to an extreme in his quest for knowledge of God. The pious or saintly character may then be a necessary level for the achievement of Maimonides' highest level, as described in the *Guide* 3:54, the total identification with and intellectual knowledge of God with concomitant negation of any concern for one's own physical or psychological self.

Maimonides is presenting a blueprint for stages of religious development, and as in all developmental schema, Maimonides understands that not everyone reaches the highest level, although it is the ultimate goal.[16] This perspective may also help to explain why Maimonides reverses himself in *Hilkhot Deot* regarding anger and pride, demanding an extreme negation of these emotions rather than the balanced middle way. The power of anger and pride have too detrimental an effect on man's ability to transcend the self and therefore must be dealt with in a more extreme fashion.[17] Maimonides the man, the practical physician and healer of the soul as well as the body, was aware that most people are unable to achieve the highest level espoused in the *Guide*. He addresses the *Guide* to his pupil, Yosef ben Yehuda, someone he believes has at least the possibility of achieving the highest level of perfection.[18] Maimonides does not diminish or negate the efforts of those who are struggling to develop a healthy soul with an inner sense of balance and self, and for them he provides the guidelines for achieving knowledge of God in *Shemonah Perakim* and *Hilkhot Deot*. These levels of religious development may also provide an insight into Maimonides' own personal religious, ethical, and moral development.

PHYSICIAN OF THE SOUL

From Maimonides' letters and medical writings there emerges a powerful composite picture of a physician who treats his patients with care and gentleness, a true dispassionate concern that comes from his total subordination of self in the quest for knowledge of God. The manner in which he addresses the Vizier Al-Malik al Fadil in both the *Regimen of Health* and the *Treatise on the Causes of Symptoms* is not that of a physician who is concerned with his own importance in the court of the ruler of his land. Maimonides' deep caring for his patient is clearly evident in these two medical treatises, despite the vizier's dissolute life-style, which was antithetical to everything Maimonides believed in. In addition to providing all the prescriptions for diet, exercises, syrups, and electuaries for the vizier's depression, anxiety, and constipation in great detail, Maimonides provides the guidance for his ethical growth in an effort to help him achieve some degree of moderation and inner balance. He gently condemns the vizier's overindulgence and focuses on the need to achieve peace of mind by efforts at restraint and limiting extremes of emotion.[19] He informs the vizier that this may be accomplished by "those who have learned and have studied philosophical virtues and moral admonitions of the religious law and the chastisements—they acquire strength of mind and they are truly strong."[20] Maimonides is able to lovingly but firmly educate the vizier:

> How many times has a rich man become impoverished and a king lost his kingdom and this occurrence became the cause of the improvement of his body and the perfection of his soul with virtuous characteristics, and the prolongation of his days, bringing him closer to the Lord his Creator and his cleavage to Him by serving Him? This is the ultimate and eternal good.[21]

One senses that Maimonides would have treated a beggar with the same gentle care as well as firm but lovingly prescribed advice. It is Maimonides himself who exemplifies the fourth and highest form of perfection.

7

The Art of Cure: A Medical Text by Maimonides

Uriel S. Barzel

Maimonides' *The Art of Cure*, otherwise known as the *Compendium of Galen*,[1] has been in existence in Arabic in manuscript form only. There are two distinct manuscripts, one in the Escurial Library in Spain and the other in Paris. The Escurial-Casiri manuscript (798) was copied in 1413 by Musa ibn Alfadil Yusuf Ibn Sasoon in a North African Arabic script. It is a plain-looking manuscript. There are no decorations, but key words are in large letters. This 155-page manuscript has numerous minor omissions: some 24 individual lines throughout the text, as well as one full page, are missing. The Paris manuscript (1023) is in Hebrew (Rashi) script, and is not dated. This manuscript has decorated captions, and the key words throughout the manuscript are written in bold script. When compared to the Escurial manuscript, the Paris manuscript is found to be missing at least 15 pages. Some extraneous material brings this manuscript to 200 pages.

In its format, *The Art of Cure* deviates from the then-usual presentation of medical subjects, and instead of discussing disorders in an organ-oriented system, it deals with classifications of disease: the definition of the disease state, wounds, diseases of paired organs, febrile disorders, and tumors.

Although Maimonides states in the text that he reproduced the writings of Galen faithfully, there is no doubt that the compendium format allowed him to select those observations that he felt were appropriate for his time and place, but the criteria for these selections are not stated in this text. Here and there he illustrates his discussion of disease with clinical examples which clearly reflect his personal experience as a physician.

Maimonides had a good knowledge of gross anatomy, which must have been developed through observation, as he says at one point in the manuscript, "we ourselves would not know the difference [between a round tendon and a nerve] were it not for the art of surgery." He recognized the difference between pulsating and nonpulsating blood vessels, but obviously had no concept of the circulation of blood, which was discovered hundreds of years after his time. Similarly, he had no knowledge of physiology as we know it today. The prevailing medical tenets of the time were the Aristotelian principle of the four qualities and the Hippocratic doctrine of the four humors. These provided the framework for the explanation of all natural phenomena as well as disease phenomena. According to these schemes, bodily health depended on the proper equilibrium between the qualities of hot, cold, dry, and wet, and on the balanced mixing of the four humors – the blood, the phlegm, the black bile (melancholy), and the yellow bile (choler) (Table 7-1). Disease states were the results of shifts in the equilibrium of the qualities, or of disturbances in the balance of the humors, or of both. Analyses of the state of the qualities and of the state of the humors provided the physician with the guidelines for his therapeutic decisions, which were meant to return the equilibrium and balance to normal.

Like all physicians of his time, Maimonides subscribed, of course, to these concepts. In his description of medical conditions and diseases, he repeatedly refers to the state of the qualities and of the humors in each condition, and explains his therapeutic prescription in these terms. Thus we read (chapter 3): "Let us assume that the wounded organ has exceeded the temperate state towards dryness by four numbers, and that the complexion of the body exceeded the temperate state towards dryness by three numbers. It is evident, then, that the organ needs a medicine that exceeds the temperate state by one number. [All this is known as guess or estimate]."

The mainstays of treatment in general were purging and phlebotomy, as well as bathing, diet control, and a variety of medications, most of which were herbals or herbal compounds available in the Mediterranean countries at the time. The choice of the latter was also dependent on their perceived effect on the qualities or on the humors in the sick body.

Table 7-1.

The four qualities	The four humors
hot	blood
cold	phlegm
dry	black bile (melancholy)
wet	yellow bile (choler)

Maimonides states that he was careful to prescribe only those treatment regimens and those medications that he found by his own experience to be useful. The specific prescription for a treatment regimen for any condition took into account not only the nature of the illness, but also the constitution of the patient, his or her age and habits, geography and climate (the town in which the patient lived), and the time of the year (Table 7-2). Thus, he individualized his therapy and prescribed different treatment regimens and different medications to suit the different circumstances of every patient. In fact, he evokes the authority of Galen and says (chapter 8): "Said the author: Galen is instructing us here that when deciding a treatment we have to observe seven things: the nature of the sickness, the nature of the patient, his age, his habits, the nature of the town, the season of the year, and the constitution of the surrounding air at that time." Examples of the attention given to the condition as well as the patient abound in the text. One such example, in the treatment of a deep wound, reads (chapter 3): ". . . you do not find even one medicine with which it is possible to cure every deep wound, but . . . the medicine is selected on the basis of the extent of moisture and filth of the wound and on the basis of the complexion of the sick man."

In contrast to these dated medical concepts, many principles enunciated by him in the treatment of injuries are still acceptable to surgeons today. For instance, he knew that a cut would heal if the parts were brought together (using one of several kinds of bandages). If the parts were separated by anything, be it air, pus, or bone, there would be no primary healing. Pus had to be dried with drying medication, and if a collection occurred, it had to be drained. If the edges of the wound appeared to become abnormal, they had to be excised to reach healthy tissues.

An injury to a pulsating blood vessel could be treated with a silk ligature. "If the vessel from which the blood bursts is very deep, study it carefully until you know clearly its location and its size, and whether it is pulsating or non-pulsating. When you know everything about the vessel, suspend it on a hook, pull it up and twist it lightly and gently" (chapter 5).

In an abdominal wound, the intestine can be returned into the cavity and

Table 7-2.

Attributes to observe in the treatment of patients

Nature of the sickness
Nature of the patient
His/her age
His/her habits
Nature of the town
Weather and season of the year
Constitution of the surrounding air

the peritoneum closed before the skin was sutured. The omentum could be excised before the intestine was returned into the cavity, provided a ligature was placed below the site of excision.

Treatment of a simple fracture has not changed over the millennia:

> When a bone breaks in two.... You must stretch the organ, whether it is an arm or a leg, with your hands if it is small, or with a rope.... Pull the two parts of the broken bone and position them.... Then loosen the rope with which you stretched the organ and allow the muscles to bring the bones together. Then feel it, and if you see anything protruding there, fix it.... It should not move.... It is best to strengthen the broken place with a bandage.... (chapter 6).

The medical treatment of hemorrhage does not meet modern-day standards: "The outburst of blood from inner vessels [i.e., from the uterus, the bladder, or the intestine] can be treated by pulling the blood to the opposite side ['attraction'], or drawing it from its place to another ['transfer'], or with the help of adhesive foods and drinks that will close and stop up the vessel, or with the help of cooling constipating medicines" (chapter 5).

Febrile diseases are attributed to an imbalance of the humors or an impairment in the digestion and utilization of food. The treatment of fever depended primarily on removing its cause and on cooling the body, all in an effort to restore the normal balance.

It is difficult for the modern physician to identify the condition described below, but it does exemplify the detail into which Maimonides goes to maximize the treatment and adapt it to the condition and to the patient's condition:

> A man suffered from a slightly dry bad humor, but the doctors who undertook his treatment gave him absinth to drink and fed him branches of banana tree and muscary and quince and sour pomegranate, and made him drink sumach. With this treatment they almost wore him out, and the moisture of his body diminished greatly. Eventually he was almost like a dead man since his stomach did not extract the food properly because of the weakness caused by the dry bad humor. The relationships of hot and cold were healthy....
>
> When I undertook his treatment I started to administer moisture to him in every possible way. I took for him a place of residence in close proximity to the public bath and I had him taken ... to the bath in a litter so that he did not have to move, which might have dried him further.... He had to remain in the water for a long time.... When he would come out of the bath I would give him to drink milk of a female donkey; I used to bring the animal to him, to his bed. If it were possible for him to suckle the milk from the donkey he would have recovered much quicker because the milk changes very rapidly.... Women's milk, which is of human nature, is the best milk, but many people reject the idea

of drinking women's milk. . . . The body in such a state as described here requires quick nourishment because the passages of food and its routes are contracting. For this reason the patient should be given the milk by itself or with a little lukewarm honey.

Maimonides then goes on to describe in great detail the honey, the milk, and the conditions under which the donkey should be maintained for optimal milk production, and continues: "I then anointed him moderately with oil, but I did that only after knowing that the milk has been digested completely, which I learned from examining his bowels and the degree of swelling of the abdomen . . ." Maimonides then goes on to discuss at length the kind and amounts of food and wine, as well as exercise, that the patient should be given. These should be done with careful attention to the patient's prior habits in terms of exercise, sleep cycle, and food preferences. Other treatment modalities are applications of tar to the abdominal wall and of warmth by having a boy with a nice body, or a puppy, sleep with the patient in his bed, always adhering to the patient's abdomen (chapter 7).

Phlebotomy was a major treatment modality. It was used in the treatment of tumors, which in this context include abscesses and lymphadenopathies. For example (chapter 13):

Assume that a tumor has begun to develop in the liver. After examining the entire body and the strength of the patient and his age, we bleed him from the basilic vein, the inside vein of the right arm, which is connected with the vena cava and has common passages with it. If you do not find this vein, bleed the median vein which lies further to the middle. If it is too hard to find, bleed the third vein of the arm which is the cephalic vein. The extent of emptying should be in accord with the extent of fullness and also relative to the age, nature, town, habits, and strength of the patient.

Eye drops, rectal enemas, and bladder catheters were used to deliver medications and treat conditions involving these organs. Medications were chosen because they were drying or wetting, softening or hardening, cooling or heating, constipating or purging. Intestinal worms were removed by "killing them with bitter medicines, and if they die, they come out with the excrement." It is of interest that hemorrhoids and asthma, which were subjects of special books, are not mentioned in this manuscript. The treatment of snake bite is mentioned briefly, however.

In all, the book enhances Maimonides' stature as a teacher of medicine. It also allows us again to recognize in him an observant and careful practitioner of medicine, one who was versed in the art and science of medicine as it was understood in his day, and who used to advantage available resources for the care of his patients.

II

Maimonides the Scientist

8

Maimonides and the Makings of Modern Science

Nachum L. Rabinovitch

The upsurge in Jewish learning in recent decades has brought with it an increased interest in Maimonides and his work. Acknowledged as the greatest halakhic authority as well as the most profound philosopher which Judaism has produced, many generations refer to the master by the title of his great work – *The Guide for the Perplexed*. Although the title is still popular indeed, few take the trouble to study the work: for one thing it seems to be truly perplexing in character. For another, many are repelled even before looking at it by its avowedly medieval form and its reputedly medieval concepts.

Does Maimonides the philosopher have anything to say to us? Before that question can even be asked, a prior one needs to be answered. Does not his medieval and Aristotelian background inevitably relegate Maimonides to nothing more than historical importance, making his thought irrelevant in the context of modern science and philosophy?

Medieval Jewish philosophy has been aptly described as the product of the attempt to reconcile religion with reason, revelation with reflection. In general terms, this approach involved distinguishing three components of human thought, making for a kind of two-tiered intellectual structure.

First, there was mapped out an area of basic truth common to both revealed religion and philosophical speculation. For example, the principle of the existence of God was thought to be demonstrable by logical argument leading to a conclusion identical with that taught a priori by faith.

On this common foundation, it was sought to erect a superstructure in which faith and reason were each assigned separate compartments in which to exercise complete and independent authority. Thus, with respect to many of the commandments, for example, tradition and revelation were the only arbiters.

On the other hand, in parts of what we call today the natural sciences, philosophy alone had the final word.

Although the precise boundaries between the disciplines vary from one thinker to another, the nature of the endeavor is usually the same. To delineate the shared realm, constructive efforts were required, namely to devise logical arguments to derive certain religious propositions from universally accepted premises.

On the other hand, criticism was the tool to mark the boundary between the independent scopes of religion on one side and reason on the other. Inevitably, as the criticism grew profounder, it tended not only to circumscribe the independent domain of each but also to narrow their common area.

Questioning the validity of religious teachings in any one area weakens the authority of revelation everywhere. This result was avoided by a procedure suited to a body of received doctrine incorporated in specific texts – the method of interpretation. It was recognized that "the Torah has seventy facets"[1] and new levels of meaning are continually to be discovered. This meant that the validity of none of the traditional material was at all in doubt. Reinterpreting its content prevented the status of Scripture being put in jeopardy.

Although, to some extent, the techniques of interpretative exegesis were applied also to the corpus of Aristotelian writings and other philosophical works, the character of philosophical inquiry itself precluded such an approach. Attention to the methods of scientific inquiry and rational argumentation in order to define their proper limits of application led to a reexamination of fundamental issues in the theory of knowledge and the nature of the laws of thought, which ultimately undermined the entire Aristotelian outlook.

A major – perhaps *the* major – concern of all Jewish thinkers is an adequate conception of the Divine Will. The Creator acts because He chooses to, not because He is an automaton. The principle of Voluntarism alone distinguishes the God of the Bible from the Prime Mover of Aristotle.

Aristotle, too, believed in the existence of God, but he thought of Him as the goal toward which everything moves, rather than as the originator of all. Aristotle's God is not an efficient cause, only a final one. He is not the Creator; both matter and the Forms are eternal. *Physis* is the Form of each thing and also the totality of all forms. It is eternal, immutable, uncreated, and rational. In Aristotle, teleology belongs to nature, "seeing that everything that Nature makes is means to an end,"[2] and "that is produced which is conducive to the end." Thus the purpose or "that for the sake of which" a process takes place is a cause – the Final Cause. Therefore to know the final cause is to understand why nature works the way it does.

Nature is orderly and unchanging. "In natural products the sequence is invariable if there is no impediment."[3] Therefore, Aristotle declared that "The proper object of unqualified scientific knowledge is something which cannot be other than it is."[4]

According to Aristotle, knowing the causes is sufficient for knowing the effects, and the ideal of science is not empirical observation but rather demonstrative reasoning. Knowledge is generated by syllogisms based upon premises which are somehow intuited. It follows, for example, that since circular motion is perfect, the heavenly bodies must move in circles.[5] If observation shows otherwise, so much the worse for observation!

Jewish thinkers had their work clearly cut out for them. To make room for the biblical idea of the Divine Will, one must find scope in the universe for purposeful acts which, not being orderly and necessary, appear arbitrary, but in reality display God's teleology. For Aristotle there was nature, which is governed by rules that hold "for the most part."[6] Of course he had to admit that there are certain phenomena which appear to be a failure of nature and seem to be due to chance and hazard. But these are uncommon and, moreover, no science or knowledge of them is possible. They are therefore best ignored.

To Maimonides, though, such exceptional phenomena were not unimportant and peripheral at all. On the contrary, they loomed large as counterexamples to the Aristotelian concept of natural necessity. If only one could discover some criterion to characterize the products of pure chance and distinguish them from the results of design and purposefulness, it might open the way to defending Divine Voluntarism.

That is exactly the line of attack that was followed. The logical weapons to press home the attack came out of the arsenal of rabbinic logic as it had developed in the Talmud and the halakhic tradition.

Most knowledge that matters is not demonstrable. Rather, it is the result of empirical observation and generalization from observation. As such, it is subject to uncertainty. This much even Aristotle and his followers would admit. But in the Talmud there is more than the dichotomy certain/uncertain. The rabbis quantified the uncertainty, or, if you like, the probability of propositions. Some propositions are less probable, and others are more probable. There is a continuous spectrum of probability ranging from zero to one. Says Maimonides in a halakhic work, *The Book of Commandments:*[7] "Among contingent things some are very likely, other possibilities are very remote and yet others are intermediate. The possible is very wide."

Thus it becomes feasible to define equal probabilities, and then it is only one step further to characterize events as due to chance only if the probabilities of all possible alternative outcomes are equal; and if they are all equally likely, it follows that all possible alternatives must in the long run be realized in about the same proportions.

Now suppose we know that two contraries are equally probable and yet only one outcome is always observed, or even preponderantly? Can we conclude anything significant about such a series of events? Maimonides formulated his "principle of particularization" for just such cases. He makes it clear that a similar principle was devised by the Kalam theologians, but it had serious weaknesses that completely falsified it. His own "principle of particularization" is as follows:

> There can be giving of preponderance and particularization only with respect to a particular existent that is equally receptive of two contraries or of two different things. Accordingly, it can be said of that inasmuch as we have found it in a certain state and not in another, there is proof of the existence of an artificer possessing purpose.[8]

Two points should be noted. The first has already been observed, namely the provision that one is dealing only with "a particular existent that is *equally* receptive of the two contraries." The second is the premise that "we have found it in a certain state and not in another." The full meaning of this condition appears when we compare it with another statement in the *Guide*:

> This is the nature of the possible, for it is certain that one of the possibilities will come to pass. And no question should be put why one particular possibility and not another comes to pass, for a similar question would become necessary if another possibility instead of this particular one had come to pass. Know this notion and grasp it.[9]

Here Maimonides points out that a single random event cannot but have only one of all the possible outcomes, and consequently it need not, on that account alone, be attributed to a cause other than chance. However, in a series of similar events (or things) each with equally possible mutually exclusive outcomes, all of the possibilities ought ultimately to be realized if chance alone were operative. If, however, this does not turn out to be so, one may infer the existence of an agent other than chance that determines the actual outcome. Now this agent cannot be "nature," for nature would give a regular unvarying outcome. The principle of particularization, according to Maimonides, states that the particularizing agent is purposeful: its action is to be identified with that of an independent will.

What Maimonides is saying can be rephrased as follows: if two possibilities are mutually exclusive and both are equally likely, then in a large number of similar events, chance alone would make for both possibilities ultimately to be realized in approximately equal proportions; so that if only one outcome is actually observed coming to pass, then we may conclude that a purposive cause is at work rather than chance.

On the basis of this principle, Maimonides reasons that the universe is the handiwork of an intelligent, purposive Creator. One of his arguments deals with the way the stars seem scattered in the sky.[10] He states that there are three possible hypotheses to explain the observed distribution of the stars in the heavens.

1. The distribution is entirely random and must be ascribed to the effects of blind chance.
2. The Aristotelian view that this "proceeded obligatorily and of necessity from the Deity" in some unknown manner, implies the existence of unsuspected and inexplicably "unnatural" properties of nature, which account for the observed irregular and asymmetric distribution.
3. It is due to design.

As for the first alternative, Maimonides says:

It is even stranger that there should exist the numerous stars that are in the eighth sphere all of which are globes, some of them small and some big, one star being here and another at a cubit's distance according to what seems to the eye, or ten stars being crowded and assembled together while there may be a very great stretch in which nothing is to be found.

What is the cause that has particularized one stretch in such a way that ten stars should be found in it and has particularized another stretch in such a way that no star should be found in it?

... How then can one who uses his intellect imagine that the positions, measures and numbers of the stars ... are fortuitous?

Aristotle had argued that regularity and symmetry preclude chance and indicate natural law,[11] but here we have neither regularity nor random distribution.

If chance is rejected, there remains either unknown necessity or design for some unknown purpose. Now teleological design is known as an efficacious cause for irregularities:

In fact you know that the veins and nerves of any individual dog or ass have not happened fortuitously, nor are their measures fortuitous. Neither is it by chance that one vein is thick and another thin, that one nerve has many ramifications and another is not thus ramified, that one descends straight down and another is bent. All this is as it is with a view to useful effects whose necessity is known.

Is it reasonable, then, to postulate unknown natural necessity to explain the strange distribution of the stars, which is clearly neither random nor regular, when there is a familiar principle at work in the world which can explain the irregularity? That would be "very remote indeed from being conceivable." On the other hand, though,

> If it is believed that all this came about in virtue of the purpose of one who purposed who made it thus, that opinion would not be accompanied by a feeling of astonishment and would not be at all unlikely. And there would remain no other point to be investigated except what is the cause for this having been purposed?

What has been accomplished by this argument? The immediate goal was to restore Providence to God, since the universe is as it is *not* because it could not be otherwise but rather because God chose to make it this way. But the end result is far more radical, and Maimonides goes on to draw some of the implications. Astronomy and cosmology, the proudest scientific attainments of man, do not yield certain knowledge. The greatness of Ptolemy's system lies in his ability to predict to a high degree of accuracy various astronomical phenomena such as eclipses.

> The truth of this is attested by the correctness of the calculations – always made on the basis of these principles [epicycles and eccentrics] concerning the eclipses and the exact determination of their times as well as of the moment when it begins to be dark, and of the length of time of the darkness.[12]

Yet Ptolemy cannot tell us the true shape of the heavenly spheres (the planetary orbits). Maimonides develops at length the contradictions between astronomical theory and Aristotle's physics, which advances in observation since Aristotle had brought about:

> If what Aristotle has stated ... is true, there are no epicycles or eccentric circles and everything revolves round the center of the earth. But in that case how can the various motions of the stars come about? ... How can one conceive the retrogradation of a star, together with its other motions, without assuming the existence of an epicycle? On the other hand, how can one imagine a rolling motion in the heavens or a motion around a center that is not immobile? This is the true perplexity![13]

Although he does not know how to solve the crisis in astronomy, Maimonides' recognition and discussion of the crisis is exceedingly important. Aristotle was unaware of various phenomena discovered subsequently. "If, however, he had heard about it, he would have violently rejected it; and, if it were to his mind established as true, he would have become most perplexed about all his assumptions on the subject."[14] Maimonides' conclusion is revolutionary: "Regarding all that is in the heavens man grasps nothing but a small measure of what is mathematical."[15]

Insofar as observation confirms the predictions made on the basis of mathematical formulas, we are entitled to use these formulas, but we must not suppose that the physical model which suggests these formulas to us is also the true form of the heavens.

Thus scientific theories are subject to revision on discovery of new empirical facts. Moreover, Maimonides maintains that the validity of scientific theories is established by probabilistic methods.[16] Alternative theories "should be examined by means of the doubts they arouse" and "when one compares the doubts . . . one should not take into account the number of the doubts but rather consider how great is the incongruity and what is their disagreement with what exists."[17] In the final analysis all our theories must be tested against the facts of observation and, as these data accumulate, our theories may well have to be changed. That a given theory is logical is no guarantee that it is true: even if it yields true predictions, it is not beyond refutation.

Thus reason is used to allow the idea of a voluntarist Deity.

Following on this, Maimonides proceeds to carve out a niche where religion can proclaim on its own authority the belief in *Creatio ex Nihilo,* for although it is not demonstrable, neither is its contrary. But in the process, the very foundations of Aristotelian philosophy have been shaken.

The ultimate conditions of the cosmic process on which everything else depends according to fixed laws—these were seen by the Aristotelians as logically deducible. Against this approach Maimonides argues that factual reality cannot be logically derived. The real world is apprehended empirically and it is only a free act of the Divine Will which gave it the form it has: He could have chosen to make it otherwise—with different qualities and patterns. It is only by empirical observation that we can obtain a description of the world, and moreover, that description cannot be other than a partial one. "For it is impossible for us to accede to the points starting from which conclusions may be drawn about the heavens; for the latter are too far away from us and too high in place and rank."[18]

If, as Aristotle maintained, the essence of natural objects is definable, it follows that their properties must be deducible by reason from the essence. But if the essence of the heavens, for example, is unknowable, as Maimonides claims, it is only the evidence of experience which suffices to tell us anything at all about them. He quotes Themistius, "That which exists does not conform to the various opinions, but rather the correct opinions conform to that which exists."[19]

Furthermore, although God's purposefulness is taken for granted by Maimonides—he ridicules the suggestion that the Divine Will is arbitrary and capricious—he makes the very decisive point that the purpose of Creation is unknowable.[20] The human intellect is debarred from comprehending God's purpose. In this way, final ends are effectively eliminated as grounds from which may be deduced conclusions concerning natural things.

Once natural science abandoned final causes, the way was open to objective observation and evaluation of all empirical data that can be marshaled. Instead of sterile speculation on ultimate purposes which were supposed to give the "why" of natural processes, scientists concentrated on the phenomena themselves, seeking to discover the "how" of events in the universe. Scientific explanation no longer dealt with purposes, rather it became an exercise in prediction and/or control. A natural process is understood to the extent that it is possible to forecast its future outcome. No other understanding is properly called "scientific." For types of processes within human reach, such scientific understanding makes possible also the controlled replication of observed phenomena, which can then be utilized for any purposes which the scientist may seek to attain. The passive observer becomes the active experimentalist and the inventive technologist.

Thus natural science becomes empirically based. There is order in nature, indeed. Maimonides vigorously opposes the Kalam view that makes all things contingent and immediately due to an act of the Divine Will, thus effectively abrogating any kind of law of nature. For Maimonides natural law is binding and expresses a unifying pattern which embraces all phenomena. Yet the features of this pattern cannot be derived a priori from metaphysical "truths." They can only be imperfectly pieced together by inference from observational data painstakingly accumulated over long periods of time. Because the contingent is not merely an appearance, human knowledge is only of "appearances."

A remarkable specific Maimonidean insight is worth noting. The laws of nature are a function of time, in the sense that the state of the universe at any particular time depends upon its earlier states. However, says Maimonides, it is an error to "draw an inference from the nature of a thing that has achieved actuality to its nature when it was only in potentia."[21] Consequently "we declare against him [Aristotle] that this nature, after it has achieved stability and perfection does not resemble in anything the state it was in while in the state of being generated, and that it was brought into existence from absolute non-existence."[22]

Modern theories of cosmogony speak of a singularity from which the universe originated in a "big bang." We can trace back the laws of physics that obtain after the "big bang," but they vanish in the singularity of the origin. Echoes of Maimonides!

Whether a particular Maimonidean proposition is invalidated after eight centuries or not is immaterial: in fact, on Maimonides' own suppositions it is to be expected that the accumulation of new information and the articulation of new theories will render some of his judgments obsolete, especially since he himself never claimed certainty for them—only that they were likely. It is the method and the philosophical stance that is of decisive import and that endures as the underpinning of the scientific outlook. No serious scientist today expects all his conclusions to endure unalterably. One theory succeeds another in every branch of investigation, but the nature of the scientific endeavor is common to all the theories.

In this connection, an excellent example is provided by the particular instance of Maimonides' reasoning which we cited above, namely the question of the distribution of the stars. Right up into our century, this was still a live issue. The eminent statistician R. A. Fisher took up the problem of computing the probability of getting a constellation like the Pleiades, where six stars cluster together, and he reached the conclusion that one must "exclude at a high level of significance any theory involving a random distribution."[23] Subsequently the problem of stellar distribution was treated from a three-dimensional point of view in a way such that the supposition of randomness can be sustained.

More recently, advances in observational techniques have opened up vast new vistas for astronomy and the issue has resurfaced on another level—that of the distribution of galaxies in the universe. Improvements in observers' ability to measure red shifts of galaxies quickly and accurately have made it possible to map galaxy distribution. Strong concentrations of numerous galaxies along a line have been found, and these are known as "God fingers." On the other hand, it appears that "... galaxies are distributed on the surfaces of 'bubble-like' structures. Empty regions or 'voids' are common ... These voids fill approximately 80% of the volume of the local universe. Clusters of galaxies lie at the interstices of bubbles. ..."[24] A recent research report sums up the situation thus: "The common occurrence of large voids has sobering implications for attempts to determine the mean properties of the galaxy distribution."[25]

Furthermore, with the spread of statistical conceptions throughout all of natural science, questions as to the randomness of this or that process have proliferated. Especially relevant to the religious thinker is whether evolution proceeds by purely random processes. This question is very much in the forefront of current scientific thinking.[26]

SUMMARY

To sum up, then, our analysis has led us to recognize two distinct but related issues through which the fundamental concerns of medieval Jewish philosophy paved the way for the rise of modern science. The method of modern science depends upon the presupposition that empirical observation can make a contribution to knowledge and that without it no knowledge at all is possible.

Secondly, recent science has made probabilistic and statistical reasoning central to all its procedures.

No philosophy can be consistent with the possibility of natural science as we know it unless it incorporates these two concepts. It is a fact of European intellectual history that the assimilation of these ideas took a long time, but it is also a well-known fact that some of the impetus for empiricist skepticism that spread through fourteenth-century scholasticism is directly traceable to the influence of the Latin translation of the *Guide*.[27]

What is not so well known, but I believe, no less a fact, is that these revolutionary conceptions which undermined the Greek outlook originated in biblical and rabbinic sources. Obviously a freely acting Divine Will was known to the scholastics directly from the Bible and is required by Christianity no less than Judaism.[28] The Jewish philosophers who sought to accommodate the Divine Will with some form of natural philosophy served as a model for Christian thinkers trying to do the same. This acquainted European savants with the rabbinic – or more precisely – halakhic concepts used by the Jewish thinkers.

It is often said that the accomplishment of the medieval Jewish philosophers was to introduce Aristotle and Greek philosophy generally into the Jewish world of ideas. Might it not be more appropriate in granting the truth of this claim to point out that a greater accomplishment of theirs was to introduce Jewish ideas into the mainstream of Western philosophy, thus paving the way for the rise of modern science?

Even on the threshhold of the modern era, Rambam's radical criticism of Aristotle was still effective. It seemed so impressive to Leibniz that he remarked on it in the margin of his copy of the Latin translation of the *Guide*.[29] Moreover some of the other marginal comments are illuminating. Leibniz was one of the architects of modern science and helped lay the foundations of probability theory, and he pointed out the importance of Maimonides' concept of possibility and the evaluation of hypotheses. The *Guide,* says Leibniz, "deserves careful reading."[30]

9

Maimonides' Stance on Astrology in Context: Cosmology, Physics, Medicine, and Providence

Gad Freudenthal

Maimonides was one of the rare medieval Jewish thinkers to oppose astrology radically. But it has not yet sufficiently been appreciated that from the viewpoint of medieval science such a stance was more problematical than might appear to a mind informed by modern science, for the universally accepted premises of contemporary physics, biology, medicine, and climatology to a considerable extent *warranted* the claims of astrology. The status of astrology in Maimonides' thought thus raises more questions than previously realized. In Maimonides' own view, medieval science indeed provided a rational basis for some of the fundamental claims of astrology. Is it conceivably possible that the author of the "Letter on Astrology" was not as opposed to astrology as he said he was? Can his admonitions against it possibly have had halakhic – i.e., social and pragmatic – significance only, without reflecting his true beliefs concerning its truth as a cosmological theory?

THE GROUNDING OF ASTROLOGY IN MEDIEVAL SCIENCE

All medieval thinkers subscribed to the doctrine that the heavenly bodies exert influences on the sublunar world: generation and corruption, indeed the very existence of sublunar substances, were taken to depend upon celestial influences.¹ Drawing on this doctrine, astrologers argued that their art had a basis in natural philosophy.

The causal influences issuing from the supralunar region were held to be of two different kinds. First, the *bodies* of the planets were held to be *efficient* causes, blending the four sublunar elements and determining their respective proportions in the composite substances. Second, the active *intellect*, one of the separate intellects moving the planets, was construed as the *formal* cause informing sublunar matter.

The first part of the theory goes back to Aristotle, who pointed to the manifest influence of the sun upon the natural sublunar processes: he argued that the sun's daily and annual motions account, respectively, for the very fact that the four sublunar elements have not settled immobile in their natural places, and for the regular growth and decay of living beings.² Aristotle also made passing mention of the influences of the moon on natural processes.³ Medieval Aristotelians, as well as astrologers (following in the footsteps of Ptolemy), generalized this claim. The sun clearly reinforces the element fire and thus increases its share in composite substances on which it acts; similarly, the moon's role in bringing about the tides was taken to demonstrate beyond doubt that it reinforces the element water. By induction, it was then concluded that *all* planets similarly influence the sublunar elements, even though the effects of most planets were admittedly less perceptible than those of the sun and the moon.⁴ The material composition of each sublunar substance was thus held to depend causally upon the celestial bodies.

Like all his contemporaries, Maimonides too subscribed to this scheme, although he proposed a slightly modified, allegedly original version of it. He grouped together the five planets in one single sphere, so that the number of spheres bearing stars was four—"the sphere of the fixed stars, that of the five planets, that of the sun, and that of the moon"⁵—each acting on one of the four elements:

> Thus the sphere of the moon moves the water, the sphere of the sun the fire, while the sphere of the other planets moves the air.... The sphere of the fixed stars moves the earth. Perhaps the earth is so sluggish in moving to receive the action being brought to bear upon it and in undergoing combinations because of the slowness of the fixed stars in their motion.⁶

The second part of the theory concerns the formal cause. Aristotle's matter is amorphous and passive; it cannot itself give rise to structured substances. Moreover, because structured substances are composed of contrary qualities (hot/cold, moist/dry), they naturally tend to decay.⁷ To account for the coming-to-be and the perseverance of structured substances, Aristotle's natural philosophy was in need of a complement. This was of momentous importance: the necessity to add to Aristotle's physical theory an account of the origin and perseverance of forms made room for a bridge, or rather a synthesis, between the theory of sublunar matter on the one hand and metaphysics and theology on the other. In fact, to account for forms, Peripatetics argued that sublunar substances having forms, notably plants and animals, come to exist and persevere because suitably mingled matter is *informed* by an external agent possessing those forms. In other words, since forms do not arise in matter spontaneously, they must be imprinted upon it and maintained by a distinct agent possessing them in actuality.[8] This agent, the formal cause of forms of sublunar substances, was identified as the active intellect, the "Giver of Forms," a notion that has its roots in Aristotle's psychology.[9]

The form of each sublunar substance was thus construed as resulting from the interplay of the efficient and the formal causes. By mingling the matter, the former produces in a given lump of matter a mixture characterized by a specific ratio *(logos)* of the elements composing it. Thereupon the Giver of Forms imprints upon the *mixtum* a form *suitable to its material composition:* the better the balance of the elements in a given mixture, the higher the form it will receive. The form of every sublunar substance is thus conditioned by its material constitution. This physical theory established the notion of God's general governance (or providence) over the sublunar world. Since the separate intellects were associated with the planets as their "motors," this governance, the sum total of the efficient and formal causes, was loosely perceived as "heavenly influences."

Astrologers eagerly drew upon a suitably modified version of the theory concerning the role of the Giver of Forms in producing sublunar substances. For them, however, it was not a transcendent intellect, but rather influences emanating from the planets themselves, that inform sublunar matter (in addition to mixing it).[10]

The physicotheological theory we have reviewed is fully endorsed by Maimonides:

> Know that there is a consensus of all philosophers to the effect that the governance of this lower world is perfected by means of the forces overflowing to it from the sphere ... and that the spheres apprehend and know that which they govern.[11]

More specifically:

> Heaven in virtue of its motion exerts government over the other parts of the world and sends to every generated thing the forces that subsist in the latter. ... Know that ... the forces that come from heaven to this world are four: [1] the force that necessitates the mixture and composition – there is no doubt that this force suffices to engender the minerals;[12] [2] the force that gives to every plant a vegetal soul; [3] the force that gives to every animal an animal soul; [4] the force

that gives to every rational being a rational faculty. All this takes place through the intermediary of the illumination and the darkness [on earth] resulting from the light in heaven and from the heaven's motion round the earth.[13]

This heavenly "governance" over the sublunar world is indispensable for its continued existence. "Just as an individual would die and his motions and forces would be abolished if the heart were to come to rest even for an instant, so the death of the world as a whole and the abolition of everything within it would result if the heavens were to come to rest."[14]

Maimonides was keenly aware of the fact that this physical doctrine – according to which, as he formulates it, the spheres and the stars are "the lords [*adonim*] of every body other than themselves" (although, to be sure, they themselves are subordinated to God) –[15] is closely related to astrology. Thus, he repeats that

> It is known and generally recognized in all the books of the philosophers speaking of governance that the governance of this lower world – I mean the world of generation and corruption – is said to be brought about through the forces overflowing from the spheres.

He then does not shun from quoting a saying from *Bereshit Rabbah* (10:6), of which the Jewish proponents of astrology were particularly fond:

> [Y]ou will find likewise that the Sages say: "There is not a single herb below that has not a '*mazzal*' in the firmament that beats upon it and tells it to grow." ... Now they also call a star: *mazzal*.[16]

Maimonides comments on this saying in a sentence that from the pen of any other writer would appear as distinctly astrological: "By means of this dictum they have made it clear that *even individuals subject to generation have forces of the stars that are specially assigned to them.*"[17]

Indeed, Maimonides himself explicitly recognized that the universally accepted Aristotelian doctrine may be taken to provide a scientific basis for astrology:

> It also is said with regard to the forces of the spheres that they overflow toward that which exists. Thus the overflow of the sphere is spoken of although the actions come from a body. Hence the stars act at some particular distances; I refer to their nearness to or remoteness from the center or their relation to one another. *From here astrology comes in.*[18]

Maimonides thus endorses even the idea that the actions of the stars upon sublunar bodies depend upon their positions with respect to one another, i.e., on what in the technical vocabulary of astrology is called their "aspects" – a distinctively astrological doctrine. And he notes that this physical thesis may appear to provide astrology with a basis in physical science. The significance of Maimonides' statement is perspicaciously perceived by Moshe Narboni, himself a mild proponent of astrology:[19] "Understand how he generalized and *verified* [*immet*] all of astrology [*mishpat ha-kokhabim*] by saying 'the stars act at some particular distances. . . . From here astrology comes in.' For this is the truth [i.e., essence] of astrology."[20]

A universal consensus thus prevailed over the doctrine that the generation and corruption of all sublunar bodies depend upon the actions of the stars and those of the immaterial intellects, lumped together as "celestial influences." These two-tiered influences were held, first, to determine the material composition of substances and, second, to endow them with appropriate forms. Now this doctrine implies that living beings, too, inasmuch as they are *natural* composite bodies, are affected by the efficient and formal causes of celestial origin. The question thus arises: To what extent does this hold of man, too? Are man's desires, aims, choices, and actions also dependent upon the ubiquitous celestial influences (as astrology would have it)? (Recall that according to Aristotelian doctrine, the forms of living beings are their souls—nutritive, sentient, rational—so that every man and woman owes even his or her rational soul to the active intellect.)

Although man is a being endowed with a rational soul and *deliberates* over his actions, the universally accepted theories of contemporary science entail a largely affirmative answer to our question. To see this we have to look briefly into two further medieval scientific theories: the doctrine of psychophysiology and the related doctrine of climatology, both of which were universally accepted, too, and which also allowed astrology to claim for itself a foundation in natural philosophy.

The Hippocratics, followed by Aristotle, held that certain physiological characteristics of the body—e.g., whether it is hot or cold—determine the character of a person.[21] This idea was elaborated in the doctrine of the four humors, whose equilibrium was held to constitute the person's "temperament," that is, to determine the sum of his or her psychical faculties, including his or her moral traits. This theory was elaborated notably by Galen, one of whose treatises, translated into Arabic, bears the title: "That the faculties of the soul depend upon the mixtures [or temperaments] of the body."[22]

This standard view, part and parcel of medieval biology and medicine, was, of course, shared by Maimonides too. In order to explain why men are psychologically so dissimilar—it is this dissimilarity that makes social organization indispensable—Maimonides said:

> [T]here are many differences between the individuals belonging to [the human species], so that you can hardly find two individuals who are in any accord with respect to one of the species of moral habits. . . . The cause of this is the

difference of the mixtures [or temperaments], owing to which the various kinds of matter differ, and also the accidents consequent to the form in question.[23]

In other words, every individual has his or her specific "mixture" of the elements or humors, his or her particular complexion or temperaments. Since the material compositions of the individuals are different, their forms (souls) are different too, and so are the accidents—particular psychical properties and dispositions, i.e., traits of character[24]—subsequent upon these forms. Individuals are thus different because they differ in their material composition. Psychical differences—character, dispositions, faculties, and so forth—ultimately depend upon differences in the *material* composition of the body.

Consider an example. The faculty of courage, Maimonides says, "varies in strength and weakness, as do other faculties, so that you may find among people some who will advance upon a lion, while others flee from a mouse." The cause of this, Maimonides goes on to explain, is that there "must necessarily exist a temperamental preparation in the original natural disposition" (the innate physical complexion or temperament) of each individual.[25] The same psycho-physiological doctrine also underlies Maimonides' theory of prophecy, according to which only an individual whose (largely innate) temperament is perfectly well balanced has the perfect imaginative faculty necessary for prophecy.[26]

This theory supplied another important building block for astrology. As we saw, the medieval philosophers held the mixture of the elements within any composite body to depend upon the heavenly bodies. Now *qua* body, man is a natural substance, a composite of the four elements. Therefore, the equilibrium of the elements within a person's body—his or her temperament—depends significantly upon the influences of the heavenly bodies (acting as an efficient cause), along with other factors (such as inherited biological traits and the influence of the environment). Since the temperament in turn determines the psychical faculties, it follows that these faculties (e.g., courage), and consequently the individual's disposition to behave in some manner (e.g., bravely), largely depend upon the heavenly bodies. Astrologers could consequently claim that by knowing how celestial influences affect the temperament, one can predict the behavior of any given person with a reasonable probability.[27] This argument was embraced by natural philosophers, too.[28] Thus the logical (although unstated) corollary of Maimonides' views is that the differences among men, and hence the need for social order, *in fine* are a consequence of the celestial influences affecting men *qua* natural substances.[29]

Maimonides was keenly aware that the theory of the dependence of physicopsychical faculties upon celestial influences is within a hairbreadth of astrology. This can be perceived, for instance, from the fact that in his *Shemonah Perakim,* the short exposition of this theory is immediately followed by a strong admonition against the follies of the astrologers and by an attempt to refute this theory by arguing that the innate temperament can be changed by a suitable "corrective therapy."[30]

The doctrine of the dependence of psychical faculties upon celestial influences underlies and comes to the fore in climatology.

In the Middle Ages, it was universally believed that the physiological equilibrium (of the elements or of the humors) inside a human body, and consequently also the individual's psychical faculties, are strongly influenced by the physical conditions of the environment,[31] some of which in turn depend on the "climate," the geographical latitude of the region, which determines its position with respect to the sun.[32] The impact of these environmental conditions is superimposed, so to speak, upon the direct influences of the heavenly bodies. The doctrine goes back at least to the Hippocratic treatise *Airs, Waters, Places,* which is echoed, for instance, in the *Kuzari,* where Yehudah Halevi puts in the mouth of the philosopher the view that in addition to characteristics a man inherits from his parents, his individual traits are determined by the "influence of winds, countries, foods and water, spheres, stars and constellations."[33] Halevi's rabbi shares this idea and draws on it to foster his view that *Eretz Yisrael* is the most suitable place for prophecy.[34] Similarly, Maimonides, in his *Pirké Moshe,* follows Galen's opinion that the differences of climate are the causes of the differences of the individual temperaments, and consequently also of the differences of the faculties of the speech organs and of the intelligence. He also agrees with al-Fârâbî that the inhabitants of the middle climates are "more perfect in their intellects and in their forms generally," their tongues being in greatest harmony with man's logic.[35] Again, in *Hanhagat ha-Beriut* Maimonides comments: "when the air changes, be it a little, the soul's inquiry changes perceptibly. This is why one finds many people in whom one can perceive how their psychic actions diminish when the air becomes corrupt: I mean that although no change can be perceived in the actions of the vital and the natural functions, yet their understanding and their memory suddenly fail."[36]

Climatology thus supplied a further argument for the astrological doctrine. The sun, the foremost heavenly body, determines the climate and through it influences the physiological temperament of the individual, on which in turn depend his or her psychical faculties. As confirmatory evidence, the astrologers invoked the purported fact, accepted as such by the natural philosophers too, that national collective traits are determined by the climate.[37] Thus even an opponent of judicial astrology as al-Fârâbî could describe the causal chain by which the celestial influences determine psychical qualities in the following general terms:

> The first natural cause for the differences among nations ... is the difference between the celestial regions. ... These bring about differences of the parts of the earth [and] differences of the exhalations. ... Subsequent upon the differ-

ences between the exhalations are differences in the air and differences of the waters.... These in turn entail differences of the vegetation [and] of the species of irrational animals, [so that] there are differences in the nutrition of [different] nations. The differences in nutrition entail differences in the matter and the sperm out of which men are constituted ... causing differences of their forms and natural faculties.[38]

Medieval philosophers of nature thus considered as indisputable the idea that by shaping the natural processes in the sublunar world the heavenly bodies to a large extent determine the "psychology" of every living being. One's temperament–the mixture of the elements (or humors) in one's body– was held to depend both directly and indirectly on the celestial bodies. First, by mixing the elements, the heavenly bodies largely determine the initial composition of every natural substance, including the innate temperament of living beings. Second, by determining the climates, the sun additionally influences the environmental conditions (air, nutrition, etc.), which (along with other factors, such as age and conduct) act upon the initial constitution and eventually modify it. From the theory according to which the temperament conditions the psychical qualities, it further followed that one's disposition to behave in one way or another to a great extent ultimately depends on celestial influences. On this basis it could reasonably be argued that the behavior of individuals is largely influenced by the celestial bodies (even if one supposes that it is not *determined* by them, inasmuch as men are supposed to remain free to behave in ways other than those dictated by their biological makeup). In a further move, it could then be claimed that on the basis of a knowledge of astral influences, the future behavior of individuals can be predicted–not with certainty, but with a degree of probability. All this, I repeat, is based on Aristotelian and medical theory accepted by all medieval philosophers of nature, including, as we have seen, Maimonides.

MAIMONIDES' REJECTION OF ASTROLOGY

In his letter to the sages of Montpellier, Maimonides unequivocally repudiates astrology:

> Know, my masters, that every one of those things concerning judicial astrology that [its adherents] maintain–namely, that something will happen one way and not another, and that the constellation under which one is born will draw him on so that he will be such and such a kind and so something will happen to him one way and not another–all those assertions are far from being scientific; they are stupidity.[39]

He rejects astrology with equal clarity and firmness in his *Epistle to Yemen*. "I note," he writes to R. Ya‘aqob ben Netan'el al-Fayyûmi, "that you are inclined to believe in astrology and in the influence of past and future conjunctions of the planets upon human affairs. You should dismiss such notions from your thoughts. Cleanse your mind as one cleanses dirty clothes. Accomplished scholars, whether they are religious or not, refuse to believe in the truth of this science. Its postulates can be refuted by real proofs on rational grounds."[40] He had made similar pronouncement in his *Mishneh Torah*[41] and, as already mentioned, in *Shemonah Perakim*. There is thus no ambiguity concerning the firmness of Maimonides' opposition to astrology.

The foregoing analysis of the basis for astrology afforded by contemporary science should make us pause, however. We should ask how and on what grounds Maimonides reconciled his acceptance of a natural philosophy from which, as he himself had noted, "astrology comes in," with his rejection of judicial astrology. Maimonides' attitude toward astrology has often been taken to be self-explanatory: it has been perceived as singularly perspicacious, rational, and modern, deriving from his ingenuity and forward-looking mind. (This approach was particularly tempting when Maimonides' stance was viewed against the background of medieval Jewish philosophy, most of whose proponents to one degree or another accepted astrology.) This, however, is a wrong way to look at the matter. Maimonides' position must be evaluated against the background of the science he himself held to be true and not by reference to later standards of argument. The fact that Maimonides' position is supported by modern science in no way explains why he propounded it some eight centuries ago. Therefore, since judicial astrology justly claimed to have roots in the tenets of natural philosophy – that is, in what is called "natural astrology" – the question we must raise is: what were Maimonides' reasons for his negative stance on judicial astrology? Or could it be that Maimonides' repeated public denial of judicial astrology is addressed to the masses and covers up a secret, "esoteric" position more favorable to this art? This question seems warranted on its own merits, by virtue of the *problematique* described above, independent of any general stance on the significance one should accord to Maimonides' statements in the *Guide* on the one hand, and in his halakhic writings on the other. It obviously gains in urgency if we adopt the Straussian interpretive paradigm. According to Leo Strauss, as is well known, "the *Guide* is 'my speech' revealing 'my opinion,' as distinguished from 'our opinion,' expressed in 'our compilation,' the *Mishneh Torah,* where generally speaking Maimonides appears as the mouthpiece of the Jewish community or of the Jewish tradition," so that "the *Guide* was not addressed to the vulgar, nor the *Mishneh Torah* to the perplexed."[42] Four considerations may *prima facie* seem to militate in favor of such a suggestion.

1. Maimonides discusses astrology explicitly only in writings intended for the masses – halakhic writings and letters to the leaders of communities. In the *Guide,* by contrast, astrology is mentioned only in one or two asides,[43] but is not made into a topic. Did Maimonides deliberately avoid the subject in his most theoretical opus in order to conceal his true views of it?

2. Maimonides nowhere attacks the postulates of judicial astrology head-on, trying to show that on the basis of Aristotelian science its claims are *false*. In his "Letter on Astrology" he insists on the dangers of astrology to the Jewish faith, i.e., on its possible religious and moral harmful consequences, but does not endeavor to *refute* that doctrine. He contents himself with the statement that "there are lucid, faultless proofs refuting all the roots of those assertions" and that "never did one of those genuinely wise men of the nations busy himself with this matter or write on it,"[44] but he does not intimate what these proofs are. In his *Epistle to Yemen*, Maimonides adduces arguments refuting the astrological theory, going back to Mâshâ'allâh (754–813) and propounded in Hebrew, among others, by Abraham Bar Hiyya (d. ca. 1136) and Abraham Ibn Ezra (1089–1164), construing the history of the world as depending upon small, middle, and great conjunctions of the planets.[45] Its statements, Maimonides shows, conflict with the historical evidence. But here, too, Maimonides does not attempt a theoretical refutation of astrology; he contents himself to show that, from the Jewish vantage point, astrology is *harmful*, but does not try to demonstrate that it is a *false* theory. Could it be that the reason for this silence is that while Maimonides regarded astrology as a dangerous doctrine, he was not all that sure of its falsity?

3. We know from Maimonides himself that he had devoted much reading to astrology, and to idolatry in general. Indeed, says Maimonides, "it seems to me [that] there does not remain in the world a composition on this subject, having been translated into Arabic from other languages, but that I have read it and have understood its subject matter and have plumbed the depth of its thought."[46] To justify this interest which runs against an explicit interdiction, Maimonides invokes his desire to understand the reasons for the precepts, whose primary intention, as he believed, is to eradicate idolatry.[47] One can nonetheless ponder the possibility that astrology, the first of these subjects he studied, also presented an intellectual challenge. This seems perfectly plausible if we remember that Maimonides shared theoretical premises from which, as he recognized, "astrology comes in." Whence again our question: could it be that Maimonides did not have *theoretical* arguments against astrology?

4. Last but not least, if we accept the view advanced by two of Maimonides' foremost interpreters, the late Shlomo Pines and Alexander Altmann, that Maimonides upheld determinism,[48] then we would have two further serious reasons to suspect that his true views of astrology were less negative than he professed. First, the causal chain which then *ex hypothesi* determines man's fate is described by the theories we have reviewed above and it cannot but have its beginning in the heavenly bodies, the "lords" (*adonim*) of every sublunar substance, which (or rather, whom) God entrusted with the governance of the lower world. But is it not then plausible to expect that this causal chain can become known to man—that even if at present astrology is deficient, it can in the future become a true science? Second, if Maimonides

believed in determinism, then one important reason he invokes in justification of his hostility toward astrology—namely the fact that it fosters fatalism—would fall to the ground; in this case, his statements about the perils of fatalism which astrology engenders must be intended only for the masses. Therefore, the one who assumes that Maimonides believed in determinism must take very seriously the possibility that he had a secret positive attitude toward judicial astrology.

For these reasons I suggest that we should earnestly examine the possibility that Maimonides harbored an "esoteric" position on judicial astrology that was more favorable to it than his public admonitions against it suggest. Even if, after reflection, we discard this possibility, we will, I believe, have acquired a better insight into the considerations that motivated Maimonides' position.

The above-mentioned doubts notwithstanding, Maimonides' stance on astrology was as negative as he said it was. The reasons for his attitude, including his silences, will become clear when we take into consideration the intellectual and social contexts in which he lived, thought, and acted.

For Muslim philosophers in the East, astrology was not at all an issue. Although natural philosophy and astrology shared quite a number of theoretical tenets, most philosophers—including al-Fârâbî and Ibn Sînâ—rejected astrology unambiguously.[49] Maimonides' position, therefore, is simply that of his cultural milieu, Peripatetic Arabic philosophy. His claim that "there are lucid, faultless proofs refuting all the roots of those assertions" was indeed founded on a consensual body of knowledge which he shared.[50] This is certainly one of the reasons why Maimonides did not deem it necessary to take up a theoretical discussion of astrology in the *Guide* or elsewhere.[51]

Maimonides' silence on the theory of astrology also has to do with the circumstances in which he goes into the matter. As we noticed, Maimonides takes up astrology not in the context of a philosophical discussion—in the *Guide* astrology is not at all discussed—but rather in halakhic works and in replies to inquiries from faraway communities seeking his guidance. This means that it is not so much Maimonides the philosopher as Maimonides the community leader who discusses astrology. His correspondents and readers, Maimonides understood, sought spiritual direction, not instruction in natural philosophy; they looked up to him as an authority on the *halakhah,* not as an expert on science of pagan and Muslim origin.

That Maimonides did not seek to refute astrology theoretically is thus primarily a consequence of the character and the objective of the writings in which he addressed the subject. He was interested in the possible religious *cum* social consequences of astrology, not in astrology as a cosmological theory. According to Maimonides, astrology presents two major dangers: it unwittingly favors star worship and (as already mentioned) it gives rise to fatalism, both of which he considered as extremely dangerous and sinful.[52] (This statement obviously remains true even if we assume that Maimonides subscribed to a secret determinist position. Maimonides could insist on the social dangers of true doctrines; in the Straussian perspective, he does so time and again.)

Nor does the assumption that Maimonides accepted determinism imply that he had a positive attitude toward astrology. For even if one supposes man's fate to be predetermined by a causal chain having its beginning in the heavenly bodies, it does not follow that man can obtain knowledge concerning it. Maimonides' epistemological skepticism, in particular his belief that the laws governing the heavenly bodies – their motions and their physical influences on the sublunar world – will never become known to man,[53] thoroughly undermines astrology. Therefore, even a determinist Maimonides would reject astrology. Indeed, according to Maimonides, whatever knowledge of the future is given to man is obtained *via* prophecy and veridical dreams, both of which derive from a divine overflow, not from a human science of the stars.[54]

Last but not least, in point of fact, as it seems to me, Maimonides did *not* uphold determinism. Rather, in his view, nature itself is indeterminate to some extent[55]; moreover, in his (and his contemporaries') view, although man's biological constitution is causally determined by celestial influences, that physiological constitution determines only one's *propensity to act* in a certain way, but not one's *actual behavior* (which may, and indeed should, be subject to the control of the intellect). These two elements of indetermination obviously undermine the possibility of predicting man's conduct and hence judicial astrology.

We may thus conclude that astrology, which was incompatible with Maimonides' philosophy, interested him first and foremost as a social, not as a scientific or intellectual, issue. Maimonides knew that although Peripatetic natural philosophy could seem to provide astrology with a rational basis, which indeed the astrologers claimed for themselves, the great Peripatetic philosophers had refuted the claims of judicial astrology which went beyond natural astrology. Nonetheless, judicial astrology was popular, in Egypt as well as in Yemen and in France, and this popular belief in astrology, which had nothing to do with its alleged theoretical foundation, appeared to him to present serious religious-social threats. To counter those threats was the goal of Maimonides' admonitions against astrology, and this aim accounts for the character of his treatments of the subject. We can, I believe, safely discard the idea that Maimonides had an esoteric doctrine that was closer to judicial astrology than his professed statements suggest.

We have seen that Maimonides had little room in which to maneuver. The received doctrine of the celestial influences on sublunar substances and processes, including man, provided the foundation for the philosophic view of God's governance of the world. This is why Maimonides dwells on this doctrine even in the "Letter on Astrology," where at first glance it may appear as counterproductive. Maimonides had to acknowledge these physical influences, to concede that the heavenly bodies are the "lords of every body," while still denying the possibility of judicial astrology. Indeed, other medieval thinkers interpreted the same evidence differently and held that judicial astrology is a perfectible art whose theoretical foundations are sound. It would be misguided and unjust to characterize them as irrational; some of these thinkers, as for instance Gersonides (see below), were perfectly rational. Nor is Maimonides' rejection of astrology a product of an ahistorical rationality. For Maimonides, astrology presented a social and religious, rather than a scientific, problem, and his views of it followed the *opinio communis* of the great Peripatetic Muslim philosophers. We can, therefore, in sum, appreciate this: Maimonides was fortunate that, at least on this issue, his scientific considerations (pertaining to *truth*) and his pragmatic ones (pertaining to social-religious *utility*) were in harmony.

Maimonides' rejection of astrology is congruent with (although not a consequence of) an essential stance of his philosophy, namely his view of the purpose *(telos)* of material existents generally, and of the celestial bodies in particular. Maimonides vehemently rejects the popular view that "the finality of all that exists is solely the existence of the human species so that it should worship God, and . . . that even the heavenly spheres only revolve in order to be useful to it and to bring into existence that which is necessary for it." According to him, all existents have only one final cause, namely, "God has wished it so, or: His wisdom has required this to be so." The consequence is this: "It should not be believed that all the beings exist for the sake of the existence of man. On the contrary, all the other beings too have been intended for their own sakes and not for the sake of something else. . . . Just as He has willed that the human species should come to exist, He also has willed that the spheres and their stars should come to exist." Therefore, the stars "do not exist for our sake and so that good should come to us from them."[56] Maimonides' stance is decidedly *anti-anthropocentric*.[57] It is absurd to suppose that the most perfect beings exist for the sake of infinitely inferior ones, the heavenly bodies and the separate intellects for the sake of man;[58] rather, they exist for their own sake, although some good overflows from them, from which man benefits.

This theological cosmology seems to have a bearing on the question of astrology. Maimonides' world picture is unfavorable to, although not strictly incompatible with, a science predicting the effects upon man of the celestial bodies. Rather, astrology is much more naturally imbedded in a worldview in which the heavenly bodies exist for the sake of man. This can be perceived from a brief comparison with the views of one of Maimonides' most brilliant followers, R. Levi ben Gershom, *Ralbag*, also known as Gersonides (1288–1344).

Gersonides explicitly rejects Maimonides' view that the spheres and their stars exist only for their own sake. Chapter 3 of Treatise V, Part II, of his *Sefer Milhamot ha-Shem* is devoted precisely to the demonstration that "the stars exist in the spheres for the sake of the things [down] here," in the sublunar world.[59] In Gersonides' view, when God created the celestial bodies, He endowed them with such natures as to allow them to perfect, as far as possible, all sublunar existents. The heavens were designed with utmost wisdom for the benefit of the sublunar existents, and particularly for that of man, the most perfect among them. Gersonides does not doubt that every particularity of each planet and of its motions follows a specific intention, for only the extreme diversity of the planetary actions can bring about the extreme diversity, and indeed great perfectness, of their effects down here.[60]

Now this anthropocentric optimism – Gersonides' view of a divine providence exercised through an "astral determinism" (as Charles Touati has fittingly called it) – is in much greater congruity with astrology than Maimonides' view. If the heavenly bodies exist, nay were *created, in order to* govern the sublunary world and particularly to exert providence over man, it is reasonable to expect, as Gersonides did, that their actions can be studied and, eventually, become known and predicted.[61] Here, obviously, Gersonides' epistemological optimism (the antipode of Maimonides' skepticism) comes into play too, for Gersonides does not doubt that the motions of the stars and the precise mode of their exercising providence can (and indeed should) be investigated empirically and that ultimately they will become known to man. It is in fact precisely this idea that underscores the value of the science of the heavens and that supplied Gersonides with the motivation to devote his days (and nights) to it.[62]

I thus suggest that Maimonides' view that the celestial bodies do not exist for the sake of the sublunar world and his rejection of astrology are related. Although there is no logical necessity here, a common tendency nonetheless seems to underlie Maimonides' views on both issues. Maimonides' is a *theo*- rather than *anthropo*-centric worldview, in which the sublunar world, including man, is of negligible significance. But if the celestial bodies do not exist for the sake of anything, if their influence on man is unrelated to their purpose – they govern the world accidentally and not essentially, so to speak – then there is little wonder that man cannot, by gazing at the skies, know his future.[63]

10

Maimonides and Gersonides on Astronomy and Metaphysics

Menachem Kellner

Maimonides (1138–1204) and Gersonides (1288–1344) shared much the same universe of discourse.[1] Their areas of disagreement, therefore, are more important than their areas of agreement.[2]

Having proved philosophically to his satisfaction that the world was created, Gersonides adds the following consideration:

> That which adds publicity and perfection to what has been made clear concerning the creation of the world is that we find that all that has been written in the sciences[3] is new and recent. We find that the early [savants] said something about each science; afterwards each was perfected during the course of time. We find sciences which did not reach their perfection till Aristotle and others which did not reach their perfection till Galen. There is another science which we do not find perfectly in the work of any of the ancients; this is the science of astronomy. [All this shows that] a science which demands more time for its perfection because of what you must determine concerning it from the senses reaches its perfection later. Thus, the mathematical sciences, such as geometry and arithmetic are found earlier than other sciences. Aristotle's predecessors already expressed them perfectly, according to what is told about them. Physical science, on the other hand, because of its greater need of the senses, reached its perfection later. Thus the art of medicine, which is more dependent upon the senses, especially with respect to what is learned in it from the senses and from dissection, reached perfection still later. But astronomy, which depends upon the senses in such a fashion that its perfection through them can come about

only after a stupendously long time, reaches its perfection even later. Since these sciences bring a man along the route to perfection, and he naturally desires them, it cannot [therefore] be said [both] that the human race is uncreated and that these sciences were discovered by them recently, for were the matter so we would be faced with a possibility which only became actualized after the passage of an infinite period of time, despite the existence of many natural implements for bringing it into actuality, and of humankind's extremely strong natural desire to actualize it. This is clearly absurd.[4]

In this text we find *an* idea of scientific progress clearly expressed. Gersonides places a great deal of emphasis on the cooperative nature of the scientific enterprise: students of nature labor, generation after generation, to add to our knowledge.[5] Alongside this view of scientific progress we see the clearly expressed view that scientific progress is not an open-ended affair: the various sciences reach perfection or closure. The mathematical sciences were perfected by Aristotle's predecessors; Aristotle himself, it seems, brought physics to perfection; Galen brought medicine to perfection; astronomy, which depends upon a huge number of difficult observations, had not, by Gersonides' day, been brought to perfection yet.[6]

MAIMONIDES' APPROACH

What is Maimonides' view on this question? Did he also believe that the sciences could or had reached closure? There is one clear-cut reason for thinking that he had. Maimonides opens the second chapter of his *Mishneh Torah* by telling us that Jews are commanded to love and fear God. "What is the way," Maimonides then asks, "that will lead to the love of Him and fear of Him?" The answer, he says, is the examination of God's work of creation. By way of helping his reader to fulfill the commandment to love and fear God, Maimonides explains "some large, general aspects of the works of the Sovereign of the Universe."[7]

Chapters three and four present an account of the physical universe as Maimonides saw it. It is a finite universe, composed of nine concentric spheres, with the earth in the center. The ninth and largest sphere "includes and encircles all things." Each of the eight internal spheres is divided into subspheres, "like the several layers of onions." These subspheres are contiguous, with no empty space between them at all. In addition to the concentric spheres which encompass the earth, there are smaller spheres (epicycles) fixed in the larger spheres. The heavens are "alive" in the sense that they are populated by living, thinking entities. The sublunar realm is the world of the four elements and of bodies composed of them. It is a world in which things strive always to return to their natural place. It is a world of constant generation and corruption, a world the most fundamental principles of which are form and matter.

Maimonides' description appears in a law code, the *Mishneh Torah,* in a section called "Laws of the Foundations of the Torah." Maimonides composed his code in an apodictic fashion because he expected it to be exactly that: a code. Furthermore, it was a work meant to translate the immutable Torah of God into a useful, manageable body of specific prescriptions. It was Maimonides' hope that the *Mishneh Torah* would be adopted as *the* binding code of Jewish law. It is reasonable to assume that Maimonides expected his vision of the physical universe to be as immutable as his codification of the laws, say, of theft.

This being the case, it would seem that Maimonides would have had to have held that the physical sciences, at least, had reached closure in his day. Otherwise, how could he present them in the apodictic fashion that characterizes his discussion in the *Mishneh Torah?* The matter, however, is not so simple. There are good grounds to think that Maimonides did not present the description of the physical universe in "Laws of the Foundations of the Torah" as the last word on the subject.

Among the reasons for supposing that Maimonides would urge us to relate to his account of the universe in the *Mishneh Torah* as being nothing more than a statement of the best science available in his day, and not as an incontrovertible account of the world as it actually is, was, and always will be, are the following:

1. The strongest reason for understanding Maimonides in this fashion is his account of how we are to relate to the scientific pronouncements of the rabbinic sages. He sharply distinguishes their role as transmitters of the Sinaitic revelation from their role as individuals reporting on their own ideas and interpretations or reporting on the best science of their day. Indeed, in two passages in the *Guide for the Perplexed* Maimonides informs his readers that the sages erred on scientific matters. If Maimonides thought that the sages could err when they relied on the best science of their day, would not Maimonides feel the same about his own reliance on the science of his day?[8]

2. Further support for this position is found in Maimonides' attitude toward Aristotle. Despite his tremendous admiration for the "chief of the philosophers," he still maintained that Aristotle could err. It is well known that Maimonides rejected Aristotle's claim that the universe was uncreated.[9] Furthermore, Maimonides held that Aristotle was indubitably correct in what he had written about the sublunar world, but wrong with respect to much of what he had to say about the celestial world.[10] Once gain, if Aristotle can be mistaken about scientific matters, would not Maimonides admit that he himself could be mistaken?

3. There is yet a further reason for thinking so. Maimonides held that

human beings progress both scientifically and in spiritual terms. Maimonides expressly taught that "the science of astronomy was not in his [Aristotle's] time what it is today," that Galen had brought anatomy to high pitch of perfection, and that his own astronomical knowledge might be superseded.[11] Without getting into the vexing question of when the idea of progress entered Western culture, we can see here that Maimonides admitted the fact of scientific development and even anticipated that science would develop beyond what he himself had been able to accomplish in it.

4a. In terms of what we can call "spiritual progress," Maimonides indicates that human beings grow and develop from generation to generation, both as individuals and as a race. As individuals, Maimonides maintained in one of the most notorious passages in the *Guide,* the generation of the Exodus was unable to worship God in a truly mature fashion and needed a sacrificial cult.[12] Our forefathers may have been religious primitives; spiritual progress had taken place since the days of the Exodus, however, and some Jews in Maimonides' day were ready to be told how to truly worship God: "it consists in setting thought to work on the first intelligible and to devoting oneself exclusively to this as far as this is within one's capacity."[13]

4b. Individual human beings have progressed spiritually to the point where they can worship God through intellectual meditation.[14] Eventually, all human beings will progress to the point where they abandon idolatry and embrace Judaic monotheism. Thanks to the intervention of Christianity and Islam, the world is being slowly monotheized, thus making possible the eventual advent of the Messiah.[15] With such human development possible, is it credible that Maimonides would think that the description of the universe presented in his *Mishneh Torah* would never become outdated?

5. Another point: Maimonides, it turns out, for all his interest in presenting the *Mishneh Torah* in apodictic terms, was not even wedded irretrievably to the details of his account of *halakhah* presented there. He recognized the fact that he could err, corrected mistakes which he caught himself, and admitted the fact when others found mistakes in the work. It seems fairly clear that if Maimonides was willing to admit that in halakhic matters the *Mishneh Torah* was not necessarily the last word, he would even more be willing to admit that such was the case with scientific matters.

COMPARING THE VIEWS OF MAIMONIDES AND GERSONIDES

If Maimonides presented the science of the *Mishneh Torah* provisionally, then an important reason for thinking that he would have agreed with Gersonides' claim concerning the closure and perfectibility of the sciences must be rejected. There is a further and even more convincing argument to the effect that

Maimonides would have rejected Gersonides' views on this subject. This has to do with another debate between them.

In his well-known monograph, *To Save the Phenomena*,[16] Pierre Duhem distinguishes between two approaches to astronomy in the Middle Ages, the formalistic and the realistic. The formalistic or instrumentalist, utilitarian approach follows Plato and Ptolemy.[17] According to it, our models of planetary motions are nothing other than mathematical constructs designed to facilitate our calculations; they are not meant to describe the "real world" as such. The formalistic approach was interested only in "saving the phenomena" (i.e., describing and calculating the occurrence of specific phenomena). The second, or "realistic" approach followed Aristotle in affirming that our astronomy ought to reflect physical reality.

On this issue Maimonides placed himself firmly in the formalistic camp,[18] while Gersonides placed himself just as firmly in the realist camp.[19] Why does Maimonides reject the opposed, realistic approach to astronomy? *"The heavens are the heavens of the Lord,"* Maimonides quotes from Psalm 115:16, *"but the earth hath He given to the sons of man."* As is well known, Maimonides places severe limits on the extent of human knowledge.[20] Knowledge of the heavens is literally beyond our ken. This is not a matter of "sagacious skepticism," as Duhem would have it, but of crucial *religious* importance to Maimonides. Insisting on the limitations of human knowledge and emphasizing the absolutely qualitatively different characters of divine and human knowledge allows Maimonides to eat his cake and have it too with respect to any number of theological problems. Breaking with the school of Andalusian Aristotelianism on this matter was thus absolutely crucial to Maimonides. It was more than simply criticizing Aristotle's celestial physics so as to make the refutation of his arguments for the eternity of the world easier; it was a central element in the edifice Maimonides was trying to construct, an edifice in which the "foundation of all foundations" was equivalent to the "pillar of all the sciences." In order to harmonize Torah and (Aristotelian) science, Maimonides had to draw narrow limits around what we can in principle know. His formalistic astronomy is a further expression of this.

Adding detail to the claims made in the previous paragraph will make my point clearer. There are a considerable number of theological problems solved by Maimonides' theory of attributes. According to this theory, terms predicated of God and human beings may be so predicated only by way of "absolute equivocation," whereby all the terms have in common is the name (e.g., God's knowledge and human knowledge have only one thing in common: the word *knowledge*).[21] Maimonides uses this theory to good effect in solving several problems. For example, the problem of evil in the world is ultimately solved by recourse to the fact that we cannot in principle know why God created the world as He did. The problem of God's knowledge of particulars vs. human freedom is ultimately solved by affirming that we can never understand how God's knowledge works; similarly for the problem of God's will. Maimonides' philosophical agnosticism concerning the creation of the universe can also be traced back to his theory of attributes.

Returning to the point under discussion, what does Maimonides' attempt to "save the phenomena" have to do with the question of his attitude toward the science he presents in the *Mishneh Torah*? We are now in the position to state categorically that superlunar science had not reached perfection or closure in Maimonides' day for the simple reason that he held that such science would never reach that stage: the full picture is beyond our abilities to apprehend. Therefore, the science he presents in the *Mishneh Torah* is, by its very nature, incomplete and provisional.

Comparing Maimonides and Gersonides on this point may illuminate the issue a bit further. Rejecting Maimonides' theory of attributes, Gersonides affirms that when the term *knowledge* is applied to God and to human beings, the equivocation is not absolute.[22] A consequence of this approach is that for Gersonides the scope of possible human knowledge is much wider than it is for Maimonides. Gersonides, additionally, affirms the following claims, all denied by Maimonides: all knowledge (not just knowledge of metaphysics) leads to felicity; we can in principle know the heavens; we can prove the creation of the universe. We study the heavens, Gersonides furthermore affirms, not just for utilitarian reasons but both in order to increase our knowledge of highly worthwhile things, thus increasing our felicity, and in order to learn about God's providence, which is most clearly expressed through the ordering of the heavens.[23] If studying the heavens adds to our felicity, then such study must produce true knowledge and not simply successful predictions. There can be no surprise, therefore, that Maimonides is a formalist in his astronomy while Gersonides is a realist.

In order to make his synthesis of religion and philosophy possible, therefore, Maimonides must claim that the science of astronomy can never be brought to perfection or closure. What we can know of astronomical phenomena must never be thought to accord with the true facts; rather astronomical knowledge is only a model which allows us to make predictions, while telling us nothing about the true state of the heavens. Maimonides is driven to this position by his theory of attributes.

In consequence, Maimonides' account of the heavens in "Laws of the Foundations of the Torah" must be understood as having been presented provisionally. Those who insist on reading Maimonides' science as canonically as they read his *halakhah*, therefore, are not, whatever they are, followers of Maimonides.

11

The Sciences as "Maidservants of the Torah" in Maimonides' Writings

Yehudah Levi

PREAMBLE

The Torah (the Jewish religious teaching) is meant to guide life in this world. Knowledge of the world in general, and scientific knowledge in particular, has always played an important role in Judaism. The talmudic sages unequivocally support the study of science.[1] Rabbi Yaakov Provencali, an outstanding fifteenth-century halakhic authority, writes: "Each of the seven sciences is praiseworthy in the eyes of our sages, who embraced them wholeheartedly. Nowhere – neither in the Babylonian, nor in the Jerusalem Talmud, nor in any *midrash* – do they disparage any science."[2]

However, in later times, some students were diverted from the Torah path due to their study of science, and this phenomenon generated opposition to such study among the more conservative elements in Jewry. Evidently these were, occasionally, excessively zealous in derogating study of science. Concerning those who shun philosophy completely because of its dangers, Maimonides writes: "... the fools and lazy ones who love to see their own shortcomings and stupidity as perfection and wisdom, and the perfection and knowledge of others as deficiency and impiety – they present darkness as light and light as darkness."[3]

Already a thousand years ago Rabbi Saadiah Gaon derided people who, on religious grounds, oppose study of science, comparing them to those who explain lunar eclipses as due to a monster which periodically swallows the moon.[4]

Five hundred years ago, Rabbi Eliyahu HaLevi, a disciple of Rabbi Eliyahu Mizrachi, severely reprimanded a person who publicly insulted a Torah scholar for studying science. Rabbi HaLevi writes that the person insulted not only the scholar, but also all those of our great masters who studied science, such as Rabbis Saadiah and Hai Gaon, Yehudah HaLevi, Avraham Ibn Ezra, and Maimonides (RaMBaM).[5]

Two hundred years ago, Rabbi Barukh of Sklov, a disciple of the Gaon of Vilna, complained about people, "some of whom have no good traits or other qualities, neither Torah knowledge, nor wisdom, nor fear of Heaven; they only hope to merit the world-to-come for not having the faintest knowledge of science. It is these who have betrayed the Jewish people regarding science, have blinded them on this issue, and made them into an object of derision in the eyes of the nations."[6]

In view of the aforementioned, it is not surprising that Maimonides, too, was obliged to defend the study of science.

INTRODUCTION

In his famous letter to Rabbi Yehonathan HaKohen of Lunel,[7] Maimonides explains that, when he studied the sciences, he took them only "as maidservants to the Torah, in order to show the nations the beauty of their mistress."

It should be of interest to demonstrate this contention by means of examples from Maimonides' writings. I have found no indication that Maimonides studied the sciences purely for the sake of knowledge. On the other hand, we shall see in the following that he indeed did use the sciences in the service of Judaism, i.e., the practice of Torah.

Maimonides also freely admits that the sources of his scientific knowledge are occasionally gentile. This is perfectly consistent with the assumption that such knowledge is simply a tool. If scientific knowledge were Torah proper, and its study was part of Torah study, use of such sources would be decried.

The Jewish Calendar and Astronomy

The first commandment given to the Jewish people is the establishment of a solar-lunar calendar.[8] This calendar is unique in that the year follows the solar cycle of the seasons, while the months follow the lunar cycle.

This calendar was maintained by the rabbinic high court (Sanhedrin) in a manner that combined astronomical calculations with eyewitness reports of sightings of the moon.[9] In accordance with Maimonides' ruling, the calculation of the possibility of a moon sighting on the thirtieth day of each month is a Torah (i.e., divine) commandment.[10] This is the basis for his devoting seven chapters in his *Code (Mishneh Torah)* to the details of the required astronomical calculations.[11]

This is the only context in which he teaches astronomy in great detail, even explaining why he uses certain approximations (either because two approximations have effects canceling each other out, or because the error introduced falls within the acceptable tolerance limits).[12]

Sukkah and Optics

The first *mishnah* in Tractate *Sukkah* deals with the density of the required ceiling cover *(sekhakh)*. If the illuminated portion exceeds the shaded portion, the *sekhakh* is unfit. Maimonides, based on the talmudic discussion on this *mishnah,* explains that if the illuminated areas on the floor of the *sukkah* are equal to the shaded areas, the *sekhakh* is fit, because this situation implies that in the plane of the *sekhakh* itself, the areas of the openings are less. This follows, according to Maimonides, "from the laws of optics, according to which the light from the sun passing through a hole illuminates, on the ground, an area greater than that of the hole."[13]

Menstrual Impurity and Anatomy

In Tractate *Niddah,* Maimonides goes into considerable anatomical detail to clarify minutiae of menstrual impurity and its practical determination.[14] He bases himself there on the secular anatomical literature.

Redemption of the Firstborn and Probability Theory

The concepts of probability were but poorly developed in ancient times and even in the Middle Ages.[15] Yet Maimonides uses these concepts in making halakhic rulings. Specifically, in connection with the *halakhah* that requires the "redemption" of the firstborn child, if it is a male, Maimonides treats the case of two women giving birth together to two boys and one girl, under conditions where it is not known which woman gave birth to which child. He rules that if one of the women had not previously given birth, her husband must pay the "redemption-charge" of five *shekel* to the *kohen,* even though his debt is not certain – his wife may have given birth to the girl first. He bases his ruling on an enumeration of the possibilities, concluding that it is considerably more probable that his wife gave birth to a boy first.[16]

Author's note:

1. There is a 50 percent probability that she is the one with the single birth, in which case there is a two-thirds probability that it was a boy.
2. If she gave birth to twins, these may have been a mixed pair, in which case there is a 50 percent probability that the boy was delivered first; but there is now the additional possibility that she gave birth to two boys, in which event her husband would certainly be obligated. Thus here, too, the chances are greater than 50 percent that he is obligated.

The probability of her having given birth to a boy first turns out to be twice as great as the reverse.

We have here a clear application of probability theory to a halakhic decision.[17]

Kilayim, Eruvin, and Geometry

The need to apply geometry to halakhic questions in the laws of *kilayim* (prohibition of planting different species in close proximity) is well known. We cite only one reference,[18] which deals with the prohibition of planting a vegetable in a vineyard and the number of vines which become prohibited as a result of such a planting. Here Maimonides goes into a considerable geometrical discussion to elaborate the *halakhah*.

A similar need exists in connection with the prohibitions to travel and to carry in the public domain on the Sabbath, where the permitted areas are defined in mathematical terms. These laws give rise to geometrical problems that Maimonides treats in some detail. We again cite just one example dealing with the maximum area of an enclosure in which carrying is permitted even though the enclosure was not made for residential purposes.[19] Here Maimonides discusses the various approximations adopted by different mishnaic authorities.

FUNDAMENTAL COMMANDMENTS

Love and Reverence of God and the Study of His Works

Love and reverence for God are arguably the most fundamental commandments of the Torah. The mode of their fulfillment affects the fulfillment of all commandments. Both the prophets[20] and the talmudic sages stress that such love and reverence must be based on knowledge of God, which, in turn, can only emanate from a study of His creations: the Torah and the physical world.²¹ But especially Maimonides emphasizes at great length the study of nature as a precondition to knowledge and love of God.

We briefly illustrate this approach by means of quotations from his *Commentary on the Mishnah,* his *Code,* and the *Guide for the Perplexed.*

In his introduction to Tractate *Avot,* Maimonides writes concerning the study of mathematics and physics: "[The student's] goal in studying them should be to acquire the ability to give logical proofs by means of which he can attain knowledge of the existence of God."²² Especially the study of medicine is very important to the attainment of self-perfection and knowledge of God; thus it can become divine service at the highest level.²³

Maimonides devotes the first four chapters of his *Code* to a description of the structure of the world. To explain his curious decision to begin his *Code* in this way, he writes: "When a person contemplates these matters and recognizes all creatures . . . and sees God's wisdom in all creatures, he increases his love of God."²⁴ Earlier he asks: "Which path should be taken to [attain] love and reverence of God? When a person contemplates His wondrous and magnificent works and creatures and deduces [from them] His limitless and infinite wisdom, he will immediately love [God] . . ."²⁵

In his *Guide,* Maimonides proclaims: "You are certainly aware of the stress put on love [of God]: 'With all your heart, with all your soul, and with all your possessions.'²⁶ We have already explained in the *Code* that such love can come about only out of a knowledge of the world as it is, and by contemplating His wisdom."²⁷

Self-Perfection and Science Study

In the introduction to his *Guide,* Maimonides presents the following list, in which each item depends conditionally on the following item: (1) the perfection of our person and society; (2) intellectual attainment, especially knowledge of God; (3) theology; (4) natural science – "for natural science borders on theology and must precede it in time."²⁸

Further on in the *Guide* he declares: "And [God] can be known only by means of His actions. . . . Hence, it is necessary for anyone who wishes to attain human perfection to prepare himself first by means of [the study of] logic . . . and afterwards natural science and then theology."²⁹

"Walking in God's Path" and Hygiene

In the commandment to walk in the paths of God, Maimonides includes the care of both mental and physical health. He used his extensive knowledge of hygiene to prescribe a regimen to guide his students toward physical health. A full chapter in his *Code* is devoted to this topic.³⁰

Torah Study and Natural Science

One of the most fundamental of the Torah's commandments is the study of Torah; Torah knowledge is an obvious precondition to the proper fulfillment of its commandments.

In this context too, Maimonides used his extensive knowledge of science to clarify talmudic passages. We present here several illustrations of such use, where we are concerned not so much with the level of his scientific knowledge, but rather with his attitude, to use his knowledge to gain insight into the exact meaning of a talmudic statement.

1. The *mishnah* refers to polished, transparent glass as *s-f/p-k-l-r-y-h*. This word seems to be related to *specula,* the Latin word for mirror. That explanation does not, however, account for the letters *l-r-y*. Therefore Maimonides suggests that the term derives from the Hebrew *"safek le-re'iyah"* ("uncertain vision"): "for a person who views [an object] behind a layer of glass, a jewel, or any other transparent material, will not see it in its correct position, as demonstrated by the science of optics."[31]

2. Another *mishnah* refers to a mouse which is half flesh and half earth.[32] Maimonides comments upon this: "The creation of a mouse from earth, such that part of it may be flesh and part mud . . . this is a very wide-spread tale, and an untold multitude have told me that they have seen it. The existence of such a creature is strange and inexplicable."

3. The Talmud rules that the halakhah proscribing the killing of an animal on the Sabbath applies only to animal species that reproduce sexually.[33] The Talmud also specifically includes fleas in this category. Using his (contemporary) scientific knowledge that fleas are generated spontaneously from dust, Maimonides concludes that such animals are considered equivalent to sexually reproducing ones.[34] (Note that here the talmudic sages are in better agreement with modern science than Maimonides.)

THE ORIGIN OF SCIENTIFIC KNOWLEDGE

Maimonides repeatedly stresses that, by its very nature, natural science may be discovered by anyone, in contrast to new Torah material, which we can accept only from a proven prophetic source (i.e., Moses). This implies that he considers natural science as distinct from Torah and not included in it.[35]

In concluding the extensive presentation of his method for ascertaining the visibility of the moon on a given day, Maimonides emphasizes that his theory is not part of divine teaching, but, rather, is based on the works of the Greeks. In defending his use of such gentile sources as a basis for religious practice, he writes: "Since all these matters are [founded on] rigorous proof . . . it does not matter whether the author was a prophet or a gentile. For any matter based on, and derived from, incontrovertible proof – [in accepting it] we are not relying on the person stating or teaching it, but rather on the proof."[36]

Similarly, he writes in his *Guide:*

> Do not expect me to demonstrate agreement between [the talmudic sages'] words and matters as they are in fact; for the sciences were, at that time, incomplete. [The sages] spoke of science, not on the basis of a tradition they had from the prophets [i.e., divine revelation], but as the scholars of their time in this area, or as having received [the information] from the scholars of their time.[37]

Maimonides' son, Rabbi Avraham, is even more explicit in differentiating between Torah, which is divinely revealed, and in which the talmudic authority is absolute, on the one hand, and scientific knowledge, which originates in the results of human research. He states:

> The superiority of the talmudic sages and the completeness of their qualifications in the exposition of the Torah, its details and the integrity of its statements, in general and in detail – all this does not imply that we must defend and uphold their statements in matters of medicine, natural science, and astronomy, and to believe them as we believe them concerning the exposition of the Torah, where they have the ultimate wisdom.[38]

On this issue, however, we find in Maimonides' writings a statement that implies the opposite, that natural science is part of Torah. In the fourth chapter of his *Code,* after completing the description of the world's structure and the nature of the soul, he writes: "The explanation of all these matters in the third and fourth chapter, is called *'maaseh bereshit.'* And our early sages enjoined us, that these matters not be taught in public; one may teach them only on a one-to-one basis."[39]

Since *maaseh bereshit* is clearly part of Torah, some authors interpret this statement to mean that Maimonides considers science part of Torah study. However, this supposition seems to be almost impossible to maintain. No other medieval halakhic authority espoused it and, to my knowledge, Maimonides himself states it in no other context. On the contrary, we have seen that both he and his son implicitly contradict this position. Furthermore, it is inconceivable that he would detail these matters in a publication accessible to the general public and, in the same breath, state that they may be taught only on a one-to-one basis.

However, if one reads his words carefully, the appearance of a contradiction vanishes. He does not call "these matters," i.e., science, *maaseh bereshit.* Rather, "their explanation," i.e., their deeper significance, is termed *maaseh bereshit.* Evidently, the significance of the interaction of spiritual matters, "the nature of the soul," with physical matter – this is *maaseh bereshit.* This may only be taught on a one-to-one basis, and this he does not publish.

CONCLUSIONS

Maimonides' claim that he studied science only in the service of Torah can be supported from the many instances in which he uses his scientific knowledge to clarify the commandments of the Torah or, directly, to fulfill such commandments. This is illustrated by means of specific halakhic issues, as well as in conjunction with the most fundamental Torah commandments.

Furthermore, Maimonides considers natural science to be distinct from Torah, so that the obligation to study Torah does not apply directly to the study of science. Rather, study of science is, to Maimonides, a tool in the fulfillment of Torah commandments. We are, indeed, obligated to study science, but only in a secondary role.

GLOSSARY

Baraita – Tannaic statement not included in Mishnah.

Eruv(in) – Halakhic device(s) joining a number of separate domains into one for the purpose of permitting the transport of objects from one domain into the other on the Sabbath.

Halakhah – rulings of religious law.

Kilayim – the mingling of different species. Specifically, the intermingled planting of different botanical species.

Maaseh Bereshit – the process of original creation. An area of study concerning this.

Rambam – Rabbi Mosheh ben Maimon, Maimonides.

Sekhakh – the ceiling covering of the *sukkah*.

Sukkah – a hut, temporary dwelling. Especially the hut used on the Sukkot holy day ("tabernacles").

12

Maimonides on the Distinction between Science and Pseudoscience

J. David Bleich

Maimonides does not present a systematic exposition of his understanding of the notion of causality. Nevertheless, he certainly understood and accepted the principle of causal relationships between empirical events. Causality is clearly invoked in his discussion of divine attributes, critique of Kalam philosophy, proof of the existence, unity, and incorporeality of God, creation, prophecy, good and evil, divine knowledge and will, and also in his philosophy of law as well as in his formulation of *taamei ha-mitzvot* (the purpose or rationale underlying the various divine commandments).[1]

Maimonides certainly believed that the universe is governed by a set of physical laws. To speak of the universe as governed by a set of laws is but another way of stating that physical phenomena occur in an orderly and predictable manner. That formulation, in turn, is actually a good working definition of the notion of causation, i.e., the principle that affirms that physical events are not merely isolated and discrete individual occurrences that happen to occur in a certain chronological order but that there is a certain intrinsic connection between them such that, *ceteris paribus*, the occurrence of one will necessarily and invariably lead to another. However, while the notion of causality as an intrinsic and necessary relationship between otherwise independent events may be an a priori concept inherent in the human intellect, specific instances of cause and effect relationships may not always be immediately discoverable; in other cases the existence of a causal relationship may be debatable. Philosophy may posit the existence of such a relationship, but it is science that must provide instantiation.

It is certainly arguable that, for Judaism, causality is not simply a philosophical construct of entirely speculative interest but is part of the axiological framework upon which *Halakhah* is predicated. The Jew is commanded to eat *matzah* on Passover, but *matzah* does not descend as manna from heaven. The obligation to eat *matzah* on Passover carries with it an obligation to prepare unleavened bread to be eaten on the festival. Implied in that commandment is the empirical principle that when flour is mixed with water and then kneaded and subsequently placed in a heated oven, *matzah,* rather than porridge, will emerge. Implied in all positive commandments requiring physical artifacts for their fulfillment is a notion that man is capable of producing or fashioning such artifacts. Man is not required to engage in random activity in the pious hope that somehow his haphazard actions will yield the necessary object, much as the Golden Calf emerged from Aaron's bonfire, but to act in an orderly, purposive manner fully confident that his endeavor, properly executed, will yield the anticipated result. Man is, in effect, commanded to accept the principle of causation; otherwise he could plead impotence in failing to fulfill the *mitzvot* imposed upon him.[2]

The principle of causality is certainly reflected in Maimonides' formulation of the principle that all measures must be taken, whether in a therapeutic context or in nontherapeutic situations, for purposes of preservation of life (*Hilkhot Rotzeah* 1:14; *Commentary on the Mishnah, Nedarim* 4:4; and *Hilkhot Nedarim* 6:8) and in his ruling (*Hilkhot Yesodei ha-Torah* 5:1–2, 5:4, and 5:6) that, with the exception of the three cardinal transgressions, all provisions of Jewish law are suspended in the effort to preserve life, even if the efficacy of the endeavor is in doubt (*Hilkhot Shabbat* 2:1).

In light of these clearly enunciated principles, Maimonides' statement, *Hilkhot Shabbat* 19:14, is problematic. The issue is whether or not an amulet may be worn on *Shabbat* while passing from a private to a public domain. Maimonides rules:

> One may go out with a tested amulet. What is a tested amulet? One which has cured three persons or which has been made by a person who has cured three persons by means of other amulets.

Maimonides' codification reflects the ruling of the Mishnah, *Shabbat* 60a, and the ensuing discussion of the Gemara, *Shabbat* 61a, and is predicated upon acceptance of the curative powers of amulets when prepared by persons proficient in such matters.[3]

Maimonides, to be sure, was well aware of the traumatic effect of withholding even useless remedies and the possibility that resultant anguish might hasten death. Thus, in *Hilkhot Avodat Kokhavim* 11:11, he rules:

> One who has been bitten by a scorpion or by a snake may recite an incantation over the site of the bite, even on the Sabbath, in order to put his mind at ease and to strengthen his heart. Even though it is entirely of no avail, since he is in danger, [the Sages] permitted it to him so that his mind not become destroyed.

Even though incantations are generally forbidden, as Maimonides clearly rules in the immediately preceding paragraph, *Hilkhot Avodat Kokhavim* 11:10, he nevertheless sanctions resorting to incantations for purposes of *pikuah nefesh*. Despite the fact that Maimonides regards incantations as intrinsically useless, he permits them because the condition of a victim of a snake bite who believes them to be of therapeutic value is such that the victim may become agitated and the danger to his life aggravated if the incantation is withheld. Maimonides does not hesitate to permit otherwise forbidden pseudoremedies when their use is indicated by virtue of psychological considerations but explicitly indicates the reason for that permissiveness. Maimonides offers no such justification with regard to the use of amulets. Moreover, as noted by *Maggid Mishneh, ad locum,* amulets are permitted even for the cure of non-life-threatening maladies on the ground that, for the sick, they are comparable to articles of clothing. Thus, Maimonides permits the wearing of amulets on *Shabbat* even in the absence of life-threatening emotional anguish. If so, why does Maimonides permit only an amulet of demonstrated efficacy or an amulet that has been fashioned by persons of demonstrated competence? At least in cases of illness posing a danger to life, even an amulet of merely possible therapeutic value should be permitted on grounds of *safek pikuah nefesh*.

A similar problem arises with regard to Maimonides' comments in his *Commentary on the Mishnah, Yoma* 8:6. The Mishnah declares:

> One who has been bitten by a mad dog should not be fed of the lobe of its liver. But R. Mattia ben Heresh permits [this practice].

The practice of prescribing the liver of the attacking dog as a prophylactic measure against contracting rabies seems to have been fairly widespread among physicians of antiquity[4] and appears to have survived in at least some primitive societies until comparatively recent times.[5] An obvious and facile analysis of that controversy is presented by R. Menahem ha-Me'iri, *Bet ha-Behirah, Yoma* 82a, who comments that R. Mattia ben Heresh permitted consumption of the liver "because he thought it to be therapeutic," while the Sages forbade the practice "because it is not a cure," even though it was categorized as such by the masses. According to this analysis, R. Mattia ben Heresh maintained that, since consumption of the dog's liver was an accepted treatment for the bite of a mad dog and was commonly recommended by physicians, the prohibition against eating the flesh of unclean animals may be disregarded. Although the therapeutic or prophylactic efficacy of this remedy could not be demonstrated, the victim was, nevertheless, permitted to eat the liver of the dog because the liver was regarded as possibly, albeit doubtfully, efficacious. The Sages, on the other hand, were convinced that the liver was devoid of any therapeutic value. A similar analysis is independently advanced by Maharam ben Habib, *Tosafot Yom ha-Kippurim, Yoma* 83a.

Assuming that the Sages maintained that the liver of a dog is of entirely no benefit in the treatment of rabies, their position is unexceptionable. Violation of proscriptions of Jewish law for purposes of saving a human life is sanctioned only when there exists at least a possible cause-and-effect relationship between the violation and the desired effect. If it is factually determined that no such relationship exists, there are not grounds upon which violation of the prohibition might be sanctioned.

Maimonides, however, does not offer this obvious analysis of the controversy between the Sages and R. Mattia ben Heresh. According to the Ibn Tibbon version of the *Commentary on the Mishnah,* Maimonides states:

> The law with regard to this is not in accordance with R. Mattia ben Heresh who permits feeding a person the liver of a dog that bites because this does not benefit other than by way of a *segulah*. But the Sages declare that one may not transgress the commandments other than in conjunction with a therapy, i.e., with regard to things which cure in accordance with Nature. That is, a true matter derived by reason or[6] experience that approaches truth. But to treat by means of things that cure by virtue of their *segulah* is forbidden because their power is weak, not [known] by virtue of reason and its [demonstrated efficacy on the basis of] experience is far-fetched; its advocacy by one who is in error is weak.

The Kapah version of the same text reads:

> But the Sages declare that one may not transgress the law other than in conjunction with therapy that is a clear matter mandated by reason or[7] simple experience[8] but not for treatment by means of *segulot* because they are weak in nature, not mandated by reason and its [demonstrated efficacy on the basis of] experience is far-fetched but is [nevertheless] advocated by its advocate.

Here, too, Maimonides' analysis presents us with the identical problem. If the efficacy of the treatment is not dismissed out of hand, why is it not permitted for purposes of *pikuah nefesh?* Maimonides' comments make it abundantly clear that, were it to be known with certainty that the dog's liver is capable of curing or preventing the occurrence of rabies, consumption of the liver by the victim of the dog bite would be sanctioned. If so, since the therapeutic or prophylactic value of that therapy has not been ruled out, consumption of the dog's liver should be permissible as a matter of *safek pikuah nefesh.*

Maimonides (*Guide* 2:22) records a series of four axioms assumed by "Aristotle and all philosophers." The first axiom states that a simple element can produce only one simple thing, while a compound can produce as many things as it contains simple elements. The second of these axioms is: "Things are not produced by others at random; there must be some relation between cause and effect. . . ." Maimonides then proceeds to ask a question: The first intellect is undoubtedly simple. "How then can the compound form of existing things come from such an intellect by fixed laws of Nature, as Aristotle assumes?" According to the laws of Nature, a compound can emanate only from a compound. Therefore, concludes Rambam, "It must now be clear that this emanation could not have taken place by the force of the laws of Nature, as Aristotle contends."

Moreover, Maimonides (*Guide* 2:19, 2:24) observes that there exists a certain lack of order in the celestial realm. Although celestial spheres move with uniform circular motion, the varied velocities of the planets have no apparent order. In some instances a sphere moving with greater velocity is above one moving more slowly, while in other instances the reverse seems to be the case. In still other instances two spheres differing in location have the same velocity. These and other celestial irregularities cannot be explained on the basis of the Aristotelian view that the universe is totally ordered.

Maimonides concludes that although the sublunar world is governed by necessary laws, i.e., cause-and-effect relationships which are intelligible to man, nevertheless, in the translunar world causality is not necessarily operative. Maimonides (*Guide* 2:22) succinctly states:

> I hold that the theory of Aristotle is undoubtedly correct as far as the things are concerned which exist between the sphere of the moon and the center of the earth. . . . But what Aristotle says concerning things above the sphere of the moon is, with few exceptions, mere imagination and opinion. . . .

Maimonides concedes that the sublunar world is governed by the laws of Nature in general and by the principle of causality in particular. But this is not the case with regard to the translunar universe. The translunar universe is not governed by the laws of Nature but, as Maimonides declares in the same chapter, by the "design and determination of a Creator in accordance with His incomprehensible wisdom." Formulation of that position makes it possible to accept the doctrine of creation rather than the Aristotelian notion of the eternity of the universe.

Although Maimonides' distinction is cast in terms serving to distinguish the sublunar world from the translunar universe, the underlying distinction may well be regarded as being essentially a distinction between the physical and the metaphysical. As such, it is not at all surprising that the laws of Nature apply only to the physical universe. One should not anticipate that physical laws are applicable to any metaphysical being or power. Accordingly, translunar celestial bodies are outside the pale of the laws of Nature, simply because those laws are limited to the sublunar universe which, by virtue of its very nature, is corporeal and physical.

The categories of the metaphysical and the physical, while essentially dichotomous, are not without points of interaction. One of the problems inherent in Aristotle's view regarding the motion of the celestial bodies is how an incorporeal intelligence may serve as an efficient cause in effecting motion in a corporeal substance. Nevertheless, Aristotle maintains that metaphysical causes have physical effects. The cosmogony of the *Kabbalah,* in which human activity plays a focal role in *tikkun,* i.e., restoration of the world of *asiyah* to its spiritual perfection, is founded upon the premise that the correlate principle is also true, i.e., that physical causes produce metaphysical effects.

The problem is mitigated considerably if it is recognized that the interaction between the physical and the metaphysical is not governed by laws of Nature, just as the realm of the purely metaphysical is not governed by laws of Nature. Thus, categories of causality as reflected in the sublunar physical world cannot fully explain those relationships. Our understanding of particular causal relationships is the product of inductive inference based upon empirical observation which, by its very nature, is limited to situations in which both the cause and the effect are observable, i.e., physical rather than metaphysical. Nevertheless, areas of interaction between the physical and the metaphysical do exist.

An example of such interaction can be found in Nachmanides' exposition of the nature of sorcery in his *Commentary on the Bible,* Deuteronomy 18:9:

> And now, know and understand with regard to the matter of sorcery, that when the Creator, blessed be He, created everything *ex nihilo* He made the higher powers to be guides for the lower powers beneath them. He placed the power of the "earth and all things that are thereon" (Nehemiah 9:6) in stars and constellations in accordance with their rotation and position as proven by the science of astrology. Over the stars and constellations He further appointed angels and "lords" who are the soul [of the stars and constellations] as guides. Now, their behavior from the time they came into existence until eternity is according to the decree of the higher power which He placed in them. However, it was one of His mighty wonders that, within the power of the higher forces, He put configurations and capacities to alter that which is under them. Thus if the gaze of the stars towards the earth be good or bad to a certain land, people or individual, the higher powers can change by their own gaze.... Therefore, the author of the Book of the Moon, the expert in necromancy said, that when the moon, termed the sphere of the world, is, for example, at the head of Aries and the constellation thus appears in a certain position, you should make a certain picture and engrave upon it the time and the name of the angel – one of the names mentioned in that book – appointed over it and then perform a certain

burning of incense in a certain specified manner and the result of the gaze [of the stars] will be for evil. . . . and when the moon shall be in a certain constellation and a certain gaze you should make the picture and the burning in a certain manner and the result will be all manner of good. . . . This then is the secret of sorcery and power. . . . Therefore it is proper that the Torah prohibit these activities in order to let the world remain in its customary way and in its simple nature which is the desire of its Creator.

It is certainly true that Maimonides, *Hilkhot Avodat Kokhavim* 11:16, negates the efficacy of sorcery and witchcraft and, *inter alia,* dismisses such practices with the observation that ". . . they are all imaginary and foolishness which attract only those that are deficient in knowledge." Nevertheless, Maimonides certainly recognized that metaphysical causes may produce physical effects. Maimonides, no less than Aristotle, accepted the principle that incorporeal intelligences are the cause of motion of corporeal bodies. Maimonides' own understanding of causality and the differing role of causation in the physical and metaphysical realms may serve to illuminate his halakhic rulings regarding amulets and nonscientific remedies.

As indicated by his comments in *Hilkhot Shabbat* and in his *Commentary on the Mishnah,* Maimonides was quite prepared to accept the therapeutic efficacy of amulets and certain remedies that he describes as *segulot.* The term *"teva"* ("Nature") that appears in the Ibn Tibbon version of the *Commentary on the Mishnah* in elucidating the dichotomous nature of the two modes of therapy reveals the crucial nature of the distinction between conventional cures and *"segulot."* The distinction is between medical remedies rooted in the laws of Nature, whose efficacy is explainable in accordance with causal connections between the medicament and the disease for which it is prescribed, and other remedies whose effects can be explained only in some nonnatural or metaphysical manner.

The thesis that, according to Maimonides, violation of halakhic restrictions for purposes of preserving life is permitted only in conjunction with the use of natural remedies, but not permitted with regard to *segulot,* is certainly an inviting one. That distinction would be justified by the contention that transgression of halakhic prohibitions is permitted only in conjunction with actions designed to yield predictable effects based upon known causal relationships present in the natural order. This, indeed, seems to be the position of Maharam ben Habib, *Tosafot Yom ha-Kippurim, Yoma* 83a. That authority seems to be of the opinion that transgression of a biblical prohibition can never be sanctioned for the purpose of administering therapy in the form of a *segulah.* This is also the manner in which Maimonides was understood by *Admat Kodesh,* I, *Yoreh De'ah,* no. 6, as well as by *Teshuvot Pri ha-Arez,* III, no. 3.[9] Those authorities were asked if a nonkosher chicken might be fed to a person suffering from some form of mental illness. The cure is described as a *segulah.* We are, however, informed that it was well known that the lives of many people were saved by means of this therapy. Although those authorities permit use of the therapy in question, they indicate that Maimonides would have forbidden the use of even a tried and tested *segulah* under such circumstances but that, according to other authorities, any known therapy, even a *segulah,* may be utilized in cases of danger. R. Chaim Joseph David Azulai, *Birkei Yosef, Orah Hayyim* 301:6, applies the same analysis to the propriety of writing an amulet on *Shabbat,* apparently even when the success of the procedure is not in doubt.[10] Similarly, R. Shlomoh Kluger, both in his *Teshuvot Tuv Taam va-Daat, Mahadura Kamma,* no. 239, and in his *Teshuvot u-Vaharta ba-Hayyim,* no. 87, forbids desecration of the Sabbath in order to secure the prayer of a saint, even if it is known with certainty that the prayer will effect a cure. Prayer, while undoubtedly efficacious, can also be described as a nonnatural cause yielding a physical effect.

R. Chaim Sofer, *Teshuvot Mahaneh Hayyim, Yoreh De'ah,* II, no. 60, explains that availing oneself of the ministrations of a physician is permitted only because of specific dispensation granted by the verse "and he shall cause him to be thoroughly healed" (Exodus 21:20). Permission to utilize medical remedies entails an obligation to use them in the preservation of life. The obligation to preserve life, in turn, serves to obviate strictures of religious law. However, asserts *Mahaneh Hayyim,* the obligation arising out of that verse is limited to utilization of natural remedies; no similar obligation exists with regard to the use of nonnatural, occult, or metaphysical powers in effecting a cure. Infractions of Jewish law are permitted for purposes of preserving life only because such measures are demanded by *Halakhah.* Accordingly, *Mahaneh Hayyim* concludes that, according to Maimonides, even *segulot* of demonstrated efficacy may not be employed, even in face of danger to life, if such use involves an infraction of a halakhic prohibition. Alternatively, the verse "It is not in heaven" (Deuteronomy 30:12) may serve to establish the principle that all human obligations are limited to employment of natural forces present in the sublunar world.

Such a principle would serve to explain why, for example, there is no absolute mandatory obligation to offer prayer on behalf of a sick person.[11] Given the phenomenon of prayer and its efficacy, it is otherwise unclear why the obligation "Nor shall you stand idly by the blood of your fellow" (Leviticus 19:16) does not establish an absolute obligation to pray on behalf of a person whose life is endangered concomitant with the obligation to administer therapeutic measures or to engage in other endeavors to preserve his life. That problem is immediately resolved if it is posited that man's obligations are limited to the physical but exclude the employment of "heavenly" or metaphysical forces.

This distinction also serves to illuminate the comment of *Rema, Yoreh De'ah* 339:1, with regard to the treatment of a *goses.*[12] Although active euthanasia is always forbidden and the hastening of death by even a matter of moments is regarded as tantamount to homicide, *Rema* rules that, in the case of a *goses*, "... if there is something that causes a hindrance to the departure of the soul such as a clattering noise or salt upon his tongue and these prevent the departure of the soul they may be removed for this involves no act whatsoever but only the removal of the impediment." These comments of *Rema* notwithstanding, *Teshuvot Shevut Yaakov,* I, no. 13, cites *Yoma* 85a as demonstrating that *Shabbat* laws are suspended for the purpose of even marginal prolongation of life. *Shevut Yaakov* declares that all recognized therapeutic remedies must be utilized in prolonging the life of a *goses*, regardless of how brief a period of time he may be expected to survive. This authority evidently distinguishes between natural remedies of demonstrated efficacy involving readily recognizable causal relationships and nonscientific *segulot* of undemonstrable causal efficacy, such as the placing of salt upon the tongue. The latter, according to this analysis, is not required in the case of a *goses*, because they are not recognized medical procedures and hence their utilization is never required as a matter of normative *Halakhah*.[13]

The rulings of the earlier cited latter-day authorities notwithstanding, the language employed by Maimonides in his *Commentary on the Mishnah, Yoma* 8:6, seems to support the view that nonnatural remedies are forbidden when their use necessitates violation of halakhic restrictions only if those *segulot* are of unconfirmed therapeutic value but that no similar restrictions are placed upon administration of tried and tested *segulot* whose value has been confirmed by experience. According to the Kapah version of the *Commentary on the Mishnah,* Maimonides distinguishes between therapy "mandated by reason or simple experience" and *"segulot"* that are "weak in nature," i.e., not mandated by reason, and whose "demonstrated efficacy on the basis of experience is far-fetched." According to the Ibn Tibbon version, one may not employ otherwise forbidden measures in attempting to cure by means of a *segulah* because "their power is weak, not known by virtue of reason and its demonstrated efficacy on the basis of experience is far-fetched."

The reference, according to both versions, to cures that are known by virtue of "reason" is clearly a reference to medicaments or procedures with regard to which there is a rational, well-understood cause-and-effect relationship between the remedy and the cure. Maimonides' reference to "experience" as an independent criterion indicates that he is willing to accept the existence of a cause-and-effect relationship on the basis of "experience" or empirical generalization, even if the underlying scientific causal relationship is not fully understood. Experience gained over a period of time indicating a chronological relationship between cause and effect is accepted for purposes of *Halakhah* as indicative of an intrinsic relationship between the events, or at least of the possible existence of an intrinsic relationship between the events, with the result that violation of *Halakhah* is sanctioned, and indeed mandated, for reasons of *pikuah nefesh*. Nevertheless, Maimonides distinguishes between "experience that approaches truth" (Ibn Tibbon) or "simple experience" (Kapah) and experience that is "far-fetched" (*rahok*), i.e., between experience that is demonstrably compelling and experience that is inconclusive.

The crucial phrase in Maimonides' exposition of the position of the Sages in refusing to permit the victim of a dog bite to eat the liver of its attacker is that the ascription of curative power to this remedy on the basis of experience is far-fetched. Apparently even putative cures attributable to such therapy were few and far between. Such experience does not serve to confirm the efficacy of the contemplated measure. Nevertheless, similar therapies may be employed, even in the absence of the evidence of experience, in situations in which use of such remedies is "mandated by reason" or known "by virtue of reason." It would appear then that, according to Maimonides, the crucial factor in suspension of halakhic restrictions in situations involving *pikuah nefesh* is the presence of a causal relationship or, more precisely, the reasonably possible presence of a cause-effect relationship. Thus, suspension of halakhic proscriptions is warranted either on the basis of a cause-and-effect relationship postulated by reason or on the basis of experience. Since, in the case of *segulot*, the human intellect cannot grasp the presence of a causal relationship, the sole basis for permitting their utilization when such use involves an infraction of Jewish law is experience. Hence, when the evidence based upon experience is "far-fetched," no basis exists for permitting such use.

Assuming that what Maimonides says with regard to the translunar world is true with regard to metaphysical phenomena as well, *segulot* cannot *ipso facto* be subsumed under causal categories. This, it would appear, is the meaning of Maimonides' statement that the power of *segulot* is "weak," i.e., ordinary causal connections are not predictable as being uniformly present. It is that element of predictability that Maimonides regards as the sine qua non for suspension of halakhic prohibitions in the face of *pikuah nefesh*. It is, of course, quite true that accepted medical remedies do not unvaryingly result in a cure. Such negative phenomena do not suggest the absence of a causal relationship since instances of failure are readily attributed to the severity or advanced state of the disease, complicating factors, or the like. However, when the putative effect is only infrequently manifested, the curative power must be ascribed, not to the causal operation of laws of nature, but to the noncausal, unpredictable operation of a metaphysical power or *segulah*.

Maimonides thus relies upon experience in establishing the existence of a causal relationship, even in situations in which no scientific explanation is discernable. The inability of the human intellect to explain the basis of a cause-and-effect relationship does not necessarily mean that no such relationship exists. Hence, if the effects of a remedy can be predicted in a reliable manner, that in and of itself is evidence that the remedy in question is efficacious because of the presence of a causal principle. Such a remedy is not to be relegated to the category of a *segulah* of unconfirmed and unsubstantiated efficacy and thus may be utilized in instances of a threat to life, even if such use would otherwise be forbidden by Jewish law.

There are, however, situations in which physical effects are generated in a manner that cannot possibly be explained in terms of the operation of laws of nature governing the physical universe. Despite the regularity and predictability of such phenomena, they are clearly the result of the operation of metaphysical causes. When there exists sufficient evidence demonstrating a regular, predictable relationship between the metaphysical cause of the physical event, e.g., in the case of a "tested amulet," the phenomenon is treated no differently than natural, i.e., physical, causal relationships.

This analysis of Maimonides' distinction is supported by *Tiferet Yisrael, Yoma* 6:32, who cites Maimonides' comments with regard to cure by means of *segulot* in the face of halakhic strictures and concludes, "Therefore, any [such remedy] whose cure is not certain is forbidden." The threshold level of possible efficacy, and hence of *safek pikuah nefesh,* is satisfied if the putative therapeutic property of the medicament in question is perceived by reason or if it has been established on the basis of experience. Since even *safek pikuah nefesh,* i.e., even doubtful or possible preservation of life, is sufficient to warrant disregard of halakhic restraints, it is not necessary that reason or experience establish therapeutic efficacy beyond cavil; it is sufficient that reason or experience point to probable, or even possible, benefit.[14] Nevertheless, in the absence of experiential evidence of past success or cogent reason to assume therapeutic value, utilization of a contemplated remedy does not rise to the level of "doubtful" *pikuah nefesh.* However, when therapeutic value has been demonstrated on the basis of experience, remedies in the nature of *segulot* are treated no differently than recognized and established medical cures.[15]

Although Maimonides maintains that events confined entirely to the translunar world are not at all governed by causal principles, he makes no specific reference to the nature of the relationship between metaphysical powers and physical phenomena such as are manifest, for example, in motion imparted to celestial bodies by incorporeal intelligences. It is therefore entirely possible that some metaphysical causes not only produce physical effects but do so in a uniform, patterned manner entirely similar to the manner in which causally connected physical phenomena occur. Since the cause is metaphysical, the rationality of the connection is unlikely or impossible to be grasped by the human intellect. Nevertheless, when such matters do recur with regularity, a causal relationship can be inferred from such experience on the basis of empirical generalization.[16]

According to this analysis, Maimonides' sanction of the wearing of an amulet on *Shabbat,* provided that the efficacy of the amulet has been demonstrated, is readily understandable. *Segulot* in the form of metaphysical cures are treated no differently from scientifically explainable remedies in those limited situations in which the effect of the *segulah* is predictable.

III

Maimonides the Philosopher

13

Medical Categories in Maimonidean Ethics

Alexander Broadie

There is much to be said for the view that the moral philosophy of Maimonides is, at least in broad outline, Aristotelian. As regards the details of the relation between the moral philosophies of the two men, there are ample grounds for uncertainty. It is however generally agreed that, at the level of detail, Maimonides is no mere echo. But if the relation is not one of echo to source, what is it? Here I shall develop a partial answer, one focused upon Maimonides' teaching on virtue and vice and upon his employment of medical categories in dealing with moral philosophical concepts. Though Maimonides follows Aristotle in employing a version of the doctrine of the mean in his discussion of moral states, his perspective upon that doctrine is substantially different from that of Aristotle. The difference, roughly stated, is that Maimonides' perspective is that of a doctor interested in restorative medicine, whereas Aristotle's perspective is that of a doctor interested in preventive medicine. I shall not seek to argue that Aristotle believed the model of restorative medicine wholly inapplicable to moral philosophy – nor do I think that such an account of Aristotle can be sustained. However, it is possible to provide a strong defense for the claim that that model plays a prominent and key role in Maimonides' moral philosophy and that, on the contrary, it plays only a minor role in Aristotle's.

My starting point is the concept of health, of which Maimonides makes free use in his discussions of virtue and vice. He writes:

> The health of the soul consists in its condition and that of its parts being such that it always does good and fine things and performs noble actions. Its sickness consists in its condition and that of its parts being such that it always does bad and ugly things and performs base actions.[1]

It is possible that these two accounts are intended to be read as definitions *per genus et differentiam* of health of soul and of its sickness. If so, the genus in each case is the condition of the soul and of its parts, and the *differentiae* are the specific features of that condition which result in the soul performing the acts it does. The acts of the healthy soul are fine and noble, those of the sick soul the opposite.

Given Maimonides' abiding interest in univocal and equivocal predication, one might wonder whether the term *healthy* is being used univocally when predicated of "body" and of "soul." It is not certain what the answer is to this question, but it is plain that he believed there to be at least a very close similarity in signification between the term *healthy* predicated of "body" and of "soul."

Maimonides speaks of vice, as we have noted, as a sickness of the soul, and he held that the proper treatment for it is formally identical with the proper treatment for physical ailments. His prescription is based upon the doctrine of the mean:

> Should [a man's] soul become sick, he must follow the same course in treating it as in the medical treatment for bodies. For when the body gets out of equilibrium we look to which side it inclines in becoming unbalanced, and then oppose it with its contrary until it returns to equilibrium. When it is in equilibrium we remove that counterbalance and revert to that which keeps the body in equilibrium. We act in a similar manner with regard to moral habits.[2]

Maimonides cites as an example the moral vice of miserliness: "If we wanted to give medical treatment to this sick person we would not order him to be liberal. That would be like using a balanced course for treating someone whose fever is excessive. This would not cure him of his sickness."

Maimonides' prescription is to make the agent repeat extravagant acts. Indeed, in order to acquire the virtue of liberality the miser needs to perform more acts of extravagance than the extravagant man needs to perform miserly acts, since it is easier to cure an extravagant man of his extravagance than a miser of his miserliness. Maimonides observes that it is generally the case that in any pair of mutually opposed vices, one of the vices tends to be harder to cure than the other. The good doctor of the soul knows which are the more difficult ones and he acts accordingly. Maimonides adds: "This subtlety is the rule of therapy and is its secret. This is the rule for the medical treatment of moral habits, so memorize it."[3]

On the basis of these considerations it is plausible to maintain that, for Maimonides, the signification of "healthy" according to which a soul is healthy is at least very close to the signification according to which a body is healthy. Perhaps when he reports that "the ancients said that the soul can be healthy or sick just as the body can be healthy or sick,"[4] he is to be understood as endorsing the view that there is an essential identity between the healthy soul and the healthy body and between the sick soul and the sick body.

This conclusion must, however, be held lightly in view of Maimonides' teaching that the term *sentient* is predicated equivocally of a human being and of a nonhuman animal.[5] It can be argued that the differences between the sentient soul of a human being and the sentient soul of a donkey are no greater than those between a human being's soul and his body. Hence, if it is only by equivocation that a human being and a donkey can be said to be sentient, it is surely only by equivocation that a human soul and a human body can be said to be healthy. This argument is not conclusive, but it shows that the question of whether Maimonides is committed to the view that "healthy" has the same signification when predicated of a human soul and a human body raises complex issues. Nonetheless, the parallels he draws between the treatment of the sick soul and the sick body are striking.

One further striking parallel to which Maimonides draws our attention provides support for my thesis concerning the relation between Aristotle and Maimonides. A virtuous person, perceiving in himself a tendency toward a given vice, routinely acts against that tendency by adopting the outer trappings of the opposing vice. Thus, a virtuous person who finds in himself a tendency toward luxurious living afflicts himself, not because a life of self-affliction is in itself good, but solely because it is an effective means to restoring, or maintaining, the balanced state – the state of virtue. But an ignorant person who sees the virtuous man behaving thus will say to himself: I too can become virtuous by afflicting myself. Maimonides comments:

> Such men can only be compared to someone ignorant of the art of medicine who sees that skillful physicians have given deathly sick people the pulp of colocynth, scammony, aloe . . . and they are cured. He, therefore, takes them and falls sick. Similarly, those with sick souls are undoubtedly so from taking medicine while they are healthy.[6]

The resulting sickness is iatrogenic, since the faulty prescription is due to the patient in the role of physician.

In the foregoing discussion there is repeated employment of the concept of a mean, and it is plain that Maimonides has Aristotle's teaching, or something very like it, in mind. There is, of course, a notorious problem here. Should not Maimonides' moral philosophy be recognizable as rabbinic, not Aristotelian? Is God's law not enough, that it has to be supplemented by Aristotelian ethics?

Maimonides holds that the doctrine of the mean is rabbinic whether or not it is Aristotelian. The first of the eleven commandments listed by Maimonides at the start of the *Hilkhot Deot* is to imitate God's ways: As Maimonides puts the matter:

> Just as He is called gracious, you too be gracious; just as He is called merciful, you too be merciful; just as He is called holy, you too be holy . . . In like manner the prophets applied all these terms to God: slow to anger and abundant in loving kindness, just and righteous, perfect, powerful, strong, and the like. They did so to proclaim that these ways are good and right, and a man is obliged to train himself to follow them and imitate them according to his strength.[7]

The relation between this teaching and the doctrine of the mean is quickly stated: "Since these terms applied to the Creator refer to the middle way that we are obliged to follow, this way is called the way of the Lord."[8] On this basis it seems that the way of the Lord is the way of Aristotle. Those who fail to imitate God suffer from either an excess or a deficiency in their character, and the step they must take is plain: "Let them go to the wise men – who are physicians of the soul – and they will cure their disease by means of the character traits that they will teach them, until they make them return to the middle way."[9]

For reasons cited below, I do not believe this doctrine to be Aristotelian. For the moment I shall merely note that even if, as Maimonides thinks, the character traits of the gracious, merciful, or holy person can be expounded in terms of their location in an intermediate position between two vices, these are not character traits upon which Aristotle dwells; neither does it seem plausible to suppose that we should have learned more from him on this matter had he provided extended discussion of the "godlike man" to whom he makes very brief reference.[10] As regards the virtue of mercifulness, it might be thought that the vice on one side is mercilessness. On the other side there is, perhaps, a disposition to show mercy to people known to be certain to do evil as a result of the mercy shown them (though this might imply that mercilessness is a disposition not to show mercy to people known to be certain to do good as a result of the mercy that would be shown them – and I do not believe that that is what mercilessness is). Perhaps, also, we should not have great difficulty in describing the character trait which is a deficiency in relation to graciousness. On the other hand it is not immediately clear what the vices are which are located on either side of the un-Aristotelian virtue of holiness. Perhaps on the one side is sanctimoniousness, but I am doubtful about this. In any case, the numerous problems in this area do not tend to undermine the claim that it is in terms of a version of the doctrine of the mean that Maimonides seeks to expound the command to imitate God's ways.

Indeed, for Maimonides, God's law must itself be expounded in terms of a mean. He quotes the psalmist: "The law of the Lord is perfect, making wise the simple, restoring the soul,"[11] and adds: "Indeed, its goal [sc. that of the law] is for man to be natural by following the middle way."[12] This teaching is quickly reinforced: "In the tradition of our prophets and those who transmit our law, we see these men aiming at the mean and at preserving their souls and bodies in accordance with what the law requires."

There is room for dispute regarding the correct interpretation of these last quotations. An interpretation which seems to me particularly plausible is the following: We must set imitation of God's ways as our goal—"You will be holy for I the Lord your God am holy"—and this goal, so far as it is in our power to achieve it, is to be achieved in our obedience to the law. The individual acts of obedience are in a sense not an imitation of God's ways, for of course God does not obey His law! Our imitation is our possession of attributes which are attributes also ascribed to God, and what constitutes in us the possession of those attributes, our being just, merciful, slow to anger, and so on, is our disposition to obey God's law, a disposition whose exercise, as we have seen, involves acting in a mean. This does not imply that the attributes in question can be predicated univocally of God and of human beings. But, as already noted, Maimonides in any case insists that the predication of justice, mercy, and so on, of God and of human beings is merely equivocal.

Yet, Maimonides appears on occasion to deny that the mean should always be followed. I wish to dwell briefly on this contentious issue before spelling out what I take to be a crucial difference between Maimonides and Aristotle regarding the doctrine of the mean. We read:

> In the case of some character traits, a man is forbidden to accustom himself to the mean. Rather, he shall move to the other [i.e., far] extreme. One such [character trait] is a haughty heart, for the good way is not that a man be merely humble, but that he have a lowly spirit, that his spirit be very submissive. Therefore, it was said of Moses our master that he was "very humble," and not merely humble.[13]

The underlying consideration is quickly provided: "all pride denies the existence of God." The thought process is obvious. We should be humble in the presence of our superiors, the proper degree of humility being proportional to the degree of our inferiority; and we are always in the presence of God. Clearly, there is something very un-Aristotelian in this argument. I am not certain that Maimonides is denying the doctrine of the mean. No doubt Aristotle would have said that there is a due attitude to adopt to other people depending upon whether they are superior, or inferior, or are on the same level. That which is due is a mean between the too much and the too little. Since Aristotle did not believe that we are permanently in the presence of an infinitely superior being, he thought that there was room for a too much and a too little in our attitude to others with respect to humility. Maimonides' faith forced him to the view, articulated also by Aristotle,[14] that in respect of some things we should not speak of a mean, for they are wrong by nature, for it is of the nature of every creature to stand in the presence of God; and for those creatures who are able to feel extreme humility, such humility is the proper attitude. If this thesis is correct, it is not the doctrine of the mean as such that is being rejected but the propriety of insisting that moderate humility is a mean *sub specie aeternitatis* as well as *sub specie civitatis*. There is, in short, no circumstance in which haughtiness or even moderate humility is appropriate, just as, to take Aristotle's examples, there are no circumstances in which spite, shamelessness, and envy are appropriate.[15] It is true that Aristotle says of these three vices that their very names imply that the states of the soul are bad, and it might seem, therefore, that he is merely making a definitional point. But the reason the names have this implication is that they name states that are bad by their nature – just as pride is, for Maimonides, and in the way just explained, bad by its nature.

It might seem, therefore, that Maimonides applied Aristotle's doctrine of the mean, exactly as Aristotle understood it, within the context of a worldview of which Aristotle himself had not the smallest inkling.

But there are obstacles in the way of this conclusion. One problem is that there is not an absolutely clear-cut doctrine of the mean in Aristotle's ethical writings. In particular, we should note that, in his discussion of virtue and vice, he gives two distinct accounts of what it is that is, or lies in, a mean,[16] and we are left to work out the precise relation between the two accounts. First, virtue is spoken of as a state of character, a *hexis,* which is intermediate between two vices, as, for example, courage is intermediate between rashness and cowardice. Secondly, virtue is described as a mean because it "finds and chooses that which is intermediate." That is, particular actions found and chosen by a virtuous person are intermediate, presumably between actions that are vicious. There is room for dispute as to whether it always makes sense to describe the actions of a virtuous person as intermediate, except in the sense that they are actions performed by a person exercising his virtuous disposition.[17]

It should be said here that Maimonides, also, speaks about the mean in relation both to dispositions and to actions. Thus, we are told that "the right way is the mean in every single one of a man's character traits. It is the character trait that is equally distant from the two extremes."[18] We are also told that "good actions are those balanced in the mean between two extremes, both of which are bad."[19] Maimonides does not tell us whether there is a criterion for identifying an action as one balanced in a mean, which does not involve identifying the action as one which expresses an intermediate character trait.

Thus far, Maimonides' account of the mean is the same as that of Aristotle's. But there is a difference of perspective, and much of the evidence for the difference has now been produced. The difference can be put as follows: For Aristotle, the doctrine of the mean enables him to provide a conceptual framework within which he can present a program of upbringing for the young. They are to be trained to be good citizens, and mistakes dare not be made in the training, for the outcome of the training is a *hexis*, a character trait which is so fixed as to be hardly alterable. In Aristotle's view, the acquisition of a virtuous character, as of a vicious one, is the acquisition of a second nature, an abiding state. This is not to say that, for Aristotle, a person cannot lose his virtuous state or rise above his previously vicious one. It is to stress the degree of fixedness of the state acquired by the initial training. For Maimonides, on the other hand, conceptualizing virtue as a mean implies a perspective from which virtue presents itself as achievable by therapeutic methods. As demonstrated in passages already quoted, the curing of vice plays a large part in Maimonides' thinking about moral matters. Aristotle pays very little attention to the curing of vice, as opposed to the training for virtue. Thus, what is central to Maimonides' approach in respect of the doctrine of the mean is not characteristically Aristotelian, even if it is not totally alien to Aristotle's approach.

Maimonides speaks, in a way reminiscent of Aristotle, of virtue becoming firmly established in the soul. Thus, his comment on Hillel's question "And if not now, when?" is:

> If I will not acquire virtues now, in the period of youth, when shall I acquire them—in the period of old age?—no, for it is difficult to turn aside from dispositions at that time because traits and attributes have become firm and permanent, whether virtues or vices. And the sage said, "Train a child in the path he should follow; even when he is old he will not turn aside from it [Proverbs 22:6]."[20]

Elsewhere he writes that "these moral virtues and vices are acquired and firmly established in the soul by frequently repeating the actions pertaining to a particular moral habit over a long period of time."[21] He immediately adds that should the soul become sick by ceasing to be in equilibrium, the person should be treated medically by becoming unbalanced on the opposite side. Maimonides persistently focuses upon the person who has a vice into which he has slid from a virtuous state, rather than a person who has a vice by upbringing. This is not a preoccupation of Aristotle's. Maimonides' persistent attention to the need to cure a person of his vice suggests that he has a view of virtue as a state upon which we can never safely rely, a state which is always more or less precarious and which we have to fight to protect. The concept of virtue as the object of a struggle emerges at several points. For example, Maimonides takes as his proof text "And how can one born of woman be just?,"[22] and writes:

> ... the perfect man needs to inspect his moral habits continually, weigh his actions, and reflect upon the state of his soul every single day. Whenever he sees his soul inclining toward one of the extremes, he should rush to cure it and not let the evil state become established by the repetition of a bad action.[23]

That we cannot afford to take our virtuousness for granted is spelled out even more clearly in a later passage in the same work:

> It is necessary for [a man] to accustom himself to good actions until he acquires the virtues, and to avoid bad actions until the vices disappear from him, if he has acquired any. He should not say he has already attained a condition that cannot possibly change, since every condition can change from good to bad and from bad to good; the choice is his.[24]

Since our virtuousness is always at risk, it does of course make good sense to place considerable emphasis, as Maimonides does, upon the role of doctor of the soul, a person who has expertise at curing those who have fallen morally. Such an expert plays no large part in Aristotle's account of the virtuous life, and neither should we expect otherwise, given that Aristotle is much more concerned with upbringing than with curing, with the training that is required if a child is to mature into a good citizen rather than with the moral rehabilitation required after backsliding. It is precisely at this point that Maimonides' perspective upon virtue and vice is radically different from that of Aristotle. Naturally, Maimonides attached great weight to the practice of preventive moral medicine, and who indeed could doubt its overwhelming importance? But his insight into the fragility of virtue, into the fact that the fight for our virtuousness is never truly won, led him to draw our attention repeatedly to the practice of a moral medicine oriented toward restoration rather than prevention.[25]

14

Well-Being of the Body or Welfare of the Soul: The Maimonidean Explanation of the Dietary Laws

Hannah Kasher

In *The Guide for the Perplexed* (3:48) Maimonides proposes the following principle: "I say, then, to eat any of the various kinds of food that the Law has forbidden us is blameworthy (Arab.: *madhmum*)."[1] He then enumerates the species of forbidden animals and the damage consumption of their flesh causes the digestive system. As a result of this passage, it is generally accepted that Maimonides' explanation for the prohibition of certain foods is based on grounds of health, his view being that the entire system of dietary laws is designed to further the proper nourishment of the observant, thanks to their abstention from kinds of meat that may harm their bodies.[2] Some support for this interpretation of Maimonides' view rests on complementary biographical evidence: Maimonides was renowned in his time as a physician, and his writings in the medical field were well known to later generations. It has indeed been demonstrated in great detail that the nutritional recommendations contained in his medical works are largely in accord with the permitted foods listed in the Torah.[3]

However, the interpretation according to which Maimonides explains the forbidden foods on a hygienic basis raises some difficulty, since it clashes with his own statement in *Mishneh Torah*. In *Hilkhot Avodat Kokhavim* 11:12, he states that the Torah does not serve as a cure for the body but for the soul:

One who whispers a spell over a wound, at the same time reciting a verse from the Torah, and who recites a verse over a child to save it from terrors and one who places a scroll or phylacteries on an infant to induce it to sleep, are not only in the category of sorcerers and soothsayers, but they are included among those who deny the Torah; for they use its words to cure the body, whereas these are only medicines for the soul, as it is said, "they shall be life unto the soul" [Prov. 3:22]. On the other hand, any one in the enjoyment of good health is permitted to recite verses from the Scriptures or a psalm, so that he may be shielded by the merit of the recital and saved from trouble and hurt.[4]

The prohibition against using words of the Torah to induce physical health might at first sight be explained as affecting only their misuse in a magical context. A person who cures himself in this way has not only contravened the prohibition of "sorcerers and soothsayers," but has also sinned in the illicit use of the Holy Scriptures themselves, as they are not intended for this purpose. This might be construed as implying that Maimonides did not necessarily object to assigning a healing role to the Torah. It is not inconceivable that, while frowning on the use of scriptural verses as useless charms, he would not deny the rational thesis that the observance of certain commandments is conducive to bodily health.[5] Hence one could well uphold a hygienic interpretation of the dietary laws.

Nonetheless, though at first sight consistent with Maimonides' viewpoint, this interpretation does not stand up to closer scrutiny. Indeed, accepting it, one would have to assume that a person who employs Scripture for therapeutic purposes is considered a "denier of the Torah" only if he does so in a useless way; but the Torah, while intended mainly for the well-being of the soul, may also be applied effectively to curing the body. None of this is said by Maimonides himself in the passage cited above. On the contrary, he is quite explicit: Those who "whisper a spell over a wound" sin not only as performers of a mere magical act, which is "chimerical and inane ... [and to which] only those deficient in knowledge are attracted" (ibid., 16). A person who utilizes Scripture for therapeutic purposes is clearly of the opinion that the Torah was designed to cure the body. But the Torah was not meant to induce physical health, whether by medical or magical means. Though Scripture indeed contributes to the body's well-being, that is not its primary purpose: the sole purpose of the Torah is to ensure the well-being of the soul.[6] Such depreciation of the Torah is tantamount to a denial of its divinity. Hence, whoever applies the Torah to curing the body is indeed to be considered a "denier of the Torah."

In view of the interpretation we have suggested, it is impossible to explain the dietary laws as intended to promote physical health. Indeed, other considerations will clearly demonstrate that these commandments have an entirely different purpose.

Maimonides' position can be summarized as follows:

1. The words of the Torah should not be used to promote physical well-being, for they exist to foster the welfare of the soul.

2. A person who believes that the Torah's words can be used to promote bodily health is counted among the deniers of the Torah.

The second of these rulings ("they are included among those who deny the Torah") brings us quite naturally to the passage in the Code (*Hilkhot Teshuvah* 3:8) where Maimonides defines the term "deniers of the Torah.":

> Three classes of people are deniers of the Torah;
> (1) he who says that the Torah is not of divine origin . . . ;
> (2) he who denies its interpretation, that is, the Oral Law . . . ;
> (3) and he who says that the Creator changed one commandment for another. . . .
> Everyone belonging to any of these classes is a denier of the Torah.[7]

It follows necessarily that any person who holds that the words of the Torah exist to cure the body must be assigned to one of these three categories. The only possible category under which it is reasonable to classify such a person is surely the first—"he who says that the Torah is not of divine origin." According to Maimonides himself, in *The Guide for the Perplexed* (2:40), a divine law is one that addresses itself not only to bodily and social perfection, but also to spiritual welfare. A person desirous of proving that his law is divinely inspired must therefore demonstrate that, in addition to the usual manmade laws, it contains provisions designed for the achievement of spiritual perfection in its adherents. Hence any negation of the Torah's function of promoting the welfare of the soul is essentially equivalent to denying its divine origin.

Maimonides' dogmatic ruling ("they are included among those who deny the Torah") may be understood in light of Maimonides' ascending scale of perfections, as described in *Guide* 3:54:

1. Perfection of possessions;
2. perfection of bodily constitution (health and strength);
3. perfection of moral virtues;
4. perfection of rational virtues.[8]

In chapter 5 of his Introduction to the mishnaic treatise *Avot*, Maimonides indicates the ideal causal relationship between these perfections: The sole worthy object of the accumulation of wealth is to insure physical health, while a healthy body enables the soul to acquire perfection. In chapter 1 of the same work, Maimonides classifies the soul's faculties in accordance with the perfections they are intended to cultivate. Thus, the contemplative intellect is aimed at acquiring perfection of the rational virtues. Through the medium of the practical intellect[9] one achieves skill in craftsmanship, such as carpentry, agriculture, and seamanship, which pertain to the perfection of possessions, or medical skill, which is concerned with the perfection of the bodily constitution. The third type of perfection (that of moral virtues), though not mentioned, is apparently the concern of the practical-contemplative intellect.

The three areas of knowledge, too, are classified in Maimonides' *Treatise on Logic* (chapter 14) in accordance with the specific perfection they are meant to cultivate.[10] Thus, theoretical philosophy is concerned with rational perfection, the highest perfection of all. The various branches of practical philosophy aim at the perfection of moral virtues, while the perfection of possessions is the object of craftsmanship, such as stonecutting and carpentry. The medical art, however, is not mentioned in this context.

Returning again to the Introduction to *Avot* (chapter 5), we find Maimonides arguing for the superiority of medicine to other professions. Medicine is concerned directly with the body – unlike carpentry and weaving, for example, whose objective is the acquisition of possessions – and through its medium a person can deliberate how best to employ the body efficiently in the service of the soul. Medicine offers man a rational criterion for the choice of material sustenance: he should be governed in his choice by the beneficial effect of specific foods on his health, not by his base desires or appetite.

Medicine grades foods according to their contribution to man's well-being; it is thus concerned with the perfection of the body, and that is why it surpasses the other professions, whose objective is the first, lowest class of perfections – of possessions. Nevertheless, it too is only a means toward a higher end: the perfection of the soul.

Previously in the Introduction to *Avot* (chapter 4), Maimonides had postulated: "Apply this test to most of the commandments: You will find that all of them educate and train the faculties of the soul." In other words, most of the commandments are oriented to acquisition of the third perfection, that of moral virtues, and one of the means Maimonides lists there to counteract the physical appetite is "the prohibition of all the forbidden foods."

In the *Guide*, too (3:54), Maimonides suggests that most of the commandments help man to attain the perfection of moral virtues. The smaller part, apparently, imparts the metaphysical truths, i.e., they promote rational perfection. Thus, the realm of the Torah may be likened to that of practical and theoretical philosophy: its concern is primarily with "political," i.e., practical wisdom and, to a lesser extent, with metaphysics. In any event, since no part of the Torah is directly concerned with the perfection of the bodily constitution, anyone attributing to the Torah such goals as the promotion of physical health is thereby detracting from its value, since a sublime thing cannot possibly serve as a means toward an inferior end (*Guide* 3:13). In Maimonides' classification of the commandments of the Torah in accordance with their reasons (*Guide* 3:35), he explains "the commandments concerned with the prohibition of certain foods": "The purpose of all this is, as we have explained in the Commentary on the Mishnah, in the introduction to Avot, to put an end to the lusts and licentiousness manifested in seeking what is most pleasurable and to taking the desire for food and drink as an end in itself."

"The desire for food and drink" and the like are destructive to both the body and society and repress "the longing for speculation" which leads to "man's last perfection" (*Guide* 3:33). Therefore, "to the purposes of the perfect Law belongs the abandonment of desires . . . so that these should be satisfied only insofar as it is necessary" (*Guide* 3:33). In other words, the reason for the prohibition of certain foods is to be sought in the sphere of moral virtues and not in the area of physical hygiene. Its purpose is to cultivate the perfection of moral virtues in man by restraining him from surrendering to his base appetites. Indeed, in the same chapter where Maimonides explains that the forbidden foods are injurious to health (*Guide* 3:48), he goes on to say: "Besides the ordinances given to us concerning the prohibition of forbidden food, ordinances have also been prescribed to us with regard to the vows by which we impose prohibitions on ourselves . . . all this being a training with a view to achieving temperance and to restraining the appetite for eating and drinking."

Therefore, the view according to which Maimonides' explanation of the dietary laws is based on considerations of health stems from a misreading of his precise wording in the *Guide* (3:48). He writes there: "Eating any of the various kinds of food that the Law has forbidden us is blameworthy." This is not to say that "eating any of the various kinds of food that the Law has forbidden us is *because* it is blameworthy." At this point, Maimonides is explaining, not the reason for the dietary laws per se, but the agreement between the object of the religious prohibition and the content of the medical recommendation. The prohibition of certain foods is indeed intended to restrain man's appetites. But this is not accomplished through arbitrary, random injunctions. The Torah directs man to wholesome – not necessarily tasty – food, thereby warning him against foods that are harmful from the medical point of view ("their food is blameworthy"). The very details of the dietary laws have the effect that man, in choosing his food, relies not on what pleases his palate, but rather on what is rationally and medically beneficial.

Abravanel, in his commentary to the Torah (Leviticus 11:13),[11] states: "Many commentators believe that the prohibition of the foods forbidden by the Torah was for reasons of the body's health and well-being, those bad foods causing noxious humors in the body. This is Nachmanides' opinion on the verse: 'The following you shall abominate among the birds' (Leviticus 11:13)."

Nachmanides indeed states that the milk of unclean animals is liable to cause infertility and the milk of swine, leprosy. The flesh of unclean birds is prohibited because it harms the perfection of moral virtues, but the reasons it does so are physiological: The composition of their blood induces excess of melancholy and this, in turn, leads to cruelty.[12]

Abravanel sharply criticizes such medical explanations, weaving parts of Isaac Arama's commentary[13] together with his own remarks:

1. Such explanations undermine religion: "The divine Torah" is not "on the level of a small medical book..."
2. They are contrary to experience: "We see with our own eyes how the gentiles, though they eat swine and abominable creatures... are still flourishing, strong as a solid mirror (Heb. בראי מוצק), none of them weary or stumbling.
3. They are exegetically unconvincing: Poisonous snakes and plants, though undoubtedly harmful to health, receive no mention in the Torah.

Abravanel then offers his own explanation, in which one hears an echo of Maimonides' words: "The reason for their prohibition is on account of the soul and not on account of the body and its health.... Thus one sees that the reason for the prohibition of these foods is on account of the perfection of the soul and its welfare and not on account of the body."

However, closer attention reveals that Abravanel's criticism of Nachmanides and the similarity between his formulation and that of Maimonides are both misleading; in this area Abravanel is closer in spirit to Nachmanides than to Maimonides.

Indeed, as we have already seen, Maimonides argues that the object of the Torah and the dietary laws is not to cure the body but to promote the welfare of the soul. Nevertheless, this end is achieved by restraining man's base desires, in particular, his appetite for food. In this context, therefore, Maimonides is still maintaining an element of dualism between body and soul.

Abravanel, however, describes the perfection of the soul as a physiological outcome of the perfect temperament of the body: this is clearly a monistic view. Proper foods "create pure and refined blood, not coarse, thick and unsmooth, as created by the forbidden foods"; thereby man attains "perfection of the soul, its radiance and purity." While Nachmanides, in his explanation of the medical grounds for the prohibition of the milk of unclean animals (as these may cause infertility or even leprosy), also alludes to the virtuous trait acquired by refraining from eating the flesh of unclean birds: The consumption of their blood, on the contrary, is conducive to excessive melancholy and cruelty. In sum, both Nachmanides and Abravanel describe the causal sequence initiated by the forbidden foods as follows:

1. Consumption and digestion of forbidden food → formation of tainted blood and humors.
2. Formation of tainted blood and humors → injury to bodily health (Nachmanides: from animals and swine).
3. Formation of tainted blood and humors → injury to the soul (Abravanel, Nachmanides – with regard to birds).

Essentially, therefore, despite Abravanel's criticism, he has not offered an alternative explanation. He still maintains his physiological explanation, according to which the forbidden foods injure the body's temperament because of their composition. His argument is simply that the outcome of the flawed temperament of the body is not damage to the body's well-being, but rather to the disposition of the soul. Thus, the bodies of gentiles, who derive their nourishment from forbidden foods, are unharmed, and there are no valid medical grounds for the dietary laws.

Maimonides, on the other hand, does not believe that the digestion of forbidden foods causes a change in the character of the person involved. The basic contribution of the dietary laws to the observant Jew is their very essence as prohibitions, which therefore teach man to curb his base desires.

15

Psychological Formulations in the Works of Maimonides

Reuven P. Bulka

Psychology is vitally interested in human behavior. Specifically, psychology is concerned with behavior that is normal, what is beyond the pale of normal, and how to correct behavior that is deviant from normal. Much of psychology relates to what is called "The Sick Model."

The sick, or defect model, focuses on what is wrong with a human being's behavior and how to correct what is wrong. A true psychology of the human being must be not only reactive but also proactive, in that such a psychology proposes a philosophy, or a vision, about what human behavior, indeed human life, should entail.

Frankl asserts that "every school of psychology has a concept of man, although this concept is not always held consciously."[1]

Allport alludes to the importance of philosophy relative to the clinical situation when he rhetorically asks, "May not [sometimes at least] an acquired world-outlook constitute the central motive of a life and, if it is disordered, the ultimate therapeutic problem?"[2] In other words, there is a definite overlap between philosophy and psychology. There is need for philosophers to make propositions that might be of therapeutic benefit. Sound philosophy is at the same time sound psychology.

In this context, Albee made the following observation:

> Conditions seem right for the emergence of a philosophical therapy.... The problems of a great many people who are seeing psychotherapists are concerned

with a search for the meaning of existence, for purpose, identity. It seems probable that a well trained Ph.D. in philosophy, particularly if the philosopher is well grounded in logic, ethics, and existential phenomenology, is well prepared to become a psychologist. I hope this development comes soon, because I believe that large numbers of clinical philosophers would be powerful allies for psychology in attempting to throw off the domination of the sickness [or defect] model.[3]

If philosophers are to be helpful in clinical situations, they must be modern twentieth-century philosophers. Pure philosophers can be of help in a clinical situation, through their own philosophical approach. But philosophers who provide insight into the psychology of how a human being behaves or should behave can speak to the modern situation even if they lived long before the twentieth century. In this vein, it is instructive to study some of the views of Moses Maimonides, outstanding Jewish philosopher, to explore possible insights that Maimonides' philosophy may offer for the health model in psychology.

In the second chapter of the first part of his *Guide for the Perplexed*,[4] Maimonides describes a question that was posed to him concerning the first human beings before and after they ate from the forbidden fruit in the Garden of Eden. Scripture states that after Adam and Eve ate from the forbidden fruit, they, and through them all humankind, were granted the capacity "to know good and evil."[5] In the words of Maimonides, "It does appear strange that the punishment for rebelliousness should be the means of elevating man to a pinnacle of perfection to which he had not attained previously." If Adam and Eve were heretofore unable to distinguish between good and evil, their having disobeyed God's command resulted in an elevation to the capacity to distinguish between good and evil. It hardly seems congruous that because one behaves in a wrong manner, one is rewarded.

The gist of Maimonides' response to this question is that before their disobedience, Adam and Eve were able to distinguish between true and false, between *emet* and *sheker*. Afterwards, their capacity to make this distinction was not elevated; it was reduced so that they were only able to discern the difference between good and evil, *tov* and *ra*. In other words, Adam and Eve previously possessed a perfect and complete intellectual capacity, which became compromised by their subsequent disobedience.

What is the primary difference between true-false and good-evil? The dimension of true-false concerns itself with absolute values, whereas the dimension of good-evil deals with relative values. In determining what is true and what is false, one deals with objective reality. Maimonides himself points out, with regard to the statement that the earth is flat, that it is not appropriate to employ the terms good and bad. Either the earth is flat or it is not, in which case the statement is either true or false. Before Adam and Eve's disobedience, all values were clearly in the category of true and false, since matters were perceived in terms of objective truth. Values were not subjective, but rather objective realities.

Once Adam and Eve submitted to self-interest, with Eve seeing that the fruit was attractive and anticipating that it would be quite tasty, they introduced a new factor into human confrontation with reality. This factor was the capacity to reduce heretofore objective truths to relative values – values subject to compromise. Judging whether a behavior was desirable or not was now reduced to whether it was good or bad, not true or false. The woman saw that the tree was good for food (Genesis 3:6) and then ate from it. Although the terms objective and subjective truths are used, Maimonides – in making the distinction between good-evil and true-false – speaks about a difference between apparent truth and necessary truth. The objective-subjective paradigm seems to correlate quite accurately with the Maimonidean distinction.

Regarding the capacity of an individual to discern between good and evil, Maimonides makes a telling statement in his *Mishneh Torah*,[6] where he asserts that every individual has the capacity to incline the self toward the good and become righteous, or to incline the self toward evil and become wicked. This thesis is suggested by the biblical verse that "the human being has become like one of us, to know good and evil" (Genesis 3:22). This means that the human species is unique in the world and there is no other comparable species in this regard. A human being, autonomously, with its volition and thought, knows good and bad and actualizes all that it desires. No one can stop a human being from perpetrating good or evil.

Maimonides categorically rejects the view that an individual's righteousness or wickedness is decided by God. Every individual has the capacity to be as righteous as Moses or as wicked as Jeroboam. An individual chooses whether to embrace the way of wisdom or the way of foolhardiness, to be either compassionate or cruel, to be either miserly or philanthropic.

Thus it is with all other character traits. No one forces or decrees any pattern of behavior upon an individual. The individual chooses which path to follow.[7] Maimonides considers this notion of free will to be a fundamental principle and a pillar of the Torah.[8]

If an individual's righteousness is a direct result of Divine decree, or if any force operates naturally within an individual to push toward either righteousness or wickedness, all the exhortations of the prophets to improve our ways or to forsake the ways of evil do not make sense. If behavior has already been preordained, the individual cannot be blamed for whatever path has been adopted. In fact, Maimonides asks what point would there be to the entire Torah? How can any wicked individual be blamed for wickedness, and how can any righteous individual be rewarded for righteousness? Maimonides then confronts another crucial point. How is it that an individual can do what the individual pleases? Is it possible that anything can occur in this world without God willing it, without God wanting it? Maimonides answers quite bluntly that it is God's will that a human being have free choice; therefore, that free choice is a reality.[9]

All that has been so far delineated belongs to the realm of philosophy, but it is a philosophy that has profound impact on psychology. Maimonides clearly states that an individual has free choice and can control the direction of life. A human being is responsible for behavior and cannot blame behavior aberrations on God or on any other force. Therapy directed toward achieving wholeness, psychological health, or, in the Maimonidean system, embracing God's way, begins and ends with the human being, who generally has the ultimate choice and therefore the power to correct wrong behavior and to adopt appropriate behavior.

Concerning self-administered therapy for the perfection of human behavior, Maimonides notes that each individual differs in character pattern from others. Some individuals are temperamental, others never get angry. Some people are arrogant, others humble. Some people are lustful and others puristic, with little or no desire for almost anything. Some people believe that they never have enough material wealth, but others are happy with whatever they have, however little. Some people are miserly and spend no money on self-indulgence, whereas other people squander all their possessions for purposes of pleasure. There are also people who embrace levity in excess and others who are depressed. Some people are cruel and others are compassionate, and so forth.[10] Maimonides also says that these character patterns may exist in an individual from birth, as part of one's nature, or they can be tendencies an individual adopts. These character patterns can be learned or self-taught behavior.[11]

At first glance it seems that Maimonides here contradicts his prior assertion that every individual has free will. But the tendencies about which Maimonides speaks here are not necessarily the same as the issue of whether an individual is righteous or wicked. Whether or not an individual has miserly tendencies does not dictate that the individual is either righteous or wicked. Whether the individual is righteous or wicked depends on how the individual expresses the tendency to frugality or to hard-heartedness, or to anger. How an individual uses the tendency is the decisive factor, and the decisive factor is rooted in choice.

Maimonides recommends that the upright path for an individual, as a general rule, is the middle path between the extremes.[12] One should not be temperamental, and also not like a dead person who has no feeling whatsoever. One should express anger regarding that about which it is fitting to be angry. One should not be tight with one's money; at the same time one should not squander it. Rather, the middle path of giving charity according to one's means and extending loans to those who are in need is the proper way. Being continually light-headed and laughing or depressed and mournful is also wrong. The proper attitude to espouse is the middle, between these two extremes; to be happy in a contented way, with a cheerful countenance. A person who follows this middle path is a wise individual.

Maimonides strongly emphasizes an individual's intellect and the individual's ability to perceive, appreciate, and intellectually apprehend the correct way. A person then employs the mental capacities to steer behavior in the intellectually superior direction. Maimonides points to the extraordinarily pious who adopt a more exacting posture, but indicates that for ordinary mortals, the middle path between extremes is the right way to espouse.[13]

Maimonides accentuates the relationship between mind and behavior in a short discourse on the biblical passage that "the imagination of the heart of the human being is evil from youth" (Genesis 8:21). When does the good inclination arise in a person? According to Maimonides, the good inclination comes when the mind is developed.[14] Before the mind matures, the person is not governed by thought processes and instead follows the emotions, by doing what the person feels like doing. Once the mind develops, it can and should take over the behavior choices made by the person. The intellect and the rational faculties allow one to attain desired, well-balanced behavior.

How does an individual achieve the goal of being well balanced between the extremes and acting in the most desired human behavior pattern? Maimonides suggests that the best way is through behavior reinforcement by repetition. Behavior should be repeated once, twice, three times, as many times as necessary, until it becomes almost automatic.[15]

In his *Commentary to the Mishnah*,[16] Maimonides says that for inculcation of good behavior patterns, repetition is the key. Thus, to implant within the self the propensity for kindness, it is much better to give a single gold coin one thousand separate times than to give one thousand gold coins at once. The amount that is given to charity is the same, but the repetition of the charitable act one thousand times makes an indelible impression and creates a behavior pattern that may be ongoing and long-lasting. From this Maimonidean statement, one cannot conclude that Maimonides espoused behaviorism. Rather, Maimonides affirms the ability of individuals to affect their own behavior through their free-willed decision to implement proper strategies for behavior adjustment.

Among many behavior patterns, Maimonides singles out the expression of anger.[17] As with arrogance and humility, where the rule of the golden mean does not apply, in that humility even in its extreme form is desirable, so too it is desirable to avoid expression of anger at all times. Even when a situation arises in which anger is appropriate, Maimonides urges the individual just to be angry, but not to express that anger in action. Maimonides suggests that one use but not lose one's temper. Control of human behavior is absolutely essential; a person who is angry is out of control. To maintain one's capacity to freely choose one's behavior, one should never submit to forces that might compromise that capacity.

Maimonides repeats his admonition that one avoid extreme levity or extreme despondency. The ideal for the individual is to greet all others with a cheerful countenance and to always maintain a happy, contented posture.[18] Since many ills are associated with despondency, despair, and depression, Maimonides' emphasis of this point is quite instructive.

In his *Guide for the Perplexed*,[19] Maimonides describes the general objective of Torah law as the well-being of the body and the well-being of the soul. Bodily well-being is established by removing violence from our midst, eliminating the pattern of everyone doing as he or she pleases, and by teaching good morals that produce a good social context. The well-being of the soul is only attained after the well-being of the body has been secured. Maimonides argues that one who suffers from hunger, thirst, heat, or cold is incapable of grasping an idea, even if communicated by others, and is even less likely to reach conclusions autonomously. However, if a person is in possession of the first perfection, i.e., well-being of the body, that individual is able to acquire the second perfection, namely the well-being of the soul. This is the intent of Torah commandments in their entirety, to effect the perfection of body and soul. In other words, the Torah is vitally concerned with the human psychological state, the state of the human psyche. All the commandments of the Torah become, in a sense, meta-clinical directives for meaningful living, for the good of humankind.

Maimonides' model of a healthy body and a healthy soul evokes comparison with Maslow's famous subdivision of deficiency needs (D) and being needs (B).[20] There are fundamental deficiency needs that must be cared for before an individual can attain the more lofty heights of meaningful existence. This does not mean that Maimonides was Maslowian or that Maslow was aware of Maimonides. Maimonides makes a simple observation of human nature and posits the argument that the thrust of the Torah is to help a human being attain the greater good to the fullest extent possible.

In another context, Maimonides sees this natural need progression as basic to successful marriage. He suggests that people who use their intellectual capacities realize that the natural chronological order is for a human being first to have a source of income, then to acquire a residence, and only then to marry. Only fools marry first, then attempt to acquire a home, and then seek a profession.[21] Marriage obviously is in the B-need category of sharing one's self with another. To address those needs without prior attention to more basic needs which, if not satisfied, impact negatively on the marital relationship, is wrong. Thus, the general principle concerning needs–indeed concerning the purpose of Torah law–has specific and practical application in real-life situations.

Maimonides offers a novel interpretation of a seemingly remote regulation that impacts on an appreciation of the human psychological state. He comments on the biblical prohibition that forbids exchanging an animal set aside for a sacred purpose for another one. Obviously, there would be no objection if the first animal is of a lesser quality than the newly sanctified exchange. However, remarks Maimonides, if an individual were given the right to exchange an inferior animal for a superior one, that individual may then exchange a superior product for an inferior one, and perhaps even think that the inferior one is actually better. For this reason, the Torah categorically forbids any such exchanges (Leviticus 27:10). All this, says Maimonides, is to rein in one's desire and to perfect one's character. In fact, says Maimonides, most of the laws of the Torah are to perfect one's character and to make all of one's actions of upright quality.[22]

Another well-known Maimonidean comment further clarifies the point he makes concerning animal exchange. In Jewish law, if a man is required to grant his wife a bill of divorce (*get*) but refuses, he is even physically coerced until he agrees to divorce her. Then the divorce is written and given and is legally valid. But how can such a bill of divorce (*get*) be valid, since Jewish law states that a man must give a divorce of his own free will? Maimonides answers this question by stating that coercion applies only to one who is forced to do something he really does not wish to do. One who is overcome by evil forces to negate a Torah obligation, or to do that which is prohibited by Torah law, and is coerced until he does that which he is obligated to do, or until he desists from that which is prohibited, is not considered to be under coercion. Rather, the evil force, which is the coercive force, is being driven away. A man who refuses to cooperate in the granting of a divorce still wants to be a member of the Israelite community. He still desires to fulfill all the affirmative commandments of the Torah and to avoid the prohibitions. His evil inclination overpowered him. Therefore, he is coerced until his evil desire weakens and he agrees to cooperate. He has thus granted the divorce of his own free will.[23]

There are forces in human beings with the potential to lead one astray and to cause refusal to live up to one's responsibility. Similarly, there are internal forces that may cause a person to rationalize away an animal exchange as a fair bargain. The Torah recognizes human frailty and seeks to give humans the tools to counter those frailties. Sometimes obstacles in the way must be forced out and eliminated by coercion. Such court-administered "therapy" allows an individual to return to where that individual had long ago chosen to be, but was temporarily driven away by the evil inclination.

Maimonides' rationale for the offering of animal sacrifices is the same that he suggests in the "animal exchange" situation described above, but in even more dramatic fashion. Maimonides asserts that:

> It is, namely, impossible to go suddenly from one extreme to the other; it is, therefore, according to the nature of man impossible for him suddenly to discontinue everything to which he has been accustomed. . . . But the custom

which was in those days general among all men, and the general mode of worship in which the Israelites were brought up, consisted in sacrificing animals in those Temples which contained certain images, to bow down to those images, and to burn incense before them; religious and ascetic persons were in those days the persons that were devoted to the service in the Temples erected to the stars, as has been explained by us. It was in accordance with the wisdom and plan of God, as displayed in the whole Creation, that He did not command us to give up and to discontinue all these manners of service; for to obey such a commandment it would have been contrary to the nature of man, who generally cleaves to that to which he is used; it would in those days have made the same impression as a prophet would make at present if he called us to the service of God and told us in His name, that we should not pray to Him, not fast, not seek His help in time of trouble; that we should serve Him in thought, and not by any action. For this reason God allowed these kind of services to continue; He transferred to His service that which had formerly served as a worship of created beings, and of things imaginary and unreal, and commanded us to serve Him in the same manner....[24]

Maimonides further explains that through the Divine plan, idolatry was effectively eradicated and the Judaic foundation of monotheistic belief firmly established, at the very time that people were not frustrated through the abolition of the worship modes to which they had become acclimatized. Maimonides is not suggesting that the negation of idolatry is the sole reason for sacrifices. Sacrifices were motivated by a recognition that without such an institution, the people might veer toward idolatry. However, since the sacrifices were allowed, they were implemented with a view toward a transcending purpose which Maimonides refers to as the realization of God's "first intention."

Maimonides anticipates the philosophical difficulties with his argument. His trend of thought indicates that the Torah commandments are not necessarily intended for their own sake, but for the sake of a plan established by God to achieve God's first intention. Why did God not give a law that reveals His first intention and, at the same time, gives human beings the capacity to actualize that law? Maimonides answers that sacrifices are not the only instance wherein God's intentions relate directly to the human condition.

Maimonides cites the example of the path taken by the Israelites in the Exodus from Egypt. The people were not ready, at that moment, to proceed from protracted servitude to the spiritual challenges facing them. They were made to wander in the desert until they could muster sufficient courage to face these challenges. The lack of normal comforts in the desert stimulates one to develop independence and courage. These same dynamics of understanding the spiritual-psychological state of the people, says Maimonides, were at work in the order of sacrifices. Maimonides argues that God has the capacity to change human nature and to bring it to a level of receptivity, but that God rejects such intervention. If God would intervene in such a manner, all law would be meaningless. Free will is the uncompromising reality that must govern human behavior. Otherwise, all human life is a charade.

This approach of Maimonides is instructive in terms of appreciating the Torah as relating, from a Divine perspective, to human reality. This perforce has profound implications for the contemporary arena. One can extend Maimonides' approach to, for example, individuals who come from totally alien backgrounds and who desire to embrace Judaism, but may have difficulty embracing the entire Torah all at once. The delicate approach of God with the Israelites is a useful precedent for the approach to the returnee. That approach would transmit the Torah in a more palatable way, so that it will be more readily understood and integrated.

A recent responsum[25] makes this point quite forcefully. It suggests that if one weighs down too heavily on the returnee, that returnee may be scared away. Thus, for example, even though Shabbat observance is more crucial, it is wise to first transmit the less vital but more easily integrated laws of *kashrut* and to work gradually toward the more difficult to observe commandments.

Maimonides offers an interesting interpretation of the biblical command to love your neighbor as yourself (Leviticus 19:18). He states:

> It is incumbent on everyone to love every Israelite as one's self, since it is said; "you shall love your neighbor as yourself." Thus one ought to speak in praise of one's neighbor and be careful of one's neighbor's property as one is careful of one's own property, and solicitous about one's own honor.[26]

Aside from respect for the property of others, Maimonides rules that one fulfills the obligation to love one's neighbor as one's self through saying nice things to others. Maimonides shows an uncanny awareness of the importance of self-esteem and that an individual should feel good about oneself.

Since Maimonides emphasizes the importance of being happy and content as the ideal mean between the extremes of melancholy and levity, it is essential to have a societal system whereby such contentedness is reinforced. There is no better way than through each individual saying nice things about others.

This great principle of the Torah, to love one's neighbor as one's self, is thus the psychological reinforcement of contentedness and feeling good. This principle makes it possible to approach one's higher purpose in life with confidence and enthusiasm. Here Maimonides, the man of reason and champion of intellect, is at his psychological best.

16

Maimonides' Philosophic Medicine

David J. Eisenman

In book E of *Metaphysics*,[1] Aristotle presents a classification of all of the branches of knowledge. He divides knowledge into three categories: practical, productive, and theoretical. The last category is further subdivided into physics, mathematics, and theology or "first philosophy." This classification contrasts with the Platonic one which divides all knowledge into the categories of logic, ethics, and physics.[2] The value of classifying the sciences is not purely academic. As Guthrie explains in his *History of Greek Philosophy*, according to Aristotle "one cannot prove theorems of one class by means of another . . . and one cannot demonstrate by passing from one genus to another."[3] The classification of a science is also important for elucidating its goals.

Maimonides, well known for his propensity to and proficiency in classification, presents a classification of the sciences in *Millot ha-Higayon*[4] that is based firmly on the Aristotelian model. He divides the sciences into the practical and the theoretical. The practical includes arts such as carpentry and sculpture. The theoretical arts are further divided into the two broad categories of theoretical and practical philosophy. Theoretical philosophy includes mathematics, physics, and theology; practical philosophy includes personal ethics, household ethics, politics of cities, and politics of nations.[5] Logic is not a science in and of itself, according to Maimonides, rather it is a tool (*örganon*) of all of the other sciences. Maimonides elaborates on each of these subdivisions and discusses their definitions, subject matter, and in some instances proximate goals.

There is no reference to medicine as an art or science in Maimonides' classification. Other medieval Jewish philosophers include medicine in their classifications of the sciences and describe its subject matter and function. Isaac Israeli, in his introduction to *Sefer ha-Yetzirah*, divides theoretical philosophy in the same way as Maimonides, and under natural sciences he lists only medicine.[6] Joseph b. Isaac Kimhi, in his introduction to *Sefer ha-Galui*, divides the sciences into those useful for this world, those to be used in the world to come, and those which have a purpose in both worlds. He lists medicine as useful to both worlds, though he fails to explain his reasoning.[7] Abraham ibn Daud describes medicine, somewhat derogatorily, as a pure *ars mechanica* which aims simply to preserve health.[8] Many Arab philosophers too include medicine in their discussions on the classification of the sciences. Al-Farabi, in his *Categories of the Sciences*, an important source for Maimonides' work, writes that medicine is an integral part of physics.[9]

Where does medicine belong in the Maimonidean classification? Does it belong in the category of the practical arts, as it does in ibn Daud's schema? Or does medicine have a more far-reaching purpose, and should it be classified as a practical or theoretical philosophy?[10] The answer to this question helps one to understand the position and function medicine held in Maimonides' life and thought. Did medicine run as a parallel line to his philosophical and theological work, accompanying them to the end yet never crossing or interacting with them? Was Maimonides' life a compartmentalized reservoir of different arts and sciences, with no portals allowing the waters to flow through and mix with one another? Or was there unity to his thought and an active meshing of his various studies to form a complex and beautiful latticework? The former is a distinct possibility often asserted, yet the latter seems more appropriate for a man of philosophy who devoted his works and life to revealing the one ultimate goal of all human endeavors.[11] That none of the works of any philosophers or legalists who also practiced medicine reveal their profession as manifestly as do Maimonides' writings, also attracts us to the latter possibility. To begin to answer these questions we must first understand the subject matter, functions, and proximate and ultimate goals of medicine as an art and science. After that we will be better able to grasp where it belongs in Maimonides' classification of the sciences and the role it plays in his thought in general. Maimonides' works do not allow for an easy or precise definition of the subject matter of medicine. In the medical treatise *Pirkè Moshe*, Maimonides discusses not only diagnostics, therapeutics, hygienics, and nutrition, i.e., "clinical medicine," but also anatomy and physiology, which are often perceived as basic sciences. That Maimonides believes all of these topics to be a part of the study of medicine is substantiated by his own enumeration of the divisions of medicine at the beginning of his *Commentary on the Aphorisms* of Hippocrates.[12] The first of the seven parts includes study of both the structure and function of the parts of the body, i.e., anatomy and physiology.[13] A problem arises, however, when we look at the study of the fundamental principles of these topics. Did Maimonides consider the study of basic physiological principles to be a part of medicine, as did Galen, or are these principles by definition included in the second part of Maimonides' "divine science," which deals with fundamental principles and causes of all sciences? Considering his general aversion for discussing matters of philosophy and "divine science" with doctors,[14] the fact that Maimonides does deal with some fundamentals of physiology in *Pirké Moshe*[15] indicates that these principles are indeed an integral part of medical science. Be that as it may, if the student of medical physiology gains insights into these fundamental principles from his study, they are willy-nilly a part of the corpus of medicine, regardless of their strict classification.

An examination of some of Maimonides' other works to see some of the parts the practice and study of medicine play in his thought will give us a better understanding of medicine's broader functions and goals. Medicine certainly played the role of the practical art in Maimonides' life. Disregarding the time he spent in the study of medical science, the practice of medicine as a profession took up a vast amount of Maimonides' time. Heschel believes medicine's greatest function is as a practical art, and sees in it the fulfillment of the ultimate goal of converting the contemplative life into one of *hesed* (loving-kindness).[16] There are many difficulties with his explanation,[17] but we still cannot deny that in one respect medicine is simply a practical art.[18] It is clear, however, that the importance of medicine for Maimonides goes far beyond its role as a practical art. Maimonides studied the science of medicine long before his brother's death forced him to take it up professionally.[19] Xenophon describes the young man with intellectual interests as having "already bought a whole library with books on architecture, geometry, astronomy, and above all medicine";[20] Aristotle talks of the "medically cultured" person in his *Politics*.[21] For the medieval philosophers as well, and Maimonides in particular, the study of medicine as a theoretical art was an important step on the road to ultimate perfection. In this respect we see medicine in many different roles and encompassing many fields.

One simple role as such is as a methodological tool. Medicine, like any other valid science, as Maimonides writes in the first section of the *Guide*, functions as a tool, like logic, in training the mind to think properly.[22] Just as Plato uses the model of medical science to develop the sciences of ethics and politics,[23] and Aristotle uses medicine as a paradigm for the method of applying universal rules to particular individuals,[24] Maimonides frequently uses medicine as a methodological paradigm.[25]

Medicine also plays an important role as a theoretical philosophy, a part of physics, and even metaphysics. Here medicine is not merely a prerequisite or propaedeutic, but is itself an active part of these sciences. Maimonides defines physics as the study of physical bodies not caused by man, found in nature (minerals, plants, and living creatures). Physics also deals with the accidents, properties, and causes of such bodies, as well as with the necessary traits of time, place, and motion that accompany them.[26] Aristotle writes in *De Sensu* that "it behooves the physical philosopher to obtain also a clear view of the first principles of health and disease inasmuch as [they] cannot exist in lifeless things."[27] The author of the Hippocratic treatise *On Ancient Medicine* goes even further than this and writes that "I do not believe that any clear knowledge of Nature can be obtained from any source other than a study of medicine."[28] Although Maimonides would not agree that study of medicine is the only way of gaining knowledge of nature, he would argue that such study plays an important role in the search for knowledge. In the *Commentary to the Mishnah* on *Pesahim*, Maimonides writes that medicine is based on the nature of all that exists, i.e., physics.[29] This idea is underscored in the treatise *The Regimen of Health*. In a discussion based firmly on Aristotle's comments in *De Sensu*, Maimonides writes that most medical failures are due to the physician's ignorance about nature.[30] Since it integrates and reflects the principles of nature, medicine is a part of physics itself, and its study is the study of physics. Furthermore, since he writes in many places in the *Guide* that there is no way to apprehend God except through the things He has made,[31] certainly the study of the nature of God's ultimate creation, the one created in His likeness, must be significant to this end.

Another aspect of medicine as a theoretical philosophy is its relation to metaphysics. Metaphysics, the divine science, concerns itself with the nature of incorporeal objects and with the fundamental abstract principles of nature and science in general, the universal laws.[32] Jaeger writes in *Paideia* that the advancement of ancient medicine came with its recognition of universal laws.[33] Such laws, writes Jaeger, were already assumed by others outside of the medical field such as Solon, who developed the theory that political crises are dislocations of health of the social organism.[34] The *Guide* is replete with examples of Maimonides operating freely and widely with this notion of universal laws, many of which have medical sources or applications. In the *Guide* (1:72) he describes some of the rules for the governance of bodies that are conglomerations of individual parts. Similar rules and laws apply to the human body, the body of the universe, and political bodies. Many of the universals found in that chapter are taken directly or indirectly from Aristotle's biological works and Galen's *De Usu Partium*.[35] In the *Guide* (2:17) he states a universal law that the nature of an object during its generation differs from that during its preservation or corruption. This universal has, among other places, Galen's *On the Natural Faculties* as a source,[36] and, in fact, the example Maimonides brings there is a medical one. In the *Guide* (3:32) we learn that all changes in nature, be they in a body or soul, must proceed gradually in order to facilitate proper adaptation. Again, a clear source for this universal is Galen's

De Usu Partium.[37] Since it integrates and serves as a source of universal laws, the proper study of medicine requires an understanding of and contributes to the study of metaphysics.[38]

Medicine's relationship with ethics is its most important in Maimonides' thought. It is not only a paradigm of methodology or a source of universal laws, but is itself, at least de facto, a part of the practical science of ethics. Ethics, as Maimonides explains in *Millot ha-Higayon,* is a branch of practical philosophy that deals with the acquisition of proper moral and ethical virtues and the expulsion of bad ones.[39] This precisely is the domain of Maimonidean medicine as well. As he explains in *Shemonah Perakim,* medicine teaches the need for moderation and disciplines the rational faculty to subdue emotional passions and thereby direct personal improvement.[40] Understanding and fulfillment of the commands of medicine requires moral discipline. This "psychological" aspect of their relationship was recognized early on by the ancients. Jaeger,[41] Edelstein,[42] and Frede[43] all point out that classical philosophers looked to medicine as an analogous mode of thought that utilized and trained the same natural faculty as their philosophic ethics. Philosophic ethics was truly the *medicina mentis.* This is the understanding implicit in the analogy of medicine and ethics found in the works of many of the medieval philosophers.[44] The relationship, however, goes even further for Maimonides. Since diseases of the soul can produce physical illness, as we learn in many places, including the seventeenth chapter of *Pirké Moshe*[45] and Maimonides' letter to Yefet on the death of his own brother,[46] perfection of the soul is a prerequisite of health. In the third chapter of *The Regimen of Health,* Maimonides writes that "passions of the psyche produce changes in the body that are great, evident, and, manifest to all," but that "people nurtured in the philosophy of morals" will not be affected as such.[47] We find an extreme example of such an affection in Maimonides' *Responsa on the Question of the Fixed Length of Life,* where he describes people dying from extreme elation or depression, the signs of an imperfect soul.[48] The converse of this relationship is also true. Maimonides explains in the *Guide* that moral virtues, which are a prerequisite for rational virtues, can be influenced and created by physical states of the body.[49] He brings an example of this in chapter 17 of *Pirké Moshe.*[50] The study of medicine, then, is important for ethical perfection, and the study of ethics is important for the student of medicine and every person interested in preserving his health. The relationship is not only psychological, it is physiological, too.

Because of his ideas of man as a "psychosome," Maimonides surpasses his predecessors in explaining medicine's role in relation to ethics. Farabi, in his *Aphorisms of the Statesman,* a work replete with the analogy of ethics and medicine, and a well-known source of the *Shemonah Perakim,* writes that "it is not the business of the doctor qua doctor to consider the health or sickness of the soul."[51] Although Maimonides does write in *The Regimen of Health* that "the physician inasmuch as he is a physician should not insist upon *his own art* as the rationale for the stratagem in removing [the] passions [of the psyche]," he nonetheless writes that "the skillful physician should place nothing ahead of rectifying the state of the psyche."[52] Since the health of the body reflects the health of the soul, the good doctor must understand how to cure both of them. Knowledge of medicine of the body cannot exist without knowledge of medicine of the soul, since the health of one is impossible without the health of the other.[53] Although formally separate sciences, medicine and ethics are not just related by way of analogy, as they are for Farabi. Medicine is an important source and expression of ethics and ethical behavior.[54] In this respect we can extend Jaeger's statement that "of all the branches of human knowledge then existing, medicine is the most closely akin to the ethical science of Socrates," to apply to Maimonides as well.[55]

With this background we can understand why Maimonides lauds medicine more than any other art as one whose study has "a great influence upon the acquisition of the virtues and of the knowledge of God, as well as upon the attainment of true spiritual happiness."[56] As Strauss explains in *Philosophy and Law*, prophecy for Maimonides, as for Avicenna, is a part of the practical philosophy of politics. The prophet, however, is superior to the regular lawgiver by virtue of his incorporation of theoretical and practical philosophy to one end.[57] So too, we may say, the ideal student of medicine – though not every student, and certainly not the average medieval physician – elevates the study of practical ethics by giving it a basis in theoretical philosophy (i.e., medical science), and elevates the study of theoretical philosophy by giving it a practical purpose. Medicine is a root of theoretical ethics, linking the distinct branches of theoretical and practical philosophy.[58]

There is a constant tension running through Maimonides' works, thought, and life between the pure Aristotelian contemplative life and a life in which a perfected rational virtue is comingled with moral action. The root of this famous antithesis is that whereas God's actions are themselves a product of pure contemplation,[59] we who try to imitate Him, but are subservient to and restrained by our association with matter, cannot duplicate His Unity as such. Action and contemplation for us must always be separate. Much of the *Guide* is devoted to the resolution and synthesis of this antithesis. Medicine is unique among the sciences in that it synthesizes the antithetical requirements of action and contemplation in one field. It breaks the boundaries of classification because it is an art and supreme act of loving-kindness, which is rooted in and sends out branches to both the theoretical (physics, metaphysics) and practical (ethics) sciences. It is a point of contact of Whitehead's Reason of Plato and Reason of Ulysses.[60] In this respect Jaeger's statement in *Paideia* is almost a paraphrase of Maimonides' words in *Shemonah Perakim*. Medicine, he writes, is for Plato "the embodiment of a professional code which is . . . a perfect model of the proper relation between knowledge and its purpose in practical conduct."[61]

17

The Cosmology of Maimonides and His Critique of the Inconsistencies and the Insufficiency of the Aristotelian Physics

Hubert Dethier

INTRODUCTION

To use a term introduced by Thomas Kuhn in his *The Structure of Scientific Revolutions,* Maimonides could be characterized as a "puzzle-solver." Puzzles are, in the entirely standard meaning employed by Kuhn, that special category of problems that can serve to test ingenuity or skill in solutions. What challenges the individual engaged on a normal research problem is the conviction that, if only he is skillful enough, he will succeed in solving a puzzle that no one before has solved or solved so well. Many of the greatest scientific minds have devoted all of their professional attention to demanding puzzles of this sort. On most occasions any particular field of specialization offers nothing else to do. But if it is to classify as a puzzle, a problem must be characterized by more than an assured solution. There must also be rules that limit both the nature of acceptable solutions and the steps by which they are to be obtained. To solve a jigsaw puzzle is not, for example, merely "to make a picture." Either a child or a contemporary artist could do that by scattering selected pieces, as abstract shapes, upon some neutral ground. The picture thus produced might be far better, and would certainly be more original, than the one from which the puzzle has been made. Nevertheless such a picture would not be a solution. To achieve that, all the pieces must be used, their plain sides must be turned down, and they must be interlocked without forcing until no holes remain. Those are among the rules that govern jigsaw-puzzle solutions. Similar restriction upon the admissible solutions of crossword puzzles, riddles, chess problems, and so on, are readily discovered.

If we can accept a considerably broadened use of the term *rule* – one that will occasionally equate it with "established viewpoint" or with "preconception" – then the problems accessible within a given research tradition display something much like this set of puzzle characteristics. The existence of a strong network of commitments – conceptual, theoretical, instrumental, and methodological – as that described by Kuhn[1] is a principal source of the metaphor that relates normal science to puzzle solving. Because it provides rules that tell the practitioner of a mature speciality what both the world and his science are like, he can concentrate with assurance, as Maimonides did, upon the esoteric problems that these rules and existing knowledge define for him. What then personally challenges him is how to bring the residual puzzle to a solution. In these and other respects a discussion of puzzles and of rules illuminates the nature of normal scientific practice. Yet in another way, that illumination may be significantly misleading. Though there obviously are rules to which all the practitioners of a scientific specialty adhere at a given time, those rules may not by themselves specify all that the practice of those specialists has in common. Normal science is a highly determined activity, but it need not be entirely determined by rule. That is why, at the start of his essay, Kuhn introduced shared paradigms rather than shared rules, assumptions and points of view as the source of coherence for normal research traditions. Rules derive from paradigms, but paradigms can guide research even in the absence of rules.

The way scientists consider "reason" can be very useful to discover the relation between rules, paradigms, and normal science. An historical investigation of a given "specialty," such as cosmology, and of the "established viewpoint" of reason at a given time can disclose a set of recurrent and quasi standard illustrations of various conflicting theories in their conceptual, observational, and instrumental applications. These are the community's paradigms, revealed in its textbooks and philosophical speculations. By studying them and by practitioning with them, the members of the corresponding community learn their trade. Despite occasional ambiguities, the paradigms of a mature scientific community can be determined with relative ease. The ambiguities of Maimonides' new configuration and alignment between the idea of God, on which Judaism is founded, and the philosophical view – a new alignment entailed by his speculations of negative theology – his preconception of reason that underlies the concrete pieces of his research and its legitimate problems and methods, his recourse also to hypothetical rules of the game, lead us to consider his underlying conception of reason as an important moment of the preparadigm stage and its subsequent evolution, let us say from Aristarchus to Copernicus.

A main theme of the *Guide for the Perplexed* concerns the contradiction between the idea of God upon which Judaism is founded and the philosophical view of God. The philosophical view for Maimonides is the conception of God as an intellect rather than as described by the speculations of *negative theology*. God, Maimonides argues, is a being of absolute perfection.[2] The divine essence is thus entirely beyond our ken. Our truest characterizations of God's being are negative, signifying divine transcendence. Positive descriptions express at best the relative perfections we know. As Joseph Albo sums up Maimonides' position: "all the attributes described to Him are assigned only by way of attributing the perfection they entail, not any of the privations they connote." Specifically, "without entailing plurality in His Being, which would be a privation relative to God"[3] Maimonides is fully aware of the crucial character of the issue and of the impossibility of achieving a true conciliation between the philosophical and the religious points of view. He remarks in the *Guide* (2:20): "For to me the combination between [the world] existing in virtue of necessity and being produced in time in virtue of a purpose in the world ... comes near to being a combination of two contraries" and points out the "very disgraceful conclusions" that follow from the philosophical view:

> Namely it would follow that the Deity, whom every one who is intelligent recognizes to be perfect in every kind of perfection, could as far as all beings are concerned, produce nothing new in any of them; if He wished to lengthen a fly's wing or shorten a worm's foot, He would not be able to do so. But Aristotle would say that He would not wish it and that it is impossible to will something different from what is; that it would not add to His perfection, but would perhaps from a certain point of view be a deficiency. [*Guide* 2:22]

Philosophers and scientists such as Maimonides confront growing difficulties in distinguishing the "scientific" component of past observation and belief from what their predecessors had really labeled "error" and "superstition." The more carefully they study, say, Aristotelian dynamics, the more certain they feel that those once-current views of nature were, as a whole, neither less scientific nor more the product of human idiosyncrasy than those current in their lifetime. If these out-of-date beliefs or "theories" are to be called "myths,"[4] then myths can be produced by the same sorts of methods and held for the same sorts of reasons that now lead to scientific knowledge. If, on the other hand, they are to be called science, then science has included bodies of belief quite incompatible with the ones we hold today. Out-of-date theories are not in principle unscientific because they have been discarded. The choices made by scientists and philosophers make it difficult to see scientific development as a process of accretion. Historical research that displays the difficulties in isolating individual inventions and discoveries gives ground – as Thomas

Kuhn and J. L. Dreyer have observed—for profound doubts about the cumulative process through which these individual contributions to science were thought to have been compounded.

THE *KALÀM* AND ITS DEFECTIVE LINES OF ARGUMENT

An important section of the *Guide* (1:71–76) treats of the *Kalàm*. According to Maimonides, the method of the *Kalàm* is copied from the Christian Fathers, who applied it in the defense of their religious doctrines. The latter examined in their writing the views of the philosophers, ostensibly in search of truth, in reality however, with the object of supporting their own dogmas. Subsequently Mohammedan theologians found in these works arguments which seemed to confirm the truth of their own religion; they blindly adopted these arguments and made no inquiry whence these had been derived.

The *Kalàm*—the system of the philosophers or Mohammedan theology—shows that God in the capacity of the Creator exists, is One, and is incorporeal, while in the first place it shows that the world has been created; but it only shows this premise by means of dialectical or sophistical arguments. The philosophers show that God exists, but they cannot prove this supposition. The two lines of argument are therefore defective. The argument of Maimonides consists in a combination of both. For, he argues, "the world is eternal—the world is created" is a complete disjunction; as the existence, the unity, and the incorporeality of God necessarily follow from the one or from the other of the two possible single suppositions, the basic truths are demonstrated by this very fact (*Guide* 1:71, 2:2). Still the conclusions drawn from the opposite premises cannot be purely and simply identical. The God whose existence is shown by supposing the eternity (of the world) is the unmoved mover, the thought that only thinks itself and that, like it, is the form or the life of the world. The God whose existence is shown by supposing the creation is the God of the Bible, who is characterized by the Will and the knowledge of which he only has the name in common with our knowledge. If we consider the situation as Maimonides sums it up, we see that that which is demonstrated by this argument is only what is common to the two different ideas of God, or what is neutral as regards the difference between God as pure Intellect or God as Will, or what is beyond this difference, or what is no more than a name in common with either the Intellect or the Will. But God, if one understands Him in that way, is precisely God as He is presented in the doctrine of the attributes; Maimonides' argument of the existence of God retrospectively clarifies his doctrine of attributes, which is entirely assertorical. Of God thus understood, one can say that He is more outside the world, not only than the God of the philosophers, but also than the God of the Bible; this way to understand God furnishes the basis for the theoretical, but also the most radical practical asceticism (*Guide* 3:51).[5]

In other words the two opposite suppositions really lead to God as the most perfect being; yet, even the Sabians consider their god, i.e., the sphere and its stars, as the most perfect being (*Guide* 3:45); to put it more generally, everyone understands by God the most perfect being in the sense of the most perfect possible being; the doctrine of the attributes, seen in the light of the argument which is then given of it, leads to God as the most perfect being, whose perfection is characterized by the fact that in Him the Intelligence and the Will cannot be distinguished from each other, because the two are identical in His essence (cf. *Guide* 1:69). Still, as the world is necessarily either created or eternal, it becomes necessary to restore the distinction between the Intellect and the Will. Let us put it in a general way: the *Guide* moves between the point of view according to which the Intellect and the Will cannot be distinguished and the one according to which they must be distinguished (and, consequently, that one should understand God more as Intelligence than as Will) according to the requirements of the various subjects which are being discussed (cf. *Guide* 2:25 and 3:25). For example, in his discussion of the Omniscience – it is in the same context that he reopens the discussion concerning the relative status of the imagination and the intellect – Maimonides solves the problem caused by the apparent incompatibility of the Omniscience and the free will of man (*Guide* 3:17) by appealing to the identity of that Intellect and the Will, while, in his discussion of the reasons of the biblical authority, he prefers the point of view according to which the authority springs from the intellect of God to the one according to which the authority originates in His will.

The reader of the *Guide* should carefully consider not only the general lines of the argument followed by Maimonides, but also all its bends and curves. The great work to which Maimonides devoted years of study and for which he sought a synthesis was organized in the esoteric mode, to be read and read again, the understanding gleaned in each reading funded into the next. Maimonides protected his philosophic world from casual perusers by the same device. While considering this the reader should never forget that the demonstration of the basic truths and the discussion of this demonstration is immediately preceded by the discussion of the Unity or that the discussion of the Unity constitutes the transition from exegesis to speculation. If the world, or to be more precise, the sphere is created, it is obvious that it has been created by some agent, but for quite a simple and stronger reason it does not necessarily follow that the creator is one, and that he is incorporeal. On the other hand, if the sphere is eternal, it follows, as Aristotle has shown, that God exists and is incorporeal; but if one makes this supposition, the angels or separate intelligences, each of which is the mover of one of the spheres, which are several, are just as eternal as God (cf. *Guide* 1:71, 2:2, 2:6). The question arises therefore whether monotheism, taken in a strict sense, is demonstrable. Maimonides affirms that the Unity and also the Incorporeality follow from certain philosophical arguments, which presuppose neither the eternity of the world nor its creation.[6] Moreover, if there were arguments of that kind, one is inclined to say that there is no need to admit the eternity of the world for the time being in order to prove the Existence, the Unity, and the Incorporeality of God; yet Maimonides asserts with much emphasis that there is a need of that kind. None of these problems or other similar ones is, however, in any way the most serious one. But here Maimonides' speculations of negative theology entail a remarkable configuration and alignment, not a synthesis between the idea of God on which Judaism is founded and the philosophical view. For, while the belief in the unity, existence, and incorporeality of God is required by the Law, this same belief, as it is compatible with the belief in the eternity of the world, is also compatible with the absolute rejection of the Law; the Law entirely depends on the belief in the creation of the world. It is therefore encumbent with Maimonides to show that Aristotle or Aristotelianism is wrong in maintaining that the eternity of the world has been demonstrated: the eternity of the world, which was the basis of the argument of the Existence, the Unity, and the Incorporeality of God, is a doubtful supposition. Still, it does not suffice to refute the claims of Aristotelianism in order to constitute the possibility of the creation as the Law understands it, for if the world is not necessarily eternal, it can nevertheless have been created from some eternal matter.

Thus Maimonides is compelled to abandon, or in any case to refine, the original disjunction ("the world is either eternal or created" is incomplete) at least to the extent where it mixes up the difference between the creation from matter and the creation from nothing. It sets off the opposition between Aristotle and the Law, but it conceals the intermediary possibility presented in Plato's *Timaeus*. The account Plato gives of the doctrine of the eternity does not conflict with the Law, for, while Aristotle's account excludes the possibility of any miracle, the Platonic account does not exclude all miracles as necessarily impossible. Maimonides does not say which miracles are excluded by Plato's teaching. One possible answer immediately comes to mind. The special providence of God for Israel, according to which Israel will prosper if it obeys and will be unhappy if it disobeys, is a miracle, of which it is not probable that it would have been admitted by Plato, whose teaching on providence seems to have been identical to that which is given in the Book of Job; providence naturally follows the intelligence of the individual human being. In conformity with the relationship existing between the Aristotelian doctrine and the doctrine of the Law, Maimonides shows by means of an extensive argument that the Aristotelian doctrine is not demonstrated and, over and above this, is not probable. As regards the Platonic doctrine, he explicitly refuses to pay any attention to the additional argument that it has not been demonstrated.[7] This argument is somewhat strange, because, according to Maimonides, the two terms of the alternative, the Aristotelian and the biblical, have not been demonstrated either. In his criticism of the Aristotelian doctrine, he uses the argument of the *Kalàm* based on a premise, which defines the possible in such a manner that it could be either the imaginable, or what is not contradictory, or that in relation to which we cannot make any definite assertion, which is the case as a result of our lack of knowledge; the premise in question excludes the view according to which the possible is what is capable of being, or what is in accordance with the nature of the matter in question or with what possesses a specific available substratum (cf. *Guide* 1:75, 2:14, 3:15).

The reader has to find out what are the premises or the premise preferred, what does Maimonides think of these premises, and whether the argument based on the premise in question does not only make the eternity of the visible universe improbable, but also the eternity of matter.

THE PHILOSOPHICAL THEORY OF THE PRIMAL CAUSE

The enumeration of 26 propositions, by the aid of which the philosophers prove the Existence, the Unity, and the Incorporeality of the Primal Cause and which forms the introduction of the second part of the *Guide,* are important when considered from this Platonic and neo-Platonic viewpoint. The principal arguments, the first and the fourth, for instance, which may be called cosmological proofs, have this in common: while proving the existence of a Primal Cause, they at the same time demonstrate the Unity, the Incorporeality, and the Eternity of that Cause. Special proofs are nevertheless superadded for each of these postulates, and on the whole they differ very little from those advanced by the Mohammedan theologians.

This philosophical theory of the Primal Cause was adapted by Jewish scholars to the biblical theory of the Creator. The universe is a living, organized being, of which the earth is the center. Any changes on this earth are due to the revolutions of the spheres; the lowest or innermost sphere, viz., the one nearest to the center, is the sphere of the moon; the outermost or uppermost is "the all-encompassing sphere." Numerous spheres are interposed; but Maimonides divides all the spheres into four groups, corresponding to the moon, the sun, the planets, and the fixed stars. This division is claimed by the author as his own discovery; he believes that it stands in relation to the four causes of their motions, the four elements of the sublunary world, and the four classes of beings, viz., the mineral, the vegetable, the animal, and the rational. The spheres have souls, and are endowed with intellect; their souls enable them to move freely, and the impulse to the motion is given by the intellect in conceiving the idea of the Absolute Intellect. Each sphere has an intellect peculiar to itself. The intellect attached to the sphere of the moon is the famous "active-intellect": "borderline, frontier, bridge and pool of consciousness" (*Sekel ha-po el*).[8] In support of this theory numerous passages are cited from both Holy Writ and from postbiblical Jewish literature. The angels (*elohim, malakhim*) mentioned in the Bible are assumed to be identical with the intellects of the spheres; they are free agents, and their volition invariably tends to that which is good and noble; they emanate from the Primal Cause and form a descending series of beings, ending with the active intellect. The transmission of power from one element to the other is called "emanation" (*shefa*). This transmission is performed without the utterance of a "sound"; if any voice is supposed to be heard, it is only an illusion, originating in the human imagination, which is the source of all evils (chap. 12).

In the first seven chapters of part III (*Guide*) Maimonides follows the exposition of the *maaseh merkabah* (Ezekiel 1), the Divine Chariot. According to him, three distinct parts are to be noticed, each of which begins with the phrase: "And I saw." These parts correspond to the three parts of the Universe, the sublunary world, the spheres, and the intelligences. First of all the prophet is made to behold the material world which consists of the earth and the spheres, and of these the spheres, as the more important, are noticed first. In the second part, in which the nature of the spheres is discussed, the author dwells with pride on his discovery and remarks they can be divided into four groups. This discovery he now employs to show that the four *hayyot* (animals) represent the four divisions of the spheres. In the third vision Ezekiel saw a human form above the *hayyot*. The world of Intelligences was represented by this figure; these can only be perceived in as far as they influence the spheres, but their relation to the Creator is beyond human comprehension. The Creator Himself is not represented in this vision.

In accordance with this doctrine, Maimonides explains that the three men who appeared to Abraham, the angels whom Jacob saw ascend and descend the ladder, and all other angels seen by man, are nothing but the intellects of the spheres, four in number, which emanate from the Primal Cause (*Guide*, chap. 10). In his description of the spheres he, as usual, follows Aristotle, a sometimes heavily neo-Platonized Aristotle. Nevertheless the spheres do not contain any of the four elements of the sublunary world, but consist of quintessence, an entirely different element. While things on this earth are transient, the beings that inhabit the spheres above are eternal.

According to Aristotle, these spheres, as well as their intellects, coexist with the Primal Cause. Maimonides, faithful to the teaching of the Scriptures, here departs from his master and holds that the spheres and the intellects (just as the human souls) had a beginning and were brought into existence by the will of the Creator. Maimonides does not attempt to give a positive proof of his doctrine; all he contends is that the theory of the *creatio ex nihilo* is, from a philosophical point of view, not inferior to the doctrine which asserts the eternity of the universe and that he can refute all objections advanced against Aristotle's theory.

In Maimonides' interpretation of the Aristotelian position, *God's will is assimilated to the divine Intellect*, which is identical with God himself, and the world may be regarded as something like an intellection necessarily produced by the Intellect. A consequence of Aristotle's theory as understood by Maimonides is that every characteristic of things existing in the world must be supposed to have a cause grounded in the natural structure of the universe (as opposed to a supernatural cause not determined by this structure). It may be added that as far as bodies are concerned, Maimonides seems to believe that in cases in which a mechanistic explanation can be found, it might provide such a cause. If this were accepted, it would mean that no part of the natural order could be, or could ever have been, different from what it actually is, for its existence is guaranteed by the immutability of divine reason. In other words, the world could not have been created in time. Maimonides' rationalist contemporaries, echoing Proclus, Aristotle, and Parmenides, also maintained that God, being perfect, must be changeless, so nature, as God's work, must exist eternally and unalterably. If so, Maimonides replies, nothing in nature can ever have changed. The doctrine not only eliminates contingency, which many philosophers cherished as the bastion of their voluntarism, but also undermines the notion of divine intelligence (wisdom), the one attribute that many rationalist philosophers, following Aristotle, held irreducible and constitutive of God's identity. These neo-Platonic Aristotelians argued that it would be somehow an admission of error or indecision for God to have created the world after not having created it.

From this point of view, Maimonides is quite consistent in describing temporal creation as the greatest of miracles and in stating that if this is admitted, the intellectual acceptance of other direct interventions of God in the natural course of events does not present any difficulties. Since it serves Maimonides' purpose to make out the best case possible for what he designates as the religious conception of God, he attempts to show that a structure of the universe which is necessary, because it is rationally determined in every respect, does not exist—or at least he seems to do so. In fact, he does not go beyond the demonstration, made at some length, that as far as the heavenly spheres are concerned, Aristotelian physics (although it gives satisfactory explanation of the phenomena of the sublunar world) is incapable of propounding a comprehensive scientific theory which can be regarded as certain and which provides cogent proof for the assumption that the cosmic order could not be different from what it actually is. In this critique of Aristotle's celestical physics he is helped by the much debated discrepancy that exists between Aristotle's natural science and the Ptolemaic system.

Maimonides also puts forward an argument of somewhat different character. He points out that man's knowledge of the order of nature is based on the empirical data of which he is cognizant. It is, however, conceivable that the existence of the data that are known to man had a beginning in time. No man who studies this problem should ignore this possibility, for if he does so, his case would be analogous to that of a person who disbelieves on empirical grounds – because he has met only adults – that human beings are brought into the world through birth after having been embryos. Arguments for eternity are mere projections of the settled order we now know; our present notions of matter, potentiality, time, and change read back into a stage of the world's history that far outleaps our limited experience.

Maimonides' critique of the inconsistencies and the insufficiency of the Aristotelian physics is pertinent within its scheme of reference. However, the doctrine of the eternity of the world does not rest exclusively upon physical theory. It is also corollary to the conception of God as Intellect, and Maimonides is aware of this. It is certainly significant, and it may be a deliberate omission, that when Maimonides is dealing with the problem of the eternity of the world in the *Guide*, he does not mention this conception, although other portions of the work proved he had adopted it.

Thus he does not allude to God as Intellect when he proclaims in the *Guide* (2:25) that he does not accept the doctrine of the eternity of the world for two reasons: (1) because it has not been demonstrated; (2) because its adoption would be tantamount to destroying the foundations of the Law, for it would mean denying the claims of the prophets and rejecting the belief in miracle.

The disappointing disagreement between Aristotle and Ptolemaic astronomy provoked a crisis which partially anticipated new sorts of problems and a pronounced failure in the normal problem-solving activity: in many cases, such as that of Maimonides, factors external to science played a large role. In the absence of crises some anticipators had been ignored. It is true that Maimonides' anticipation didn't concern directly heliocentric astronomy, but it made scientists aware of new problems in the field of cosmology, and drew the attention on the part of philosophical speculation in the elaboration of scientific theories. The only complete anticipation is also the most famous, that of Copernicus by Aristarchus in the third century B.C.E. It is often said that if Greek science had been less deductive and less ridden by dogma, heliocentric astronomy might have begun its development eighteen centuries earlier than it did.[9] But that is to ignore all historical context. When Aristarchus's suggestion was made, the vastly more reasonable geocentric system had no needs that a heliocentric system might even conceivably have fulfilled. The whole development of Ptolemaic astronomy, both its triumphs and its breakdowns, falls in the centuries after Aristarchus's proposal. Besides, there were no obvious reasons for taking Aristarchus seriously. Even Copernicus's more elaborate proposal was neither simpler nor more accurate than Ptolemy's system. Available observational tests provided no basis for a choice between them. Under these circumstances, one of the factors that led astronomers to Copernicus (and one that could not have led them to Aristarchus) was the recognized crisis that had been responsible for innovation in the first place. Maimonides' speculations and observations made a large contribution to that crisis. Ptolemaic astronomy had failed to solve its problems; the time had come to give competition a chance.[10]

THE DETOUR

We already mentioned that in the *Guide* (2:25), Maimonides shows that God's will and wisdom are not reducible to one another, as Muslim intellectualist philosophers had supposed. His argument takes the form of a spirited dialectical defense of biblical creationism. The rationalist philosophers, echoing Proclus, Aristotle, and Parmenides, had maintained that God, being perfect, must be changeless, so nature, as God's work, must exist eternally and unalterably.[11] Such a doctrine, Maimonides replies, undermines the notion of divine intelligence (wisdom), the one attribute that many rationalist philosophers, following Aristotle, held irreducible and constitutive of God's identity. The same neo-Platonic Aristotelians argued that it would be somehow an admission of error or indecision for God to have created the world after not having created it.

Here Maimonides turns the tables and introduces subreptively a subtle way to think differently about nature: the very notion of divine intelligence is attenuated to irrelevance unless God is regarded as having made the world better than it might have been.[12] To argue, as Muslim rationalist philosophers did, that all determinations in nature have a reason, are determined for the best by divine wisdom,[13] is to assume that God had a choice.[14]

Divine determination has no meaning unless room is allowed for a wholly undetermined state of pure possibility—unlimited even by the condition of matter as we know it, or any surrogate thereof.[15] It follows, Maimonides argues, that we must think of the world in creationist terms, as once lacking all definition (which in Greek philosophical terms means lacking existence absolutely) and then having been created, acquiring the nature we now study in the sciences.[16] Arguments for eternity, as we remarked previously, are mere projections of the settled order we now know—our present notions of matter, potentiality, time, and change, read back into a stage of the world's history that far outleaps our limited experience.

CHANCE AND ORDER

In discussing chance, Maimonides defers to Aristotle's conception: chance events are causally determined, but not by the causes we rightly expect when we think of the general classes of natural concomitances. They are *coincidences*. It is in this sense that they depart from nature's general causal pattern. Thus the distinction between chance and other causally determined events (like that among God's attributes) is subjective, a result of the finitude of our intelligence.

> Everything which comes to be in time must have some proximate cause which brings it into being; this cause too must have a cause, and so until the series ends at the First Cause of all things, which is the Will and Choice of God. . . . Chance, as has been made clear, is the outcome of a superfluity of natural causes, and most of it is accounted for by nature or by choice or by will.[17]

God's determination of the character of nature can be understood in terms of an act of will whose ultimate wisdom, being infinite, will always answer to, yet always continue *to elude,* our categories of comprehension. Within nature, events that we cannot reduce to causal order are not uncaused but are effects of causes we do not grasp. They have patterns we do not, or cannot follow, as when they involve causes that tend in divergent directions with forces too equally balanced for us to anticipate the exact character of their resultant. We see events as arbitrary primarily when we find their outcomes unpredictable. Biblically all events are ascribed to God's act – whether to will or rational choice is immaterial, since in God there is in fact neither will nor intelligence in any human sense: these are only two different ways we have of interpreting natural events.[18] The "random" then may be understood as representing a rational pattern beyond our present knowledge.

Complementing Maimonides' argument, we can say, as L. E. Goodman points out in his remarkable contribution to the Essays in Honor of Arthur Hyman,[19] that *not only is randomness a superfluity of causes, but causality is a superfluity of randomness* – as, for example, in the kinetic law of gases, where materials approach ideal behavior more closely as randomness increases in the motion of their particles, or in genetics, where the ratios of offspring approach their expected values as conditions of random mating are approached.

Maimonides remarks that God's attributes or acts are His work in the world of matter and form.

Both creation and revelation would be inconceivable from a human standpoint without assigning God an arbitrary aspect.[20] Plainly matter must represent that aspect. As the principle of individuation, matter was the one level of differentiation that could not be accounted for simply by reference to the forms. Matter was indeed the principle of differentiation, by which the universe was freed from absolute simplicity. Maimonides recognized these givens when he referred to matter, following Galen, as the basis of individuality and the resultant vulnerability of the body, and when he referred to matter in the heavens, following Philoponus, as the ultimate basis of the claim that the heavenly bodies are not simplex but differentiated and hence (from our viewpoint) arbitrarily determined.[21]

THE UNIFYING INTENT

The thesis of Goodman's paper was that Spinoza learned from Maimonides to overcome the disparity between *mind and body,* form and matter, which he reconceived as thought and extension, by treating both as attributes of God. Goodman's contention is that Maimonides identified matter with the will of God and thought or form with the traditional attribute of wisdom, both of which he believed to be mere human ways of recognizing God's act. In the absoluteness of creation we detect God's infinite perfection. The objects of creation—matter and form, organized as body and mind, constituting nature—express, through their finitude and relative perfection, an Identity *(Dhàt)* transcendent of all limitation and definition (*Guide* 1:57, S. Munk, ed., Paris, 1956-66).

Maimonides' position, Goodman observes, is not identical with Spinoza's. Spinoza defined "attribute" as "that which the intellect apprehends of substances as constituting its essence" and spoke of the attributes as objectively constitutive of the actual essence of the divinity. He clearly departed from Maimonides' rejection of the notion that there are "attributes" proper to God's Identity. Spinoza is plainly influenced here by Descartes' theses that *res extensa* and *res cogitans* are clearly and distinctly apprehended, and that the intellect is not deceived in what it clearly and distinctly apprehends. But in supplementing Maimonides' subjective treatment of God's attributes with his own objective treatment, Spinoza does not depart from Maimonides' unifying intent. The plurality of thought and extension remains subjective. Spinoza has accepted Descartes' argument that what is clear and distinctly conceived must be as it is conceived, but he has rejected the inference that *res cogitans* and *res extensa* must be substances.

An ambiguity in the word *distinct* may have allowed Descartes to pass beyond the mutual irreducibility of mind and matter to an affirmation which entails the self-sufficiency and self-intelligibility of finite being. We can appreciate Spinoza's preference for the expression "adequate idea" to Descartes' "clear and distinct idea." Spinoza's thought and extension are clearly distinct, but they are not for that reason separate distances: their absoluteness is a subjective illusion.

Spinoza, then, learned from Maimonides *a method of resolving* some aspects of the ancient paradox of the one and the many. Specifically, he learned a system of aligning the two irreducible features of nature: (1) matter/extension and (2) form/thought—as philosophic interpretations of the medieval philosopher's two irreducible attributes of God, wisdom and will. The expedient of *subjectivizing* troublesome aspects of experience is not unfamiliar. Freedom, good and evil, substances, selves, plurality, potentiality, and chance have been accorded similar treatment by one philosopher or another.[22] Hume and Kant used such an approach in addressing problems about time, space, and causality. This treatment is not unrelated to the present one. *Space,* after all, is Kant's version of Descartes' extension; and *causality* is the modern surrogate for that dimension of necessity that Aristotelians sought to comprehend in formal terms.

Plotinus treated time, space, and causal process as projections of the subjectivity of Soul. Ghazali made them categories of human consciousness inapplicable in the spiritual realm. Hume and Kant complete Ghazali's project when they seek objectivity for these categories in the very fact of their structural subjectivity. But although Hume, Kant, and Ghazali made space and causality subjective, they did not treat them as attributes of God–despite Ghazali's admonition that the true monotheist sees God in everything.

Maimonides and his sometimes wayward follower, Spinoza, more faithful to the monist spirit, made space (that is, extension matter) and "causality," at least on its conceptual level (that is, the formal, causal order, called wisdom or intelligence by Maimonides and transformed to "thought" by Spinoza) both attributes of God.

Newton was severely censured by Leibniz and others for essays in a similar direction. But it seems clear that only through efforts of this type can we achieve the objective of seeing all of nature as an expression of the divine.

Within philosophy, and also more specifically within cosmology, dialectics get categorized only to be developed in depth by Fichte, Schelling, and Hegel according to Maimonides' methodology. Poetic thought is dialectic. It does not make necessarily an appeal to the riddle, the paradox, the inner contradiction: rather, it is ironic. Irony is an essential characteristic of poetic thought (as is irony the actual dialectic). Socrates' irony was therefore not coincidental, and neither was Plato's, whereas Aristotle's logic was utterly serious. Hegel, too, is ironic, although he averses from the false or Romantic irony, which is nihilistic–it is the irony of an empty subjectivity that deems itself way above the insignificance of the world. Hegel's irony, on the other hand, is the dialectic cunning of reason which achieves its goal through side issues, by roundabout ways. Irony is the detour, not the direct and straight road, for this leads to nowhere; it is without a way out. The dialectic is the reasoning of the escape hatch, it is the thought with which something can be accomplished. Is it the thought for new thoughts, for a higher self-awareness? This is what Hegel thought. Marx thought further: it is the praxis, the revolutionary, reforming, changing thought. Poetic thought in Marx is the dialectic of the praxis or the mobile unity of theory and practice in the production relationships.

Maimonides' method centers around the detour, the "shortest way." A detour can, however, also be a wrong track. One may aim at a certain point and take a track that leads away from it. One is following a wrong track and realizes this only after a lapse of time. One slides farther away from one's aim, until suddenly one realizes that one finds oneself at the very point at which one aimed to be.

Since philosophy takes detours, it cannot help wandering. Wandering is a substantial element in philosophy and science, and the more intense philosophy gets, the higher the chances of choosing wrong tracks. These wrong tracks, however, incorporate direction of truth. The wandering gets lost on the right track, which is a perfect definition of Maimonides' fundamental reasoning. Being prepared to take wrong tracks causes fear, not of an inhibiting or passive nature, but active fear, allowing, according to Maimonides, for temerity, boldness, risk, and wager.

18

Some Insights into Maimonides' Approach to Mental Health Issues

Mordechai Reich

HOLISTIC APPROACH TO HEALTH

Maimonides addresses the connection between mind and body in many of his writings. Perhaps the clearest expression of this holistic approach to psychological and physical health is found in his letter to the sultan, son of Saladin the Great, whose reign began in 1198. The sultan turned to Maimonides, at that time one of the court physicians, with complaints of constipation, hard and painful stools, loss of appetite, indigestion, depression, and thanatophobia, or fear of dying. Maimonides' reply to him, later published as a manual for healthful living, addresses the areas of nutrition, digestion, and elimination, but also focuses on the sultan's psychic pain. In his reply to the sultan, Maimonides attempts to guide all physicians who would follow him, toward a better understanding of their patients' physical and psychological difficulties.

After explicating the mind-body connection and the effects of emotions on the patient's physical state, Maimonides continues:

> And let the physician remember that every ill person's heart is constricted and every healthy person's heart is broadened. Therefore, let the physician relieve the patient of his psychological problems which bring him to despondence. This will strengthen the patient's general health and is the first step in the treatment of any ill person.

Certainly, when the patient's illness is primarily of a psychological nature, for example hypochondriasis or melancholia, attention to the patient's psychological state is even more necessary.[1]

Maimonides demands much from the physician and the patient. He expects the physician to be a reservoir of knowledge concerning ethical, philosophical, and religious approaches to living, as well as an expert in diagnosis, understanding of the body, and pharmacotherapy. First, the physician needs to obtain a clear understanding of the patient's subjective world and secure a diagnosis of the patient's psychological distress. Even if psychological distress is not manifest, it is assumed to exist, and the physician is required to search for it. Only after this "psychological workup" can the physician begin with a medical intervention. Of the patient, Maimonides demands a willingness to undertake an introspective process and adhere strictly to the regimen that the physician would formulate. Once the patient and physician embark upon a carefully directed program which includes an examination of thoughts, feelings, and philosophy of life, as well as any necessary medical interventions, a partial or total cure is likely. Maimonides expects that the patient's "spirits would be raised and depressive and self defeating thoughts would decrease in frequency or vanish."[2]

While many of Maimonides' prescriptions for psychological health are behavioral, the approach he posits in his letter to the sultan is much broader in nature. The patient and physician must attempt to explore deep-seated emotions and the patient's philosophy of life. At the same time, a cognitive approach is taken where negative or self-defeating thoughts are identified and confronted. Stress is to be avoided, particularly during meals or afterwards while the digestive process is underway, and moderate exercise is recommended for stress reduction and general fitness. In fact, Maimonides seems to be in favor of a multimodal therapeutic approach which includes elements of analysis, behavioral and cognitive therapy, rational-emotive therapy, stress reduction, and even logotherapy. Finally, speaking to the sultan, and through him to a large religious Muslim population, Maimonides unabashedly prescribes faith in God as a significant factor in reducing anxiety and fostering emotional well-being and a sense of equanimity.

THE GOLDEN MEAN

In his major treatise, the *Yad ha-Hazakah,* a halakhic compendium which addresses every aspect of Jewish observance, Maimonides devotes a whole section to *Hilkhot Deot* (Laws of Ethics), in which he discusses varieties of character types and behaviors, as well as medical and psychological issues. That these chapters find their way into a work which is essentially a treatise on Jewish law is no surprise, for Maimonides firmly believed that a healthy body and a healthy mind were prerequisites for the service of God.

Beginning with a discussion of temperament and behavioral patterns, Maimonides addresses himself to the nature-nurture issue, and essentially takes a middle-of-the-road position. He points out that people are often born with a particular temperament. Consequently, certain people are more prone to particular behaviors or emotional states due to their inherent temperaments. At the same time, Maimonides asserts that much of our behavior is acquired through learning and the modeling of others, and sometimes we adopt certain behavioral patterns as a result of conscious decisions or a particular philosophy of life. After accentuating the variations of character traits, emotions, and behaviors reflected in human beings, Maimonides focuses on common goals which will insure healthful living. One must maintain a constant introspective process regarding his behavior and emotions and work to strike a healthful balance in terms of behavior and emotions. One must not be prone to anger, but one cannot be lifeless and unfeeling. One must be charitable and giving, but not give beyond his means. For every behavior and feeling a balance must be achieved and extremes must be avoided, except for humility, which should be practiced to the utmost. When a person feels out of synch, or when one becomes cognizant of a particular imbalance in emotion or behavior, Maimonides prescribes a visit to the prime psychotherapists—the *Hakhamim* (sages)—who then conduct an assessment of their "patients'" behavioral, ethical, and emotional patterns, and advise necessary adjustments.

Up to this point, Maimonides requires an extraordinary amount of introspection and insight. First, there is the constant effort on the part of the individual to strike a healthful balance in his behavior and emotions. Secondly, one must recognize when things are not going well and when there is an imbalance. All this calls for a strong observing ego and a good deal of willpower. Interestingly, Maimonides does not really address the issue of resistance. The assumption is that a person who recognizes that he is in trouble and needs help will seek out the aid he requires. If one recognizes specific problems and refuses to secure help, he is in the category of "Wisdom and ethics the foolish have scorned" (Proverbs 1:7). What Maimonides suggests for the patient unwilling to accept responsibility for his behavior and visits the therapist's office because "other people tell me I have problems," is not clear. Similarly, the treatment for the patient who is eager to accept responsibility for all the ills of the world is not outlined. Obviously, both for the character-disordered patient who tends to blame others and for the neurotic, guilt-ridden patient, preliminary work has to be done around issues of self-evaluation and the parameters of responsibility for one's actions.

What is Maimonides' approach toward instilling healthful behavior and achieving a beneficial balance in everyday living? Initially he takes a straightforward behavioral approach. Maimonides is a firm believer that repetitive behaviors can induce lasting changes. That is to say, repeated conscious efforts at entrenching particular behaviors can induce beneficial, long-term changes in one's personality and emotional makeup. A person with a tendency toward stinginess is adjured to repeatedly do acts of kindness; after a while, he will in fact become kind and charitable. For the person manifesting a gross imbalance in one or more areas of emotions or behavior, Maimonides presents a more extreme approach reminiscent of the "flooding" technique used in treating phobias. For example, when dealing with a patient's fear of snakes, actual or fantasy-guided exposure to snakes, perhaps accompanied with relaxation exercises, may be helpful. In the case of a person who is constantly angry, Maimonides recommends that he conduct himself in such a manner that even if he is cursed or struck, he will learn to feel nothing. Even more dramatic, for the person who is haughty, Maimonides recommends dressing in rags and conducting himself in occupations far below his social standing in order to achieve humility. Ultimately the negative trait, emotion, or behavior will be uprooted, and the person can return to the middle way. Maimonides states that this radical therapy may in fact take a long time, but will ultimately succeed.

One of Maimonides' premises—that we are responsible not only for our behaviors, but for our feelings as well—would clearly be rejected by many psychotherapists today. Maimonides clearly makes this point in the seventh chapter of Laws of Repentance, in the *Yad ha-Hazakah:*

> Do not say that repentance concerns only those transgressions which involve action such as sexual impropriety or theft. Just as a person must repent of these misdeeds, so must he search his negative character traits and emotions and repent for his anger, his envy and jealousy, his pursuit of money and honor, and the pursuit of culinary gratifications. All these require repentance. These issues are more difficult than those which involve specific activities, for when one is involved with them, it is difficult to separate from them. And, thus the verse says "Let the evil man desert his path and the transgressor leave his *thoughts* behind."[3]

Obviously, Maimonides' prescription for mental and spiritual health is quite demanding. Repenting for thoughts and emotions is not an easy process. For Maimonides, repentance includes recognition of one's sin, feelings of regret, and a commitment not to repeat the error. In most modern therapists' offices one is likely to hear "Look, you can think or feel whatever you like as long as you don't act out on every impulse." Maimonides asks for more. He asks for introspection and awareness, control of emotions and thoughts, a willingness to overcome resistance to the point where a therapeutic alliance is assumed, and even a willingness to undergo a radical form of "flooding" or behavioral therapy when one is in a severe state of emotional or behavioral imbalance.

In addition, Maimonides is quite direct in describing his vision of healthful living. A "healthy" man is happy and able to deal with others in a pleasant manner. He is honest with himself and others, and his heart feels the words of his mouth. He communicates openly with others. When he harbors negative or angry feelings, he expresses them in a direct but sensitive manner. He comes to love his fellow man as well as love and appreciate himself. He has the strength of will to assert his sense of self and personal values even when assailed by a negative environment, and he seeks out models who help him in his striving for health.

Maimonides was one of the leading religious personalities of his time. In his view, a healthy body and healthy mind are prerequisites for the ultimate goal – service of the Creator. Every word of Maimonides is infused with a deep belief in God and a commitment to religious observance. Indeed, the Torah and all its commandments are a blueprint for a healthful and meaningful life.

In discussing his prescription for healthful living, Maimonides points to the biblical imperative *ve-halakhta bi-drakhav,* "And you shall walk in His ways" (Deuteronomy 28:9). Maimonides offers the rabbinical interpretation of the verse: Just as He is called Merciful, so too, you shall be merciful. Just as He is called Holy, so too, you shall be holy. Similarly, with all the other attributes of God, man should strive to imitate his Creator, *imitatio dei.* Maimonides maintains that the more we attempt to imitate and acquire God's attributes, the more wholesome a life-style we lead.

Maimonides identifies faith in God as a cornerstone for the treatment of anxiety and depressive thinking. He posits that depressive thoughts and anxiety arise from one of two causes: either a focus on past events which generally involve loss or separation, or a focus on the future in which a person imagines catastrophic or harmful events. After describing some cognitive therapeutic approaches which could work to negate depression and anxiety, Maimonides turns to the most significant weapon in his therapeutic armamentarium – belief in God. A strong belief in Divine Providence is a powerful factor in dealing with anxiety about the future and coming to terms with losses and separations of the past. If one is able to place himself firmly behind Rabbi Akiva's words: *Kol man de Rahmana avid le-tov avid,* "Whatever the Merciful One does is for good," one is prepared to deal more effectively with the stresses, losses, and vicissitudes inherent in living life as a sensate being.

Aside from viewing a general belief in Divine Providence as a potent force in achieving psychic equilibrium, Maimonides introduces the idea that individual *mitzvot,* or commandments, contribute significantly to character development and appropriate behavior. In his work *The Eight Chapters,* a prelude to talmudic tractate *Avot,* Maimonides outlines the effects of some commandments on our state of psychological health and emotional makeup. For example, the negative commandment not to take revenge and the positive commandment to come to the aid of one's enemy when his beast of burden falls under its load, enables a person to confront and deal more effectively with anger. The commandments to reprove the person who has done one a wrong, or not to be fearful when called upon to pass judgment, are viewed as helpful in increasing self-confidence and assertive behavior.

Maimonides formulates the ultimate goal to which man should aspire—constant awareness of God and service of God through even the most mundane activities. Eating, drinking, and sexual relations are all for the sake of Heaven. One fortifies himself with food in order to better serve his Creator. One sleeps in order to awaken refreshed for the study of Torah and the performance of commandments. Maimonides was not an ascetic, and he does not demean the pleasure accompanying physical activities. In fact, Maimonides, in the *Yad ha-Hazakah*, describes the intensity of one's love of God in terms of a man, smitten with love for a woman, who can neither eat nor sleep nor concentrate, and who is totally involved only in thoughts of his beloved.[4] For Maimonides, sexual relations are an integral part of healthful living, and the love and intimacy shared by a man and his wife are a model for the love relationship between man and God. Maimonides admits that total devotion to God through one's physical and emotional activities is a goal which few people attain. However, for Maimonides, pursuing that goal is our life's work, and the effort involved in maintaining a constant awareness of God brings in its wake physical, mental, and spiritual health and enables us to achieve the ultimate in self-actualization.

For Jewish patients experiencing psychological distress, it is clear that Maimonides requires a Jewish therapist who is deeply committed to religious observance and belief in God. Short-term goals might include alleviation of presenting symptoms, but long-term goals are clear and specific—bringing the patient to a point where he or she can become committed to full religious observance and achieve a deep and constant awareness of God. The process may indeed be slow, but the therapeutic goals are not open-ended.

While Maimonides addresses himself to a variety of therapeutic approaches—analytic, cognitive, behavioral, rational, emotive—he does not directly address what we might call developmental arrest and the all-pervasive problem of lack of self-esteem. Would Maimonides view the *baal gaavah* (the haughty person) as a manifestation of a narcissistic personality disorder? Similarly, Maimonides focuses a good deal more on neurosis and character disorder than he does on psychotic or borderline disorders. Is the white-hot fury of the borderline personality disorder also included in Maimonides' description of the negative emotion of anger that must be vanquished? One can assume that in his work as a physician, Maimonides did in fact confront the full range of psychological disorders. Undoubtedly, a deeper and more comprehensive understanding of his approach to treatment issues can be acquired through further research of the writings of our master and teacher, Rabbi Moshe ben Maimon, Maimonides.

IV

On and Around Maimonides

19

Remarks on Eight Pseudo-Maimonidean Treatises

Fred Rosner

INTRODUCTION

It is not surprising that many writers in medieval and modern times would not only try to emulate Moses Maimonides, but even attach his name to their own writings. Such is the case for several famous works, including the well-known and widely quoted "Prayer of Maimonides" for physicians, which was actually written by Marcus Herz in Germany in 1783, although he never asserted that the prayer was composed by Maimonides.[1]

Other treatises have also been falsely attributed to Maimonides for a variety of reasons. These works have never been available to the English-speaking world and, although spurious, are important for those interested in medieval Judaism in general and Moses Maimonides in particular. It is also important to emphasize and demonstrate, once and for all, that works commonly spoken of as Maimonidean, such as the *Treatise on Eternal Bliss (Pirké ha-Hatzlahah)*, the *Book of Remedies (Sefer Refuot)*, his *Last Will and Testament (Shaare ha-Musar)*, the *Scroll of the Unrevealed (Megillat Setarim)*, and *The Letter on the Messiah of Isfahan* are all medieval fabrications and not written by Maimonides.[2]

Three additional works attributed to Maimonides deal with the existence and Unity of God and were published in 1990.[3] *Maamar ha-Yihud (Treatise on the Unity of God)* may well have been authored by Maimonides himself; *Sefer ha-Nimtza (Treatise on the One Who Exists)* is probably spurious; and *Tishah Perakim mi-Yihud (Nine Chapters on the Unity of God)* was certainly not written by Maimonides.

I will briefly describe the *Sefer ha-Nimtza* and the *Tishah Perakim Mi-Yihud* and present evidence to support my thesis that these are spurious works. Later, I will discuss several additional pseudo-Maimonidean treatises, including the renowned *Physician's Prayer*.

TREATISE ON THE ONE WHO EXISTS (*SEFER HA-NIMTZA*)

Sefer ha-Nimtza is a small and somewhat obscure medical-moral work attributed to Moses Maimonides, first published in 1596. The work begins with an introductory plea in very flowery language for moral conduct, not at all typical of Maimonidean writings. The work itself starts with praises to God the Creator who "is everything and bears everything and everything is dependent upon Him." Galen and Plato are cited. The physical and spiritual parts of the human body are described and analogies are made between the sun and the planets of the "large world" and the heart and other major organs of the "small world." The spirit and the soul, the powers of imagination, thought, and memory, the four fundamental elements—fire, air, water, and earth—and the medieval concept of body humors as the modulators of health and disease are cited. The heavenly constellations, signs of the Zodiac, and seasons of the year are all briefly discussed.

The second half of *Sefer ha-Nimtza* is devoted to medical rules and regulations for the preservation of health. Large sections of these rules seem to be taken verbatim or only slightly modified from chapter 4 of the laws of temperaments (*Hilkhot Deot*) in Maimonides' *Mishneh Torah*. Some quotations cited exactly from *Hilkhot Deot* are commented upon, sometimes at length. Others are just paraphrased or modified or cited without comment. The last third of chapter 4 of *Hilkhot Deot* is not quoted at all or paraphrased in *Sefer ha-Nimtza*. No reason is apparent for this omission.

The original publisher, Abraham Akara, as well as the subsequent editors, Gabriel Polak and Judah Leib Maimon, consider Maimonides as the author. This view is also supported by other scholars such as Shlomo Rapoport. On the other hand, the renowned Hebrew bibliographer Moritz Steinschneider, as well as other scholars such as Zaks and Zabara, consider *Sefer ha-Nimtza* to be spurious and falsely attributed to Maimonides.

Although there is considerable controversy among scholars as to the authenticity of *Sefer ha-Nimtza* as a Maimonidean work, some confusion about the meaning of the word *nimtza*, and even the erroneous suggestion that *Sefer ha-Nimtza* is identical with Maimonides' *Maamar ha-Yihud*, because of considerable similarities in both works, I considered it important and worthwhile to translate the *Sefer ha-Nimtza* into English and to present it together with a translation and analysis of Maimonides' *Maamar ha-Yihud,* which is probably an authentic Maimonidean work.

THE NINE CHAPTERS ON THE UNITY OF GOD (*TISHAH PERAKIM MI-YIHUD*)

The work entitled *Nine Chapters on the Unity of God* attributed to Moses Maimonides was published in Hebrew in 1950 by Georges Vajda in the periodical *Kobetz Al Yad.*[4] Three years later, Vajda published, in French, an analysis of this work, which he called a pseudo-Maimonidean treatise.[5]

Vajda clearly proves the spurious nature of the *Nine Chapters* by showing that it is an abbreviated adaptation of the kabbalistic *Ginnat Egoz* of Rabbi Joseph Gikatila (also known as Siciliano), which was published in Hanover in 1615. The *Nine Chapters* is clearly a kabbalistic work or was profoundly influenced by Kabbalah. Many passages are borrowed from the *Book of Creation (Sefer Yetzirah).* The combination of the letters that comprise the Tetragrammaton and the isopsephies *(gematria)* differ significantly with the subject of Divine names in Maimonides' *Guide for the Perplexed.* Further, the constant repetition and belaboring of the same points is evidence that the *Nine Chapters* was not written by Moses Maimonides. Maimonides writes in short, clear language and does not repeat himself. Any seeming repetition turns out, on closer scrutiny, to be a clarifying or qualifying phrase that modifies or adds to what he originally said.

Vajda discusses by whom and when the *Nine Chapters* was written and why it was attributed to Maimonides. He considers it unlikely that Gikatila wrote it and suggests that Meir Aldabi may have been the author. Vajda dates the composition of this work to the year 1300. He suggests that the *Nine Chapters* was attributed to Maimonides in order to strengthen the position of the kabbalists, who were attempting to justify their legitimacy as sacred scientists. Be that as it may, the *Nine Chapters on the Unity of God* was almost certainly not written by Maimonides.

Although the *Nine Chapters* has been wrongly attributed to Moses Maimonides, it is nevertheless an important work of historical interest and was, therefore, published together with two other works on the unity and existence of God attributed to Maimonides.[6]

TREATISE ON ETERNAL BLISS (*PIRKÉ HA-HATZLAHAH*)

The *Treatise on Eternal Bliss* attributed to Moses Maimonides was published in a critical Arabic and Hebrew edition in 1939 by Davidowitz[7] and includes textual and philological corrections and explanatory notes by Baneth.

The *Treatise on Eternal Bliss*, known in Hebrew as *Pirké ha-Hatzlahah* or *Perakim be-Hatzlahah* (literally: *Chapters on Eternal Bliss*), was first cited in the middle of the fourteenth century by Joseph ben Eleazar, the famous commentator of Ibn Ezra, as "a short essay" composed by Maimonides *(maamar katzar she-hiber)*.[8] Davidowitz asserts that this unusual citation indicates that even then there was doubt about the true name of the treatise, or else they just did not know.

In 1897, Bacher[9] published an in-depth analysis in English of the *Treatise* with his explanations of the allegory of the sanctuary, especially of the candlestick, the ceremonial commandments and prayer, ecstasy, repentance, the allegorical interpretation of Psalm 45, the symbol of the delights of eternal salvation *(hupah)*, the biblical evidences for the continuation of the soul after death, and miscellaneous remarks on eternal salvation. Bacher was convinced of the authenticity of the *Treatise on Eternal Bliss* as a Maimonidean work, although he admits that the generally adopted view of most writers is that Maimonides was not the author.

Bacher and Steinschneider[10] stand alone in their support of the authenticity of the *Treatise on Eternal Bliss* as a Maimonidean work. In 1869, Schmiedl[11] wrote that the mania of using allegory in medieval writings resulted in the attribution of some allegorical works to Maimonides, including the apocryphal *Treatise on Eternal Bliss*. Similarly, continues Schmiedl, to increase the prestige of Kabbalah, it would not have been surprising for writers to attribute kabbalistic works to Maimonides.

The strongest evidence of the spuriousness of the *Treatise on Eternal Bliss* is provided by Davidowitz in his critical edition of this work. The style and character and contents of the book are not those of Maimonides. The very complicated and involved style has no comparison in the *Guide for the Perplexed*, although the *Treatise* was for years considered to be a codicil for *The Guide*. Davidowitz cites six major areas in the *Treatise on Eternal Bliss* where the contents are at variance with or totally contradictory to Maimonides' statements in the *Guide for the Perplexed*. Davidowitz then offers numerous stylistic reasons why he concludes that the *Treatise on Eternal Bliss* is a spurious work that did not come from the pen of Maimonides.

All the above facts, asserts Davidowitz, lead one perforce to the conclusion that the *Treatise on Eternal Bliss* was not authored by Maimonides and should not be considered among his authentic writings. One should also not think that an unintentional error of the printer or publisher attributing this work to Maimonides led people for generations to falsely believe it to be authentic. Rather, the character, contents, and style of the *Treatise* clearly indicate that the author intentionally tried to create the impression that the *Treatise* emanated from Maimonides. The author who added Maimonides' name to the *Treatise* is not guilty of ordinary literary plagiarism, where the author substitutes *his* name for that of the true author. It is possible that this falsification was perpetrated with the best of intentions to aggrandize the name of God and to strengthen Jewish beliefs and practices. In those days, many people had come under the influence of Aristotle and his followers. The author of the *Treatise on Eternal Bliss*, perhaps an ardent admirer of Maimonides, tried to justify the contents of Maimonides' *Guide for the Perplexed* and defend it against jealous critics by calling the *Treatise* "the conclusion of the *Guide*."

BOOK OF REMEDIES (*SEFER REFUOT*)

In 1900, Menashe Grossberg published a booklet entitled *Sefer Refuot le-Rabbenu Moshe Maimon Z"l, Rofeh le-Melekh Mitzrayim* (Book of Remedies of Moses Maimonides, Physician to the King of Egypt).[12] The title page indicates that the booklet "is being published for the first time based on a manuscript in the British Museum in London."

Grossberg was convinced of the authenticity of the work as a Maimonidean writing, as he described in the foreword to the 1900 edition. However, there is serious doubt as to the accuracy of Grossberg's hypothesis. It seems likely that the *Book of Remedies* has been falsely attributed to Maimonides and was probably authored by Raymond Lull in the thirteenth century, as was proven by the elegant research of Benjamin Richler.[13]

In the Hebrew publication *Kiryat Sefer*, Richler discusses a *Book of Wisdom* or *Book of Raminos* and its relationship to the fifty sections (literally: gates) attributed to Maimonides. The *Book of Raminos* is described by Richler as a book of remedies from the thirteenth century, or perhaps somewhat earlier, that is almost unknown in the Jewish medical literature of the Middle Ages. Internal evidence alludes to its composition outside Germany. The book consists of the search for wisdom by young Raminos, who was accepted as a student of philosophy and medicine by Arimon in Chaldea. The book gives general recommendations for the preservation of health. One chapter is followed by the following statement: "Behold, I am adding to all this fifty sections [literally: gates] which I call fifty gifts. Conceal them as much as you can and do not teach them to any person." Richler points out that his friend, Shmuel Ashkenazi, told him that these fifty sections are identical with the composition by this name attributed to Maimonides in the London manuscript that was published in London in 1900 by Menashe Grossberg. It is still not clear whether the fifty sections are part of the original book or whether they were added by one of the copyists. Early evidence points to the fact that at the end of the thirteenth century they were already considered to be part of the *Book of Raminos*.

My own view is that the *Book of Remedies* is spurious. There is no extant Arabic manuscript, and it is known that with the exception of the *Mishneh Torah*, all of Maimonides' writings were composed in Arabic. The text itself is not similar to other writings of Maimonides with which I am familiar, including his ten authentic medical treatises. The *Book of Remedies* is full of errors, and the author jumps from topic to topic. Many of the statements contradict what Maimonides wrote in the fourth chapter of his *Hilkhot Deot* and elsewhere. For example, section 43 asserts that all purgatives are harmful, but Maimonides recommends them. Finally, the *Book of Remedies* is not mentioned at all by Steinschneider, Kroner, or Muntner, the renowned Maimonidean scholars. For all of these reasons, I believe that the *Book of Remedies* has been falsely attributed to Maimonides.

THE PHYSICIAN'S PRAYER (*TEFILLAT HA-ROFE*)

The Physician's Prayer attributed to Moses Maimonides is a lofty and beautiful prayer that first appeared in print in a German periodical in 1783.[14] The editor of this journal, Heinrich Christian Boie, and his associate, Christian Wilhelm Dohn, provide no notes or commentaries or any indication as to who the author is. The prayer bears only the title, "Daily prayer of a physician before he visits his patients: From the Hebrew manuscript of a renowned Jewish physician in Egypt from the twelfth century." Since the 1783 German edition, numerous versions, abbreviations, or excerpts thereof have been presented in English, German, Hebrew, French, Dutch, and Spanish. There are undoubtedly others. Much heated debate exists among various writers and scholars concerning the true authorship of the prayer. Elsewhere, I presented the controversy chronologically[15] and concluded, based mainly on the work of Leibowitz[16] that the evidence strongly favors the concept that the physician's prayer attributed to Maimonides is a spurious work, not written by Maimonides but composed by an eighteenth-century writer, probably Marcus Herz. Absolute proof is, however, lacking, and may never be discovered.

LAST WILL AND TESTAMENT (*SHAARE HA-MUSAR*)

The first mention I found of a "Last Will and Testament" of Moses Maimonides was in an appendix to the 1800 book *Lekah Tov* by Abraham Yagal, published in Warsaw. The title of the will is "A very beautiful moral instruction by Moses Maimonides to his son the Sage Rabbi Abraham." The same title was used in a collection of responsa and letters of Maimonides published in 1859 in which the will was reprinted.[17]

In 1926, Israel Abrahams published "The Gate of Instruction Attributed to Maimonides" (*Shaare ha-Musar ha-Meyuhas le-ha-Rambam*) in a collection of Hebrew Ethical Wills[18] in Hebrew and English. Abrahams hypothesizes that, although the manuscript is a fifteenth-century copy, it points to an older origin. In several places, the copyist must have had an old and faded manuscript before him, as he frequently was unable to read the original. It seems most probable, continues Abrahams, that the text is a product of the early thirteenth century and was thus written soon after Maimonides' death. The writer adopts several of the most prominent Maimonidean views, including the doctrines of free will and the mean or golden path. Abrahams concludes that the text is unmistakably not by Maimonides because the writer addresses his *children* in the plural, yet we know of only one child of Maimonides, his son Abraham.

In 1957, Jacob Minkin reprinted Abrahams' English translation of Maimonides' Ethical Testament as an appendix to his (Minkin's) book, *The World of Moses Maimonides*.[19] Minkin admits that scholars such as Steinschneider, Graetz, and Abrahams consider the testament to be spurious. Yet Minkin tries to justify its authenticity because its moral and ethical teachings are similar to those of Maimonides.

In 1970, David Margalith reprinted the Hebrew version of the Testament.[20] He concludes, as do Steinschneider and Abrahams, that the *Last Will and Testament* of Maimonides is a spurious work but worthy of being studied. Margalith states that its style differs from the style of Maimonides' *Guide for the Perplexed* and other works "like the distance from East to West."

SCROLL OF THE UNREVEALED (*MEGILLAT SETARIM*)

The *Megillat Setarim,* attributed to Maimonides, is essentially a letter with kabbalistic views that are foreign to all known authentic writings of Maimonides. Although the true author is unknown, it was clearly not written by Maimonides. Since the contents deal primarily with the secrets of the Torah and mystical and kabbalistic statements, it is better translated *Scroll of the Unrevealed.*

Megillat Setarim was first published in 1778 in Karetz in the kabbalistic work entitled *Shoshan Sodot (Rose of Secrets).* This book, whose author is not named, is said to have originated with the disciples of Moses Nachmanides and was printed by John Anton Krieger. Within this book is a statement by the author on page 31a that he found a letter called *Megaleh Amukot (Revealer of Profundities)* that was sent by Moses Maimonides to his distinguished disciple and scholar Rabbi Joseph.

The author of *Shoshan Sodot* calls this letter "the voice of Maimonides in his beautiful language" but then asserts that the contents of the letter concern matters that seem to be the words of kabbalists and astrologers. He therefore suggests that the letter may be by one of Maimonides' disciples, who wrote it in his teacher's name.

In 1856, Zvi Hirsch Edelman published a book in Koenigsberg entitled

Hemdah Genuzah (Concealed Delight) containing a variety of "dear and esteemed treatises" that heretofore had been unavailable, which he edited and annotated from various manuscripts and other sources. Within this book, on pages 42 to 45, is a "Letter attributed to Moses Maimonides, and known by the name *Megillat Setarim [Scroll of the Unrevealed]*." Edelman clearly states that his intent was not to support or negate the attribution of authorship to Maimonides and leaves it "up to the judges to judge."

In 1988, Shilat published a collection of Maimonides' letters in a two-volume work.[21] In a discussion of six spurious works attributed to Maimonides, Shilat discusses *Megillat Setarim,* whose main contents comprise "praises of Kabbalah and its preference over philosophy, instructions in practical Kabbalah and the use of holy [that is divine] names."

Shilat cites the various published editions of *Megillat Setarim,* including the first version in 1778, in *Shoshan Sodot.* He states that according to Azulai (also known as *Hidah*) in his work *Shem ha-Gedolim,* the author of *Shoshan Sodot* is Rabbi Moshe ben Jacob of Kiev, who lived about 350 years after Maimonides. Shilat also expresses doubt whether Rabbi Moses Alshakar, who mentions *Megillat Setarim* in his Responsa 117, seriously attributed this letter to Maimonides or whether he used it only to protest against those who were disrespectful of Maimonides.

According to Shilat, "there is not even a shadow of a doubt" that *Megillat Setarim* is a forgery, and he offers a series of reasons.

In a general way, concludes Shilat, one can say that legends like "at the end of his day, Maimonides reverted [to Kabbalah]" do not add honor either to Maimonides or to Kabbalah. The proper way to compare the philosophical teaching of Maimonides with the wisdom of Kabbalah is to descend into the depths of the divine perceptions of both and to openly examine and compare them, as was done by many sages and kabbalists throughout the generations, and not by artificial coercion of one over the other.

LETTER ON THE MESSIAH OF ISFAHAN

In 1881, Adolf Neubauer published a pseudobiography in Hebrew of Moses Maimonides, based on manuscript no. 1767 of the *Bet ha-Midrash* in London.[22] The following year Neubauer published, in Hebrew and in French translation, an analogous apocryphal document that he considered of much greater interest because of the pseudomessianic movement of David Alroy, which is described therein with numerous details.[23] It consists of a pseudobiographical account of the life of Maimonides and includes a letter supposedly written by Maimonides to the Jewish community in Fez, about the Messiah who appeared in Isfahan. The letter states that the reason the Messiah is delaying the redemption of the Jewish people is that the time for the messianic redemption has not arrived, but is near. Maimonides describes how he investigated the authenticity of the Messiah by eighteen talmudic questions on Jewish law that he sent him.

In 1892, David Kaufmann wrote that the false letter, edited and published by Neubauer in 1882, exemplifies one of many historical or literary movements that tried to find support for their position in the writings of Maimonides and, therefore, falsified letters and whole books that they attributed to him.[24] Similarly, false passages were interpolated into authentic Maimonidean writings in order to support an opinion or accredit an impostor. Thus, Kabbalah tried to make Maimonides one of its partisans, as mentioned above about the *Nine Chapters* and the *Scroll of the Unrevealed*.

There is obviously a similarity between the spurious letter to the Jews of Fez concerning the Messiah of Isfahan and the authentic Maimonidean work *Epistle to Yemen* in that both deal, at least in part, with the Messiah. It is also understandable why the Jews of Provence were not aware of the *Epistle to Yemen*. In the year 1194 there was no Hebrew translation of the *Epistle to Yemen* and the Arabic original had not yet reached them.[25] Most scholars conclude that the Messiah of Isfahan is Menachem ben David Aldagi, better known as David Alroy.

I have found many biographical errors in the letter to the Jews of Fez about the Messiah of Isfahan which prove beyond a doubt that the letter is a hoax. The biography states that Maimonides and his father and brother sailed from Fez to Alexandria, whereas they actually sailed to Acco, Palestine. The biography states that Maimonides lived hidden in a cave for several years. There is no mention in any other source to support this fantasy. The entire story of Maimonides' servant and the interpretation of the king's dream is not found in any biography of Maimonides and is no doubt a fabrication. The biography states that the king gave Maimonides a wife from among the women of Fez and that he had a son named David, but there is no evidence to support this claim. Maimonides, as far as is known, had only one son, Abraham. The biography states that David, the brother of Maimonides, died of a serious illness, whereas in actuality he died in a shipwreck at sea.

The average day in the life of Maimonides, as described in the pseudobiography, is totally at variance with the authentic description by Maimonides himself of his busy schedule, found in his famous letter to Samuel Ibn Tibbon. Finally, the biography erroneously states that Maimonides died in the year 1202 instead of the known 1204 and that he was buried in Egypt instead of Tiberias, where his gravesite can be visited by all.

CONCLUSION

The *Treatise on the One Who Exists* is a small and somewhat obscure medical moral work. Part of its obscurity lies in its flowery language, which is a telltale clue that sets it apart from the plain, precise prose of Maimonides. The *Nine Chapters* includes passages from the kabbalistic work called the *Book of Creation*, which is never mentioned or alluded to in any Maimonidean work and which clashes with ideas and concepts in the *Guide for the Perplexed*. The author of the *Treatise on Eternal Bliss* intentionally tried to create the impression that the treatise emanated from the pen of Maimonides, perhaps to dissuade people who were influenced by Aristotle and others. In spite of the fact that these and the other above-discussed works were not written by Maimonides, they are important to be made known to the English reader.

20

The State of Maimonidean Scholarship Today and Prospects for the Future

Jacob I. Dienstag

The time has come to make an inventory of the state of Maimonidean scholarship. The source for this so-called inventory is my bibliography of Maimonidean scholarship, at which I have labored for the last several decades. Unlike other Jewish philosophers and sages, Maimonides has been the subject of research, not only by Jewish but also by Christian and Moslem scholars.

PHILOSOPHY AND THEOLOGY

Let us begin with philosophy and theology. My bibliography is divided into two parts: subjects or topics, alphabetically arranged, from Allegorical interpretation to *Zohar,* and personalities, also arranged alphabetically, from Abravanel to the kabbalist Menahem Zion. The table of contents for topics occupies 14 pages and includes about 500 topics.

The table of contents for the second part, personalities, occupies 19 pages and includes 630 personalities. To sum up: there are more than 10,000 entries in the field of philosophy and theology. Sample sections of both divisions have been published in various scholarly journals and Festschriften.[1]

HALAKHAH

I do not, in this survey, touch on the subject of *halakhah*. I believe that in order to avoid duplication, Maimonides as a halakhist must be researched simultaneously with the *Talmudic Encyclopedia*. Practically every entry in the *Encyclopedia* refers (in the footnotes) to Maimonides' works: *Mishneh Torah, Sefer ha-Mitzvot, Commentary to the Mishnah,* and *Responsa*.[2]

THE LITERATURE ON MAIMONIDEAN MEDICINE: A SURVEY

The literature on Maimonidean medicine consists, of course, of the works by Maimonides written in Arabic – about eleven works. The definitive Hebrew editions were edited by the late Professor Suessman Muntner;[3] German translations by Hermann Kroner and others;[4] English translations by Professor Fred Rosner and others.[5] *The Extracts of Galen* was recently translated by Professor Uri Barzel.[6]

There are also translations in Italian,[7] Spanish,[8] and French.[9] Of singular interest is a Russian translation of the *Regimen Sanitatis* which was published during the Stalin regime (1930).[10]

Another field in Maimonidean medical scholarship is the literature on specific subjects: anatomy, botany, cardiovascular system, chest diseases, circumcision, dentistry, dermatology, epilepsy, gynecology, heart disease, melatherapy (music therapy), metabolism, ophthalmology, pharmacology, psychosomatics, sexual hygiene, surgery, tuberculosis, urology, veterinary medicine, zoology.

The literature also includes the various personalities in Maimonidean thought and scholarship: Aristotle, Galenus, Harvey, Hippocrates, Zahalon, and many others – about 100 more names.

Quite a literature is dedicated to Maimonides the physician in folklore and legend, also in fiction and poetry.

We are also enriched by artistic representation of Maimonides the physician.

Spurious works were attributed to Maimonides, e.g., *The Prayer for Physicians* and the *Sefer Refuot,* now translated into English by Professor Rosner.[11]

The list of works by and about Maimonides the physician runs to about 1,500 entries. It would amount to about 300 pages in print.

MAIMONIDES' HYGIENIC PRINCIPLES

The neglect of one's health is regarded as a sin in Judaism, where physical well-being is looked upon as a religious command. "And live through them, but not die through them" (*Yoma* 85b, based on Leviticus 18:5) is the principle applied to all the laws of the Bible. Maimonides accordingly dedicated a special section to hygiene or health laws, entitled *Hilkhot Deot* (Laws of Moral Disposition) (chapter 4).

"One should aim to maintain physical health and vigor in order that his soul may be upright," the sage writes, "in order to know God . . . Whoever follows this course will be continually serving God."[12]

My bibliography on this section is organized according to the following subdivisions:

1. editions and translations (arranged by language);
2. commentaries on *Hilkhot Deot,* chapter 4;
3. essays and studies on *Hilkhot Deot*;
4. versifications of these hygienic principles.

MAIMONIDES THE SCIENTIST

Unlike the art of medicine, which Maimonides chose as the means of earning his livelihood, his interest in science for its own sake is displayed by various excurses throughout his rabbinical writings on botany, chemistry, technology, zoology, and astronomy. The sage's treatise *On the Theory of the Calendar* and the astronomical chapters of his *Laws Concerning the Sanctification of the New Moon* deal with one of the most difficult problems of ancient and medieval astronomy, namely to determine in advance the visibility of the new crescent.[13]

A pioneer in the struggle against astrology, he was inspired to write his famous *Epistle to the Rabbis of Marseilles* on this subject. This section, too, has been the subject of scholarly research since the thirteenth century.[14] Besides the commentaries on the above-mentioned *Sanctification of the New Moon,* attention has been given by modern scholars and historians of science to such subjects as agriculture, alchemy, chemistry, ecology, genetics, horology, international date line, metrology, numismatics, physics, space, time, vacuum, and many others. Like the previous disciplines, this subject also includes a section on personalities in the history of science and its relation to Maimonides, e.g., Aristotle, Einstein, Euclid, Ptolemy, and others.

My bibliography includes about 900 entries.

ART

Since the *Mishneh Torah* is supposed to be the constitution of the Jewish State in Messianic times, *Hilkhot Bet ha-Behirah,* the laws of the Temple, are included.

Maimonides was therefore obliged to describe its architecture. This section of Maimonides' *Code* was ignored by rabbinic scholars. The obvious reason is that they were not architects. Secondly, it is also due to the fact that it belongs to *Hilkheta li-Meshihah*, laws deferred to the messianic days.

However, attempts were made to study Maimonides' description of the Temple by the late Professor Rachel Wischnitzer (1885–1989)[15] and by the late Helen Rosenau (1900–1984).[16]

What surprised me was the fact that the architect whose name is associated with the Louvre in Paris got involved in a commentary on Maimonides' *Laws Concerning the Temple*. I am referring to Claude Perrault (1613–1688), who was invited by Ludovicus de Compiegne de Veil to comment on his Latin translation of the *Laws Concerning the Temple*.[17]

Veil, who converted to Catholicism and afterward to Protestantism, was a descendant of Rabbi Jacob Weil of Nuerenberg. To his credit, however, is the very idea of inviting the famous architect, Perrault, to comment on Maimonides' description of the Temple.[18] Unfortunately, nowhere will you find Perrault's name in classical Jewish scholarship.

Like Professor Otto Neugebauer, a German non-Jew, the foremost historian of astronomy, who wrote an astronomic commentary to the English translation of Maimonides' *Sanctification of the New Moon*,[19] Perrault brought his architectural knowledge to this subject.

Unfortunately, Perrault wrote his work in Latin and escaped the attention of Jewish scholars, but not the famed philosopher Leibniz[20] and scientist Isaac Newton.[21] An English translation of his commentary would be a welcome contribution to Maimonidean scholarship.

Very little has been written on this subject. We would welcome the contributions of scholarly architects.

PROSPECTS FOR THE FUTURE

In surveying the vast literature, one gets the impression that specialized studies in the various disciplines we referred to will continue ad infinitum. "With so many trees one does not see the forest." Maimonides has become a discipline in itself.

The time is therefore ripe for the compilation of a Maimonides encyclopedia.

The work, which would have articles on all the topics and personalities we referred to, should also include, in the same alphabetical arrangement, a directory of scholars and their contributions to Maimonidean scholarship.

Scholars in Israel, Europe, and America are qualified to undertake this project.

21

Maimonides and the Cure-all Book

Yehudah Gellman

The *Mishnah* in *Pesahim* 4:10 relates that King Hezekiah concealed a *sefer refuot*, a "book of remedies," and that the wise men of his generation concurred in this act. In his commentary to this *Mishnah*, Maimonides offers two explanations as to what the "book of remedies" was: (1) It was a book of talismanic cures, concealed because such treatment is forbidden; (2) the book contained antidotes to poisons, and was concealed when people began to use it to gain information on how to poison their enemies.[1]

My interest here is not in Maimonides' own interpretation of the Mishnah, but on his rejection of an alternative explanation, cited by Rashi and Nachmanides, of what the "book of remedies" was, and why it was concealed. This alternative explanation states that the Mishnah refers to a book, written by King Solomon, that any person suffering from any illness could consult, do as instructed, and become cured. In other words, the *sefer refuot* was a "cure-all" book. However, since people depended on the book instead of turning to God to be cured, King Hezekiah concealed the cure-all book, restoring public piety to its proper place.

Maimonides objects to this explanation for two reasons. The first is that it is a "nothingness" and is "hallucinatory" in character, the Arabic term here, *hathiyan*, akin to the Hebrew word *hazayah*, meaning "hallucination."

Maimonides' second objection is that just as a person thanks God for the bread God gives him, so too he thanks God after being cured by a medicine.

There is, therefore, no reason to think that a cure-all book weakens one's sense of dependence on the Creator. On the contrary, a cure-all book reinforces a believer's faith in God.

I will here limit myself only to the first objection of Maimonides to the cure-all book, which is that the interpretation in terms of a cure-all book is "hallucinatory" in character. The discussion will focus on what Maimonides meant by "hallucination" and why he thought this rejected explanation was involved in such an hallucination.

Ibn Tibbon, Hebrew translator of Maimonides' *Guide for the Perplexed* from Arabic, translates *hathiyan* as equivalent to "hallucination" or "craziness." Shlomo Pines, in his English translation of the *Guide*, renders it as "raving" or "crazy imagining." And in his list of Hebrew philosophical terms translated from the Arabic, Ibn Tibbon defines the Hebrew equivalent for *hathiyan, hazayah*, as follows: "It means the speaking of nonsense, devoid of substance, in the manner of those who speak confusedly in their sleep, or in the case of some sick people."[2]

Maimonides used *hathiyan* in a *technical* way, to denote strings of words that are conceptually incoherent. In particular, Maimonides' use of this term relates to word strings that contain metaphysical category-mistakes. This thesis is suggested by the word's occurrence in Ibn Tibbon's list of philosophical terms, and confirmed by examining three places in the *Guide* where Maimonides employs the term *hathiyan*.

Maimonides' first objection to the cure-all book is not based merely on its implausibility as an actual historical reality, but on the claim that the very thought that there *could* be such a thing is conceptually incoherent.

In the *Guide for the Perplexed* (3:34), Maimonides contrasts medicine with Torah in regard to their respective scopes of applicability.[3] Torah legislation, says Maimonides, does not vary its laws for differences between individuals. Medicine does. Medicine is as variegated as variations between people, climates, ages, and so forth. Maimonides explains the difference between medicine and Divine legislation as follows:

> For in everything that it wishes to bring about, [the Law] is directed only toward the things that occur in the majority of cases and pays no attention to what happens rarely or to the damage occurring to the unique human being because of this way of determination and because of the legal character of the governance. . . . The general utility [of the Law] . . . necessarily produces damages to individuals. You will not wonder at the fact that the purpose of the Law is not perfectly achieved in every individual and that, on the contrary, it necessarily follows that there should exist individuals whom this governance of the Law does not make perfect. *For not everything that derives necessarily from the natural specific forms is actualized in every individual.* [p. 534, my emphasis]

Maimonides wishes to convey here that the Divine legislation is perfectly suited to bring the form of man to a full embodiment. However, not every individual can embody the form of man to the same extent. The greater the potential in an individual for the embodiment of the form of man, the greater the congruence of the Divine legislation to the situation of that particular individual.

Here we meet a crucial principle: "Not everything that derives necessarily from the natural specific form is actualized in every individual." That is, a given person may not have the potential to successfully embody the form of man. The reason for this proposal, in turn, is a principle attributed to Galen in *Guide* 3:12, where Maimonides writes:

> Everything that is capable of being generated from any matter whatever, is generated in the most perfect way in which it is possible to be generated out of that specific matter; the deficiency attaining the individuals of the species corresponds to the deficiency of the particular matter of the individual. [p. 444]

Individuals are composed of form and matter. The specific matter of which a given individual is composed may resist by its very nature the embodiment of the species-form in it. In principle, in such a case the form will not be perfectly or fully realizable in that individual. So Maimonides writes of individuals who are mere copies of real men.

Galen's principle is perfectly general, applying to all species compounded of form and matter, and expresses, for Maimonides, a general metaphysical truth that whereas form, metaphorically speaking, tries to impose its will on matter, matter has a mind of its own.

This principle occurs again in *Guide* 2:19, which states that there is "great latitude with regard to quantity and quality," in individual embodiment of species forms (p. 304).

Returning to *Guide* 3:34, Galen's metaphysical principle explains why there are individuals not benefited or even harmed by Divine legislation, even though the latter is perfectly congruent to the form of man. This is because the specific matter of which such individuals are composed cannot adequately embody the form of man. Hence the ends of Torah legislation become thwarted. It is a matter of sheer metaphysical necessity that there be such individuals, because of the contribution of matter to species-instantiation.

The Torah is absolute and universal for Maimonides, not in that it applies to every individual in an optimal way to guide him to individual perfection, but in the sense in which its authority is binding on every individual, regardless of whether or not all individuals are perfected by it. Given Galen's principle, Maimonides says that Torah legislation is perfectly rational, no better legislation being possible.

Medicine accommodates prescriptions for action to individual needs. Given Galen's principle, there must be anomalies in the embodiment of the human form by individuals. Medicine, as opposed to Torah, addresses itself to the entire range of form-embodiment, including those resulting from the recalcitrance of specific matter.

But Galen's principle is only one source of anomalies in men. If we call the anomalies resulting from Galen's principle "structural anomalies," we may say that Maimonides recognizes a second type of anomaly in addition to structural ones. In his *Treatise on Asthma,* Maimonides writes that it can happen that

> the physician does everything he is supposed to do to great perfection, without error, neither from him nor from the patient, and the patient does not improve and get healthy, which is the goal. This is because that which acts in us is not medicine alone, but medicine and nature together. And sometimes nature does not listen to many causes, some of which we have mentioned in this treatise. Similarly, one who works the earth, will do everything in the right way, and the seed may not succeed. And so the sailor steers his ship in accordance with the best sort of sailing, and builds the structure, and goes to sea at the appropriate time, and the ship may be wrecked. And the reason for all of this is that the goal in each case comes from two agents, and whereas one does everything in the right way, the other comes up short.[4]

It is a mistake to interpret Maimonides as attributing the failures of the physician, farmer, and sailor, respectively, to a deficiency in their knowledge of nature, because Maimonides repeats in each instance that the agent in question acted correctly. Furthermore, in none of the cases is reference made to unforeseen circumstances. The sailor sets sail at the right time. No storm rises to defeat his best efforts. The ship simply breaks apart at sea. The farmer's seed is not defeated by drought or disease. It just does not grow. The physician is not being mocked for thinking he knows all there is to know. The patient is just not cured. Maimonides' point is not about our epistemological limitations, but about nature's metaphysical limitations.

Maimonides is saying here that nature, of itself, manifests anomalies that cannot be correlated with lawlike generalizations of any kind. This type of anomaly defies not only species-correlative generalizations, but any detailed generalizations about individuals. In the case of medicine, these anomalies defy all formulations, however detailed, including factors of age, bodily constitution, climate, and whatever else one includes. Let us call such anomalies "deep anomalies." Deep anomalies, like their structural cousins, result from species-composition in which specific matter resists law-likeness.

Thus species-embodiment yields deviation from generalizations in two ways: first, through structural anomalies resulting from wide differences in the degree to which specific matter can successfully receive a given form; and secondly, through deep anomalies, deeper than the level of form, defying all detailed generalizations.

We can now appreciate the two-tiered conceptual incoherence Maimonides thought to reside in the "hallucinatory ravings" of there having been a cure-all book.

First, to think that a single book can list the cure for every illness fails to see that structural anomalies are a metaphysical necessity in the species of man, individuals displaying wide variations in "quantity and quality." Therefore, no single book can contain all remedies. It could not be long enough to include all possible variations in the human condition. In his *Treatise on Asthma*, Maimonides says that even to only give the details of this one illness (asthma) would be too long for a single treatise.[5] A cure-all book is impossible, unless one thinks of medicine as a legislation, universal and absolute, that does not attend to individual differences. Then the cure-all book would be something like a medical Torah scroll. This approach, though, would be conceptually incoherent with the idea of medicine.

Secondly, to think that everyone without exception can be cured by a cure-all book is to fail to recognize deep anomalies in the human species. Specific matter can defeat the application of every generality, even the most individualized, as we saw in the *Treatise on Asthma*. To deny this necessity is to lapse into the conceptual incoherence of thinking of matter as being as round and smooth as form.

My interpretation of the term *hathiyan* is corroborated by a review of its occurrence in three places in the *Guide*. With each, the allusion is to the same conceptual incoherence, namely, the conceptual mistake of failing to recognize that a form might be imperfectly realizable in matter because of both structural and deep anomalies.

The first instance occurs in the previously mentioned chapter on evil in *Guide* 3:12. The relevant passage reads as follows:

> Every ignoramus imagines that all that exists exists with a view to his individual sake; it is as if there were nothing that exists except him. . . . However, if man considered and represented to himself that which exists and knew the smallness of his part in it, the truth would become clear and manifest to him. For this extensive *raving* entertained by men with regard to the multitude of evils in the world is not said by them [except with regard to] some individuals belonging to the human species. [p. 442, my emphasis]

The word translated by Pines as "raving" is *hathiyan*. Later in this chapter, Maimonides replies to the view that everything exists for the sake of the individual, by stating that individuals exist with their ills for the sake of the species. Because of Galen's principle, if the species of man exists at all, deficient individuals exist. The species' existence is so valuable that evils inherent in individuals from defective matter are justified. Maimonides says:

> Now the true way of considering this is that all the existent individuals of the human species and, all the more, those of the other species of the animals are things of no value at all in comparison with the whole that exists and en-

dures.... The greater part of the evils that befall its individuals are due to the latter, I mean the deficient individuals of the human species. [pp. 442, 443]

So the problem of evil generated by the view that the universe exists for the sake of the individual and that, therefore, the individual's ills are not justified, is answered in part for Maimonides by saying that the individual ills exist for the sake of the existence of the species as a whole.

Notice, now, how the view that everything exists for the sake of the individual, and, therefore, individual imperfections are unjustified, becomes a conceptual error of a metaphysical sort. It violates Galen's metaphysical principle that the instantiation of a species is beholden to the whims of matter and pretends that the ways form becomes embodied have nothing to do with whether and to what extent specific matter is capable of embodying the form. It treats matter as uniform and smooth as form. This is an incoherent "raving."

The second reference to hallucination is in *Guide* 2:25, where Maimonides explains why he rejects the eternity of the world in favor of creation *ex nihilo*. The text reads as follows:

> The belief in eternity the way Aristotle sees it – that is, the belief according to which the world exists in virtue of necessity, that no nature changes at all, and that the customary course of events cannot be modified with regard to anything – destroys the Law in its principle, necessarily gives the lie to every miracle, and reduces to inanity all the hopes and threats that the Law has held out, unless ... one interprets the miracles figuratively also, as was done by the Islamic internalists; this, however, would result in some sort of *crazy imagining*. [p. 328, my emphasis]

The term translated here as "crazy imagining" is the same as translated elsewhere as "raving" or "hallucination."

The Aristotelian view that there are no miracles is, for Maimonides, the same conceptual mistake as the previous ones we have examined. The reason can be summarized in five points:

1. Galen's principle that matter can defeat the instantiation of form applies to all species composed of matter, not only to man.
2. It follows that a metaphysically necessary corollary of the existence of nature is the existence of anomalies within all species.
3. Maimonides works within an Aristotelian framework in which the law-likeness of nature is reducible to the shared potencies of objects. Likeness of potencies makes for uniformity of nature.
4. The corollary of that reduction is that Galen's principle entails the

nonabsolute uniformity of nature, since potencies of objects are a result of the embodiment of forms.

5. Hence, the supposition that miracles do not exist involves a conceptual error exactly the same as that involved in the previous two uses of the term for hallucination. To say that miracles do not occur is equivalent to denying that objects deviate from generalizations constructed from shared potencies. And to deny that is to fail to recognize the necessity of such deviations.

Such a reading of Maimonides' criticism of Aristotle on miracles imposes a striking uniformity upon his use of the term "hallucination." Maimonides forges a strong link between the idea of miracle and the idea of metaphysically necessary deviations from the generalities of shared potencies. This approach leads to a rethinking of several passages in which Maimonides deals with the topic of miracles.

The third appearance of *hathiyan* is in the introduction to the *Guide,* where Maimonides describes two types of philosophical parables. In the first, every element in the parable corresponds to an element in the interpretation, yielding *isomorphic interpretation.*

In the second type of parable, not every element in the parable corresponds to an element in the intended interpretation. The parable contains elements that merely embellish the image or help conceal the true meaning. Such parables are interpreted only as to their overall idea. Maimonides then says that most parables are of this second type, and warns against attempting to interpret every element of a parable:

> The assumption of such an obligation would result in *extravagant fantasies* such as are entertained and written about in our time by most of the sects of the world, since each of these sects desires to find certain significations for words whose author in no wise had in mind the significations wished by them. [p. 14, my emphasis]

The term for "extravagant fantasies" is *hathiyan.*

Consider now Maimonides' examples of the two types of parables. He illustrates isomorphic interpretation with the parable of Jacob's ladder, which in *Guide* 1:15 Maimonides explains to be about the prophet who gains knowledge of God and who then descends to teach the people. His example of nonisomorphic interpretation is the parable of the harlot, in Proverbs 7, which Maimonides explains to be about matter hindering individuals from reaching their perfection.

How wondrous are Maimonides' words! His example of an isomorphic interpretation concerns matter perfectly embodying the form of man. The prophet comes to knowledge of God, matter not interfering, as with the angels, who for Maimonides are disembodied intellects (*Guide* 2:10). His example of a nonisomorphic parable concerns the opposite: the failure of matter to embody form. These examples, then, perfectly illustrate the topic: the fit of parable to interpretation.

Maimonides thinks of a parable as analogous to matter and of the intended philosophical interpretation as analogous to the form which the parable is to embody. Sometimes matter embodies form perfectly, as in the prophet and as in isomorphic interpretation. But most of the time matter is faithful to the form only roughly and with wide variations, as with a harlot and as with the parable that does not fit the interpretation isomorphically. In such cases, elements of the parable are dictated by the nature of the parable itself, and not by elements of the interpretation. In those cases, matter has a mind of its own, not shaping itself wholly around the contours of the form.

Furthermore, the parable of the ladder itself contains the notion of which Maimonides writes. The prophet ascends to the realm of knowledge of forms, and then descends to the realm of parable which he employs to convey his knowledge to the masses.

This passage, therefore, resembles an Escher painting, turning on itself again and again. The topic of parable and interpretation is reflected in the choice of illustrations of each type of parable, and again in the structure of the illustrations themselves.

To think, therefore, that most parables have isomorphic interpretations is a mistake analogous to thinking that matter does not have a mind of its own. Hence, believing in isomorphic interpretation for the majority of parables is an "hallucinatory raving."

22

Maimonides' Approach to Jewish Bioethics in the Areas of the Treatment of the Critically Ill and Abortion

Daniel B. Sinclair

INTRODUCTION

This chapter deals with two passages in Maimonides' *Mishneh Torah,* one of which concerns the killing of a person suffering from a fatal organic defect and the other dealing with therapeutic abortion. In both passages, Maimonides appears to deviate from the definitive talmudic sources and formulate his ruling on the basis of moral principles. Both rulings have strongly influenced modern *halakhah* in the areas of the treatment of the critically ill and abortion. Therefore, their analysis is vital for an understanding of contemporary Jewish bioethics in these areas.

MORALITY AND LAW IN RELATION TO THE TERMINALLY ILL

According to the Talmud, the killer of a *terefah,* a person suffering from a fatal organic defect,[1] is exempt from the death penalty.[2] Underlying this exemption is the principle that capital punishment is not administered for taking the life of an individual who would have died in any case.[3] R. Menahem Meiri uses this exemption in order to derive a novel ruling in relation to the case in the *Tosefta* of a group of travelers who are threatened by brigands and given the choice between death and delivering up one of their number to the slaughter.[4]

According to the *Tosefta*, a person may be handed over, provided that a specific request was made for that person. This provision is immediately qualified. According to one view, the specified individual may be delivered up only if the whole group – including the individual specified – is faced with certain death unless the brigands' request is met. Another view maintains that the person singled out is only to be delivered up if he is guilty of a crime. R. Meiri makes the following observation regarding this case: "It goes without saying that in the case of a group of travelers, if one of them was a *terefah* he may be surrendered in order to save the lives of the rest, since the killer of a *terefah* is exempt from the death penalty."[5]

According to R. Meiri, the exemption of the killer of a *terefah* from the death penalty indicates that the *terefah*'s life is inferior to that of a viable individual in situations such as that of the travelers' case.

R. Meiri's position is supported by R. Joseph Babad, who explains that the reason for not sacrificing one person for the sake of saving the life of another is the talmudic dictum: "How do you know that your blood is redder? Perhaps the blood of the other person is redder?"[6] In the case of a *terefah*, this reason does not apply, since his blood is indeed "less red" than that of a viable person. The life of a *terefah* may, therefore, be sacrificed in order to preserve that of a viable individual.[7]

This view was rejected by R. Ezekiel Landau, who maintains that the fact that there is no capital punishment for taking the life of a *terefah* does not mean that he can be killed for the sake of saving a viable person: "The very idea that a *terefah* might be killed for the sake of preserving a viable life is unheard of."[8] In a case in which one member of a group under threat is a *terefah*, the correct solution is to remain passive and not to give up a *terefah* to certain death.

Later authorities discuss the possibility of applying R. Meiri's recommendation,[9] which has assumed fresh significance in the era of cardiac transplants. In analyzing the halakhic permissibility of such transplants, one modern scholar suggests that a key question is whether or not R. Meiri's position is halakhically valid. Clearly, the removal of a heart from a *terefah* donor would be far less problematic for the school of R. Meiri than it would for that of R. Landau.[10] The notion that the exemption of the killer of a *terefah* from capital punishment is a relevant factor in permitting heart transplants is not an unfamiliar one in contemporary halakhic writing, and it has also been read into the Israeli Chief Rabbinate's decision to permit such operations.[11]

For the purposes of the present discussion, however, it is not necessary to draw conclusions on this matter. All that needs to be shown is that the talmudic statement regarding the killing of a *terefah* provides a basis for arguing that in certain situations, it is legitimate to consider sacrificing a *terefah* for the sake of saving viable life. The next step is to demonstrate how Maimonides formulates this talmudic ruling in such a way that it no longer serves as a basis for any such argument.

In Maimonides' *Laws of Homicide*, the talmudic provision concerning the killing of a *terefah* is codified in the following terms: "If one kills another who suffers from a fatal organic disease, he is exempt from human law even though the victim ate and drank and walked out on the streets. But every human being is presumed to be healthy, and his murderer must be put to death unless it is known for certain that he had a fatal organic disease."[12]

The phrase, "exempt from human law" indicates that the killer is nevertheless subject to Divine punishment. What is Maimonides' source for the notion that the killer of a *terefah* is liable under Divine law?

In the same chapter of the *Laws of Homicide*, Maimonides invokes Divine penalties for committing murder by proxy, indirect homicide, and suicide. This time, he states his source for this provision:

> How do we know that this is the rule? Because Scripture says, "Whoever sheds man's blood, by man shall his blood be shed" (*Genesis* 9:6) referring to one who commits murder himself and not through an agent; "And surely your blood of your lives will I require" (*Genesis* 9:5) referring to suicide; "At the hand of every beast will I require it" (*Genesis* 9:5) referring to one who places another before a wild animal for it to devour; "And at the hand of man even at the hand of every man's brother will I require the life of man" (*Genesis* 9:5) referring to one who hires others to kill someone. In these last three cases, the verb "require" is used expressly to show that their judgment is reserved for Heaven.[13]

There is no precise talmudic or midrashic precedent for this exegesis. Indeed, some scholars maintain that any texts of the *Midrash Rabbah* on Genesis which mention Divine punishment for these offenses were, in fact, amended in the light of Maimonides' ruling and are not original.[14] Now, the *Talmud* does cite Genesis 9:5 as a proof text for R. Elazar's view that suicide constitutes a prohibited act.[15] There is, however, no mention of any Divine sanction against suicides, and the focus of the discussion is the establishment of a prohibition on self-injury.[16] There is also the view of Shammai the Elder that one who sends his agent to kill a man is liable to the death penalty. The Talmud concludes that this view would be unanimously acceptable if death penalty meant "at the hands of Heaven."[17] This conclusion, is not, however, supported by any of the texts cited by Maimonides in his ruling on murder by proxy.

It is important to note that what is at stake here is not merely the literary pedigree of Maimonides' ruling concerning those exempt from capital punishment, but the conceptual basis of this ruling. Maimonides extends the notion of Divine retribution for offenses for which there is no death penalty to many more cases than those derived from Genesis 9. Moreover, Maimonides invokes the extralegal jurisdiction of the king, as chief executive officer, to put to death those exempt from capital punishment as a result of insufficient or technically defective evidence or lack of a formal warning. He also calls upon the court to employ its discretionary jurisdiction to impose serious penalties upon such killers.[18] Once again, the question of a talmudic or midrashic precedent for these far-reaching provisions arises and, again, its resolution remains elusive both on the literary and conceptual levels.

R. MEIR SIMHA COHEN'S THEORY OF NATURAL LAW IN MAIMONIDES' LAWS OF HOMICIDE

An important clue to Maimonides' thinking on these issues is afforded by R. Meir Simha Cohen of Dvinsk, author of the *Or Sameah* on the *Mishneh Torah*. According to R. Cohen, Maimonides' requirement that the king execute all those who escape the death penalty by virtue of legal technicalities is based upon the following principle: ". . . an Israelite king is authorized by virtue of his role as the preserver of the social order to act according to the general Noahide code, and this is a rational principle."[19]

R. Cohen isolates two important elements. One is the Noahide code and the other is the notion of rationality *(inyan muskal)*. The Noahide code is the code which, according to Jewish tradition, bound the whole of mankind prior to the giving of the Torah on Mt. Sinai and continues to bind all non-Jews.[20] This code consists of seven major norms: the prohibitions on bloodshed, theft, immorality, idolatry, blasphemy, and tearing a limb from a living creature, and the positive obligation to set up a court system. These norms are complemented by others, and the whole system is known as the Noahide code, since the earliest known laws in the Bible were those given by God to Noah and his family on their emergence from the ark after the flood. The biblical passage outlining these laws is in Genesis 9 – the very passage cited by Maimonides as his basis for invoking Divine sanctions against murderers by proxy, indirect killers, and suicides! If R. Cohen is correct, Maimonides treats the Noahide code as binding upon Israelites and as empowering the Israelite king to execute those who infringe its provisions, at least in the instance of the prohibition on bloodshed. In principle, however, only non-Jews are bound by the Noahide laws in the post-Sinaitic period. On what basis does Maimonides incorporate the Noahide prohibition on bloodshed into Israelite law?

The answer to this question lies in the second element in R. Cohen's principle, i.e., rationality. The idea that the Noahide code comprises the natural law of Judaism is indicated in various rabbinic statements.[21] The classic doctrine of natural law is that of a universal law, binding by virtue of its rational appeal.[22] Maimonides states quite categorically that the seven laws of Noah are "inclined to by reason."[23] It is, therefore, arguable that Maimonides regards the dictates of the Noahide code as principles of a rational nature which are universally binding by virtue of that very rationality. Hence, even though Israelites are bound by the Torah, they are still liable to obey the precepts of the natural law. Revelation does not supersede rationality – it simply adds to it. Thus there is no objection to complementing the provisions of Jewish criminal law with those of the Noahide code. The only question which must be asked is whether or not a particular norm is indeed a universal, rational one. In relation to bloodshed, it is difficult to imagine a negative response. In this respect, it is noteworthy that the positivist H. L. A. Hart was prepared to entertain the notion of a "minimum content of Natural law" which would definitely embrace a prohibition on homicide.[24] A combination of the traditional canon of Noahide laws and the rational force of the prohibition on bloodshed constitutes – according to R. Meir Simhah – the literary and conceptual underpinning of Maimonides' approach to the punishment of killers exempt from human sanctions.

In fact, the idea that the Noahide offense of bloodshed binds Israelites even after the giving of the Torah is found in the *Midrash Halakhah*. According to Exodus 21:14: "If a man come presumptuously upon his neighbor to slay him with guile, you shall take him from My altar that he may die." The sages deduce from the term *neighbor* that an Israelite who kills a heathen is exempt from the death penalty, since only a fellow-Jew is included in that category. The following objection to this exegesis is then posed by one of the sages:

> Issi b. Akabyah says: Before the giving of the Torah, we had been warned against shedding blood. After the giving of the Torah, whereby laws were made stricter, shall they be considered lighter? In truth, the Sages said: He is free from judgment by the human court, but his judgment is left to Heaven.[25]

Issi b. Akabya's objection rests upon the premise that the Noahide offense of bloodshed constitutes a moral threshhold below which the *halakhah* cannot fall. The sages accept his argument and complement the technical exemption of the killer of a heathen from the death penalty with a Divine sanction,[26] and this is the definitive halakhic position.[27]

It must be emphasised that Maimonides' invocation of Divine sanctions – on the basis of the Noahide laws – against killers who are exempt from human punishment is conceptual and not merely literary. This emerges quite clearly from the fact that he applies these sanctions to cases which are not subsumed by the tradition under the provisions of the Noahide code. The murder of a *terefah* is one such case, and the commentators on the *Mishneh Torah* have been perplexed by the lack of any precedent for including the killing of a *terefah* in the list of offenses constituting bloodshed in the Noahide laws.[28] In conceptual terms, however, Maimonides' ruling is clear. Killing a *terefah* is an act of bloodshed and, as such, falls into the minimum natural law rubric of the *halakhah*. The exemption of the killer from regular criminal sanction notwithstanding, Divine penalties and the extralegal powers of the king and court are still applicable to him.

The rational element in the crime of bloodshed in Maimonidean jurisprudence is particularly evident in the following passage from the *Mishneh Torah* in which Maimonides refers to the talmudic requirement that murderers who escape capital punishment by virtue of a technical defect in the testimony against them nevertheless be severely punished for their deeds: "For although there are worse [in the theological sense] crimes than bloodshed, none causes such destruction to civilized society as bloodshed. Not even idolatry, nor immorality, nor the desecration of the Sabbath is the equal of bloodshed."[29]

Maimonides justifies the harsh measures taken against murderers who escape the death penalty on the basis of the rational principle of the preservation of civilized society. It is also noteworthy that Maimonides justifies the whole Noahide code in terms of preventing the world becoming corrupt and, undoubtedly, the offense of bloodshed plays a fundamental role in this justification.[30]

Maimonides' categorization of all forms of bloodshed as morally heinous and halakhically forbidden acts, together with his invocation of Divine sanctions against killers who are halachically exempt from the death penalty, constitute the major bar to the use of the *terefah* category in the context of terminating the treatment of the critically ill in modern Jewish bioethics. A good illustration of this point is the following statement of R. Moses Feinstein in a responsum on the question of permitting hazardous medical procedures for a fatally ill patient:

> The prohibition on killing a *terefah* applies equally to a Jew as to a Noahide by virtue of the Talmudic principle, "There is nothing permitted to an Israelite yet forbidden to a Noahide." Moreover, Maimonides explicitly provided that the killer of a *terefah* is exempt from human jurisdiction, implying that he is liable to Divine punishment in addition to having committed a transgression.[31]

Rabbi Feinstein's formulation is typical of the views of many modern authorities, and in this respect, Maimonides' subtle formulation of the talmudic material in his *Mishneh Torah* successfully thwarted any attempt to articulate a euthanasia policy based upon the *terefah* model. There are few finer examples of Maimonides' synthetic approach to morality and law in the *halakhah* than his treatment of killers exempt from capital punishment. Whether or not the Maimonidean synthesis is the only legitimate response to the serious moral problems posed by the terminally ill in modern medicine is, however, a separate question.

MAIMONIDES ON FETICIDE AND ABORTION

According to R. Meir Simha Cohen, the argument that renders the killer of a *terefah* liable to death at the hands of Heaven would also apply to one who commits feticide. Feticide is a capital crime under Noahide law.[32] It is also a form of bloodshed, although there are excellent moral arguments for justifying it in certain circumstances such as a threat to the mother's life. Feticide carries no positive sanction in Jewish criminal law.[33] R. Cohen concludes that any Israelite who carries out an unjustified abortion is liable to Divine retribution, since the act offends against both the Noahide code and the natural-law element of traditional Jewish jurisprudence.[34]

This line of reasoning is alluded to by the *Tosafot,* who argue that although an Israelite who kills a fetus is exempt from punishment, "nevertheless, it is not permitted."[35] The basis for this ruling is the principle that Jewish law cannot be more lenient than the provisions of the Noahide code.[36] Throughout the ages, various authorities have sought to flesh out this ruling in more substantive terms, but with little success. Clearly, the issue is one of morality rather than pure legal doctrine, and the point is nicely made by R. Yehiel Weinberg, who writes that "feticide is prohibited, but we simply do not know the nature of the prohibition."[37]

Maimonides himself does not specifically indicate in any place in his works that feticide is the subject of death at the hands of Heaven. He does, however, formulate the mishnaic ruling on therapeutic abortion in terms that make it as restrictive as possible. Therapeutic abortion is permitted in the following mishnah:

> If a woman is in hard travail, one cuts up the child in her womb and brings it forth, member by member, because her life comes before that of the child. But if the greater part has proceeded forth, one may not touch it, for one may not set aside one person's life for that of another.[38]

The standard justification for this ruling is that a fetus is not a person *(nefesh)* for the purposes of Jewish criminal law, and it may therefore be killed in order to save the mother.[39] Maimonides, however, provides an entirely different justification. He invokes the pursuer principle, i.e., the *halakhah* that if A is pursuing B to kill him, then C is required to prevent A from carrying out his evil design, even if this requires him to kill A:

> This is also a negative precept, namely, not to have compassion on the life of a pursuer. Therefore, the Sages ruled regarding a pregnant woman in hard travail, that it is permissible to dismember the fetus in her womb, whether by means of drugs or by hand, but if it has already put forth its head, it may not be touched, for one life may not be set aside for the sake of another one and this is the natural course of the world.[40]

This formulation is problematic in that the pursuer principle ought to apply to a baby after birth and not only prior to the emergence of the head. It ought to be permissible to kill a baby whose head has already emerged, if by so doing, the mother's life will be saved. Nevertheless, Maimonides restricts therapeutic abortion to the period prior to the head emerging from the woman's body. Moreover, the application of the pursuer principle to therapeutic abortion during childbirth would appear to be specifically rejected in the Babylonian Talmud.[41] In addition to these internal inconsistencies, the very analogy between a fetus and a pursuer is open to question. Surely, an important element in the pursuer principle is that the pursuer intends killing the individual being pursued! Is this the case in relation to a fetus? Does not Maimonides himself admit that the threat to maternal life is the result of "the natural course of the world"? These difficulties have exercised many scholars, and the general consensus would appear to be that Maimonides adopted a strictness in relation to feticide which requires a stronger justification for therapeutic abortion than the claim that the fetus is not a person.[42] The pursuer principle serves, therefore, as a reminder that fetal life is not to be taken lightly, even in a therapeutic context. Maimonides uses the pursuer analogy in order to shift the starting position from the nonpersonhood of the fetus to the proposition that the decision to kill a fetus is similar to the one made to kill a formed, viable pursuer. In the same way that great care is taken before the latter decision is operated on, so the former one ought only to be put into operation when all other options have failed. In this manner, Maimonides builds the natural-law/Noahide principle of protection of life into the very source of the permission to perform therapeutic abortions in Jewish law.

The extent to which Maimonides' restrictive view of therapeutic abortion has influenced contemporary *halakhah* may be gauged from a remark made by R. Moses Feinstein in an essay concerning the abortion of a fetus suffering from Tay-Sachs syndrome. R. Feinstein attacks the permissive view of R. Eliezer Waldenberg who was, at the time, the decisor for the Shaare Tzedek Hospital in Jerusalem and President of the Rabbinical Court of Appeals. R. Waldenberg permits the abortion of a fetus suffering from Tay-Sachs syndrome, a fatal genetic condition affecting Jews of Eastern European origin, causing physical and mental retardation, loss of sight and hearing, and death by the age of three or four years.[43] In addition to asserting that at least two of R. Waldenberg's sources are "scribal errors" and that others are simply wrong, R. Feinstein makes the following point regarding the difficulties inherent in Maimonides' strict view of therapeutic abortion: "We do not nullify the words of Maimonides on the basis of difficulties posed by lesser authorities. Maimonides was undoubtedly capable of clearing these difficulties up and his words may not be disregarded because of such difficulties."[44]

Other authorities also base themselves upon Maimonides' approach and adopt a strict view regarding therapeutic abortion, permitting it only in the case of a direct threat to maternal life.[45]

Abortion is, therefore, another area in which Maimonides shaped the *halakhah* in accordance with his strong views regarding the value of human life and the moral heinousness of taking it, in any shape or form.

MAIMONIDES AND CONTEMPORARY JEWISH BIOETHICS

If anything can be learned from Maimonides on killing a *terefah* and feticide, it is that morality plays a role in the *halakhah* governing these issues. In this respect, Isaiah Leibowitz's remarks concerning the Quinlan trial are most illuminating.[46] According to Leibowitz, the answer to the question of whether or not to disconnect the artificial respirator should be in the negative, and the halakhic permission to remove any impediment to death should be ignored.[47] Invoking the principle that there are certain *halakhot* which should be concealed from public knowledge *(halakhah ve-en morin ken)*,[48] Leibowitz bases himself on the moral principle of the supremacy of human life and cites Maimonides as an authority for the absolute nature of this principle.[49]

All this is at the level of methodology. Maimonides teaches us that we must plumb the depths of the whole tradition in order to bring the whole spectrum of traditional Jewish values to bear on issues of life and death. The substantive answers are, however, more elusive today than they were in Maimonides' time. The area of terminating the treatment of critically ill patients is highly complex, and in many instances, the moral high ground is shared by those who would condone cessation of treatment and those who reject any such move. Abortion is another morally complicated area. Not only is the criterion of maternal welfare highly complex, but issues such as fetal brain transplants to save viable people from debilitating and fatal diseases pose the problem in very different moral terms to those of the past. The Maimonidean methodology in bioethics presents us with the challenge of going beyond legal doctrine to the ethics of Jewish bioethics. It is up to rabbis and scholars alike to pursue this challenge with integrity.

23

Maimonides, An Enemy of Authoritarianism

Alfred Soffer

Are there messages of current relevance that can be obtained from the writings of a philosopher who lived eight centuries ago? Do the anti-authoritarian admonitions of Maimonides *(Rambam)* have meaning for our day? I suggest that there is a particular and urgent necessity to remember and to heed the writings of Maimonides. Recall the warning of Tony Thulborn, who wrote:

> The plain truth is that a handful of Bible thumping extremists have corrupted what little the public knew of science in the first place. Today nine out of ten adult Americans are "scientifically illiterate"; half of them reject outright the very thought of human evolution, and in some parts of the United States, almost half of biology teachers favor the introduction of creationism in high schools.[1]

In Israel, Rabbi Menachem Hacohen described the imminent danger of the rise of reactionary religious fundamentalism. Rabbi Hacohen stressed:

> Quotations [from the Scriptures] must be viewed within the context of time, place, and circumstance. The [spirit of] *halachah* [Jewish Law] of Judaism is completely contrary to a [fundamentalist] view of scriptural passages ... Only ignorant people, and there are many of them in the Knesset representing the religious parties, adopt a literal view of Scripture and halachic passages.

Let us first consider Maimonides the rabbi. A recent report from Jerusalem had this headline, "Lenient *Rambam* rule okays banned conversions." The first sentence of the article noted, "A disposition by Maimonides is making it possible for those non-Jews who married Jews to be able to convert without objection from Israel's Orthodox hierarchy." The basis for precluding conversion when it is prompted by marriage to a Jew is deeply embedded in traditional Jewish practice. According to the Talmud, if a man lives with a non-Jewish woman who later converts, she is forbidden to marry him even then. This would affect Jews who had been married in civil ceremonies. Rabbi Eliahu quoted a ruling by Maimonides to the effect that, "In our age, if he does not marry her, we have to assume that he will continue to live with her. Therefore, you should marry her according to the law."

In a controversy with Samuel Bar Ali Halevi, Maimonides suggested that law must be interpreted differently for the age and the milieu in which the individual Jew lived. Maimonides therefore sanctioned travel on the Shabbat on the Tigris and Euphrates rivers, pointing out that they were unusually large rivers and that new precedents were necessary. This decision highlighted Maimonides' contention that rabbinical authority was not irrefutable and that deletions and additions were necessary as new needs arose. Quite correctly, Leon Roth suggests that Maimonides felt it to be the duty of thought to interpret authority. The essence of such a philosophy, according to Roth, is that "The ultimate standard is the human mind."[2] Consistent with this approach, Maimonides proved himself to be a rationalist, even at the expense of breaking with tradition.

We have witnessed in recent days raging debates about the requirements for conversion to Judaism. Fundamentalists criticize rabbis who do not require of the candidate "acceptance of the entire Torah." However, infinitely more compassionate and flexible anti-authoritarian guidance is provided by Maimonides. In his *Mishneh Torah* (*Issurei Biah* 14:1), he urges that the court accept the convert "immediately" upon hearing the willingness of the candidate to identify himself or herself with this people "confounded and beset by suffering." The candidate is to be acquainted with "the basic principles of Judaism, i.e., the unity of God and the prohibition against idolatry." The candidate is to be informed of some of the less and more weighty commandments, "but we do not enlarge on these matters. We do not confront the candidate with numerous commandments nor do we enter into detail, lest we drive him away and turn him from a good path." The tone of Maimonides' codification of the conversion procedure is noteworthy. The court, he adds, should inform the prospective convert of the punishment for transgression, but the convert should be told of the rewards of observance, and that performance of these commandments vouchsafes for a Jew the life of the world to come.[3]

Newspaper headlines in February 1989, described the attacks of Islamic fundamentalists on freedom of expression. Resurgence of reactionary fundamentalism in a number of Moslem countries reminds us of historical episodes which threatened the creative efforts – and indeed the very lives – of Jewish, as well as Islamic, scholars.

A particularly dramatic occurrence of such intolerance deeply affected the life and writings of Maimonides. On July 23, 1191, Maimonides wrote one of the most unusual essays of his career. This *Treatise of Resurrection* was, in essence, an apology and detailed explanation of the philosopher's views of resurrection of the dead. In the treatise, Maimonides defends his faith in this fundamental tenet of Judaism. The tone suggests that unwarranted pressure had been exerted upon this giant in philosophy, medicine, and theology. In the past eight centuries, thoughtful readers have wondered: Why would Maimonides posit return of the immortal soul to the body for only a finite period to be followed then by the death of the body and return of the soul to immortal life? Were outside influences a factor in making it necessary for Maimonides to defend himself?

This sad episode in the life of one of the greatest Jewish scholars in the past 2,000 years is described by David Hartman in these words: "Forcing a person like Maimonides to defend the miracle of resurrection is, to use a Maimonidean metaphor, like drawing a king away from his regal activities in order to play ball in the street."[4] Abraham Joshua Heschel described the events as follows:

> Pious and anti-philosophical Jews and Moslems accused the *Guide* [*for the Perplexed*] of "misleading" people to impiety, a charge which could have serious effects in this area of reactionary religion. By ignoring the dogma of resurrection when going through his reasons for the idea of immortality, Maimonides reinforced suspicions against himself.[5]

Maimonides was beloved by both Moslems and Jews. One of his highest honors and responsibilities was being physician to the court of the Sultan of Cairo. The sultan (Saladin) had become a very Orthodox Moslem somewhat late in life. At about the time that Maimonides wrote his *Treatise on Resurrection*, Suhraawardi, an Arab mystic, had been killed by the sultan for expressing "independent views." The sultan's new orthodoxy was in keeping with the mode of the Arab populace, who believed fervently in resurrection. Joshua Finkel suggests that Maimonides had to defend his belief in the concept of resurrection to save his own life. However, Finkel concludes that, "Circumspect as he was, Maimonides was the only medical philosopher, Jew or Arab, who dared to commit himself openly and unequivocally on the incorporeality of ultimate existence."[6]

The recent statement of principles of Conservative Judaism, *Emet ve-Emunah*, includes some comments about such fundamentalism. In the chapter, "The Messianic Hope," the authors note:

The dominant eschatological voice today is clearly revolutionary – in Islam, in American fundamentalist and evangelical Christianity and among certain groups of Jews in Israel and throughout the world. We understand the concerns that impel communities to resort to such programs. We are also convinced of their dangers; exclusivism, triumphalism, radical political action and, in the extreme, militarism and even terrorism.[7]

We recall the Golden Age of Spain, during which there was a flowering of independent scholarship, poetry, and the arts. We honor the Islamic leaders who made possible such freedom of thought and print. One can but deplore the waves of reactionary fundamentalism that drove Maimonides from his home in Cordova in 1148 and returned to harass him several times during the rest of his life. We can hope that once again the world will have the opportunity to praise and to honor Islamic contributions when the current scourge of reactionary authoritarianism is spent.

Perhaps what we admire most in the medical career of Maimonides is his empathic approach to the study of man. The word *disease* (dis-ease) means simply the absence of ease. The term indicates that physical ailments are always accompanied by emotional counterparts. Dr. Harry Friedenwald and Professor Paul Haupt stress that the primary meaning of the Hebrew *rafo* (to heal) is to ease. Indeed the Hebrew word *nefesh* denotes both physical and mental life. Maimonides not only described the relationship between emotional and physical well-being, but he also practiced this in his approach to medicine. In his *Regimen of Health,* Maimonides wrote, "The physician should notice accordingly that every sick person is depressed whereas every healthy person is cheerful. He should therefore remove the mental effects which cause that depression for in this way health is maintained." The emotional and physical aspects of the placebo effect were clearly understood by him. For example, Maimonides sanctions the use of charms for poisonous snake bites, even on the Sabbath. Though he considered the use of charms to be a worthless superstition, he realized that credulous patients could derive invaluable emotional comfort from using amulets.

Centuries before neuroses and psychoses were described in textbooks, Maimonides provided prescient observations. The concept that "no man can in law brand himself a criminal" is a fundamental principle in Jewish criminal law. Maimonides defended this dictum by explaining that depressed patients may confess to imagined aggression as a manifestation of exaggerated feelings of guilt. Today, criminologists recognize the truth of this concept. They report scores of emotionally disturbed patients who confess to every publicized major crime. In a reply to Sultan AlMalik Al Afdhal's letter (1200 C.E.), Maimonides remarked, "I have had occasion to treat some patients whose disease followed the ways of kings suffering from melancholia, viz, that it turns into mania, that is, raving madness." Surely this is an accurate description of manic-depressive psychosis.

Maimonides urged that there be maximum flexibility in the treatment of patients because of the differing emotional needs of individuals. Therefore, he avoided rigid or routine medical regimens, in each case considering the physical constitution and the emotional state of the subject. This happy avoidance of rigidity in therapy and his awareness of the indissoluble link between the psyche and bodily ills impressed both the Arabic and Jewish worlds. The medieval Arabic poet Al-Said al Mulk wrote, "Galen's art healed only the body, but Abu Imran's [Maimonides] the body and the soul."

As the greatest physician of medieval Jewry, Maimonides considered medicine to be a study of health, as well as disease, with the stress laid on the former. This represented a profound recognition of the practice of preventive medicine.

Accused of nihilism regarding drugs, Maimonides said, "Most doctors err in their treatment. In endeavoring to assist nature, they weaken the body with their prescriptions." A view commonly held by nonphysicians (and perhaps, unfortunately, by some of our modern colleagues) is that there is something contradictory between science and humanity, between technology and compassion. Glick believes that we may still be suffering from a "hold-over from the classic Cartesian mind-body dualism, with compassion representing the mind or soul and science the body and the two somehow antagonistic."[8] This thesis is reemphasized by Oreopoulos, who notes:

> In the middle of the 17th century, Descartes undermined the idea of the unity of man, by separating body and soul and set the stage for the natural but pernicious separation of technology and humanity, and of the science and ethics . . . This chain of events excluded the physician from the ministry of the soul. Now he is a scientist, with the single mission and obligation of detecting and curing disease. No more is the patient's suffering his responsibility.[9]

The philosophy of Maimonides is an effective antidote to such narrowness of mind. We recognize today that diseases such as tuberculosis are as much a social problem as a medical one. Environmental factors are key elements in prevention and treatment. Maimonides understood these relationships. Medicine to him (as it was to Hippocrates) was more than a science; it was a social science. Among giants of medicine who understood the indissoluble link between the psyche and bodily ills, Maimonides stands out as a great pioneer. His compassionate guide to patient care is ageless, and there is much that today's young physician can learn from him. His high idealism and the elevation of medicine to a holy calling, to a profession of great spiritual and humanitarian values, is a continuing source of inspiration.

Maimonides, the theologian-philosopher, wrote, "Let not the ignorant fall into the error that any man is responsible for the establishment of a great truth. Religious laws are made not by individuals but by the concerted judgment of many generations of thinkers."

In his *Mishneh Torah,* Maimonides changes the order of the biblical commandments which had been posited by the Gaon Rabbi Simon Kahira. In defense of this move he said, "For this is the feeling among the educated men of our time and surely among the multitude. They do not examine a statement by its contents but by its conformity to the statement of the previous author without having evaluated the former statement."

When French rabbis quote talmudic authorities who laud the value of astrology, Maimonides, a life-long enemy of that pseudoscience, stresses that these talmudic citations are individual opinions. He urges Jews to be guided by the science of their day and not by the opinions of yesterday. "Let us never cast our reason behind us," Maimonides pleaded.

In theology as in medicine, Maimonides was original in interpretation and insisted upon constant testing of "accepted" beliefs. With bitter satire Maimonides describes the disease of the intellectuals: "If they are applauded they think they know all branches of knowledge and suddenly become authorities. No one opposes them and their popularity increases; so likewise does the disease itself become aggravated."[10]

May one borrow not only from one's own faith, but from civilizations outside of Judaism in the establishment of philosophic truths? "In our quest for the fruits of science it makes no difference whether we apply to the prophets or to the wise men of the gentile world. Indeed, we can find wisdom even among the idol worshippers."

The assertion that only in a majority culture can truly Jewish values be developed, or the opposite claim that an ethnic minority must avoid contact with the secular world about it, was foreign to Maimonides' thought. "Some foolish rabbis go so far as to exclude a good Arabic in favor of a bad Hebrew poem. The important thing is not the language but the content of a psalm. A noble poem is divine in any language. A vicious poem is mean in Hebrew."

Although Maimonides was a codifier of ancient rituals, he also pioneered in providing new meanings to rituals. He created creeds, yet was fearful of changing dogma. Although devout in observance, he was novel in interpretation. Perhaps, therefore, we can call Maimonides "The Devout Iconoclast." Perhaps the most radical element in his philosophy was his assertion that the emotional growth of a people must proceed in stages. In an incisive evaluation of animal sacrifices he argues that as emotional maturity of the Jewish people grew, they no longer required animal sacrifices. Were Maimonides alive today he would undoubtedly sanction continual interpretation of Jewish tradition and law as applicable to the modern situation. "The gates of interpretation are not closed to us," he emphasized.

Fearlessly he stressed the emotional immaturity of the multitude at Sinai. In his *Treatise on Resurrection,* Maimonides noted, "It is well known that those people to whom the Almighty wished to have the Torah understood in their time adopted erroneous ideas. It was said of them at the end of 40 years of desert wandering, after they had seen all the miraculous acts of God: But the Lord has not given you a heart to know and eyes to see and ears to hear until this day." Maimonides explains that in view of this immaturity, God did not tell the Israelites about the tenet of the resurrection of the dead. Instead, He utilized a process of gradual understanding of new concepts.

In the beginning of this chapter I asked, "Are there messages of current relevance that can be obtained from the writings of Maimonides?" Fox asked the same questions: "Have we any reason apart from pure historical curiosity or antiquarian interests to study Maimonides with enthusiasm? Does his thought have any contribution to make to contemporary Judaism and to the resolution of religious dilemmas of contemporary Western society?"[11] Fox answers his questions with a resounding affirmative response.

> We can learn first, and most importantly, from Maimonides an uncompromising and fearless intellectual honesty in all matters having to do with religion. At a time when the forces of closed-minded intellectual timidity have managed to gain a position of some prominence in certain Jewish circles, the example of Maimonides is of great interest. While protecting the integrity of the system of Jewish law, he left room for the intellect to develop its own best understanding concerning the fundamental questions of faith.
>
> In his interpretation of the Bible he battled against literalist fundamentalism, finding his justification in the long-established tradition of nonliteral midrashic interpretation. The law is necessarily fixed, because the integrity of society demands that the precepts of the law must be obligatory. But the human effort to grasp the ultimate nature of things must, in Maimonides' view, never be totally constricted or suppressed. We can command patterns of behavior, and we rightly expect people to subordinate their private inclinations to legal norms. It is dangerous and self-defeating, however, to command conformity in the formulation, understanding, or apprehending of ultimate philosophical or theological matters. Here the human mind must be left free to find its own way. If, by chance, we were to succeed in preventing people from thinking, we would also rob them of what is essential to their humanity.[12]

Maimonides as rabbi, physician, and philosopher fought rigid, unchanging approaches to human needs. He identified such inflexibility as a negation of the spirit of Judaism and one that connotes insecurity and the fear of differing views.

24

The State of Arabic Medicine at the Time of Maimonides According to Ibn Ǧumayʿ's Treatise on the Revival of the Art of Medicine

Paul B. Fenton

INTRODUCTION

Though not strictly dealing with the works of Moses Maimonides, this chapter has nonetheless a direct bearing on the subject of the practice and status of medicine at the time of the "great eagle of Israel." Indeed we are fortunate in possessing a remarkable social and professional document in the form of a treatise on the history of medicine and its contemporary practice written by a Jewish physician and colleague of Maimonides, which throws an interesting light on the medical deontology of the time.

We cannot think of a work on this subject worthier of exposition than the *Treatise on the History and Revival of the Art of Medicine,* composed by Ibn Ǧumayʿ (ob. 1198). This work deals with the decline of medicine in the author's time and the incompetence of its practitioners, while exposing the sorry state into which the profession had deteriorated at a time when there were no real criteria to ensure proper medical training.

IBN ǦUMAYʿ

Though Maimonides, in his *Pirké Mosheh,* shares some of these criticisms, there is no evidence that he knew his contemporary or quoted his work.

However it can be safely assumed that he would have been personally familiar with both, since it seems that Maimonides and Ibn Ǧumayʿ resided in the same neighborhood in Fosṭāṭ.[1] Moreover, his elder colleague, whose full name was al-Muwaffiq Abû l-ash-Shâʿir Hibatallah ibn Yûsuf ibn Zayn ibn Ḥasan ibn Ifrâʾîm ibn Yaʿqûb ibn Ismaʾîl Ibn Ǧumayʿ al-Isrâʾîlî, was one of the foremost physicians of his time. Known in Hebrew as Nethan'el ben Efrâîm, he was one of eight Jewish practitioners, including Maimonides, in the service of the Ayyūbide court. Born in Fostat, Old Cairo, he first became physician to the last Fāṭimid caliph of Egypt, al-ʿAdîd (ob. 1171), who had bestowed upon him in addition to *al-Muwaffiq* ("the Successful"), the honorific title of *Shams ar-riyâsa* ("Luminary of the Chief Physicians").

It is possible to say that Ibn Ǧumayʿ, who was known as the "Master of his generation" *(ustâdh zamânih),* can in himself be considered a paradigm of the state of medicine in Maimonides' time. We owe most of our knowledge of his personal details to the notice Ibn Abî Uṣaybîʿa, the historian of Arabian medicine, devoted to Ibn Ǧumayʿ in his biographical dictionary, *ʿUyūn al-anbâʾ fî ṭabaqāt al-aṭibbâʾ.*

> [Ibn Ǧumayʿ] was widely conversant with the sciences and greatly exercised in the art of medicine, which he practised skilfully and in which subject he composed excellent works. Born and bred in Fosṭāṭ, Egypt, he entered the service of Saladin Yusuf ibn Ayyub, whose esteem he enjoyed . . . he headed a general council which directed medical affairs and he was possessed of noble aims . . . He also had a grasp of the Arabic tongue and accuracy in matters of linguistics. Thus he would never read without al-Ǧawhari's dictionary at hand. He would never bypass a word whose exact meaning escaped him, without looking it up.[2]

Furthermore, Ibn Abî Uṣaybîʿa goes on to say that he was an enthusiastic teacher and gave public lectures to medical students. He gained considerable reputation by reviving a man who, having suffered an attack of catalepsy, had been taken for dead. As the man's bier passed by his surgery, he observed that his feet protruding from beneath the hearse-cloth stood erect and not flat, as those of a corpse. The individual whom he then saved from being buried alive eventually regained consciousness and subsequently lived to a ripe old age.

Ibn Ǧumayʿ studied under the Syrian al-Muwaffiq Abû Naṣr ʿAdnân Ibn al-ʿAynzarbî, a court physician who died in Cairo in 1153. Another of the latter's disciples, the Karaite Jewish doctor, David ben Solomon Ibn Abî l-Bayân, later studied with Ibn Ǧumayʿ.[3] He was the very teacher of Ibn Abî Uṣaybîʿa and, while he taught at the Nâsirî hospital, wrote the famous *Dustûr al-Bimâristânî* (The Hospital Canon).

Among Ibn Ǧumayʿ's distinguished functions was his being especially commissioned by the sultan to prepare the all-heal and alexipharmic of

Mithridates, known to the Arabs as the theriac *al-Fârûq*. Besides his interest in medical matters, he assiduously cultivated Arabic literature and prided himself in speaking the language with much eloquence. Ibn Abî Uṣaybîʿa's report that he had as his continuous companion a famous Arabic dictionary no doubt explains Ibn Ǧumayʿ's exquisite style. The vizir Ibn Maṭrûḥ called him the best of the later physicians, contrasting him with Ibn Riḍwân, known as the best of the earlier ones. He is said to have died in 1198, while at work on the final version of the most renowned of his works, the *Irshâd*, or "Guide," which was subsequently completed by his son, Abû Ṭâhir Ismaʿîl.

HIS WORKS

In modern times the first author to mention Ibn Ǧumayʿ was Eliakim Carmoly, who devoted an entry to him in his history of Jewish physicians.[4] Following Ibn Abî Uṣaybîʿa, Carmoly credits him with the composition of a "Treatise on the Climate of Alexandria" (1. *Risâla fî ṭabʿ al-Iskandariyya*), which in fact has survived as an Istanbul manuscript, as well as a "Guide to the Welfare of Souls and Bodies" (2. *Kitâb al-irshâd li-maṣâliḥ an-nufûs wal-aǧsâd*). The latter, his most important work, is a compendium of the entire science of medicine, anatomy, physiology, hygiene, and pharmacology culled from the most authoritative sources of the times. The work, of which numerous manuscripts have been preserved in the libraries of Europe and the East, is dedicated to the qâḍî ʿAbd ar-Raḥîm who hailed from Bet Shean in the Holy Land, protector of several Jewish practitioners, including Maimonides. It is copiously quoted by later authorities and in particular by Abû l-Munâ ha-Kôhen al-ʾAṭṭâr, in his *Minhâǧ ad-dukkân*.[5]

Ibn Abî Uṣaybîʿa lists six other works by our author:

3. *Kitâb at-tashrîḥ bil-maknûn fî tanqîḥ al-qânûn*, glosses on Avicenna's Canon, which is extant in at least three manuscripts. There is even a supercommentary on this work by one Fakhr ad-dîn Khogandî.[6]

4. *ar-Risâla fî tadbîr ḥaythu la yaḥḍuru ṭ-ṭabîb* (Epistle on First Aid When No Doctor is Available), dedicated to the Qâḍî al-Makîn Abî l-Qâsim ʿAlî Ibn al-Ḥusayn. This treatise has been preserved in an Istanbul manuscript.

5. *al-Maqâla fî l-Limûn wa-sharâbihi wa-manâfiʿhi* (Treatise on the Beneficial Properties of the Lemon). Quoted by Ibn al-Bayṭār, as far as we know, this work has not been preserved in the original though, hitherto, its Latin translation by Alpagus was the only work of Ibn Ǧumayʿ to have been published.

6. *al-Maqâla fî r-Rawund wa-manâfiʿih* (Treatise on the Beneficial Properties of Rhubarb). Also used by Ibn al-Bayṭār.

7. *al-Maqâla fî l-Ḥadaba* (Treatise on Tuberosity).

8. *al-Maqâla fî 'ilâğ al-qawlanğ* (Treatise on the Treatment of Colics) also called *ar-Risâla as-Sayfiyya fî l-adwiya al-mulûkiya*.

THE REVIVAL OF THE ART OF MEDICINE

However, the present chapter is based on yet another of Ibn Ğumay''s works entitled "A Treatise for Şalâḥ [ad-Dîn] on the Revival of the Art of Medicine" (9. *ar-Risâla aṣ-ṣalâḥiyya fî iḥyâ' al-'ulûm aṣ-ṣiḥḥiyya*). As indicated by its Arabic title, styled slightly differently in the Istanbul manuscript, *al-Maqâla aṣ-ṣalâḥiyya fî iḥyâ' aṣ-ṣinâ'a aṭ-ṭibbiyya*, this work was dedicated to the Sultân Şalâḥ ad-Dîn al-Ayyûbî, known to the West as the famous Sultan Saladin, who reigned over Egypt and Syria from 1171 to 1193. Surprisingly, this work is not actually listed by Ibn Abî Uṣaybi'a; this omission is perhaps due to the fact that it does not strictly deal with a medical issue but rather with the social and ethical aspects of medicine.

The treatise first received attention in modern times by the renowned historian of Arabic medicine, Max Meyerhof, who, in an appendix to his article "La Surveillance des Professions Médicales et Para-Médicales chez les Arabes,"[7] reported his discovery of a unique manuscript of this hitherto unknown work. The following year, Meyerhof provided an account of the work together with a partial translation of the second chapter in a study devoted entirely to Ibn Ğumay',[8] in which he announced his intention of publishing the treatise in collaboration with Paul Kraus, professor of Semitic languages at Cairo University.

Shortly thereafter, Kraus published copious extracts from the manuscript in two articles which appeared in the Egyptian weekly, *ath-Thaqâfa*.[9] However, Kraus's tragic death in 1945, followed closely by the demise of Meyerhof himself, definitively put an end to their joint project. Unfortunately, no one knows what became of Meyerhof's copy, or for that matter the fate of his entire library, which reputedly contained many rare works on Arabic medicine, painstakingly collected during his protracted stay in Egypt. Meyerhof's manuscript, although incomplete, contained 46 pages and had been copied in the year 576 of the Higra or 1180–1181, i.e., during the author's lifetime.

It was not until 1966 that the existence of a second manuscript of the work came to light. Discovered by A. Dietrich in the medical *magmû'a N°2136* of the Ahmet III Library at the Topkapi Sarayi, its location was reported in his study of Arabic medical works in Turkish libraries.[10] The fact that this copy, dating approximately from the thirteenth century and containing 33 folios, neighbors two other treatises by Ibn Ğumay', lends credence to the principle of his authorship. In 1970 an Israeli Arab announced her intention of editing this manuscript; however, her project remained fruitless.[11]

Our own interest in this work was aroused by the fortunate purchase we made in 1979 of an additional manuscript of this interesting work from a Paris bookseller. This copy, containing 29 pages, had once belonged to the famous French mathematician Michel Chasles (1793–1880). It had previously been the property of one Nathan Noah, a Jewish physician from Damascus[12] for whose library the copy had been transcribed in Ğamādī 1112 of the Hiğra (October 1700) into Hebrew Oriental cursive from an original manuscript, which bears the same date as that of Meyerhof's, i.e., Ramadan, 576 (1181 C.E.).[13]

We were intending to prepare an edition of this interesting work when Hartmut Fähndrich published his edition and English translation of Ibn Ğumayʿ's treatise.[14] Notwithstanding its having been based solely on the Istanbul manuscript, Fähndrich's text is nonetheless reliable and exhibits few variant readings in relation to our manuscript. His English translation, upon which we shall copiously draw and adapt, though at times lacking in elegance, is thoroughly sound.[15]

THE CONTENTS

Ibn Ğumayʿ's treatise is not so much a history of medicine but an account of its decadence as a result of the incompetence of its practitioners. According to the introduction, the composition of the treatise was occasioned by a conversation held with the author's sovereign, Saladin, about the circumstances which had led to the decline of the medical art and the measures it was advisable to take in order to remedy the sorry state of contemporary medicine.

In his response, Ibn Ğumayʿ adopts the literary tradition of the Epistle (risâla), frequently employed by medical authors. Stylistically the work is couched in an eloquent prose interspersed with poetic quotations and anecdotes, as is customary with Arabic authors. His work is divided into three long chapters, preceded by an introduction, addressed to Saladin, "subduer of the worshippers of the Cross," in which he explains the circumstances which motivated his composition.

The opening chapter is subdivided into two sections, the first of which is entitled "Declaration of the excellence of medicine, of its great utility and its inevitable necessity," and the second, "Indication of the arduousness of the art of medicine and an explanation of difficulties of obtaining perfection therein, the scarcity of excellent practitioners and the incompetence of the majority of doctors." Chapter two, entitled "Indication of the reasons for the decline of the medical art and the disappearance of its virtues," presents a concise history of medicine from the Greeks to the time of the Arabs and analyzes the reasons for its ensuing decay. The final chapter, which bears the title "Indication of the means to revive and renew the medical art," provides practical advice to rulers on how to invigorate the medical profession by ensuring a proper training of students and practitioners.

A closer analysis of the content of these three chapters reveals a certain freshness, though they were written eight hundred years ago.

Ibn Ğumay' counts medicine among the "practical arts" whose aim is to attain perfection of a material base. Since their nobleness depends on the preciousness of the material with which they work, medicine is thus by far the most noble of arts, since its object is none other than man, who is the noblest of creatures. Moreover, health is the most exalted benefit which can accrue to man, since without it there is no enjoyment of things material or spiritual and, therefore, it is on a par with religion. These ideas on the centrality of man and the elevated rank of medicine are commonplace in the Arabic philosophy of the medieval period. The traditional Jewish view of medicine as expressed earlier by the Talmud is far less laudative.

The veritable virtues of medicine are evidently not the material benefits which fall to the lot of doctors, nor even the heavenly reward for those who deal kindly in relieving pain, but they are the triumph over the evils of disease, which medicine alone is capable of vanquishing. At this point, Ibn Ğumay' poses a theological question. If God is the creator of disease and cure, what is then the virtue of medicine? He answers curtly that God is also the creator of the medical art, which is therefore divinely inspired.

As for the second part of this chapter dealing with the hindrances to the acquisition of a sound grasp of the discipline, Ibn Ğumay' attributes the difficulties of medicine to the vastness of its scope. Its correct application requires intimate knowledge of the elements and the human body, as well as deep understanding and experience. The author of our treatise insists upon the necessity of acquiring these qualities, for a medical practitioner who has no theoretical knowledge is like one who acts blindly and whose success, if any, is purely accidental.

Medicine also requires the knowledge of disciplines which are external to medical science, such as logic necessary to arrive at a correct diagnosis, or astronomy for the determination of climatic conditions. He insists on the keen distinction to be drawn between astronomy and astrology, thus indicating that he was not an adept of medical astrology. All of these requirements necessitate the convergence of numerous virtues in the practitioner, such as intelligence and patience, as well as the choice of a competent master. The difficulty of cultivating so many qualities explains the scarcity of good doctors.

THE CAUSES IN THE DECLINE OF MEDICINE

The Greek Heritage

Ibn Ğumay''s second chapter is the longest of the treatise. As a preliminary to the elucidation of the causes in the decline of Arabic medicine, he provides a summary of the transmission of medical science from the ancient Greeks to the Arabs. Like Ibn Abî Uṣaybîʻa after him, he draws, it seems, on Isḥâq b. Ḥunayn's *History of Physicians,* beginning his account with the ascription of the origins of medicine to Asclepius, whom he interestingly identifies with the biblical Enoch. Medicine was an esoteric and hereditary discipline down to the generation of Hippocrates, situated by Ibn Ğumayʻ at the time of King Ataxerxes of Persia. Through fear of its extinction, Hippocrates was the first to commit medical science to writing, albeit in an enigmatic and abstruse form, so that only those worthy of it would be able to learn it. This motif also appears in Jewish sources such as in the introduction to the *Book of Asaph the Physician,* and apparently goes back to a Hermetic tradition, in which Asclepius plays an important role.

As medical knowledge spread among the Greeks, opinions multiplied and became corrupt and Hippocrates' writings were eventually disregarded until Galen arose some six hundred years later. He investigated all medical methods and found Hippocrates' to be the only sound one. Dismissing the others, he strove to purge the works of his illustrious predecessor from the adulterations to which they had fallen prey and then set about editing and commenting upon them, thus facilitating the apprenticeship of the medical art.

Ibn Ğumayʻ then describes the state of medicine in the centuries preceding the rise of Islam. This period was characterized by a general decline in medicine and science. He blames the rise of Christianity and the aversion of the Christian rulers toward intellectual matters for the ensuing decadence which set in and the discarding of the works of Hippocrates and Galen, who clearly embody in his eyes the acme of medical science.

Then came Oribasius, who attempted to remedy matters by popularizing the medical art and spreading instruction, lest it vanish completely. He compiled compendia, abridgements, and summaries of the works of the Ancients, which, considered too laborious to study, eventually fell into oblivion. This situation prevailed even in the most important of schools – that of Alexandria, where only a fraction of Galen's and Hippocrates' works were taught.

THE ARABIC COMPENDIA

This curriculum persisted until the time of the Arab conquest of Egypt, when the seat of instruction was transferred from Alexandria of Egypt to Antioch and Harran in Northern Syria, until the sciences were revived by the Caliph al-Maʼmûn, son of the famous Hârûn ar-Rashîd. But for him, observes Ibn Ğumayʻ, medical science might have entirely waned away, just as it had done in the lands of the Greeks, where it had previously been so prominent.

This narrative of how Greek medicine was transmitted to the Arabs is derived from the reports of the great ninth-century translator Hunayn b. Ishaq, who in turn no doubt inherited it from Syriac Christian sources. It had become well known by Ibn Ğumayʿ's time, mainly through Ibn Abî Uṣaybîʿa's *History of Physicians,* which devotes no less than one hundred pages to the history of Greek medicine.[16] He too ascribes the origins of medical art to Hermes, whom he equates with the biblical Enoch, and states that Asclepius was his son. Furthermore he describes the decay of the Alexandrian school, which he attributes to the Christian Byzantine hostility toward the heathen philosophers of Antiquity.

No doubt it is from earlier Arabic sources that Ibn Ğumayʿ derived his account of the transferral of the Alexandrian medical academy to Antioch and Harran, such as Masʿûdi's *Tanbihât* or *Book of Admonition,* one of the first authors to mention the story. It is noteworthy that this school had maintained itself until the Arab conquest. In his article on the *Risâla aṣ-ṣalâḥiyya,* Meyerhof had suggested that the move to Northern Syria was motivated by the latter's nearness to the Byzantine Empire, where it would be easier to renew the Greek tradition by obtaining Greek and Syriac manuscripts.[17]

The author of the *Risâla* does not do justice to al-Ma'mûn's prime importance in reviving the sciences, since he does not make the slightest mention of the Caliph's pains to obtain Greek manuscripts and translate them into Arabic. During his rule (813–833) he patronized the aforementioned scholar Ḥunayn b. Isḥâq, whose translation of over three hundred Greek scientific and philosophical works put the Arabs in possession of the essentials of Ancient science.

On the other hand, our author is perhaps less harsh than other Arabic historians in his criticism of the Alexandrian synopsis. The latter, he says, comprised sixteen of Galen's works, including his *Minor Science, On the Pulse, Method of Therapy, On the Natural Faculties, Minor Anatomy, Book of Causes and Symptoms, On Fevers,* and *On Crisis,* as well as four works of Hippocrates: his *Aphorisms, Prognostics, Regimen in Acute Diseases,* and his book on *Air, Water and Climates.*

Ibn Ğumayʿ intimates that it was hardly the intention of Oribasius, or his successor Paulus of Aegina, or, for that matter, the Alexandrians to restrict the knowledge of medicine to these works, as is assumed by ignorant physicians, but their ambition was to arouse the interest of their readers and prompt them to undertake further study and perfect the art. Indeed many an indispensable subject, such as the anatomy of the brain, the liver, and the stomach, are absent from these works. However, the author of the *Risâla* remarks that latter-day physicians who compose compendia are of the opinion that their works dispense with the study of the Ancients, and it is for this reason that they give their abridgements deceitful titles such as "The Complete Work" (*al-Kâmil*), the "Self-contained" (*al-Mughni*), and the "Sufficient" (*al-Kâfi*). This led their readers astray from the works of Hippocrates and Galen, so that some would-be doctors would embark upon a medical career after having read but a small compendium such as ar-Râzi's *Ma-sûrî* or Ḥunayn's *Masâ'il,* while they considered study of the Ancients a waste of time.

Ibn Ǧumay' is unjust in his criticism of abridgements, for they played an important part in charting the unmapped seas of Greek medicine. Indeed, Hippocrates' and Galen's works are at times verbose to the point of prolixity and at others concise to the point of obscurity. As to the compendia to which he refers, the *Kâmil* is none other than the standard encyclopedia covering the entire field of medicine by the Persian doctor Ali al-Magûsi, who lived in tenth-century Bagdad. The *Mughni* is by another Bagdadi, Sa'id ibn Hibatallah, who died in 1101, whereas the *Kâfi* referred to is by none other than Ibn Ǧumay''s own teacher, the Egyptian Ibn al-'Aynzarbi. As for Ḥunayn's *Questions on Medicine,* it was one of the most widely read medical works in the Islamic world, while the *Manṣûri,* by the outstanding clinician Rhazes (865–930), was one of the most skillfully conceived compendia of the entire science of medicine, which has recently been critically edited in Kuwait.

This being the case for the most illustrious medical compendia, our author would no doubt have had a negative opinion of Maimonides' medical epitomes, such as his compendium of the chapters of Hippocrates.

One could speculate that Ibn Ǧumay''s attitude to Maimonides' *Extracts of Galen,* composed in 1188, would have been entirely negative, albeit bearing in mind that any criticism on his part would have rung rather hollow when it is recalled that he himself composed a work with the rather pompous title "The Guide to the Welfare of Souls and Bodies," which is nothing more than one such compendium!

THE INCOMPETENCE AND DECEIT OF CONTEMPORARY DOCTORS

Having enumerated the historical circumstances which led to the decline of medical science, Ibn Ǧumay' then proceeds to describe the consequences which the resulting incompetence held for the practice of medicine at his time. He sarcastically portrays the various expedients to which practitioners would resort in order to mask their professional shortcomings.

> As this kind of person is inadequate in the art of medicine and is unable to attain fame through excellence and skill in its practice, he resorts to deception and falsehood. Some deceive the masses by means of pompous attitude in clothing, appearance, use of perfume and the like, while others deceive the people by endearing themselves to them, by currying favor with them, by winning over their wives through suitable and commercial items such as aphrodisiacs and contraceptives, drugs for gaining weight [corpulence was an appreciated femi-

nine quality in Arab society] or hair-growth, and by arranging with the lady-companions, the hairdressers, the nurses and the like that they should praise and extol their medical and human qualities.

Others deceive the rich by waiting at their doors, by contacting their servants and by being on friendly terms with their companions and friends.... Then they gain knowledge of the weakness to which each is prone, in order to win them over. If he has a weakness for women, they go about him by way of women, if he has a weakness for servants they go about him by way of servants.... This is obviously the way animals are caught.[18]

Our author continues:

If such a rich one falls ill such a physician who has become friends with him will not suggest the most suitable treatment for healing his patient, for in truth he is ignorant of that, instead he will treat the patient in the manner he finds more pleasant. Moreover even if he knew the correct treatment but the latter proved to be unpleasant, he would not employ it.[19]

Ibn Ǧumayʿ's social criticism of the medical profession is not without a touch of humor on more than one occasion. Indeed, he tells us how some of these would-be doctors owe their success not to their medical proficiency but to their ability to entertain at parties, to tell jokes and stories. Notwithstanding their deceit, such doctors even achieve renown. When, despite the physicians' erroneous prescriptions, one of their patients happens to recover and survives thanks to his own natural resistance, the doctors nonetheless attain fame and celebrity and their shortcomings go undiscovered.

THE SELF-ACCLAIMED PHYSICIAN

Ibn Ǧumayʿ denounces the ills of charlatanry in no unclear terms:

In view of most people's innate aversion to hardship and exertion and their will to pursue a goal in the shortest way, no wonder that most self-acclaimed physicians have chosen this profession as the quickest path to fame and riches. Those who loved the art for its own sake were few and far between and they were spurned by their colleagues....

To be sure, doctors of this kind are more harmful than a raging plague and more disastrous than a band of robbers, for people are wary of the latter and take measures to protect themselves against them, whereas they readily and passively deliver their persons into the hands of a physician.[20]

One of the major causes behind the proliferation of bad doctors, claims our author, is not only their profound ignorance of medical know-how but their sheer unawareness of what the latter really entails. He wonders at this state of affairs, which is so unlike the situation in other easier and less-demanding professions.

> Would these so called doctors who have observed a tailor making a shirt over a hundred times ever dream of tailoring one themselves? He would still take his piece of cloth to a tailor and yet the risk of making a mistake is so minimal as to be altogether negligible, whereas in medicine this risk is so serious it can lead to sudden death.[21]

THE IGNORANT AND THE COWARDLY DOCTOR

Ibn Ǧumay' then scornfully derides the inexperienced doctors who claim to understand the taking of a pulse. Did not Galen spend many years investigating the pulse with considerable assiduity?

However not only the doctors are guilty of this state of affairs, but the patients themselves are often at fault through their indiscriminate confidence in all those claiming to profess the art of medicine. Indeed, they are unaware that there are practitioners of varying quality. Still others choose their doctors for reasons not remotely connected with their competence. They naturally take it for granted that a rich doctor is more excellent than a poor one, without inquiring whether his prosperity is proportionate to his proficiency. Where affability is the sole criterion, the author of our treatise remarks, not without sarcasm, that a physician who spends most of his days entertaining his patients cannot have much time to study and deepen his understanding of medicine.

Ibn Ǧumay' wonders that some people seem to have more concern for their pets than for themselves. Indeed, when the health of their animals is at stake, they prefer to consult a skilled veterinarian with whom they are unacquainted rather than a veterinarian familiar to them but of less competence.

Moreover, he expresses extreme surprise at people's reluctance to change doctors, even when they are of questionable competence. To illustrate the point, he relates an amusing anecdote from his own experience. When, during an illness, the judge Ibn Qadûs turned for advice to Ibn Ǧumay''s master, Ibn al-Aynzarbi, the judge's former physician reproached him. Ibn Qadûs cynically replied to his criticism with the following poem:

> Woe to him who says "I can heal as with the miracles of Jesus"
> And yet how many has he smitten or sent to their graves?
> He scolds me for turning from him to someone more competent.
> Forgive me if I desert you, it so happens it is *my* life which is at stake.[22]

Ibn Ǧumayʿ submits that sometimes a physician's fame rests on the gentleness of his treatments, though the latter do not necessarily arise from commiseration. Indeed, instead of prescribing the required drugs because of their potency, this breed of doctors cowardly prefers to administer a "gentle treatment" so as not to cause discomfort to their patients and forfeit thereby their favor. These unscrupulous doctors restrict themselves to administering rose-water, or draughts of hot water, trusting that the patients' natural physical resistance will come to the rescue. When, as sometimes transpires in such cases, nature of itself is able to overcome the disease and the patients' health is restored, they believe their recovery to be due to the ignoramuses who treated them, upon whom they then heap undeserved praise. Ibn Ǧumayʿ stresses, however, that it is incorrect to assume that if the so-called "gentle treatment" does not do any good, it neither does any harm. On the contrary, treatment can be considerably beneficial when correctly applied, but can also be considerably harmful if wrongly administered. He observes curtly "how many a draught of cold water used in a difficult illness such as dropsy, has meant death?"

The following passage concludes this section of the book:

> It has been shown why people's ignorance of the complexity of medicine has become one of the reasons behind its decay. As to their poor examination of its practitioners it too has become one of the reasons for its effacement because it forces the practitioners of this art to turn from the endeavour to attain excellence to the pursuit of selling their services to the people and to waste their lives with this occupation.[23]

CRITICISM AND THE LITERARY TRADITION

Ibn Ǧumayʿ's criticism of the medical profession at a time when there was no real guarantee of professional proficiency was not a new phenomenon. The author's ruthless reprehension of mediocre physicians stands firmly in a long tradition dating back to the time of Galen. One of the latter's works of which the original Greek has been lost is entitled *The Examination of the Best Physician;* according to the extracts reproduced by Ibn Abî Uṣaybîʿa and other Arabic authors, it consisted of a list of admonitions directed against dishonest doctors.[24]

Similar noncomplimentary descriptions of physicians are also found in works of social criticism, such as the writings of ninth-century author al-Ǧâḥiẓ, who is particularly scathing in his critique of Christian and Jewish doctors. He wrote a special book in which he belittles both medicine and doctors to such a degree that the great physician Abû Bakr Rhazes deemed it necessary to write a refutation. Rhazes was the physician who did most to expose the misdeeds of his fellow physicians in his writings on this subject, such as the *The Reason why Ignorant Physicians, Commoners and Women are more successful than Scholars*. Furthermore, Ibn Ǧumayʿ's own teacher Ibn ʿAynzarbi also authored a still-unpublished work bearing the title *On the Scarcity of Good Physicians and the Abundance of Bad Ones*.

SUGGESTIONS FOR REFORM

Of particular interest is his third and final chapter, where Ibn Ǧumayʿ submits to his sovereign Saladin a number of proposals aimed at improving the standard of medical practice. It reads very much like a modern-day board of education report. He returns to the reasons enumerated in the previous chapter and suggests the remedial measures that should be taken to improve each deficiency. Firstly, initial deterioration had set in as a result of the rulers' disinterest in the medical profession. Thus, the authorities should show concern not only for the quality of teachers and students but also for the standards of subject matter taught. Teachers and students should be selected among the most talented and promising elements. Ibn Ǧumayʿ also makes suggestions as to the introduction of a revised curriculum of medical studies with compulsory examinations imposed by the rulers. The best form of training is fieldwork carried out in the hospitals *(bimâristânât)*,[25] where doctors and students are directly confronted with the ailing. Perhaps this is a forerunner of our modern residencies and medical student clerkships. Retribution and competition also have their part to play in the encouragement of excellence.

The author of our epistle then proceeds to elaborate at length on the criteria in the selection of personnel to supervise instruction. Examiners must be on their guard not to be deluded by outward appearances such as pompous clothing and bearing. Even the moral comportment of likely candidates should be investigated, in order to ensure that their time is not spent in frivolous activities. Hippocrates said, "Life is short and the art is long."

Ibn Ǧumayʿ explains this adage as an evolutionary process based on the philosophical idea of the Perfect Man, or, in this case, the Perfect Physician:

> All that has so far been attained in the field of medicine has been attained by thousands of men during thousands of years; if each of the later [physicians] assimilates what earlier ones have discovered, trims and classifies it, thus arriving at all he can possibly attain and he adds to it what he himself has discovered until the art is completed, then someone who grasps all that his predecessors have attained and follows their tracks is like someone who lived the totality of his life and experienced all his struggles. . . . Therefore, the path of

someone whose aim and ambition are sensual enjoyment is not the path of someone whose concern is human perfection.[26]

In view of Ibn Ǧumayʿ's admiration for Hippocrates and Galen, it comes as no wonder that he advocated as an elementary prerequisite for any practitioner, perfect familiarity with their writings almost to the total exclusion of latter-day authors who, he claimed, had distorted them. Another criterion in selecting a good physician is the latter's ability to prognosticate accurately as to the development of a patient's condition. This entails a mastery of the knowledge of fevers and diet. Therefore, Galen said, "Correct treatment depends on prognosis and prognosis on correct treatment."

> This does not mean that the skilled physician must know in advance everything that will happen to every sick person from the first day of any disease to its end: medicine does not entail this and the doctor does not have to know it. But what it does entail and what the doctor must know is the knowledge of the condition of the disease and its likely development.[27]

These are the criteria to be applied if the prince is intent on reviving the art of medicine and preventing the ignorant from practicing it and bringing harm upon the people. Finally, Ibn Ǧumayʿ's treatise ends on a democratic note which may reflect his own humble origins:

> Medicine should not be taught solely to those who happen to be rich nor should students be allowed to reap immediate reward from its practice. Rather, all students who are poor should be sufficiently supported during their studies until they can teach it. Only the best should be rewarded and praised in order that, through competition, they strive for excellence.[28]

CONCLUSION

Notwithstanding Ibn Ǧumayʿ's amusing and florid style, the *Risâla* cannot make claims to be of outstanding literary originality. The definitions of medicine, the account of its development and decline, the anecdotes about famous physicians, and his proposals for the improvement of the medical art had all been presented before him in medical works of various types, several of which are still awaiting publication.

Furthermore, we are completely in the dark as to whether Ibn Ǧumayʿ's treatise had any impact on the course of medical training in his time. There is no evidence that his suggestions were in fact implemented by Saladin. What appears to be Ibn Ǧumayʿ's significance is his contribution to the clear and systematic presentation of this material, especially in light of the comparative scarcity of similar works of introductory and deontological character in medieval Arabic literature.

Finally, the work also holds considerable historical interest as a social document, insofar as it provides a lucid insight into the attitudes of a prominent physician toward his profession in twelfth-century Egypt, attitudes which no doubt would have been partly shared by his great contemporary, Moses Maimonides.

Notes

PREFACE

1. H. Friedenwald, *Jews and Medicine; Essays* vol. 1 (New York: Ktav Publishing House, 1967) [First ed. Johns Hopkins Press, 1944], p. 194.
2. J. O. Leibowitz and S. Marcus, eds., *Moses Maimonides, On the Causes of Symptoms* (Berkeley, CA: University of California Press, 1974), p. 13.
3. F. Rosner and S. Muntner, trans. and ed., *The Medical Aphorisms of Moses Maimonides* (New York: Yeshiva University Press, 1970), pp. 25-26 [with slight changes].

CHAPTER 1

1. F. Rosner, "The Medical Writings of Moses Maimonides," *N.Y. State J. Med.* 87(1987):656-61.
2. F. Rosner, "The Physician's Prayer Attributed to Maimonides," *Bull. Hist. Med.* 41(1967):440-54.
3. F. Rosner, "Maimonides, the Physician: A Bibliography," *Bull. Hist. Med.* 43(1969):221-35; "Maimonides the Physician: A Bibliography," *Clio Medica* 15(1980):75-9.
4. U. Barzel, "The Art of Cure: A Non-Published Medical Book by Maimonides," *Harofe Haivri* 2(1955):82-83 (Hebr.) and 165-77 (Eng.).
5. M. Steinschneider, "Die Vorrede des Maimonides zu seinem Commentar über die Aphorismen des Hippokrates," *Ztschr. d. deutsch. Morgenland, Gesellsch.* 48(1894): 213-34.

6. M. Z. Hasida (Bocian), *Perush le-Pirké Abukrat shel Ha-Rambam. Hassegullah* (Jerusalem) 1934–5, nos. 1–30 (Stencil) (Hebr.).

7. S. Muntner, *Moshe ben Maimon, Commentary on the Aphorisms of Hippocrates, Perush le-Pirké Abukrat* (Jerusalem: Mosad Harav Kook, 1961).

8. A. Bar Sela and H. E. Hoff, "Maimonides' Interpretation of the First Aphorism of Hippocrates," *Bull. Hist. Med.* 37(1968):347–54.

9. F. Rosner, "The Introduction of Maimonides to his 'Commentary on the Aphorisms of Hippocrates,'" *Clio Medica* 11(1976):59–64.

10. F. Rosner, *Moses Maimonides' Commentary on the Aphorisms of Hippocrates* (Haifa: Maimonides Research Institute, 1987).

11. Z. Magid, ed. *Medical Aphorisms of Maimonides (Pirké Moshe)* (Vilna: L. Matz, 1888) (1st ed., Lemberg 1834) (Hebr.).

12. S. Muntner, *Moshe ben Maimon (Medical) Aphorisms of Moses in Twenty-Five Treatises (Pirké Moshe bi-Refuah)* (Jerusalem: Mosad Harav Kook, 1959) (Hebr.: Eng. summary).

13. J. O. Leibowitz, "Maimonides' Aphorisms," *Koroth* 1(1955):213–19 (Hebr.); I–III (Engl. Summary).

14. J. O. Leibowitz, "The Latin Translations of Maimonides' Aphorisms," *Koroth* 6(1973):273–81 (Hebr.); XCIII–XCIV (Engl. summary).

15. W. Steinberg and S. Muntner, "Maimonides' Views on Gynecology and Obstetrics," *Am. J. Obst. Gynec.* 91(1965):443–48; F. Rosner and S. Muntner, "Moses Maimonides' Aphorisms Regarding Analysis of Urine," *Ann. Int. Med.* 71(1969): 217–20; "The Surgical Aphorisms of Moses Maimonides," *Amer. J. Surg.* 119(1970): 718–25; F. Rosner, "Moses Maimonides and Diseases of the Chest," *Chest* 60(1971): 68–72.

16. F. Rosner and S. Muntner, Studies in Judaica, *The Medical Aphorisms of Moses Maimonides* (New York: Yeshiva University Press, 1970), vol. 1, p. 267; ibid., (Yeshiva University Press, 1971), vol. 2, p. 244.

17. F. Rosner and S. Muntner, Studies in Judaica, *The Medical Aphorisms of Moses Maimonides,* vol. 1 and vol. 2 (New York: Bloch Publishing Co., for Yeshiva University Press, 1973), pp. 264 and 244.

18. F. Rosner, "The Medical Aphorisms of Moses Maimonides," in J. O. Leibowitz, *Memorial Volume in Honor of S. Muntner* (Israel Inst. Hist. Med. Jerusalem, 1983), pp. 6–30.

19. H. Kroner, "Die Haemorrhoiden in der Medizin des XII und XIII Jahrhunderts," *Janus* 16(1911):441–56 and 644–718.

20. L. J. Bragman, "Maimonides' Treatise on Hemorrhoids," *New York State Med. J.* 27(1927):598–601.

21. S. Muntner, *Moshe ben Maimon. On Hemorrhoids (Birefuot Hatechorim)* (Jerusalem: Mosad Harav Kook, 1965) (Hebr.).

22. F. Rosner and S. Muntner, *The Medical Writings of Moses Maimonides. Treatise on Hemorrhoids and Maimonides' Answers to Queries* (Philadelphia: Lippincott, 1969).

23. F. Rosner, *Moses Maimonides' Treatises on Poisons, Hemorrhoids, and Coitus.* (Haifa: Maimonides Research Institute, 1984).

24. H. Kroner, *Ein Beitrag zur Geschichte der Medizin des XII Jahrhunderts an der Hand Zweier Medizinischer Abhandlungen des Maimonides auf Grund von 6 unedierten Handschriften* (Oberdorf-Bopfingen: Itzowski, 1906).

25. H. Kroner, "Eine Medizinische Maimonides Handschrift aus Granada. Ein

Beitrag zur Stilistik des Maimonides und Charakteristik der Hebräischen Ueberzetzungsliteratur," *Janus* 21(1916):203–47.

26. U. DeMartini, Maimonides, *Segreto dei segreti* (Rome: Istituto di storia della Medicina dell'Universita de Roma, 1960).

27. M. Gorlin, *Maimonides "On Sexual Intercourse" (Fi'l-Jima)* (Brooklyn, NY: Rambash, 1961).

28. E. Chelminski, "Notas introductorias al 'Guia sobre el contacto sexual' de Maimonides," *Anales de ars Medici* (Mexico) 5(4)(1961):240–48.

29. S. Muntner, *Moshe ben Maimon on the Increase of Physical Vigour (Maamar al hizuk koah ha-gavrah)* (Jerusalem: Mosad Harav Kook, 1965), pp. 35–65 (Hebr.).

30. S. Muntner, "Pseudo-Maimonides on Sexual Life," in *Sexual Life, Collection of Medieval Treatises (Maamar al razei ha-chajim ha-miniyim)* (Jerusalem: Geniza, 1965.

31. F. Rosner, *Sex Ethics in the Writings of Moses Maimonides* (New York: Bloch Publishing Co., 1974).

32. F. Rosner, *Moses Maimonides' Treatises on Poisons, Hemorrhoids, and Coitus*.

33. S. Muntner, *Moshe ben Maimon* (Maimonides). *Sefer ha-Katzeret* (The Book on Asthma) (Jerusalem: Rubin Mass, 1940).

34. S. Muntner, *Rabbi Moses ben Maimon. Sefer ha-Katzeret or Sefer ha-Misadim* (The Book on Asthma) (Jerusalem: Geniza, 1963).

35. S. Muntner, *Moshe ben Maimon on Asthma (Sefer ha-Katzeret)* (Jerusalem: Mosad Harav Kook, 1965), pp. 67–119 (Hebr.).

36. S. Muntner, *The Medical Writings of Moses Maimonides. Treatise on Asthma* (Philadelphia: Lippincott, 1963).

37. S. Muntner and I. Simon, "Le Traité de L'Asthme de Maïmonide (1135–1304) Traduit Pour la Premiere Fois en Français d'Après le Texte Hébreu," *Rév. d'Hist. Méd. Héb.* 16(1963):171–86; 17(1964):5–13, 83–97, 127–39, 187–96, 18(1965):5–15.

38. F. Rosner, "Moses Maimonides' Treatise on Asthma," *Thorax* 36(1981): 245–51; *J. Asthma* 21 (1984).

39. F. Rosner, "Moses Maimonides' Treatise on Poisons," *J.A.M.A.* 205(1968): 914–16.

40. M. Steinschneider, "Gifte und ihre Heilung," *Virchows Arch. F. Path. Anat.* 57(1873):62–120.

41. I. M. Rabbinowicz, *Traité des Poisons* (Paris: Lipschutz, 1935), 1st ed. 1865.

42. L. J. Bragman, "Maimonides' Treatise on Poisons" *Med. J. and Rec.* 124(1926): 103–7.

43. S. Muntner, *Moshe ben Maimon* (Maimonides), *Samei ha-mavet ve-ha-refuot kenegdam* (Poisons and their Antidotes, or "The Treatise to the Honored One") (Jerusalem: Rubin Mass, 1942).

44. S. Muntner, *The Medical Writings of Moses Maimonides*, vol. 2: *Treatise on Poisons and Their Antidotes* (Philadelphia: Lippincott, 1966).

45. F. Rosner, "Moses Maimonides' Treatise on Poisons," *N.Y. State J. Med.* 80(1980): 1627–30.

46. F. Rosner, *Moses Maimonides' Treatises on Poisons, Hemorrhoids, and Coitus*.

47. S. Bloch, "Michtav ha-Rav Rabenu Moshe ben Maimon Be'ad ha-Sultan," *Kerem Hemed* 3(1838): 31–39.

48. D. Winternitz, *Das Diatetische Sendschreiben des Maimonides* (Rambam) *an den Sultan Saladin* (Vienna: Braumueller and Seidel, 1843).

49. I. K. Shmukler, *Pismo Moiseh Maimonida K Egipefskomu Sultanu*. Gugienicheskie

Sovetia Perevod S Drevneevreiskogo Doctora I. K. Shmuklera (Kiev). Otdelnii Ottisk Iz, "Vrach Dela" #14–15 and 16. Charkov. "Nauchnaja Misl." Uchr. NKZ. UKSSR (1930).

50. E. Chelminsky, "La Preservacion de la Juventud" de Maimonides, Version Castellana, *Anales de Ars Medici* (Mexico) 5(1961):303–44.

51. H. Kroner, *"Fi tadbir as sihhat,* Gesundheitsanleitung des Maimonides fur den Sultan al-Malik al-Afdhal," *Janus* 27(1923): 101–16, 286–330; 28(1924): 61–74, 143–52, 199–217, 408–19, 455–72; 29(1925): 235–58.

52. H. Kroner, *Die Seelenhygiene des Maimonides, Auszug aus der 3, Kapital des diatetischen Sendschreibens des Maimonides an den Sultan al Malik Alafdahl* (ca. 1198) (Frankfurt A.M.: J. Kauffmann, 1914).

53. L. J. Bragman, "Maimonides on Physical Hygiene," *Ann. Med. Hist.* 7(1925): 140–43.

54. H. Savitz, "Maimonides' Hygiene of the Soul," *Ann. Med. Hist.* 4(1932): 80–86.

55. C. E. Butterworth, "On the Management of Health," in R. L. Weiss and C. E. Butterworth, eds., *Ethical Writings of Maimonides* (New York: New York University Press, 1975), pp. 105–111.

56. S. L. Skoss, "The Treatises of Maimonides on Health Care," in *Portrait of a Jewish Scholar; Essays and Addresses* (New York: Bloch, 1957), pp. 99–116.

57. S. Muntner, *Moshe ben Maimon, Hanhagat ha-Briyut,* Regimen sanitatis, Letters on the hygiene of the body and of the soul (Jerusalem: Mosad Harav Kook, 1956).

58. J. I. Dienstag, "Translators and Editors of Maimonides' Medical Works: A Bio-Bibliographical Survey," in J. O. Leibowitz, ed., *Memorial Volume in Honor of S. Muntner* (Jerusalem: Israel Inst. His. Med., 1983), pp. 95–135.

59. H. L. Gordon, *Moses ben Maimon, The Preservation of Youth,* Essays on Health *(Fi Tadbir As-Sihha)* (New York: Philos. Lib. 1958).

60. A. Bar Sela, H. E. Hoff, and E. Faris, *Moses Maimonides' Two Treatises on the Regimen of Health* (Philadelphia: Am. Philos. Soc. [Trans. n.s. vol. 54, pg 4], 1964).

61. S. Muntner, *Regimen Sanitatis oder Dietetik fur die Seele und den Korper mit Anhang der Medizinischen Responsen und Ethik des Maimonides* (Basel: S. Karger, 1966).

62. H. Kroner, "Der Medizinische Schwanengesang des Maimonides," *Janus* 32(1928): 12–116.

63. A Bar Sela, H. E. Hoff, and E. Faris, *Moses Maimonides' Two Treatises on the Regimen of Health.*

64. F. Rosner and S. Muntner, *Treatise on Hemorrhoids and Maimonides' Answers to Queries.*

65. S. Muntner, *Regimen Sanitatis.*

66. S. Muntner, *Moshe ben Maimon, Biyur Sheimot Ha-Refuot* (Lexicography of Drugs, and Medical Responses) (Jerusalem: Mosad Harav Kook, 1969).

67. J. O. Leibowitz and S. Marcus, *Moses Maimonides On the Causes of Symptoms* (Berkeley, CA: University of California Press, 1974).

68. M. Meyerhof, "Sur Un Glossaire de Matière Médicale Arabe Composé par Maïmonide," *Bull. Inst. Egypte* 17(1935): 223–35; "Sur Un Ouvrage Médical Inconnu de Maïmonide," *Mélanges Maspéro* 3(1935–1940): 1–7.

69. J. Meyerhof, *Un Glossaire de Matière Médicale, Composé par Maïmonide (Sarh Asma al'Uqqar),* vol. 41 (Cairo: Mem. Inst. Egypte, 1940).

70. S. Muntner, *Moshe ben Maimon. Hanhagat habriyut.*

71. F. Rosner, *Moses Maimonides' Glossary of Drug Names* (Philadelphia. Amer. Philosoph. Soc., 1979).
72. F. Rosner, "Moses Maimonides (1135-1204)" *Ann. Int. Med.* 62(1965): 373-75.

CHAPTER 2

All quotations from the works of Maimonides have been newly translated from the cited texts for this paper, unless otherwise stated.

1. F. Pfaff, "Rufus aus Samaria," *Hermes* 67(1932):356-59.
2. See G. Bergsträsser, "Ḥunain ibn Isḥāq, Über die syrischen und arabischen Galen-Übersetzungen," *Abh. fuer d. Kunde des Morgenlandes* 17(1925); *ibid.*, "Neue Materialien zu Ḥunain ibn Isḥāq's Galen-Bibliographie," *Idem.*, 19(1932).
3. See E. Lieber, "Asaf's *Book of Medicines:* a Hebrew encyclopedia of Greek and Jewish medicine, possibly compiled in Byzantium on an Indian model," *Dumbarton Oaks Papers* 38(1984):233-49.
4. For the biography of Maimonides as a physician, see E. Lieber, "Galen: physician as philosopher, Maimonides: philosopher as physician," *Bulletin of the History of Medicine* 53(1979): 268-85. On his stipend see pp. 276-7.
5. M. Steinschneider, ed., "Die Vorrede des Maimonides zu seinem Kommentar ueber die Aphorismen des Hippokrates," *Z.D.M.G.* 48(1894): 218-34. As the editor notes, the Arabic and Hebrew texts are very corrupt; F. Rosner, tr., *Maimonides' Commentary on the Aphorisms of Hippocrates* (Haifa, 1987), p. 12.
6. A. Bar-Sela, H. E. Hoff, and E. Faris, "Moses Maimonides' two treatises on the regimen of health," *Trans. Amer. Philosoph. Soc., N.S.* 54, pt. 4, see p. 16. For Arabic text see H. Kroner, "Fī tadbīr aṣ-ṣiḥḥat, Gesundheitsanleitung des Maimonides," *Janus* 21 (1923-5):101-16, 286-300; 28:61-74, 143-52, 199-217, 408-19, 455-72; 29:235-58.
7. Bar-Sela, pp. 32-40. Reproduced in *Moses Maimonides on the causes of symptoms,* J. O. Leibowitz and S. Marcus, eds. (Berkeley: University of California, 1974), with Arabic text, ed. H. Kroner.
8. Bar-Sela, p. 40.
9. M. Meyerhof, "L'oeuvre médicale de Maimonide," *Archeion* 11 (1929):136-55.
10. F. Klein-Franke, "Der hippokratische und maimonidische Arzt," *Freiburger Zeitschrift fuer Philosophie und Theologie* 17 (1970): 442-49.
11. See Leibowitz and Marcus, eds., pp. 150-51.
12. H. Kroner, "Die Haemorrhoiden in der Medizin des XII. und XIII. Jahrhunderts," *Janus* 16 (1914): 441-56, 645-718; F. Rosner, tr., *Treatises on Poisons, Hemorrhoids, Cohabitation* (Haifa: Maimonides Research Institute, 1984); S. Muntner, tr., *Moses Maimonides: Treatise on Asthma* (Philadelphia: Lippincott, 1963).
13. M. Meyerhof, tr., "Šarḥ asmā' al 'uqqār' l'explication des noms de drogues," *Mém. prés. à l'Inst. d'Egypte,* 41 (Cairo, 1940).
14. M. Steinschneider, "Gifte und ihre Heilung," *Virchow's Archiv* 57 (1873):62-120; see Rosner, *Treatises on Poisons.*
15. See Bergsträsser, "Ḥunain ibn Isḥāq, nos. 87-102, pp. 32 ff."
16. On the Galenic "Canon," see E. Lieber, "Galen in Hebrew," in V. Nutton, ed.,

Galen, problems and prospects (London: Wellcome Institute, 1981), pp. 167-86, esp. pp. 172-79.

17. Steinschneider, "Die Vorrede des Maimonides"; Rosner, *Aphorisms of Hippocrates,* p. 12.

18. Muntner, *Treatise on Asthma* chap. XIII, sect. 30, pp. 88-9.

19. Lieber, "Galen in Hebrew," pp. 182-83. There exist many brief "descriptions" of this collection of works, most of which wrongly maintain that it consisted of a single volume. As far as I know this is the only account that correctly summarizes our knowledge of these works up to the present day, although certain aspects are expertly dealt with in greater detail by S. M. Stern, "Ten autographs by Maimonides," in S. D. Sassoon, *Maimonidis Commentarius in Mischnam,* vol. 3 (Copenhagen, 1961), pp. 11-29: see p. 18.

20. J. O. Leibowitz, "The Latin translations of Maimonides' Aphorisms," *Koroth* 6 (1973), 273-81 (Hebrew) and XCIII-XCIX (English).

21. P. Kahle, ed. and tr., "Moses Maimonides' Aphorismen (Fuṣūl), Einleitung," in H. O. Schroeder, ed., *Galeni in Platonis Timaeum Commentarii Fragmenta* (Leipzig, 1934), pp. 89-96; F. Rosner and S. Muntner, tr., *The Medical Aphorisms of Moses Maimonides,* 2 vols. (New York: Yeshiva University Press, 1970-1971), p. 24.

22. This part of chapter 25 of the *Aphorisms* has been published separately, with the Arabic text and English translation: J. Schacht, M. Meyerhof, "Maimonides against Galen, on philosophy and cosmogony," *Bull. Fac. Arts of the University of Egypt* 5, Arabic Section (Cairo, 1937), 52-88. Repd. in *Max Meyerhof, Studies in Medieval Arabic Medicine,* ed. P. Johnstone (London, 1984), Section IX. See Galen's *De usu partium,* Book 11, G. Helmreich, ed., 2 vols., (Leipzig, 1907, 1909); English trans.: M. T. May, *Galen on the usefulness of the parts of the body,* 2 vols. (Ithaca, NY, 1968). On Galen's other comments on the monotheistic religions, see R. Walzer, *Galen on Jews and Christians* (London, 1949), and on this polemic in particular, pp. 11-13 and 23-37.

23. Schacht and Meyerhof, "Maimonides against Galen," fol. 240a: p. 64 (trans.), p. 77 (text).

24. *Ibid.,* fols. 269a-b: pp. 75-6 (trans.), pp. 87-8 (text).

25. S. Pines, tr., *Moses Maimonides, The Guide of the Perplexed,* 2 vols. (Chicago, 1974), pt. II, chap. 13: vol. II, p. 281.

26. *Ibid.,* Introduction to pt. I, 5b. Quoted from vol. I, p. 9.

27. Maimonides, *Eight Chapters,* Introduction. The latest English translation is by R. L. Weiss and C. E. Butterworth, *Ethical Works of Maimonides* (New York: New York University Press, 1975), pp. 59-104, Introduction, p. 60.

28. See *Encyclopaedia Judaica* (Jerusalem: Keter, 1971), s.v. "Maimonidean controversy," vol. 11, cols. 745-54, esp. 742-50; "Hillel b. Samuel," vol. 8, see col. 488; "Talmud, Burning of," vol. 15, col. 769.

29. J. C. Bürgel, "Averroes contra Galenum," *NAWG* (1967): 265-340.

30. Steinschneider, "Die Vorrede des Maimonides."

31. A. Bar-Sela, H. E. Hoff, "Maimonides' interpretation of the first aphorism of Hippocrates," *Bull. Hist. Med.* 37(1963): 347-54.

32. See F. Rosenthal, " 'Life is short, the art is long': Arabic commentaries on the first Hippocratic aphorism," *Bull. Hist. Med.* 40 (1966): 226-45; L. G. Westerink, ed. and tr., *Stephanos of Athens Commentary on Hippocrates' Aphorisms,* I 2, *CMG,* XI 1,3,1 (Berlin, 1985), pp. 43-9.

33. *De cognoscendi curandisque animi morbis,* V 1-57, K.; P. W. Harkins, tr., *Galen on the passions and errors of the soul* (Ohio, 1963), p. 62.

34. W. H. S. Jones, *Hippocrates,* Loeb Class. Libr., vol. I, *Precepts,* pp. 303–33; *Ibid.,* vol. II, *Law,* pp. 255–65, *Decorum,* pp. 266–301, *Physician,* pp. 302–13. *Testament* (known only in Arabic), trans. in F. Rosenthal, *Das Fortleben des Antike im Islam* (Zurich, 1968), p. 253.

35. S. E. Taschkandi, ed. and tr., *Kitāb at-Tašwīq aṭ-Ṭibbī Sāʾid ibn al-Ḥasan* (Bonn, 1968), pp. 71–3.

36. This is the impression that I myself have given in an earlier paper (see Lieber, "Galen"). David Eisenman has rightly noted, in an unpublished paper, that in his *Eight Chapters* Maimonides described the study of medicine as a religious activity, since it helps toward a knowledge of God. However, this is never subsequently repeated by Maimonides, who later merely echoes Aristotle's view, that it serves "to sharpen the mind."

37. See Muntner, *Treatise on Asthma,* Sect. 30, pp. 88–9.

38. This is a subject of its own, which cannot be pursued further here, but on which I am preparing a separate paper.

CHAPTER 3

1. See D. Gourevitch: "Un thérapeute accompli; Note sur l'adjectif *téleios,*" *Revue de Philologie* 61:1 (1987): 95–99. Also F. M. J. Waanders, *The History of télos and teléo in Ancient Greek* (Amsterdam: Grüner, 1983).

2. Aristotle, *Metaphysics* v. 16;1021b 14–17.

3. *Definitions,* 25.

4. Ibid., 26.

5. Maimonides uses sometimes the term *muvhak* (lit., "brilliant") with the meaning of "excellent," but it is not quite germane to *aristos,* which means "superior."

6. *Lev* (or *levav*) *shalem:* cf. 1 Kings 8:61; 15:14; Isaiah 38:3; 1 Chronicles 28:9, etc.

7. *Genesis Rabbah* 79:2. *Shalem* is related to *shalom* (peace), another category of perfection, toward which man is striving, but which he achieves only after death (cf. *Berakhot* fol. 64a; *Moed Katan* fol. 29a).

8. This is the last chapter of the *Guide.* Maimonides' exposition is based "on ancient and modern philosophers."

9. *Ha-maalot ha-hegioniot* (the high degrees of logic) is explained by Maimonides as meaning the intellectual representations that lead to a true appreciation of the divine. Some have translated "intellectual faculty," others "rational virtues." I prefer "intellectual excellence."

10. Galen's Commentary to Plato's *Timaeus,* a work that is not listed in Galen's own list of his works, but was known in a translation by Hunain and by Isaac his son, and was only preserved in its Arabic version (cf. P. Kraus and R. Walzer, Corp. Platonicum Medii Aevi. Plato Arabus I [London, 1951]).

11. In this case, the physician who does not commit errors (or commits a minimum of errors) is perhaps better characterized by the term *aristos* as we defined it above.

12. Maimonides, *Book on Asthma,* chap. 13.

13. Cf. A. Z. Iskandar, *Galen on Examination by which the best physicians are recognized,* ed. of the Arabic version, with English translation and commentary [Corpus Medicorum Graecorum, Supplementum Orientale IV] (Berlin: Akademie Vg., 1988). The Latin title of this treatise being, *De Optimo Medico Cognoscendo.*

14. "That the best physician should be also a philosopher" (Quod optimus medicus

sit quoque philosophus), cf. *Cl. Gáleni Pergameni Scripta minora,* J. Marquardt & coll. eds. vol. 2, (Leipzig: Teubner, 1891).

15. Cf. O. Temkin, "Greek Medicine as Science and Craft," *Isis* 44:3, no. 137 (1953), see p. 225.

16. Al-Said Ibn Sina Almulk (1165-1212) lived in Cairo. Ibn Abi Usaibi'a, the famous historian of Arabic medicine, was a friend of Maimonides' son Abraham.

17. See *Pirké Moshe* 18:2. Chapter 18 is devoted to the topic "exercise" (*hitamelut*). The source is Galen's small treatise on the "game of the small ball."

18. See S. Muntner's essay "Psychic treatment" (*Ripui be-derekh ha-nefesh*) in Maimonides' *Regimen Sanitatis* (Jerusalem: Mosad Harav Kook, 1957), pp. 181-233 [Hebr.].

19. Anxiety, from *ango* = to squeeze, to tighten (*angor*).

20. See J. O. Leibowitz, "Maimonides on Medical Practice," *Bulletin of the History of Medicine* 31 (1957): 309-17.

21. Biblical ethics: *ha-musar ha-torii,* in the translation of Ibn Tibbon.

22. W. Osler, *Aequanimitas, with other addresses* (Philadelphia: Blackiston, 1932), pp. 3-11 [1st ed. 1904]. Osler's address was delivered in 1889.

23. Cf. Maimonides, *Regimen Sanitatis* 2:14. See also *Pirké Moshe* 18:3.

24. Aristotle, *De Sensu* I, 436a 20. Also "On Respiration," 480b 23-30.

25. Maimonides, *Guide for the Perplexed* 1:34.

26. Here Maimonides quotes from Ecclesiastes 10:10 and Proverbs 19:20.

27. Al-Farabi, "Commentary on Analytica Posteriora" (lost). See Muntner's edition of Maimonides' *Commentary on Hippocrates' Aphorisms,* p. 8.

28. Cf. Iskandar, *Galen on Examination* 9:22.

29. Ibid, 11:1. *Hemoptysis,* spitting of blood (coming from the lungs), once a dreaded symptom of serious tuberculosis, was considered in ancient medicine, before Galen, as a sign expressing an incurable disease.

30. Galen, *Prognosticon,* 1, 1-7.

31. See also Maimonides, *Commentary on Hippocrates' Aphorisms,* S. Muntner, ed. (Jerusalem: Mosad Harav Kook, 1961, Hebrew), p. 15.

32. In the thirteenth chapter of his *Treatise on Asthma,* Maimonides gives more detail on his conception of the perfect physician: He should be quick and perfectly knowledgeable, he should remember the essentials of medical theory. Second, he should be able to differentiate between cases that should be left to their natural course and diseases that must be treated before they become more serious and beyond control. Third, in case of doubt he should refrain from any immoderate initiative and let nature work. Fourth, even in case he knows what is going on, the physician should essentially follow the action of nature, according to the teachings of Hippocrates and Galen.

33. *Pirké Moshe* 25:59. In Muntner's edition (1958), p. 363.

34. Maimonides, *Treatise on Asthma,* S. Muntner, ed. (Philadelphia: Lippincott, 1963), pp. 86-87.

35. In the Hebrew paraphrase of the Hippocratic Oath, the constant rehearsal of medical knowledge is underlined by being placed by the unknown adapter at the very end of the oath. See S. Kottek, J. O. Leibowitz, and B. Richler, "A Hebrew Paraphrase of the Hippocratic Oath," *Medical History* 22(4) (1978): 438-45.

36. Maimonides, *Eight Chapters* (Introduction to the Commentary to the Mishnah, Tractate *Abot*), chap. 4.

37. Cf. *Mishnah Kiddushin* 4:14. A great number of diverse interpretations have been

forwarded. See my essay, "The best of Physicians to Gehenna," *Assia* 4 (3)(1976): 5–12 [Hebr.].

38. "A joint consultation is beneficial, whereas consultation of several physicians, one after the other, is highly disreputable and should be avoided" (ibid.).

39. See also Maimonides, *Regimen Sanitatis* 2:4 [Muntner ed. (1957) p. 45].

40. Maimonides, *Mishneh Torah, Hilkhot Deot,* chap. 4.

41. Maimonides, "Letter to R. Joseph b. Judah Ibn Aqnin," in A. Lichtenberg, ed., *Kovetz Teshuvot Ha-Rambam,* pt. III (Leipzig, 1858) [Hebr.], pp. 30–31.

CHAPTER 4

1. For bibliographical information on sex and health in Maimonides, see F. Rosner, *Sex Ethics in the Writings of Maimonides* (New York: Bloch, 1974). This useful little book also provides English translations for most of the Maimonidean texts cited in my presentation.

2. Maimonides, *Treatise on Asthma* 1:4; in S. Muntner, ed., *The Medical Writings of Moses Maimonides: Treatise on Asthma* (Philadelphia: Lippincott, 1963), p. 7; *Sefer ha-Katzeret* (medieval Hebrew translation, Rabbi Samuel Benveniste), ed. S. Muntner (Jerusalem: Mosad Harav Kook 1965), p. 74.

3. Maimonides, *Pirké Mosheh* [Medical Aphorisms] 17:8 (medieval Hebrew translation, Rabbi Nathan ben Eleazar of Cento), ed. S. Muntner (Jerusalem: Mosad Harav Kook, 1961), p. 213. Rosner translates: "The indulgence in sexual intercourse is one of the requirements for the maintenance of health" (*Sex Ethics,* p. 72).

4. Maimonides, *Fī Tadbīr al-Ṣiḥa (The Preservation of Youth),* 4:9, trans. H. L. Gordon (New York: Philosophical Library, 1958), pp. 80–81. A. Bar-Sela, H. E. Hoff, E. Faris, "Moses Maimonides' Two Treatises on the Regimen of Health," *American Philosophical Society Transactions,* n.s. 54, pt. 4(1964):29. Maimonides, *Hanhagat ha-Beriut* (medieval Hebrew translation, Rabbi Moses ibn Tibbon), ed. S. Muntner (Jerusalem: Mosad Harav Kook, 1957), pp. 74–75.

5. Maimonides, *Fī al-Jimā',* English translation in Rosner, *Sex Ethics,* pp. 17–40. Maimonides, *Maamar al Hizzuk Koah ha-Gavra* (medieval Hebrew translation, Rabbi Zerahiah ben Isaac ben Shealtiel Hen), ed. S. Muntner (Jerusalem: Mosad Harav Kook, 1965). This treatise, written for Saladin's nephew, the Sultan of Hama, advises how to increase sexual potency. Maimonides must have had mixed feelings when he composed it, since (as we shall see) he was very far from advocating sexual profligacy. Cf. also the Hebrew treatise on sex based on Maimonides' writings, recently published by M. L. Wilensky, "Health Conduct in Intercourse Taken from Rabbi Moshe Maimon," *Proceedings of the American Academy for Jewish Research* 56(1990):101–10.

6. S. Muntner, Editor's Introduction, *Sefer ha-Katzeret* (old edition) (Jerusalem: Rubin Mass, 1940), p. 59.

7. See M. Idel, "*Sitre Arayot* in Maimonides' Thought," in S. Pines and Y. Yovel, eds., *Maimonides and Philosophy* (Dordrecht: Martinus Nijhoff, 1986), pp. 79–91.

8. The androcentrism goes beyond the comments about the semen and the testicular cords. The Hebrew verb *bo'el,* translated blandly here as "to have sexual intercourse," designates the act of the male, not the female and is related to the noun *baal,* which *inter alia* designates owner, master, husband, and the male fertility idol. I

reluctantly settled for the bland "to have sexual intercourse" only when I could not find in English a suitably virile term which would not be considered too discourteous.

9. The rooster simile reappears in *Mishneh Torah*, Book of Holiness, *Issure Biah* 21:11.

10. See my "Ethics and Meta-Ethics, Aesthetics and Meta-Aesthetics in Maimonides," in Pines and Yovel, eds., *Maimonides and Philosophy*, pp. 131-38.

11. See Leo Strauss, *Persecution and the Art of Writing* (Glencoe, IL: Free Press, 1952), pp. 75-6; Shlomo Pines, Translator's Introduction, *Guide of the Perplexed*, trans. Pines (Chicago: University of Chicago Press, 1963), p. lxii; Michal Aharoni, "Beyn Kedeshah le-Mekuddeshet: Zenut ve-Nesu'im be-Mishnat ha-Rambam," masters' thesis (Jerusalem: The Hebrew University of Jerusalem, 1989), p. 1. Cf. Pseudo-Nahmanides, *Iggeret ha-Kodesh*, ch. 2; English translation in Seymour J. Cohen, ed. and trans., *The Holy Letter* (New York: Ktav, 1976), pp. 40-3.

12. *The Preservation of Youth*, p. 81. "Moses Maimonides' Two Treatises," p. 29. *Hanhagat ha-Beri'ut*, p. 75.

13. See *Yevamot* 63b, where the excuse is given by Ben Azzai, but not endorsed by the rabbis. Cf. Aharoni, "Beyn Kedeshah le-Mekuddeshet," pp. 77-8.

14. See my "Ethics and Meta-Ethics, Aesthetics and Meta-Aesthetics in Maimonides"; and my "Maimonides and Spinoza on the Knowledge of Good and Evil" (Hebrew), *Iyyun* 28(1978):167-85 (English adaptation in Joseph Dan, ed., *Binah: Studies in Jewish Thought*, vol. 2 (New York: Praeger, 1989), pp. 131-46).

15. The term *ravished (shogeh)*, used positively in Proverbs 5:19 and negatively in Proverbs 5:20, is used negatively in *Hilkhot Teshuvah* 3:4.

CHAPTER 5

1. The author wishes to thank the Syndics and the Librarian of the Cambridge University Library for having granted permission to publish the manuscript appearing in this article.

2. S. Muork, "Notice sur Joseph ben Iehouda disciple de Maimonide," *Journal Asiatique* 14(1842):5-17.

3. H. Friedenwald, *The Jews and Medicine*, vol. 1 (New York: Ktav, 1944), p. 198, n. 19.

4. P. Fenton, "A meeting with Maimonides," *BSOAS* 45(1982):1-3.

5. See text, verso line 12.

6. With most correspondences of the *Genizah* it is customary to find at the beginning of letters such religious invocations and pleas.

7. Rabbenu Yitzhaq is most probably identical with Isaac ben Sason, a contemporary of Maimonides who held a prominent position in Cairo-Fusṭāṭ. See Jacob Mann, *The Jews in Egypt and Palestine under the Fāṭimid Caliphs* (New York: Ktav, 1970), vol. 1, p. 286. Mann had succeeded admirably in describing the sociopolitical life during what he called the "The Maimonides Period."

8. S. D. Goitein, *A Mediterranean Society*, vol. 5 (Berkeley, CA: University of California Press, 1988), p. 105.

9. Nūr al-Dīn Maḥmūd Ibn Zengī, an energetic Turkish sultan who fought the

Crusaders and built the Nuri hospital in Damascus in 1154. M. Meyerhof, *Studies in Medieval Arabic Medicine,* pt. 6 (London: Variorum Reprints, 1984), p. 103.

10. Al-Qifṭī, *Akhbār al-Ḥukamā'* (Cairo: Sāda Press, 1908), p. 210.

11. Ḥusn means literally "beauty," but in this case one should associate such "beauty" with shining of the face of learned men, *hakhmat adam ta'ir panav* (Ecclesiastes 8:1). However, nothing authentic has been recorded as to Maimonides' exterior or physical characteristics. In his famous lecture on Maimonides (*Life and Work of Maimonides* [London: Wertheim, Adine Chambers, 1847], p. 50 n32), Dr. A. Benische had this to say: "On the supposed likeness of Maimonides, copied by Reggio, from which copy that subsequently engraven at Berlin was taken, we quote the opinion of the Italian scholar, as given to Herr Solomon Stern in Berlin. We translate it from German: – 'In the celebrated work *Thesaurus Antiquitatum Sacrarum Blasei Ugolini, Venetiis,* 1744 in the first volume p. 384, is found the likeness of Maimonides, which the author says, was taken *ex antiqa tabula,* without, however, stating more fully and circumstantially how he came to the possession of this tabula, where it existed, and if any one bore testimony to the authenticity of the likeness. However, as Ugolinus is known as an industrious, honorable man, acquainted with the subject, and who cannot be easily suspected of fraud, there is nothing against assuming the probability that at the publication of his work he had really before him such a tabula.'"

12. It is interesting to note that "to read" was then in usage to mean "to study" an academic subject. Such usage is still in practice in some old English universities.

13. Al-Muwaffaq was most probably al-Shaykh al-Muwaffaq Ibn Jumay', a contemporary court physician of Maimonides. He also used to hold meetings (seminars) for students to read medicine under his supervision. See Ibn Abi Useibia, *Herausgegeben von August Müller,* vol. 2 (Leipzig), pp. 112–3. Another al-Muwaffaq who was also a contemporary of Maimonides was al-Muwaffaq Ibn Shu'a, but he did not have the title of al-Shaykh (Ibid., vol. 2, p. 116).

14. H. D. Isaacs, "Some clinical methods used by the Arabs in the Middle Ages," *Proceedings of the XXIII International Congress, History of Medicine,* 2–9 Sept. 1972 (Aberdeen University Press, 1974), p. 82.

15. R. Major, *A History of Medicine,* vol. 1 (Springfield, IL: Charles C Thomas, 1954), p. 281.

16. Hippocrates, *Aphorisms* VII, 31–35; see also F. Rosner and S. Muntner, *The Medical Aphorisms of Moses Maimonides,* vol. 1 (New York: Bloch Publishing Company, Yeshiva University Press, 1973), 5th treatise, pp. 93–97.

17. Maimonides speaks of harmful substances that are removed from the body by the urine. See J. O. Leibowitz and S. Marcus, *Moses Maimonides on the Causes of Symptoms* (Berkeley, CA: University of California Press, 1974), p. 20.

18. Arturo Castiglioni, *A History of Medicine* (New York: Alfred Knopf, 1941), p. 60.

19. Ibn Sīnā, *al-Qānūn fī al-ṭibb,* Būlāq, ed., vol. 1 (Cairo, 1294/1877), pp. 123–35. See also E. G. Browne, *Chahar Maqala,* E. J. W. Gibb Memorial, vol. 11 (London: Luzac, 1921), p. 140.

20. F. Rosner and S. Muntner, *Medical Aphorisms,* vol. 1, pp. 82–92.

21. Dryness is associated with fever, or may be due to constant emesis (ibid., vol. 1, p. 74). Desiccation of the body was considered serious enough to necessitate immediate treatment. Body heat consumes the body's moisture and steadily dries it out. Other causes of desiccation include hyperacidity, insomnia, excessive evacuation and coitus, all of which lead to dehydration. In his *Medical Responsa,* Maimonides refers to "dryness

of melancholic humors." See F. Rosner and S. Muntner, *The Medical Writings of Moses Maimonides* (Philadelphia: Lippincott, 1969), p. 71.

22. F. Rosner and S. Muntner, *Medical Aphorisms,* vol. 1, pp. 151-2. Barley is largely used as an article of diet for the sick and convalescent. Barley water is a demulcent food beverage for those suffering from excessive thirst and diarrhea. *"Kishk* is a gruel of a grain or groats saturated with sour milk or yoghurt for many days, then dried in the sun or on the terrace of a house." M. Levey and N. al-Khaledy, *The Medical Formulary of al-Samarqandī,* (Philadelphia: University of Pennsylvania Press, 1967), p. 212.

23. Leibowitz and Marcus, *Moses Maimonides,* p. 21.

CHAPTER 6

1. S. Muntner, *The Medical Writings of Moses Maimonides: Treatise on Asthma* (Philadelphia: Lippincott, 1963).

2. S. Muntner, *Moshe ben Maimon. Hanhagat Habriut. Regimen Sanitatis,* Letters on the Hygiene of the Body and of the Soul (Jerusalem: Mosad Harav Kook, 1957); F. Rosner, *Moses Maimonides' Treatises on the Regimen of Health* (Haifa: Maimonides Research Institute, 1990).

3. J. O. Leibowitz and S. Marcus, *Moses Maimonides On the Causes of Symptoms* (Berkeley, CA: University of California Press, 1974); F. Rosner.

4. Leibowitz and Marcus, chap. 19.

5. I. Shailat, ed, *Iggerot Harambam* (Letters and Essays of Moses Maimonides), vol. 1 (Jerusalem: Maaliyot Press, 1987), pp. 229-30.

6. M. M. Brayer, "The Concept of Insanity in Rabbinic Law and in Psychiatry," *Proceedings of the Association of Orthodox Jewish Scientists* 10(1990):27-33.

7. Y. Bazak, *Achrayuto Haplilit Shel Halakuy Benafsho* (Jerusalem, 1972), pp. 227-31.

8. See also *Hilkhot Shekhitah* 2:12.

9. *Kohelet Rabbah* 2:17 is a midrashic source for this as well.

10. Shailat, p. 154.

11. Ibid., vol. 1, p. 160.

12. Ibid., vol. 2 (Jerusalem: Maaliyot Press, 1988), p. 489.

13. I. Twersky, *Introduction to the Code of Maimonides (Mishneh Torah),* (New Haven, CT: Yale University Press, 1980), p. 463.

14. S. Pines, *Moses Maimonides. The Guide of the Perplexed* (Chicago: University of Chicago Press, 1963).

15. Twersky, pp. 459-68; N. Lamm, *Ha-Hakham ve-ha-Hasid be-Mishnat ha-Rambam, Sefer Zikaron le-Shmuel Belkin,* Samuel Belkin Memorial Volume (New York: Yeshiva University Press, 1981), pp. 11-28; H. A. Davidson, "The Middle Way in Maimonides' Ethics," *Proceedings of the American Academy of Jewish Research* 44(1987):31-72.

16. Twersky, p. 470.

17. Lamm, pp. 18-19.

18. Pines, p. 3.

19. Rosner, 3:13.

20. Ibid., 3:14.

21. Ibid., 3:15.

CHAPTER 7

1. C. Brockelman, *Geschichte der Arabischen Literature,* Erster Supplement (Band Leiden, 1937), pp. 893-4, no. 3.

CHAPTER 8

1. *Bamidbar Rabbah* 13:16 (ed. Mirkin, Tel Aviv: Yavneh Publications,) 1965, vol. 10 p. 70).
2. *De Partibus Animalium* i 1; 641b.
3. *Physica* ii 8; 199a-b
4. *Analytica Posteriora* i 1; 71b
5. *De Caelo* i 4; 270b
6. *Physica* ii 5; 197a
7. Negative Commandment no. 290. For a detailed treatment of this aspect of rabbinic logic see my book, *Probability and Statistical Inference in Ancient and Medieval Jewish Literature* (Toronto: University of Toronto Press, 1973).
8. Maimonides, *The Guide of the Perplexed,* trans. S. Pines (Chicago: University of Chicago Press, 1963), 1:74, p. 219.
9. Ibid., 3:26, p. 509.
10. Ibid., 2:19, pp. 309-10. I have paraphrased the argument, quoting verbatim salient passages.

The distribution of the stars seems to have long been the subject of speculation. In his commentary to Exodus 23:20, R. Abraham Ibn Ezra (died 1167) raised a similar question. Going back even further, to *Seder Eliyahu Rabbah* (which may be pretalmudic, at least in parts), we find the following passage: "What is the character of the Pleiades? It consists of seven stars in the firmament all close together. Scripture teaches the way of the world to the generations so that a man shall not say to himself, 'Why is not the firmament thick with stars?' They explained it with a parable etc" (chap. 2, ed. Friedmann, p. 9).

11. *Physica* ii 4; 196a, b.
12. Maimonides, *Guide* 2:24, p. 326.
13. Ibid., p. 325.
14. Ibid., p. 326. I have discussed Rambam's position on this issue in greater detail in my commentary *Yad Peshuta, Hilkhot Yesodei Hatorah* (Jerusalem: Maaliyot Press, 5750), chap. 3.
15. The distinction between physical and phenomenological descriptions, as between physical and mathematical models, was taken over by Aquinas and entered the mainstream of European science. To identify the two became the challenge of science. Copernicus argued that in his heliocentric theory the physical interpretation was true also. The triumph of Newtonian mechanics was its ability to deduce planetary motions from the laws of physics. See, for example, O. Pedersen, and M. Pihl, *Early Physics and Astronomy* (London: McDonald and James, 1974), pp. 267-78 and pp. 315-16. In modern physics, the distinction is again important. For Aquinas' depen-

dence on Maimonides, see Etienne Gilson, *Le Thomisme* (Paris: Vrin, 1923), especially pp. 27, 47, 59ff., 111.
    16. Maimonides, *Guide,* 2:22–23.
    17. Ibid., p. 321.
    18. Ibid., 2:25; p. 327.
    19. Ibid., 1:71; p. 179.
    20. Ibid., 3:13; see especially p. 454.
    21. Ibid., 2:17; p. 295.
    22. Ibid., p. 296.
    23. R. A. Fisher, *Statistical Methods and Scientific Inference* (Edinburgh: Oliver and Boyd, 1956), p. 39.
    24. J. Huchra, M. Geller, V. de Lapparent, and R. Burg, "The Center for Astrophysics Redshift," in J. Audouze, M. C. Pelletan, and A. Szalay, ed., *Large Scale Structures of the Universe,* Proceedings of 130th Symposium of International Astronomical Union (Dordrecht: Kluwer, 1988), p. 105. I am indebted to Dr. Benjamin Svetitsky for this and the next reference.
    25. M. I. Geller, "Two Questions about the Large-Scale Distribution of Galaxies," ibid., p. 256.
    26. See, for example, P. S. Moorehead and M. M. Kaplan, eds., *Mathematical Challenges to the Neo-Darwinian Interpretation of Evolution,* (Philadelphia: Wietar Institute Press, 1967).
    27. See, for example: Julius R. Weinberg, *Nicolaus of Autrecourt* (Princeton, NJ: Princeton University Press, 1984), pp. 84ff.
    28. See, for example, M. B. Foster, "The Christian Doctrine of Creation and the Rise of Modern Natural Science," *Science and Religious Belief,* ed. C. A. Russell (London: University of London Press 1973), pp. 294–315; also R. Hooykas, *Religion and the Rise of Modern Science* (Edinburgh: Scottish Academic Press, 1972).
    29. A. Foucher de Careil, *Leibnitii observationes ad Rabbi Mosis Maimonidis Librum qui inscribitur Doctor Perplexorum* (Reprint Gregg Int. Publ., 1969), p. 28.
    30. Ibid. superscript at the beginning.

CHAPTER 9

    1. This subject has received increasing attention in recent years. Cf., e.g., J. D. North, "Medieval Concepts of Celestial Influence: A Survey," in P. Curry, ed., *Astrology, Science and Society. Historical Essays* (Woodbridge/Wolfeboro: Boydell Press, 1987), pp. 5–17; E. Grant, "Medieval and Renaissance Scholastic Conceptions of the Influence of the Celestial Region on the Terrestrial," *Journal of Medieval and Renaissance Studies* 17(1987):1–23. Cf. also T. Litt, *Les corps célestes dans l'univers de Saint Thomas d'Aquin* (Louvain: Publications universitaires; Paris: Béatrice-Nauwelaerts, 1963).
    2. Aristotle, *De gen. et corr.,* II.10; F. Solmsen, *Aristotle's System of the Physical World* (Ithaca, NY: Cornell University Press, 1960), pp. 379–89.
    3. Aristotle, *De gen. anim.* IV.10, 777b26 ff. Aristotle was unaware that the moon causes the tides.
    4. The argument is found in Ptolemy's *Tetrabiblos* I.2 and is repeated by most medieval proponents of astrology. Cf., e.g., R. Lemay, *Abu Ma'cshar and Latin Aristotel-*

ianism in the Twelfth Century (Beirut: American University of Beirut, 1962), pp. 50 ff., 55 ff. All natural philosophers, including those who rejected judicial astrology, endorsed this argument and in fact invoked the astrologers as supplying corroborating evidence for it. Consider Ibn Rushd's exposition. After reporting Aristotle's view that the sun's motion along the ecliptic is the efficient cause of generation and corruption (it brings about the four seasons), he goes on to argue:

> This latter movement is not limited to the sun alone, but is also that of the moon and of all the planets, although actually it is more apparent in the case of the sun. For the effect of the sun upon the alteration of the four seasons in its course along its inclined circle is precisely that of *each star* in its course along its specific circle. For although the particular affect which each one of the stars exerts upon things about us is hidden from us, a comprehensive account would reveal that they do have a bearing upon generation and corruption to the extent that if we were to imagine the removal of any star or its movement, generation as a whole or the generation of some beings could not be completed. Indeed, it may be observed that some things are attributed to the action of this or that star. We therefore find that those who have observed the stars since ancient times [the reference is doubtlessly to the astrologers] divided all things into kinds according to them and characterized one thing as stemming from the nature of one star and another thing as stemming from the nature of another star.

Averroes, *Epitome on Aristotle's 'De generatione et corruptione'*, English translation by S. Kurland (Cambridge, MA: The Medieval Academy of America, 1958), p. 133.

5. All quotations are taken from M. Maimonides, *The Guide of the Perplexed*, translated with an Introduction and Notes by S. Pines (Chicago: University of Chicago Press, 1963); here 2:9, p. 269.

6. Ibid., 2:10 pp. 270 f.

7. I will argue these theses in detail in a forthcoming book on Aristotle's "chemistry" and its aftermath, to be published by Oxford University Press.

8. Cf. Maimonides, *Guide* 2:12.

9. For a masterly history of these ideas, cf. H. A. Davidson, "Alfarabi and Avicenna on the Active Intellect," *Viator* 3(1972):109–78; *idem*, "Averroes on the Active Intellect as a Cause of Existence," *Viator* 18(1987):191–225.

10. Lemay, pp. 66 f., 74–85.

11. Maimonides, *Guide* 2:5, p. 260.

12. This specific claim was controversial, for some thinkers held that minerals too receive their forms from the "Giver of Forms." Maimonides' view is shared by Averroes: cf. H. Blumberg, ed., *Averrois Cordvbensis Compedia librorun Aristotelis qui Parva naturalia vocantvr*, Arabic version (Cambridge, MA: The Medieval Academy of America, 1972), p. 76; Hebrew version, ed. by *idem* (Cambridge, MA: The Medieval Academy of America, 1954), p. 50; English translation by *idem:* Averroes, *Epitome of Parva naturalia* (Cambridge, MA: The Medieval Academy of America, 1961), p. 44 f. Since Maimonides elsewhere says that *all* forms originate in a separate intellect (*Guide* 2:12, p. 278), his view is apparently that minerals do not have properties beyond those they have by virtue of their components. As Shem-Tov, in his commentary on the *Guide*, points out, Avicenna and al-Ghazâlî were of the opposite opinion. Cf. *Sefer More Nebukhim . . . im Shlosha Perushim . . . Efodi, Sem-Tov, Ibn Qresqas . . .* (Vilna, 1902; reprinted Jerusalem, 1960), p.

112. Their view was also that of Gersonides. Cf. my "Human Felicity and Astronomy: Gersonides's Revolt Against Ptolemy" (in Hebrew), *Daat* no. 22(Winter 1989):58. H. A. Wolfson compares the views of J. Halevi and Maimonides on this issue in his "Halevi and Maimonides on Design, Chance and Necessity" (1941), reprinted in I. Twersky and G. H. Williams, eds., *Studies in the History of Philosophy and Religion,* vol. 2 (Cambridge, MA: Harvard University Press, 1977), pp. 26–34.

13. Maimonides, *Guide* 1:72, pp. 186 f.

14. Ibid.

15. Ibid., 2:6, p. 261.

16. Ibid., 2:10, pp. 269 f. Qalonymos ben Qalonymos, writing at the beginning of the fourteenth century, ironizes on precisely this saying: "... *nikkar sho'a lifney dal, lefi she-yesh lo mazzal mi-le-mala, makke oto pizey oheb we-omer lo: gedal.*" A. M. Habermann, ed., *Eben Bohan* (Tel Aviv: Mahbarot Le-Sifrut, 1956), p. 48.

17. Maimonides, *Guide* 2:10, pp. 269 f.

18. Ibid., 2:12, p. 280.

19. Cf. C. Sirat, "Moïse de Narbonne et l'astrologie," *Proceedings of the Fifth World Congress of Jewish Studies,* vol. 3 (Jerusalem: World Union of Jewish Studies, 1972), pp. 61–72.

20. Moshe Narboni, *Be'ur le-Sefer Moreh Nebukhim,* ed. Y. Goldenthal (Vienna: K. K. 1852 Hof- und Staatsdruckerei, 1852), p. 29^r.

21. Cf., e.g., R. Sorabji, "Body and Soul in Aristotle," in J. Barnes, M. Schofield, and R. Sorabji, eds., *Articles on Aristotle,* vol. 4: *Psychology and Aesthetics* (London: Duckworth, 1979), pp. 42–64; F. Nuyens, *L'évolution de la psychologie d'Aristote* (Louvain: Publications Universitaires, 1948).

22. H. H. Biesterfeldt, "Galens Traktat 'Dass die Kräfte der Seele den Mischungen des Körpers folgen' in arabischer übersetzung," *Abhandlungen für die Kunde des Morgenlandes,* vol. 40 (Wiesbaden: F. Steiner, 1973), p. 4. On the great currency of the theory in both Arabic medicine and Arabic philosophy cf. *idem,* "Gâlînûs Quwâ n-nafs, Zitiert, adaptiert, korrigiert," *Der Islam* 63(1986):119–36. The entire theory received its classical exposition in R. Klibansky, E. Panofsky, and F. Saxl, *Saturn and Melancholy* (Cambridge: Cambridge University Press, 1964).

23. Maimonides, *Guide* 2:40, p. 381.

24. Galen devotes his book *Peri Ethon* precisely to these kinds of "accidents," which he denotes by that name, for example, anger, desire, fear, love. Cf. the English translation of the Arabic version of the work: J. M. Mattock, "A Translation of the Arabic Epitome of Galen's Book *Peri Ethon,*" in S. M. Stern, A. Hourani, and V. Brown, eds., *Islamic Philosophy and the Classical Tradition: Essays presented . . . to Richard Walzer* (Oxford: Cassirer, 1972), pp. 235–60.

25. Maimonides, *Guide* 2:38, p. 376.

26. Ibid., 2:36.

27. This argument is adduced, e.g., by Ptolemy, *Tetrabiblos,* I.2, ed. and trans. by F. E. Robbins (London: Heinemann; Cambridge, MA: Harvard University Press [The Loeb Classical Library], 1940), p. 13: "Why can we not, too, with respect to an individual man, perceive the general quality of his temperament from the ambient at the time of his birth . . . and predict occasional events, by the use of the fact that such and such an ambient is attuned to such and such a temperament and is favorable to prosperity, while another is not so attuned and conduces to injury." Cf. also 3:1, pp. 223 f.

28. Cf., e.g., such an opponent of judicial astrology as al-Fârâbî. Referring to the effects of the rays of the stars, he states:

> On en vient ensuite à examiner l'influence que ceux-ci excercent sur les humeurs des hommes. On peut alors connaître l'influence que ces humeurs excercent sur les actes volontaires. Si on prédit de quelque façon en fonction des corps célestes quelque chose de ce qui concerne un acte volontaire, il se peut qu'on fasse une prédiction [i.e., a correct prediction!] à propos d'actions volontaires dépendant d'humeurs.

Al-Fârâbî then argues that some voluntary actions entirely proceed from deliberation; on these the heavenly bodies have no influence. Quoted from T.-A. Druart, "Le second traité de Fârâbî sur la validité des affirmations basées sur la position des étoiles," *Bulletin de philosophie médiévale* 21(1979):51. The argument is also put forward in Levi ben Gershom, *Sefer Milhamot ha-Shem* 2:2 (Leipzig, 1866), p. 96, quoted in G. Freudenthal, "Levi ben Gershom as a Scientist: Physics, Astrology and Eschatology," *Proceedings of the Tenth World Congress of Jewish Studies,* Division C, vol. 1: *Jewish Thought and Literature* (Jerusalem: World Union of Jewish Studies, 1990), pp. 67–8.

29. This consequence is judiciously drawn by R. Levi ben Gershom who, in accordance with his general philosophy, transforms it into yet another argument from design. Cf. his *Milhamot ha-Shem* 2:2, p. 97 and Freudenthal, "Levi ben Gershom as a Scientist."

30. Maimonides, *Shemonah Perakim,* chap. 8. Cf. also the chapter "Hanhagat Beriut ha-Nefesh," in *Hanhagat ha-Beriut* in S. Muntner, ed., *Moshe ben Maimon (Maimonides), Medical Works* (in Hebrew), vol. 1 (Jerusalem: Mosad Harav Kook, 1987), p. 58 ff. On Maimonides' differing conceptions of what the "healthy" state of the soul in fact is, and consequently of the aims of the "corrective therapy," cf. H. A. Davidson, "The Middle Way in Maimonides' Ethics," *Proceedings of the American Academy for Jewish Research* 54(1987):31–72.

31. More precisely: an environment that is not perfectly balanced will always cause the equilibrium within a composite substance to shift; this is why states of equilibrium do not last. Cf. G. Freudenthal, "The Theory of the Opposites and an Ordered Universe: Physics and Metaphysics in Anaximander," *Phronesis* 31(1986):197–228.

32. The classical study of this doctrine is E. Honigmann, *Die Sieben Klimata* (Heidelberg: C. Winter, 1929).

33. *Kuzari* 1.1; H. Hirschfeld's translation quoted from I. Heinemann, ed., *Jehuda Halevi, Kuzari,* in *Three Jewish Philosophers* (New York: Atheneum, 1977), p. 28.

34. Ibid., 2.10 ff. Cf. the excellent article by the late A. Altmann, "The Climatological Factor in Yehudah Hallevi's Theory of Prophecy" (Hebrew), *Melilah* 1(1944):1–17. This paper gives a concise but broad overview of the issues to which I briefly allude here in a single paragraph. Cf. also A. Melamed, "The Land of Israel and Climatology in Jewish Thought" (Hebrew), in M. Hallamish and A. Ravitzky, eds., *The Land of Israel in Medieval Jewish Thought* (Jerusalem: Yad Izhak Ben-Zvi, 1991), pp. 52–78.

35. Maimonides, *Pirké Moshe* 25:57–58, *Medical Works* 2:361 f. Maimonides, as he himself indicates, here follows Galen and al-Fârâbî.

36. Maimonides, *Hanhagat ha-Beriut* 4:1, *Medical Works* 1:66.

37. The argument is put forward in Ptolemy, *Tetrabiblos* II.2.

38. Al-Fârâbî, *Sefer ha-Hat'halot,* ed. Z. Filipowski (Leipzig, 1849), p. 33, quoted after, Melamed, "The Land of Israel and Climatology in Jewish Thought," p. 55 f. n. 11.

39. A. Marx, "The Correspondence Between the Rabbis of Southern France and Maimonides About Astrology," *Hebrew Union College Annual* 3(1926):351; Y. Shailat, ed., *Iggerot ha-Rambam,* vol. 2, (Jerusalem, 1988), p. 481; translation cited from R. Lerner, "Maimonides, Letter on Astrology," in R. Lerner and M. Mahdi, eds., *Medieval Political Philosophy: A Sourcebook* (Ithaca, NY: Cornell University Press, 1963), pp. 229 f.

40. A. S. Halkin and B. Cohen, ed. and trans., *Moses Maimonides' Epistle to Yemen* (New York: American Academy for Jewish Research, 1952), pp. 64–65 (texts), p. xiii (translation).

41. Maimonides, *Mishneh Torah, Hilkhot Akum,* 11.

42. L. Strauss, "The Literary Character of *The Guide for the Perplexed,*" *Persecution and the Art of Writing* (1952) (reprinted: London and Chicago: The University of Chicago Press, 1988), pp. 84, 94.

43. One of them was quoted above; another is at *Guide* 3:37.

44. Marx, "The Correspondence," p. 351; Shailat, *Iggerot,* p. 481 f.; translation cited from Lerner, "Maimonides, Letter," p. 230.

45. For an overview and bibliography cf. B. R. Goldstein and D. Pingree, *Levi ben Gerson's Prognostication for the Conjunction of 1345,* in *Transactions of the American Philosophical Society* 80, pt. 6, 1990, particularly p. 3 ff.

46. Marx, "The Correspondence" p. 351; Shailat, *Iggerot,* p. 480 f.; translation quoted from Lerner, "Maimonides, Letter," p. 229 f.

47. For the same reason Maimonides postulates that the members of the Sanhedrin must be knowledgeable, among other things, in astrology and "other stupidities of idolatry." This is necessary "in order that they be able to sit to judgment over them." Maimonides, *Mishneh Torah, Sefer Shoftim, Hilkhot Sanhedrin* 2:1. This is not sufficiently appreciated in R. Lerner, "Maimonides' Letter on Astrology," *History of Religions* 8(1968):148.

48. S. Pines, "Excursus. Notes on Maimonides' Views Concerning Free Will," included in his "Studies in Abu'l-Barakât al-Baghdâdî's Poetics and Metaphysics," *Scripta Hierosolymitana* 6(1960):195–8; A. Altmann, "The Religion of the Thinkers: Free Will and Predestination in Saadia, Bahya and Maimonides," S. D. Goitein, ed., *Religion in a Religious Age* (Cambridge, MA: Harvard University Press, 1974), pp. 25–51, reprinted in Altmann, *Essays in Jewish Intellectual History* (Hanover and London: University Press of New England and Brandeis University Press, 1981), pp. 35–64.

49. T.-A. Druart, "Astronomie et astrologie selon Fârâbî," *Bulletin de philosophie médiévale* 20(1978):43–47; idem, "Le second traité de Fârâbî sur la validité des affirmations basées sur la position des étoiles"; A. F. Mehren, "Vue d'Avicenne sur le rapport de la responsabilité humaine avec le destin," *Le Muséon* 3(1884):383–403. For a recent overview cf. B. Radtke, "Die Stellung der islamischen Theologie und Philosophie zur Astrologie," *Saeculum* 39(1988):259–67.

50. This point has been well taken by A. Halkin. Cf. *Moses Maimonides' Epistle to Yemen,* Hebrew Introduction, p. xxiii.

51. For this point I am grateful to the late Professor S. Pines.

52. Maimonides' perception of the connection between astrology, star worship, and fatalism is elaborated in Y. T. Langermann, "Maimonides' Repudiation of Astrology," forthcoming in *Maimonidean Studies* 2. The fatalism to which astrology is prone to give rise is delightfully described by al-Fârâbî: if all events were predetermined, hope

and fear would cease and all incentive to do anything on behalf of one's future would be thwarted. For want of fear, no one would anymore obey his superiors and social order would be subverted. Cf. F. Dietirici, ed., *Al-Fârâbî's philosophische Abhandlungen aus Londoner, Leidner und Berliner Handschriften* (Leiden: Brill, 1890), p. 105, translated in *idem, Al-Fârâbî's philosophische Abhandlungen aus dem Arabischen übersetzt* (Leiden: Brill, 1892), p. 174. Al-Fârâbî did not anticipate that some six centuries after his time, Calvinistic and Puritan doctrines of predestination would, according to M. Weber's and R. K. Merton's analyses, play a major role in giving rise to capitalism and modern science. Cf. my review of F. Klein-Franke, *Vorlesungen über die Medizin im Islam* (= *Sudhoffs Archiv*, Beiheft 23) (Wiesbaden: Franz Steiner, 1982), in *History and Philosophy of Life Sciences* 9(1987): 119–22.

53. Cf. *Guide* 2:24, and, generally, S. Pines, "The Limitations of Human Knowledge According to Al-Farabi, Ibn Badja, and Maimonides," in I. Twersky, ed., *Studies in Medieval Jewish History and Literature* (Cambridge, MA: Harvard University Press, 1979), pp. 82–109.

54. Maimonides, *Guide* 2:37.

55. Cf. A. Funkenstein, "Maimonides: Political Theory and Realistic Messianism," *Miscellanea Mediaevalia* 11(1977):88–90; *idem, Maimonides: Nature, History and Messianic Beliefs* (Hebrew) (Tel Aviv: Ministry of Defense, 1983), pp. 30–33; and *idem, Theology and the Scientific Imagination* (Princeton: Princeton University Press, 1986), pp. 227–39.

56. Maimonides, *Guide* 3:15, pp. 451–2.

57. This crucial point has been forcefully and repeatedly stated by Y. Leibowitz, notably in his *The Faith of Maimonides* (New York: Adama, 1987), chap. 3.

58. Cf. Maimonides, *Guide* 3:15, p. 455.

59. Cf. Levi ben Gershom, *Milhamot ha-Shem*, p. 194 ff.; Ch. Touati, *La pensée philosophique et théologique de Gersonide* (Paris: Editions de Minuit, 1973), p. 306.

60. *Milhamot ha-Shem*, bk. 5, pt. 2, chaps. 7–9.

61. Ibid., bk. 2, chap. 2, pp. 95–98; Freudenthal, "Levi ben Gershom as a Scientist."

62. Cf. G. Freudenthal, "Human Felicity and Astronomy."

63. For helpful remarks on a draft of this paper I am grateful to Professors Bernard R. Goldstein (Pittsburgh) and Samuel Kottek (Jerusalem). To Dr Y. Tzvi Langermann (Jerusalem) I am grateful for a prolonged exchange of views on the issues discussed here and for having sent me prior to its publication a copy of his paper, "Maimonides' Repudiation of Astrology," forthcoming in *Maimonidean Studies* 2.

CHAPTER 10

1. On Gersonides, see my "Bibliographia Gersonideana," in G. Freudenthal, ed., *Studies on Gersonides: A Fourteenth-Century Philosopher-Scientist* (Leiden: E. J. Brill, 1922), pp. 367–414.

2. A word about the history of this short essay is in order. I was invited to attend the Fourth International Symposium on Medicine and Bible in the Talmud in Jerusalem in 1990. I prepared a paper for that conference. Due to the fact that in the end I was unable to attend the conference, and due to the fact that the paper I prepared grew much beyond the bounds of the conference proceedings, I submitted it elsewhere,

under the title, "On the Status of the Astronomy and Physics in Maimonides' *Mishneh Torah:* A Chapter in the History of Science," *British Journal for the History of Science* 24(1991): 453-63. Professor Samuel Kottek kindly asked me to prepare a smaller paper for the conference proceedings, and the present essay is the result. It represents independent development of one idea in the longer essay. Further on this subject see my "Maimonides on the Science of the *Mishneh Torah:* Provisional or Permanent?" *AJS Review,* forthcoming. For detailed background on many of the issues raised here, see the longer essay. I would like to thank Professor Kottek and his colleagues for inviting me to the conference and for soliciting the present study. I would also like to thank the Memorial Foundation for Jewish Culture for its support during the time I worked on this paper.

3. *Hokhmot;* plural of *hokhmah.*

4. Gersonides, *Wars of the Lord* VI.i.15. In the Leipzig, 1866 (reprint: Berlin, 1923) edition of the *Wars,* the passage appears on p. 356.

5. The idea is repeated frequently in Gersonides' commentary on Song of Songs. See, for example, the following comment on 1:2:

> The third impediment – our ignorance of the way that leads to perfection – will also be overcome in this fashion. This is so because while each of those who endeavor to achieve this apprehension by themselves will either apprehend nothing or very little, when what all of them has apprehended is gathered together, a worthy amount will have been gathered. Either by virtue of himself or by virtue of his directing those who see their words towards the achievement of the truth in this. Therefore, one must always be aided in one's research by the words of those who preceded him, especially when the truth in them has been revealed to those who preceded him, as was the case during the time of this sage, for the sciences were then greatly [perfected] in our nation. The matter being so, our perfected predecessors guide us in speculation in a way which brings us to perfection, either through their speech or writing, by virtue of the natural desire they have for proffering this influence, and will make known to us concerning each thing the way in which it should be researched, and what they have understood concerning it, together with the assistance [concerning it] which they have derived from their predecessors.

For literature on this subject, see G. F. Hourani, *Averroes on the Harmony of Religion and Philosophy* (London: Luzac, 1961), pp. 46-47. See further, R. Nisbet, *History of the Idea of Progress* (New York: Basic Books, 1980), pp. 86-88.

6. This understanding of scientific progress is unfashionable today, and derided as "whiggish" by many students of the history of science circles. By imputing this view to Gersonides (and, as shall be seen, Maimonides) I do not mean to express either approval or disapproval of it.

7. Maimonides, *Mishneh Torah,* "Laws of the Foundations of the Torah," in Moses Hyamson, trans., *Book of Knowledge* (Jerusalem: Feldheim, 1974).

8. Maimonides, *Guide of the Perplexed* 2:8 and 3:15. In the translation of S. Pines (Chicago: University of Chicago Press, 1965), pp. 267 and 459, respectively. It might be argued, of course, that Maimonides could attribute error to the sages on scientific matters while being sure that he himself did not err in like fashion simply on the grounds that the sciences, while deficient in the times of the sages, had reached perfection and completion in his own times. That in fact Maimonides did not indeed

adopt this position is noted below and proved in my paper cited above.

9. This, at least, is Maimonides' publicly expressed position (*Guide* 2:15-18). Many of his medieval and modern interpreters, however, maintain that Maimonides adopted a view at variance with his publicly expressed position. On this, see my *Dogma in Medieval Jewish Thought* (Oxford: Oxford University Press, 1986), p. 242 n. 223.

10. Maimonides, *Guide* 2:22, pp. 319-20.

11. See ibid. 2:19, p. 308, and *The Medical Aphorisms of Maimonides*, vol. 2, translated and edited by F. Rosner and S. Muntner (New York: Yeshiva University Press, 1971), p. 205.

12. Maimonides, *Guide* 2:32, p. 526.

13. Ibid., 3:51, p. 621.

14. This last point was suggested to me by J. J. Ross. See "Maimonides and Progress—Maimonides's Concept of History," Y. Cohen, ed., *Hevrah ve-Historiah* (Jerusalem: Israel Ministry of Education and Culture, 1980), pp. 529-42 (Hebrew).

15. "Laws of Kings" 11:4 (uncensored edition); I cite the translation of A. M. Hershman, *Book of Judges* (New Haven: Yale University Press, 1949), pp. xxiii-xxiv.

16. P. Duhem, *To Save the Phenomena: An Essay on the Idea of Physical Theory from Plato to Galileo,* trans. E. Doland and C. Maschler (Chicago: University of Chicago Press, 1969).

17. Or so Duhem thought; he was apparently wrong about Ptolemy. See B. R. Goldstein, "The Arabic Version of Ptolemy's *Planetary Hypotheses,*" *Transactions of the American Philosophical Society* (ns) 57(1967):1-55.

18. See Maimonides, *Guide* 2:24, p. 326.

19. See G. Freudenthal, "Human Felicity and Astronomy: Gersonides' Revolt Against Ptolemy," *Daat* 22(1989):55-72 (Hebrew).

20. For discussion on this, see S. Pines, "The Limitations of Human Knowledge According to Al-Farabi, ibn Bajjah, and Maimonides," in I. Twersky, ed., *Studies in Medieval Jewish History and Literature,* vol. 1 (Cambridge, MA: Harvard University Press, 1979), pp. 82-109, and A. Altmann, "Maimonides on the Intellect and the Scope of Metaphysics," in his *Von der mittelalterlichen zur modernen Aufklaerung* (Tuebingen: Mohr, 1987), pp. 60-129.

21. See H. A. Wolfson, "Maimonides on Negative Attributes," *Studies in the History and Philosophy of Religion II* (Cambridge, MA: Harvard University Press, 1977), pp. 195-230.

22. See N. Samuelson, "Gersonides' Account of God's Knowledge of Particulars," *Journal of the History of Philosophy* 10(1972):399-416.

23. On all this, see the article by Freudenthal in *Daat* cited above.

CHAPTER 11

1. E.g., "Ponder His works, for this will lead you to recognize the Creator." *Baraita* quoted in Responsa of Maimonides (no. 150, in J. Blau edition, Jerusalem, 1961); "It is a *mitzvah* to make astronomical calculations." *Shabbat* 75a. For an extensive survey, see my *Torah Study* (Jerusalem: Feldheim, 1990), pt. 7, chap. 2.

2. "Responsum Regarding the Study of the Sciences," in *Divrey Hakhamim,* R. E. Ashkenazi, ed., p. 71. The esteem Rabbi Yaakov enjoyed may be inferred from the fact

that he is one of those who were asked to endorse *Sefer ha-Agur,* an important fifteenth-century halakhic compendium.

3. Maimonides, *Guide* 1:32.

4. Rabbi Saadiah Gaon, *Emunot WeDe'ot,* Introduction, in R. Y. Kapach, ed., sec. 6.

5. R. E. HaLevi, *Zekan Aharon,* no. 25.

6. R. Baruch of Sklov's translation of Euclid, Introduction.

7. E.g., Maimonides, *Responsa,* J. Blau, ed. vol. 3, (Jerusalem, 1961), p. 57.

8. Exodus 12:2; Maimonides, *Book of Commandments,* pos. no. 153. Cf. also Rashi, Commentary on the Torah, beginning.

9. Maimonides, *Code,* "Sanctification of the New Moon," 1:6.

10. Ibid., 1:7.

11. Ibid., chaps. 11–17.

12. Ibid., 11:5.

13. Maimonides, Commentary to *Sukkah* 1:1. See Y. Levi, *Kovetz Hidushey Torah,* vol. 2 (Jerusalem: Jerusalem College of Technology, 5749), pp. 145–6, for a treatment of the nontrivial optical aspects.

14. Maimonides, Commentary to *Niddah* 2:5.

15. E.g., N. L. Rabinovitch, *Probability and Statistical Inference in Ancient and Medieval Literature* (Toronto: University of Toronto, 1973).

16. Maimonides, *Code,* "First Fruits," 11:30.

17. See extensive discussion by L. N. Rabinovitch in "Rambam as Scientist," *Encounter,* H. C. Schimmel and A. Carmell, eds., (Jerusalem: Feldheim, 1989).

18. Maimonides, Commentary to *Kilayim* 5:5.

19. Maimonides, Commentary to *Eruvin* 2:5.

20. E.g., Isaiah 40:26.

21. E.g., *Sifrey* to Deuteronomy 6:6, and *Baraita* of R. Meir brought in op. cit.

22. Maimonides, *Shemonah Perakim,* 5.

23. Loc. cit.

24. Maimonides, *Code,* "Foundations of the Torah," 4:12.

25. Ibid., 2:2.

26. Deuteronomy 6:5.

27. Maimonides, *Guide* 3:25.

28. Ibid., Introduction (p. 8 in Y. Kapach edition).

29. Ibid., 1:34.

30. Maimonides, *Code,* "Personality Traits" *(Deot),* chap. 4.

31. Maimonides, Commentary on *Kelim* 30:2.

32. Ibid., *Hullin* 9:6.

33. *Shabbat* 107 b.

34. Maimonides, *Code,* "Shabbat," 11:2. Cf. Ramban's (Nachmanides') comment quoted in *Maggid Mishneh* ad loc.

35. Maimonides, "Thirteen Principles [of Faith]," Commentary to *Sanhedrin,* chap. 10, introduction, principle no. 8.

36. Maimonides, *Code,* "Sanctification of the New Moon," chap. 17, end.

37. Maimonides, *Guide* 3:14, end.

38. R. Avraham, son of Maimonides, *Maamar al Odot Derashot Hazal,* s.v. *da ki atah hayav* (printed in many editions of *Eyn Yaakov,* at the beginning.)

39. Maimonides, *Code,* "Foundations of the Torah," 4:10, ref. to *Mishnah Hagigah* 2:1.

CHAPTER 12

1. See Arthur Hyman, "Maimonides on Causality," *Maimonides and Philosophy*, Shlomo Pines and Yirimiyahu Yovel, eds. (Boston, 1986), p. 157.

2. The source of all causal power is, of course, the Deity. Attribution of all causal power to God may culminate in occasionalism rather than a strict notion of physical causation. Occasionalism is the doctrine that events that occur in the world are occasions for the application of God's power which produce the phenomena we perceive as effects of those events. This does not necessarily mean that God must engage in a constant series of miraculous interventions in the natural order. The concept "The Holy One, blessed be He, stipulated a condition with the works of creation" *(tenai hitneh ha-kadosh barukh hu im maasei bereishit)*, formulated in *Pesikta Zutrata* 3:24 and *Bereishit Rabbah* 5:4, implies that *ab initio*, in the act of creation, God established a series of coordinated developments. The divinely decreed coordination between those events is perceived as causal in nature. In explaining this notion, a seventeenth-century philosopher, Arnold Geulincx, offered the example of two clocks perfectly adjusted to keep the same time. One has a dial showing the hour; the second strikes to tell the hour. It appears that the second strikes because the hand of the first has reached the hour. The appearance of a causal connection between the clocks is, in fact, the result of precise prearrangement. Volitional acts on the part of human beings and their intended results are also synchronized by God. Occasionalist theories differ from a strict notion of causality in that the latter posits an intrinsic physical factor inherent in the corporeal object which is responsible for the causal connection. No attempt is made in this discussion to adjudicate between those theories and the conventional notion of causation or to determine whether or not Jewish philosophers of the medieval period adopted one or another occasionalist theory of causation.

3. Elsewhere, in *Guide for the Perplexed*, book 1, chap. 61, Maimonides writes:

> You must beware of sharing the error of those who write amulets. Whatever you hear of them or read in their works, especially in reference to the names which they form by combination, is utterly senseless; they call these combinations *shemot* [names] and believe their pronunciation demands sanctification and purification and that by using them they are able to work miracles. Rational persons ought not to listen to such men nor in any way believe their assertions.

These comments negating the efficacy of amulets seem to contradict the clear ruling of the Mishnah, *Shabbat* 60a. Indeed, Shem Tob, in his commentary on the *Guide, ad locum*, indicates that Maimonides intended to negate error that might arise on the basis of that mishnaic comment. However, Shem Tob seems to be unaware of Maimonides' own seemingly contradictory comments in the *Mishneh Torah, Hilkhot Shabbat* 19:14. See also the comments of Jacob I. Dienstag, *Talpiyot*, vol. 4, no. 1–2 *(Tammuz 5709)*, p. 261. Maimonides' negative comment in *Hilkhot Mezuzah* 5:4, cited below, although somewhat ambiguous, seems to refer to treatment of *mezuzot* as amulets rather than to amulets themselves and is interpreted in that matter in the Hyamson translation of the passage.

This contradiction might perhaps be resolved by positing that Maimonides accepted the ruling of the sages regarding entering a public thoroughfare on *Shabbat* while wearing the objects described in the Mishnah, *Shabbat* 60a, even though he regarded them as devoid of any therapeutic efficacy. Maimonides might have assumed that the sages ruled in this manner because, since the masses accepted their efficacy, albeit erroneously, such items acquired the status of articles of clothing or of ornaments simply by virtue of being customarily worn as a cure or prophylaxis. See Rashi, *Shabbat* 60a. Alternatively, Maimonides may have regarded the practice as being permitted because, in light of the fact that the items in question "are not carried in the usual manner," no transgression of a biblical prohibition is involved. See *Teshuvot ha-Radbaz, Le-Leshonot ha-Rambam,* V, nos. 63 (1,436) and 153 (1,526); and the comments of the interlocutor as reported in *Teshuvot Shemesh Zedakah,* no. 29. Since no biblical prohibition is entailed, and since the masses were desirous of wearing amulets because of their misplaced beliefs regarding therapeutic properties ascribed to such amulets, the sages did not choose to disturb the practice with an interdiction against wearing them on the Sabbath.

Those explanations, however, are entirely unlikely. However, another resolution of Maimonides' conflicting comments does suggest itself. In context, Maimonides' comments in the *Guide* occur in the course of a discussion of the various names of God and indicate that only the tetragrammaton is the *nomen proprium* of the Deity, while all other appellations are simply reflective of divine attributes indicating the relationship of certain actions to Him but are in no way reflective of the divine essence. Moreover, Maimonides insists that all divine attributes are negative in nature and are designed to negate the possibility of certain actions or qualities but tell us nothing of the nature of Deity in a positive sense. Maimonides' critical comments concerning amulets may, then, have been directed only against writers of amulets containing various divine names or various combinations of divine names and their ascription of supernatural properties to those names. Indeed amulets written during the medieval period were of that nature. Since Maimonides denies that those divine names define the essence of the Deity, he categorically rejected the efficacy of amulets employing such names. Those names neither reflect the essential nature of the Deity nor do they reflect His qualities or attributes in any positive sense. Thus they cannot conceivably be endowed with any mystic power. It is noteworthy that in *Hilkhot Mezuzah* 5:4 Maimonides decries the practice of inscribing on the inside of the *mezuzah* "the names of angels, holy names, a biblical verse or seals . . . as if it were an amulet for their own benefit as has occurred to their foolish minds that this is something that yields benefit with regard to the vanities of the world." The amulets described in the Talmud, to which he refers in *Hilkhot Shabbat,* may well have been of an entirely different nature. Their nature is, of course, unknown to us. But those amulets, when demonstrated to have been efficacious, were accepted by Maimonides and their curative power acknowledged by him.

It must be noted that *Bi'ur ha-Gra, Yoreh De'ah* 179:13, asserts that Maimonides denies the efficacy of amulets and declares that Maimonides was misled by his philosophical speculations. If the foregoing analysis of Maimonides' ruling in *Hilkhot Shabbat* is correct and Maimonides did acknowledge the therapeutic powers of the amulets described in the Mishnah, *Bi'ur ha-Gra's* criticism of Maimonides must be understood as directed toward Maimonides' invective against amulets composed of divine names. Such criticism would then be based upon *Bi'ur ha-Gra's* own conviction of the efficacy of such amulets, and hence of his certainty that the amulets to which the Talmud refers were of such nature, rather than Maimonides' putative rejection of explicit talmudic attestation of their validity.

4. See sources cited by Julius Preuss, *Biblical and Talmudic Medicine,* trans. Fred Rosner (New York: Sanhedrin Press, 1978), p. 196, note 90.

5. Ibid., note 91. Preuss himself regards use of the liver of the rabid dog as a form of antitoxin treatment; see ibid., p. 196.

6. The *vav* appearing in the text is ambiguous. It may serve as a *vav ha-hibbur* and mean "and" or as a *vav ha-pirud* meaning "or." I believe that it is correctly rendered "or."

7. See above, n. 6.

8. The term is presumably used in the sense of "common experience."

9. See also *Teshuvot Shemesh Zedakah*, no. 29.

10. See also R. Chaim Joseph David Azulai, *Hayyim Shaal*, II, no. 38, sec. 81.

11. Cf., however, 2 Chronicles 16:12 and this writer's discussion of that verse in *Judaism and Healing* (New York, 1981), pp. 5–6.

12. A *goses* is a moribund patient as defined by criteria posited by *halakhah*. For a fuller definition of the state of *gesisah*, see this writer's *Judaism and Healing*, pp. 141–42.

13. This also seems to be the position of *Teshuvot Hatam Sofer, Yoreh De'ah,* no. 338 and *Bi'ur Halakhah, Orah Hayyim* 329:2. However, other authorities, most notably, *Teshuvot Bet Yaakov,* no. 59, followed by *Iggerot Mosheh, Yoreh De'ah,* II, no. 174, apparently make no such distinction and rule that it is forbidden to prolong the life of a *goses* by any means whatsoever. Cf. R. Eliezer Waldenberg, *Tzitz Eliezer,* XIII, no. 89, sec. 14; ibid., VIII, no. 15, chap. 3, sec. 16; ibid., IX, no. 47; idem, *Ramat Rahel,* no. 28; and idem, *Assia, Nisan* 5738, p. 195.

14. Maimonides, *Guide* 3:37, certainly accepts the medical efficacy of therapy "that has been verified by experiment, although it cannot be explained by analogy." Included in that category are wearing the egg of a certain species of locust, a fox's tooth, and a nail from the gallows of an impaled convict, each of which was worn as a putative remedy for a specific disorder. Those therapies are specifically permitted according to the normative opinion of R. Meir recorded in the Mishnah, *Shabbat* 67a. Maimonides, in the *Guide,* explains that "the ways of the Amorite" are forbidden "because they are not arrived at by reason, but are similar to the performances of witchcraft, which is necessarily connected with the influences of the star," but that the earlier enumerated therapies are permitted nevertheless because "these things have been considered in those days as facts established by experiment." On the basis of Maimonides' remarks in his *Commentary on the Mishnah* in *Yoma* and in the *Guide,* it might be argued that Maimonides assumes that whenever medical efficacy is confirmed by experience it must be presumed that the therapy is in accordance with the natural order even though the nature of the causal relationship between the medicament and the cure is not understood. This analysis of Maimonides' position cannot be accepted for a number of reasons: (1) Other medieval authorities clearly recognized that the items enumerated by the Mishnah in *Shabbat* had no natural therapeutic properties; see, for example, *Teshuvot ha-Rashba,* I, no. 411. (2) Maimonides, in the *Guide,* comments, "They served as cures, in the same means as the hanging of the peony over a person subject to epileptic fits, or the application of a dog's excrement to the swellings of the throat, and of the vapors of vinegar and marcasite to the swelling of tumors." The clear implication is that the enumerated remedies were recognized as nonnatural *segulot*. (3) Most significant is Maimonides' explicit categorization in his *Commentary on the Mishnah, Shabbat* 67a, of the practices referred to by the Mishnah as remedies advocated by *"baalei ha-segulot."* Moreover, and perhaps most significantly, Maimonides, as has been shown, maintains that when there is cogent scientific reason to believe that a proposed therapy will even possibly be effective, it must be assumed that such therapy constitutes *safek pikuah nefesh* even though the hypothesis lacks experimental confirmation. See also *Teshuvot ha-Radbaz le-Leshonot ha-Rambam,* no. 63, and R. Isaac Joseph Nunez-Vaes, *Siah Yitzhak, Yoma* 83a.

15. It is quite possible that *Tosafot* espouse a position similar to that of Maimonides but require that the therapeutic power of a *segulah* be known with "certainty" in any situation in which its use involves violation of a halakhic prohibition. The Talmud declares that Elijah and Phineas were one and the same person. *Tosafot, Bava Mezia* 114b, questions the permissibility of Elijah's conduct in resuscitating the son of the widow of Zarephath. Since Phineas was a priest, he was forbidden to defile himself through tactile contact with a corpse. How, then, was he permitted to revive the dead child? *Tosafot* answers that since Elijah was certain of the success of his endeavor, violation of the priestly code was permissible. *Tosafot*'s comment is puzzling since the general principle is that halakhic strictures are suspended even on the mere chance that the procedure may succeed in saving a life. R. Abraham Jacob Neumark, *Eshel Avraham* (Tel Aviv, 5708), *Pinot Genosar*, no. 23, cites Maimonides' discussion of remedies in the nature of a *segulah* and, asserting that according to Maimonides a *segulah* may be employed in face of halakhic strictures only if its curative powers are known with certainty, explains that Elijah's use of prophetic powers was also a "nonnatural" therapy and hence was justified only because of his certainty of success. See also R. Iser Yehudah Unterman, *Ha-Torah ve-ha-Medinah*, IV, 25 f., and *idem, Shevet me-Yehudah, Shaar Rishon*, chap. 7. For other interpretations of *Tosafot*'s thesis see *Contemporary Halakhic Problems* 1:389–91.

16. It is indeed quite possible that Maimonides may have regarded physical cause-and-effect relationships as the manifestation of powers intrinsic in corporeal objects whereas metaphysical phenomena may have no intrinsic relationship to the physical effects that follow in their wake but that the effect is each time generated by divine powers. This is testament to speculating that the causal relationship between metaphysical causes and physical effects is of the nature described as occasionalism; see *supra*, n. 2. On such an analysis, the distinction between a *segulah* such as the liver of a rabid dog and a tested amulet is also readily understandable on the basis of the relative likelihood of the metaphysical cause being the occasion for the manifestation of a physical effect. When the metaphysical phenomenon is only infrequently the occasion for the physical effect, the relationship is not at all analogous to causality inherent in the operation of the laws of nature. However, when the metaphysical event is regularly and predictably the occasion for subsequent manifestation of a physical event, the phenomenon is treated in a manner identical to that of natural causal relationships.

CHAPTER 13

1. Maimonides, *Eight Chapters*, chap. 3, pp. 65–6. In this paper the translations of passages from the *Eight Chapters* and the *Laws concerning Character Traits (Hilkhot Deot)* are taken from R. L. Weiss and C. E. Butterworth, *Ethical Writings of Maimonides* (New York: New York University Press, 1975).
2. Maimonides, *Eight Chapters*, chap. 4, p. 68.
3. Ibid., chap. 4, p. 69.
4. Ibid., chap. 3, p. 65.
5. Ibid., chap. 1, p. 62.
6. Ibid., chap. 4, p. 70.

7. Maimonides, *Hilkhot Deot,* chap. 1, p. 30.
8. Ibid., chap. 1, p. 30.
9. Ibid., chap. 2, p. 31.
10. Aristotle, *Nicomachean Ethics,* VII 1, 1145a27–28.
11. Psalm 19:18.
12. Maimonides, *Eight Chapters,* chap. 4, p. 70.
13. Maimonides, *Hilkhot Deot,* chap. 2, p. 31.
14. Aristotle, *Nicomachean Ethics,* 1107a8–21.
15. Ibid., 1107a10–11.
16. Ibid., 1106b36–1107a6.
17. See Sarah Broadie, *Ethics with Aristotle* (New York: Oxford University Press, 1991), pp. 96 ff.
18. Maimonides, *Hilkhot Deot,* chap. 1, p. 29.
19. Maimonides *Eight Chapters,* chap. 4, p. 67.
20. Commentary on the *Mishnah Avot* 1:14. Translation taken from M. Maimonides, *The Commentary to Mishnah Abot,* tr. Arthur David, (New York: Bloch, 1968), p. 15.
21. Maimonides, *Eight Chapters,* chap. 4, p. 68.
22. Job 25:4.
23. Maimonides, *Eight Chapters,* chap. 4, p. 73.
24. Ibid., chap. 8, p. 88.
25. I am grateful to Sarah Broadie for criticism of an earlier draft of this paper.

CHAPTER 14

1. Maimonides, *The Guide of the Perplexed,* trans. S. Pines (Chicago: Chicago University Press, 1963).
2. This is the most commonly advanced explanation. See, e.g., I. Heinemann, *Taamei ha-Mitzvot be-Sifrut Yisrael,* vol. 1 (Jerusalem: 1959), p. 89 (Heb.). See also the interesting comment of I. Twersky, *Introduction to the Code of Maimonides* (New Haven: Yale University Press, 1980), p. 483, n. 319.
3. On this point cf., in detail, J. S. Levinger, *Ha-Rambam ke-filosof u-posek* (Jerusalem, 1989), pp. 112–124 (Heb.).
4. Maimonides, *Mishneh Torah. The Book of Knowledge,* trans. M. Hyamson (Jerusalem: Feldheim, 1962), pp. 84b–85a (with slight changes).
5. I. Twersky, " 'Halakhah u-Madda': Hebbetim ba-Epistemologiah shel ha-Rambam," *Shenaton ha-Mishpat ha-Ivri* 14–15 (1988–1989):135, 137 (Heb.).
6. It is noteworthy that in his Commentary on the Mishnah, in the Introduction to *Perek Helek* (Treatise *Sanhedrin*), Maimonides comments that he who whispers a spell over a wound has no portion in the world to come, but this applies specifically when "accompanied by spitting, since this constitutes disrespect to God." *Perush ha-Mishnah la-Rambam,* trans. R. J. Qafih (Jerusalem: Mosad Harav Kook, 1963–1969), (Heb.). In the later work *Mishneh Torah,* the disrespectful spitting is not mentioned. Nevertheless, it is clear from the context that a person whispering a spell over a wound recites a biblical verse, and the very use of biblical verses for such purposes constitutes a denial

of the Torah. It is this denial that makes the person unworthy of the world to come (*Hilkhot Teshuvah* 3:6).

7. Maimonides, *Book of Knowledge* etc. (supra, n. 4), p. 79b. Cf. M. Kellner, *Dogma in Medieval Jewish Thought* (Oxford, 1986), p. 32.

8. See A. Altmann, "Maimonides' Four Perfections," *Israel Oriental Studies* 2(1972):15–24; A. Melamed, "Philosophical Interpretations of Jeremiah 9:22-23 in Medieval and Renaissance Jewish Thought," *Mehkerei Yerushalayim be-Mahashevet Yisrael* 4 (1984–1985):31–82 (Heb.).

9. On the practical intellect see M. Kreisel, "The Practical Intellect in the Philosophy of Maimonides," *HUCA* 59 (1988):189–215.

10. I. Efros, ed., *Maimonides' Treatise on Logic* (New York: American Academy of Jewish Research, 1938).

11. Y. Abravanel, *Commentary on the Torah* (Jerusalem, 1969).

12. Nachmanides on Leviticus 11:13, acc. to *Torat Hayyim*, Leviticus (Jerusalem 1990).

13. Y. 'Arama, *Aqedat Yitzhak* 60, 197:1; S. Heller-Wilensky, *Rabbi Yitzhak Arama u-Mishnato ha-Filosofit* (Jerusalem-Tel Aviv, 1956), pp. 57, 208 (Heb.).

CHAPTER 15

1. V. Frankl, *The Doctor and the Soul: From Psychotherapy to Logotherapy* (New York: Bantam Books, 1967), p. xvi.

2. R. May, ed., *Existential Psychology* (New York: Random House, 1961).

3. G. Albee, "To thine own self be true." *American Psychologist* 30(1975):1157.

4. Maimonides, *The Guide for the Perplexed*, M. Friedlander, trans. (New York: Dover, 1904).

5. Quoted from *The Holy Scriptures*, 2 vols. (Philadelphia: Jewish Publication Society, 1917).

6. Maimonides, *Mishneh Torah, Hilkhot Teshuvah*, 6 vols. (New York: M. P. Press, 1962), 5:10.

7. Ibid., 5:2.
8. Ibid., 5:3.
9. Ibid., 5:4.
10. Ibid., *Hilkhot Deot* 1:1.
11. Ibid., 1:2.
12. Ibid., 1:4.
13. Ibid., 1:5, 6.
14. Maimonides, *Guide* 3:22.
15. Ibid., 1:7.
16. Maimonides, *Commentary to Tractate Avot*, 3:19, in *Rambam La-Am*, vol. 19 (Jerusalem: Mosad Harav Kook, 1969).
17. Ibid., 2:3.
18. Ibid., 2:7.
19. Maimonides, *Guide* 3:27.
20. A. H. Maslow, *The Farther Reaches of Human Nature* (New York: Viking Press, 1972).

21. Maimonides, *Hilkhot Deot* 5:11.
22. Maimonides, *Hilkhot Temurah* 4:13.
23. Free translation of *Hilkhot Gerushin* 3:20.
24. Maimonides, *Guide* 3:32.
25. M. Sternbuch, *Responsa Teshuvot ve-Hanhagot* (Jerusalem: Netivot ha-Torah ve-ha-Hesed, 5746), no. 350.
26. Maimonides, *Hilkhot Deot* 6:3.

CHAPTER 16

1. Aristotle, *Metaphysics,* VI, ch. 1, 1025b.1.19 ff.
2. cf. H. A. Wolfson, "The Classification of Sciences in Mediaeval Jewish Philosophy" (Hebrew Union College Jubilee Volume, 1925), p. 263. This article will herein be referred to as "Classification." In *Topics,* however, Aristotle himself hints at this same tripartite division. Cf. Aristotle, *Topics,* book 1, chap. 14, 105b, 1.19.
3. W. K. C. Guthrie, "The Divisions of Knowledge," *The History of Greek Philosophy,* vol. 6 (Cambridge: Cambridge University Press, 1962), pp. 130–34.
4. Maimonides, *Treatise on Logic (Millot ha-Higayon),* trans. I. Efros, *PAAJR* 8(1938):62–65. All references to *Millot ha-Higayon* will be to this edition (*PAAJR* 8[1938]:34–65).
5. On the meaning of these last two terms, see H. A. Wolfson's article, "Note on Maimonides' Classification of the Sciences," *JQR* 26(1936):369–77. This article will herein be referred to as "Note."
6. Quoted in Wolfson, "Classification," p. 267. Cf. Wolfson's discussion of Israeli's opinion. He may simply be using medicine as a paradigm for all the natural sciences.
7. Cf. Wolfson, "Classification," p. 279.
8. A. ibn David, *Emunah Ramah,* Introduction, p. 45, quoted in Wolfson, "Classification," pp. 314–15.
9. Wolfson, "Classification," p. 289. On the relationship between Alfarabi's work and chap. 14 of *Millot ha-Higayon,* see Wolfson's "Note."
10. We cannot, and will not, discount the possibility that medicine serves more than one role in Maimonides' thought. In fact, in Solomon ben Immanuel Dapiera's Hebrew translation of Abu 'Imram Moses Tobi's Al-Saba 'niyyah (*Batte ha-Nefesh,* ed. H. Hirschfeld, Report of the Judith Montefiore College, 1894), medicine is divided right away into two different categories, i.e., theoretical medicine and practical medicine. Cf. Wolfson's "Additional Notes to the Article on the Classification of the Sciences," *Hebrew Union College Annual* 3(1926):371–75, n. to pp. 283–5, 373.
11. There are many discussions of and allusions to this question. Among the "separatists" cf. E. Lieber, "Galen: Physician as Philosopher, Maimonides: Philosopher as Physician," *Bull. Hist. Med.* (1979):268–85; I. M. Ullmann, *Islamic Medicine* (Edinburgh: Edinburgh University Press, 1978), p. xi.; I. Twersky, *Introduction to the Code of Maimonides (Mishneh Torah)* (New Haven, CT: Yale University Press, 1980), p. 2, n2. Among the "unifiers" cf. D. Yellin and I. Abraham, *Maimonides* (New York: Hermon Press, 1972), chap. 3; E. Bar-Sela, et al., "Two Treatises on the Regimen of Health," Transactions of the American Philosophical Society, Philadelphia, 1964, p. 6.

The problem of analyzing the relationship of the medical writings to Maimonides' other works is compounded by the fact that the relationship between some of his other works themselves, specifically his legal and philosophic writings, is a much debated topic. We will assume as a general rule that all of his writings were written with one voice and all enhance one another and contribute to understanding his thought. This, of course, does not mean that there is no esotericism in his writings; it simply excludes some of the more extreme or "thoroughgoing" esoteric positions.

12. S. Muntner, ed. and trans., *Commentary on the Aphorisms of Hippocrates* (Jerusalem: Mosad Harav Kook, 1961), p. 8.

13. Or more precisely, the subject matter both of Galen's *On Anatomical Procedures* and his *On the Usefulness of the Parts (De Usu Partium)*.

14. On Maimonides' view of the majority of the doctors of his time, see the letter to Ibn Tibbon in A. Marx, ed., "Texts by and about Maimonides," *JQR* 25(1935):378.

15. See, for example, discussion of the ruling parts of the body at the very end; Maimonides, *Pirké Moshe*, 2nd ed., ed. S. Muntner (Jerusalem: Mosad Harav Kook, 1982), p. 392. (All references to *Pirké Moshe* will be to this edition.) Cf. Maimonides, *Guide of the Perplexed*, trans. S. Pines (Chicago: University of Chicago Press, 1963), 1:46, 1:72, 2:30. All references to the *Guide* will be to this edition.

16. A. J. Heschel, *Maimonides*, trans. J. Neugroschel (New York: Farrar-Strauss-Giroux, 1982), p. 243.

17. The greatest difficulty with this idea is that if it were true, we should see Maimonides rejoicing in his practice of medicine at the end of his life, while instead we see him lamenting and describing with disdain the excessive time he puts into his profession. Cf. the letter to Joseph b. Judah in *Iggerot haRambam*, ed. Y. Shelat (Jerusalem: Maaliyot Press, 1987), no. 20, 2:2, p. 299; the letter to ibn Tibbon (cited above n. 15), pp. 376–77 (also in Shelat, p. 550). Furthermore, whether this is the type of life which Maimonides is describing in *Guide* 3:54 is not at all clear. The numerous opinions on the role of the *vita activa* in human perfection in Maimonides' thought can generally be divided into three groups, i.e., the moral, political, and halakhic schools. This issue is discussed at length most recently in M. Kellner, *Maimonides on Human Perfection*, Brown Judaic Studies, no. 202 (Atlanta: Scholars Press, 1990).

18. We should point out, however, that insofar as it is a practical art, medicine should not necessarily be viewed with disdain, even if it is not the fulfillment of the ultimate human perfection. This *is* the approach taken by Lieber in the article cited above (n. 11). She asserts that Maimonides shows an Aristotelian tendency in his opinions on manual labor (cf. Aristotle, *Politics*, bk. 8). In the *Mishneh Torah*, however, he presents quite a different view. See Maimonides, *Mishneh Torah*, Laws of Talmud Torah, 3:10–11 (though the relevance of this passage can, of course, be disputed from certain esoteric positions).

19. Maimonides frequently refers to the medical teachings of the Andalusians, the implication being that he studied medicine in Spain before his brother's death. Cf. M. Meyerhof, "The Medical Work of Maimonides," in S. Baron, *Essays on Maimonides* (New York: Columbia University Press, 1941); H. Friedenwald, "Moses Maimonides the Physician," *Bull. Hist. Med.* 3(1935):555–84.

20. Xenophon, *Memorabilia*, 4.2.8–10.

21. Aristotle, *Politics*, 3.11.1282a, pp. 1–7.

22. Maimonides, *Guide* 1:34; cf. 1:5.

23. Plato, *Gorgias*, 464b, 465a, 501a ff.

24. Aristotle, *Nicomachean Ethics,* 10.10.1180b7, 2.5.1106a26-32, 1106b15, and 1106b27.

25. Cf. Maimonides, "Eight Chapters" *(Shemonah Perakim),* ed. J. Gorfinkle (New York: Columbia University Press, 1912), *passim* (all references to *Shemonah Perakim* will be to this edition); *The Code of Maimonides (Mishneh Torah)* (New Haven, CT: Yale University Press, 1949), *Hilkhot Deot,* chaps. 1-4 (all references to the *Mishneh Torah* will be to this edition unless otherwise noted); *Guide* 1:72.

26. Maimonides, *Millot ha-Higayon,* chap. 14, p. 63.

27. Aristotle, *De sensu,* 436a-b, chap. 1. W. D. Ross, ed., *The Works of Aristotle in English,* vol. 3, p. 1931, Parva naturalia, trans. J. I. Beard (Oxford: Clarendon Press, 1908).

28. G. E. R. Lloyd, ed., "Tradition in Medicine" (or "On Ancient Medicine"), *Hippocratic Writings* (Middlesex: Penguin Books, 1983), pp. 20, 83.

29. Maimonides, *Commentary to the Mishnah,* ed. J. Kafih (Jerusalem, 1963), *Pesahim* 4:10.

30. Maimonides, "The Regimen of Health," ed. and trans. E. Bar-Sela et al. (above n. 11), 21.

31. Maimonides, *Guide* 1:34, 1:55, and *passim.* This refers both to celestial and physical bodies. Cf. also Pines' introduction to his edition of the *Guide,* p. cxxi.

32. Maimonides, *Millot ha-Higayon,* ch. 14, p. 63.

33. W. Jaeger, *Paideia: the Ideals of Greek Culture,* trans. G. Highet, vol. 3 (Oxford: Basil Blackwell, 1945) p. 5.

34. Ibid.

35. E.g., on the discussion of the ruling parts of the body, cf. Aristotle, *De Partibus Animalium,* II.1, 647a25, and *De Somno,* 455b, pp. 34 ff. On the discussion of parts of the body that are consequences of other intended parts, cf. Aristotle, *De Generatione Animalium,* V.1, *De Partibus Animalium,* I.5 (645b1), and Galen, *De Usu Partium,* V.3, XI.14, and XVII.1. On this entire chapter of the *Guide,* cf. *Al-Farabi on the Perfect State,* trans. and comm. R. Walzer (Oxford: Clarendon Press, 1985), chaps. XI and XV. This analogy was common in the medieval period. (I am indebted to Prof. Michael Schwarz for this reference.)

36. Galen, *On the Natural Faculties,* trans. A. J. Brock, Loeb Classical Library (Cambridge, MA: Harvard University Press, 1916), I.5, pp. 17 ff.

37. Galen, *De Usu Partium,* I.17, II.3, XI.2.

38. For other examples see II:30 (p. 355), cf. *De Usu Partium* XI:13; III:8 (p. 431), and III:12 (p. 444), cf. *De Usu Partium* III:10; III:34, and Crescas' comment there.

39. Maimonides, *Millot ha-Higayon,* chap. 14, p. 63.

40. Maimonides, "The Eight Chapters," chap. 5, p. 70.

41. Jaeger, *Paidiea,* vol. 3, pp. 3-27.

42. "The Relationship of Ancient Philosophy to Medicine," in *Ancient Medicine,* eds. O. Temkin and C. L. Temkin (Baltimore: Johns Hopkins University Press, 1967), p. 349.

43. Michael Frede, "Philosophy and Medicine in Antiquity," in *Essays in Ancient Philosophy* (Minneapolis: University of Minnesota Press, 1987), p. 225.

44. See, for example, Farabi's *Aphorisms of the Statesman,* ed. D. M. Dunlop (Cambridge: Cambridge University Press, 1961), pp. 27 ff.

45. Maimonides, *Pirké Moshe,* chap. 17, pp. 214 ff.

46. Shelat, p. 224.

47. Bar-Sela, et al., pp. 25–6.
48. *Teshuvat ha-Rambam bi-She'elat ha-Ketz ha-Katzuv la-Haim,* ed. M. Schwarz (Tel Aviv: Papyrus, 1979), B1–2, pp. 28–9.
49. Maimonides, *Guide,* 1:34, 77.
50. See above, n. 45.
51. Al-Farabi, *Aphorisms of the Statesman,* p. 23. On Farabi's work as a source of the *Shemonah Perakim,* see H. Davidson, "Maimonides' *Shemonah Perakim* and Alfarabi's *Fusul al-Madani,*" *PAAJR* 31(1963):33–51.
52. Bar Sela, et al., p. 25.
53. Cf. F. G. Bratton, *Maimonides: Medieval Modernist* (Boston: Beacon Press, 1967), pp. 71–2.
54. Cf. Jaeger, vol. 3, p. 26: "Through its concentration on one Realm of human life, that of the body, it makes discoveries of the most vital importance to philosophy in its task of working out a new picture of human nature, and thereby it assists in moulding the individual more closely to the ideal of humanity."
55. Jaeger, vol. 3, p. 3.
56. Maimonides, *Shemonah Perakim,* chap. 5, p. 70.
57. L. Strauss, *Philosophy and Law,* trans. F. Baumann (Philadelphia: Jewish Publication Society, 1987), pp. 100 ff.
58. And we see from the last chapter of the *Guide* (3:54) that there is a vast difference between practical/moral behavior before and after intellectual perfection.
59. Cf. Maimonides, *Guide,* 1:51–53.
60. A. N. Whitehead, *The Function of Reason* (Boston: Beacon Press, 1958), p. 10.
61. Jaeger, vol. 3, p. 3.

CHAPTER 17

1. T. Kuhn, "The Structure of Scientific Revolutions," second and enlarged *International Encyclopedia of Unified Science,* vol. 2, no. 2, p. 36 sq.
2. Maimonides, *Guide for the Perplexed,* 1:56–60.
3. J. Albo, *Sefer Ha-Ikkarim,* 2.21. 8.9, I. Husik, ed. and trans. (Philadelphia: Jewish Publication Society, 1929), 2.128, lines 8–11; see *Guide* 1:47, 2:38.
4. We are conscious here that Maimonides makes a pertinent distinction between out-of-date scientific knowledge and myth.
5. Cf. L. Strauss, *Maimonides,* Série Epiméthée, P.U.F., 1988.
6. To say the least, one does not see quite clearly whether the arguments in question do not in fact presuppose the eternity of the world (cf. *Guide* 2:2 with 2:1).
7. Maimonides, *Guide* 2:13, 2:25–27, 2:29, 3:18; (Epître au) Yémen, 24, 7–10 (E.p. 64, 22–27); *(Traité de la) Resurrection* (par. 48–51); *Lettre sur l'Astrologie,* par. 19ss. (p. 354s.).
8. References in Arabic, the original language of the *Guide,* would have been preferable, but given the context of my presentation, the use of Hebrew will probably suffice.
9. For Aristarchus's work, see T. L. Heath, *Aristarchus of Samos: The Ancient Copernicus* (Oxford, 1913), part II. For an extreme statement of the traditional position about the neglect of Aristarchus' achievement, see A. Koestler, *The Sleepwalkers: A History of Man's Changing Vision of the Universe* (London, 1959), p. 50.

10. Kuhn, *Structure*, pp. 75 sq.
11. See L. Goodman's "Ghazali's Argumentation from Creation," *International Journal of Middle Eastern Studies* 2(1971):67–85, 168–88.
12. Maimonides, *Guide* 2:21.
13. Paradigmatically, Ibn Rushd, *Tahàfut-al-Tahàfut,* M. Bouygas, ed. (Beirut: Catholic Press, 1930), pp. 41–52, 88; trans. by Van den bergh (London: Luzac, 1954), pp. 230, 251: "The direction which the body of the universe is compelled to follow through its nature is the best one, because its body is the best of bodies, and the best among the moving bodies must have the best direction" (Bouyges, p. 50, lines 5–6);

"Whoever concedes of this will understand that any world posited can only be of such bodies as these" (Bouyges, p. 46, line 9).

"You might as well say the crab could have the same direction of movement as man" (p. 50, line 2);

"To imagine the world to be larger or smaller does not conform to the truth but is impossible" (p. 88, line 3);

See *De Caelo*, II, 2, 3, 5; *Phaedo* 97–98; *Metaphysics,* I, 3 (984 b, 985 a); *De Part An.* IV, 10 (687a).
14. Maimonides, *Guide* 2:19, 2:21–22; see L. Goodman's *Maimonides and Leibniz*.
15. See Ghazali, *Tahàfut al-Falàsifa* 3,4,10 (Beirut: Catholic Press, 1962), p. 182; "The Philosophers believe that the world is eternal yet claim that it has a maker. This position is self-contradictory and requires no refutation." See Maimonides, *Guide* 2:15, 2:17, 2:21.
16. Maimonides, *Guide* 2:17.
17. Ibid., Munk ed., II; see *Physics 2.6;* Rhetoric 1.10.
18. Maimonides, *Guide* 3:13.
19. L. Goodman, *Matter and Form as Attributes of God in Maimonides' Philosophy,* ed. Ruth-Link Sølinger (New York: Peter Lang, 1929).
20. Ibid., 2:32: "People's views on prophecy correspond with their views on the eternity/creation of the world"; cf. 2:6.
21. Ibid., 3:12, 3:22.
22. For two medieval precedents, see L. Goodmann's "Bahya on the Antinomy of Free Will and Predestination," *Journal of the History of Ideas* 44(1983); and *Tahàfut al-Falàsifa* (Beirut, 1962), p. 67; *Tahàfut al-Tahàfut* (Bouyges ed.), p. 76; Van den Bergh, ed., p. 43, citing *Categories,* 6(5a 27–30).

CHAPTER 18

1. Maimonides, *Hanhagat ha-Beriut,* S. Muntner ed. (Jerusalem: Mosad Harav Kook, 1957), III:13, p. 59.
2. Ibid., III:15, p. 62.
3. Maimonides, *Yad ha-Hazakah, Hilkhot Teshuvah,* Laws of Repentance 7:3.
4. Ibid., 10:3.

CHAPTER 19

1. F. Rosner, "The Physician's Prayer Attributed to Maimonides," *Bulletin of the History of Medicine* 41(1967):440–54.

2. F. Rosner, *Six Treatises Attributed to Maimonides* (Northvale, NJ: Jason Aronson, 1991).
3. F. Rosner, *The Existence and Unity of God–Three Treatises Attributed to Moses Maimonides* (Northvale, NJ: Jason Aronson, 1990).
4. G. Vajda ,"Tishah Perakim mi-yihud ha-meyuhasim le-ha-Rambam," *Kovetz al Yad* (Jerusalem: Mekitze Nirdamim, 1950), New Series, vol. 5, pp. 103–37.
5. G. Vajda, "Le traité pseudo-Maïmonidien: Neuf chapitres sur l'Unité de Dieu," *Archives d'Histoire Doctrinale et Littéraire du Moyen Age* 28(1953):83–98.
6. See Rosner, *Existence and Unity.*
7. H. S. Davidowitz, *Perakim be-Hatzlahah ha-Meyuhasim le-Rambam* (Jerusalem: Mekitze Nirdamim, 1939), pp. xxxi and 39.
8. Joseph ben Eleazar Tov Elem (Bonafil), *Ohel Joseph* (commentary on Ibn Ezra on the Torah), in the book *Margalit Tovah* (Amsterdam: 1721), p. 13:1, no. 233.
9. W. Bacher, "The Treatise on Eternal Bliss attributed to Moses Maimuni *(Pirké ha-Hatzlahah),"* *Jewish Quarterly Review* 9, old series (1896–1897):270–89, 1896–7.
10. M. Steinschneider, *Catalogus Librorum Hebraerorum in Bibliotheca Bodleiana* (Berlin: A. D. Friedlander, 1852–1860), pp. 1719 and 1917; *Die Arabische Literatur der Juden* (Frankfurt: A. M. Kauffmann, 1902), p. 209.
11. A. Schmiedl, *Studien über jüdische, insonders jüdisch-arabische Religionsphilosophie* (Vienna: Herzfeld und Bauer, 1869), p. 233.
12. M. Grossberg, *Sefer Refuot le-Rabbenu Moshe Maimon* (London: Metzik, 1900), 23 pp. [Bound with *Sefer Hevel Menasheh,* pp. 27–61].
13. B. Richler, "Sefer Haskamah o Sefer Raminos," *Kiryat Sefer,* vol. 58 (Jerusalem: Hebrew University, 1983), pp. 624–25.
14. "Taglisches Gebet eines Arztes bevor er seine Kranken besucht–Aus der Hebraische Handschrift eines berühmten jüdischen Arztes in Egypten aus dem zwölften Jahrhundert," *Deutsches Museum* 1(1783):43–45.
15. See Rosner, "The Physician's Prayer."
16. J. O. Leibowitz, "Tefilat ha-Rofé Meyuchas le-Rambam," *Dapim Refuim* 13(1954):77–81.
17. *Kovetz Teshuvot ha-Rambam Veiggrotav* (Leipzig, 1859 [5619]), pp. 38–40. Reprinted in Jerusalem in 1967 (5727).
18. I. Abrahams, *Hebrew Ethical Wills* (Philadelphia: Jewish Publication Society, 1926), pp. 101–16. Reprinted in 1976.
19. M. Minkin, *The World of Moses Maimonides with Selections from His Writings* (New York and London: Yoseloff, 1957), pp. 421–27.
20. D. Margalith, *Derekh Yisrael bi-Refuah* (Jerusalem: Academy of Medicine, 1970), pp. 197–204.
21. Y. Shilat, *Iggerot ha-Rambam,* vol. 2 (Jerusalem: Maaliyot, 1988 [5747]), pp. 595–96.
22. A. Neubauer, "Pseudo-Biographie von Maimonides," *Israelitische Letterbode* (Amsterdam: Van Es and Joachimsthal, 1881–1882), 7:14–17.
23. A. Neubauer, "Une pseudo-biographie de Moise Maïmonide," *Revue des Etudes Juives* (Paris) 4(1882):173–88.
24. D. Kaufmann, "Une falsification dans la lettre envoyée par Maimonide aux Juifs du Yemen," *Revue des Etudes Juives* (Paris) 24(1894):112–17.
25. A. S. Halkin, *Moses Maimonides' Epistle to Yemen,* the Arabic original and the three

Hebrew versions, with an English translation by Boaz Cohen (New York: American Academy for Jewish Research, 1952).

CHAPTER 20

1. a) TOPICAL: J. Dienstag, "God; Eretz Israel," *Studies in Bibliography and Booklore* 5(1961):16-27; 28-29 (Hebrew section), 187 entries;
"Eschatology," in J. I. Dienstag, ed., *Eschatology in Maimonidean Thought* (New York: Ktav, 1983), pp. 242-71, 206 entries;
"Providence," *Da'at* 20(1988):17-28, 97 entries;
"The Biblical Exegesis of Maimonides," *Gvaryahu Jubilee Volume* (Jerusalem: Biblical Society, 1989), pp. 346-66, 158 entries;
"Maimonides and the Cabalists," *Da'at* 25(1990):53-84; 26(1991):61-96, 653 entries;
"A Selected Bibliography of Maimonides and Law," in N. Rakover, ed., *Maimonides as Codifier of Jewish Law* (Jerusalem, 1987), pp. 309-25, 193 entries.
b) PERSONALITIES: J. Dienstag, "Isaac Abravanel and Plato," *Studies in Bibliography and Booklore* 5(1961):15-16; 27 (Hebrew section), 30 entries;
"The Relationship of St. Thomas to the Philosophy of Maimonides," in J. I. Dienstag, ed., *Studies in Maimonides and St. Thomas Aquinas* (New York: Ktav, 1975), pp. 334-45, 87 entries;
"The Relationship of Spinoza to the Philosophy of Maimonides," *Studia Spinozana* 2(1986):375-416, 248 entries;
"The Relationship of Gersonides to Maimonides," *Da'at* 23(1989):5-13, 68 entries;
"The Relationship of Nahmanides to Maimonides," *Da'at* (forthcoming);
"The Relationship of R. Joseph Caro to Maimonides," *Da'at* (forthcoming);
"Abraham Maimuni's Role in the Maimonidean Controversy," in *Abraham Maimonides' The Wars of the Lord,* trans. and annot. by Fred Rosner (Northvale, NJ: Jason Aronson (forthcoming).
2. The index volume which appeared a few years ago does not include references to Maimonides' works. Is it possible that another volume is to appear which will include references to the master's works?
3. Maimonides, *The Book on Asthma* (Jerusalem, 1938, 2nd ed.; Jerusalem: "Geniza," 1963); *Poisons and Their Antidotes* (Jerusalem: Rubin Mass, 1942).
The complete Hebrew editions, edited by Muntner, were published in Jerusalem by Mosad Harav Kook in cooperation with the Israel Medical Association: *Poisons and Their Antidotes* (1965); *Commentary on the Aphorisms of Hippocrates* (1961); *Regimen Sanitatis* (1957); *Aphorisms of Moses* (1959); *On Hemorrhoids; On the Increase of Physical Vigour On Asthma* (1965); *Lexicography of Drugs; Medical Responses* (1969); reprinted several times.
4. H. Kroner, *Ein Beitrag zur Geschichte der Medizin des XII. Jahrhunderts.* (Oberdorf-Bopfingen, 1906); "Eine medizinische Maimonides-Handschrift aus Granada," *Janus* 21(1916):203-47; *Die Haemorrhoiden in der Medizin des XII und XIII Jahrhunderts* (Harlem: De E. F. Bohn, 1911); *Die Seelenhygiene des Maimonides* (Frankfurt a. M.: J. Kauffmann, 1914); *Gesundheitsanleitung des Maimonides fuer den Sultan al-Malik al-Afdal* (Leiden: E. J. Brill, 1925); "Der medicinische Schwanengesang des Maimonides," *Janus* 32(1928):

12–116; S. Muntner, *Regimen Sanitatis* . . . Deutsche Uebersetzung (Basel: S. Karger, 1966; reprinted, 1968); M. Steinschneider, "Gifte und ihre Heilung," *Archiv fuer Pathologische Anatomie und Physiologie* 57(1873):62–120; "Die Vorrede des Maimonides zu seinem Commentar ueber die Aphorismen des Hippocrates," *Zeitschrift der Deutschen Morgenlaendischen Gesellschaft* 48(1894):218–34; "Maimonides ueber Galen," in his *Al-Farabi* (St. Petersburg, 1869; facs. repr., Amsterdam: Philo Press, 1966), pp. 230–38; D. Winternitz, *Das diaetetische Sendschreiben des Maimonides an den Sultan Saladin* (Vienna: Braumueller und Seidel, 1843); G. Weil, *Maimonides ueber die Lebensdauer* (Basel and New York: S. Karger, 1953).

5. F. Rosner, "Moses Maimonides' Responsum on Longevity," *Geriatrics* 23(Oct. 1968):170–78; *Treatise on Hemorrhoids; Medical Answers* (Philadelphia: J. B. Lippincott, 1969); *The Medical Aphorisms of Moses Maimonides* (New York: Yeshiva University Press, 1970–71; reprinted 1973); *Sex Ethics in the Writings of Moses Maimonides* (New York: Bloch, 1974); *Glossary of Drug Names* (Philadelphia: American Philosophical Society, 1979); "The Introduction of Maimonides to his 'Commentary on the Aphorisms of Hippocrates,'" *Clio Medica* 11:1 (1976):59–64; *Treatises on Poisons, Hemorrhoids, Cohabitation* (Haifa: Maimonides Research Institute, 1984); *Maimonides' Commentary on the Aphorisms of Hippocrates* (Haifa: Maimonides Research Institute, 1987); H. L. Gordon, *The Preservation of Youth* (New York: Philosophical Library, 1958); Ariel Bar Sela, H. E. Hoff, and E. Faris, *Two Treatises on the Regimen of Health, Transactions of the American Philosophical Society*, n.s. 54, pt. 4 (July 1964); M. Gorlin, *Maimonides on Sexual Intercourse* (Brooklyn, NY: Rambash Publishing Co., 1961); M. Meyerhof and J. Schacht, "Maimonides against Galen, on Philosophy and Cosmogony," *Bulletin of the Faculty of Arts of the University of Egypt* 5, part 1 (May 1937):53–88. Part of treatise 25 of the *Aphorisms* in which Maimonides criticizes Galen for theological views. Arabic text with English translation (pp. 64–76).

6. *The Art of Cure.* Translated by Uri Barzel. With bibliography by J. I. Dienstag (Haifa: Maimonides Research Institute, 1992).

7. S. Balossi in collaboration with A. Di Giovanni, *La Lettera al Soldano di Mose Maimonide* (Pisa: Casa editrice Giardini, 1966), translation of the *Regimen Sanitatis* and *Causes of Symptoms;* U. de Martini, *Segreto dei segreti di Maimonide* (Roma: Istituto di storia della medicina dell'Universita di Roma, 1960), translation of the two works on sexual hygiene based on Kroner's German translation (1906); severely criticized by S. M. Stern, "Medical Works [of Maimonides]," in *Maimonides Commentarius in Mischnam,* vol. 3 (Hafniae: Sumptibus E. Munksgaard, 1966), p. 17 n. 10.

8. E. Chelminsky, "La Preservacion de la Juventud" de Maimonides, version Castellana, *Anales de Arts Medici (Mexico)* 5:6 (Nov. 1961):303–44. The odd title seems to reflect the one given by H. L. Gordon to his English translation of the *Regimen Sanitatis,* entitled "The Preservation of Youth" (1958). Chelminsky also translated Maimonides' treatise on sexual hygiene (shorter version), first published by H. Kroner (see n. 4): El "Guia Sobre el Contacta Sexual" de Maimonides, *Anales de Arts Medici* 5(1961):240–48.

9. M. Meyerhof, *Un Glossaire de Matière Médicale compose par Maïmonide* (Le Caire: Imp. de l'Institut Francais d'Archeologie Orientale, 1940), reviewed by J. M. Millas Vallicrosa, *Sefarad* 1(1941):443–46; S. Muntner, *Harefuah* 20:10(1941):77–78; G. Sarton, *Isis* 33(1941):527–9;

I. M. Rabbinowicz, *Maimonide, Traité des Poisons* (Paris: A. Delahaye, 1865; 2nd ed., Paris: Lipschutz, 1935);

I. Simon, "Le Traité de l'Asthme de Maimonide," *Rev. d'Histoire de la Médecine*

Hébraique 62(Dec. 1963):171-86; 63-66(1964):5-13, 83-97, 127-39, 187-96; 67(Mar. 1965):5-15.

10. Pis'mo Moiseia Maĭmonida k egipetskomu sultanu. Gigisiapcheskie sovety. Perevod s drevneevreĭskogo d-ra I. K. Shmuklera (Kiev). Otdel'nyĭ ottisk iz "Vrach. Dela," no. 14-15 i 16. Khar'kov: "Nuauchnaĭa Mysl'." Uchr. NKZ USSR. [1930].

11. F. Rosner, *"Physician's Prayer"; "Sefer Rephuot, The Book of Remedies,* in *Six Treatises Attributed to Maimonides,* trans. and annot. by Fred Rosner (Northvale, NJ: Jason Aronson, 1991).

12. M. Maimonides, *Hilkhot Deot* III, iii, 3. For an excellent discussion on this theme, see D. M. Feldman, *Health and Medicine in the Jewish Tradition* (New York: Crossroad, 1986), pp. 15 ff.

13. J. I. Dienstag, "Maamar ha-Ibbur *(Treatise on Intercalation* – A Bibliography," *A.M. Haberman Memorial Volume,* ed. Z. Malachi (Lod: Haberman Institute, 1983), pp. 267-71.

14. J. I. Dienstag, "Maimonides' Letter on Astrology – A Bibliography," *Kiryat Sefer* 61(1986):147-58. For a comprehensive survey of the entire literature on science, see the first installment of my "Science and technology in Maimonidean thought – a classified annotated bibliography," *Torah u-Madda Journal,* vol. 4 (forthcoming).

15. R. Wischnitzer, "Maimonides' Drawings of the Temple," *Journal of Jewish Art* 1(1974):16-27.

16. H. Rosenau, *Vision of the Temple* (London: Oresko Books, 1979).

17. De Cultu Divino ex R. Mosis Majemonidae (Paris, 1678). For the other volumes of the *Mishneh Torah* translated by Lud. de Compiegne de Veil, see my "Christian Translators of Maimonides' *Mishneh Torah* into Latin," *Salo W. Baron Jubilee Volume,* vol. 1 (Jerusalem: American Academy for Jewish Research, 1974), pp. 302-4.

18. For Perrault's work, see R. Wolfgang Herrmann, "Unknown Designs for the 'Temple of Jerusalem' by Claude Perrault," *Essays in the History of Architecture Presented to Rudolf Wittkower* (London: Phaidon Press, 1967), pp. 143-58; idem, *The Theory of Claude Perrault* (London: A. Zwemer, 1973).

19. *The Code of Maimonides,* Book III, Treatise 8: *Sanctification of the New Moon,* trans. by Solomon Gandz, and an astronomical commentary by O. Neugebauer (New Haven, CT: Yale University Press, 1956), pp. 113-49. Cf. the critical notes on this commentary by E. Wiesenberg in *The Code of Maimonides,* Book III, *Book of Seasons,* trans. by S. Gandz and H. Klein (New Haven, CT: Yale University Press, 1961), pp. 577-82.

20. G. W. Leibniz, *Saemtliche Schriften und Briefe* (Darmstadt, 1923) ff. 1 Reihe, vol. 2, pp. 475 f. Cf. W. Herrmann, *Unknown Designs,* p. 143.

21. I. Newton, "whose *Description of the Temple of Solomon* was posthumously published in 1728, knew Perrault's designs from his own copy of Veil's translation" (Herrmann, *Unknown Designs,* p. 152 n. 70). On Newton's acquaintance with Maimonides' works, see J. I. Dienstag, "Maimonides in English Christian Thought and Scholarship," *Hebrew Studies* 26(1985):273-74.

CHAPTER 21

1. *Mishnah with The Commentary of Maimonides* (Hebrew), vol. 1 (Jerusalem: Mosad Harav Kook, 1976), pp. 112-13.

2. Ibn Tibbon, *The Meaning of Foreign Words* (Hebrew), printed together with the Hebrew translation of the *Guide* (Jerusalem, 1960), p. 4 of Ibn Tibbon's list.

3. All quotations from the *Guide* are from Maimonides, *The Guide of the Perplexed*, trans S. Pines (Chicago: University of Chicago Press, 1963).

4. Maimonides, *Treatise on Asthma* (Hebrew) (Jerusalem: Mosad Harav Kook, 1965), p. 107.

5. Maimonides, *Treatise on Asthma*, p. 71.

CHAPTER 22

1. The definition of a human *terefah* is open to question. It clearly embraces a fatal organic defect, e.g., a pierced gullet or windpipe. Whether or not it covers any fatal disease is not quite as clear. Several modern authors are of the opinion that it is applicable to internal diseases such as cancer. See *Resp. Ahiezer, Yoreh Deah*, no. 16; R. M. Hirschler, "The Obligation to Save Life," (Heb.), *Halakhah Urefuah* 2(5741):49; R. I. Jakobovits, "Concerning the Possibility of Permitting the Precipitation of the Death of a Fatally Ill Patient in Severe Pain," (Heb.), *Hapardes* 31(5717):43; R. E. Katz, "Regarding the Issue of Disconnecting a Fatally Ill Patient from a Respirator," (Heb.), *Tehumin* 3(5741):29.

2. *Sanhedrin* 78a.

3. *Yad Remah, Sanhedrin* 78a; *Minhat Hinukh*, no. 34; *Resp. Rivash*, nos. 251, 338; H. Cohn, "On the Dichotomy of Divinity and Humanity in Jewish Law," *Medico-Legal Library*, no. 2, *Euthanasia*, ed. A. Carmi (Berlin: Springer-Verlag, 1984), p. 38.

4. *Tosefta, Terumot* 7:20. Also see: *Hilkhot Yesodei Hatorah* 5:5; *Shulhan Arukh, Yoreh Deah*, no. 157.

5. *Bet ha-Behirah, Sanhedrin* 74a.

6. Ibid.

7. *Minhat Hinukh*, no. 296.

8. *Responsa Noda Biyehuda* 2, *Hoshen Mishpat*, no. 59.

9. *Responsa Bet Yitzhak* 2, *Yoreh Deah*, no. 162; *Responsa Yabia Omer* 4, *Even ha-Ezer*, no. 1.

10. R. Judah Gershuni, *Kol Tzofayikh* (Jerusalem, 5740); R. M. Halperin, "Heart Transplants According to the *Halakhah*" (Heb.), *Sefer Assia*, vol. 5 (Jerusalem 5746), pp. 68ff.

11. R. M. Halperin, "The Legal Implications of the Chief Rabbinate's Decision Regarding Heart Transplants," (Heb.), *Assia* 47–48(1989):112.

12. Maimonides, *Laws of Homicide* 2:7.

13. Ibid., 2:3.

14. *Bereshit Rabbah*, ed. J. Theodor and H. Albeck, p. 324 n. 8.

15. *Bava Kamma* 91b.

16. cf. *Torah Temimah*, Genesis 9, no. 8.

17. *Kiddushin* 43a.

18. Maimonides, *Laws of Homicide* 2:4–5.

19. Maimonides, *Or Sameah*, Maimonides, *Laws of Kings* 3:10.

20. See M. Elon, ed., *The Principles of Jewish Law* (Jerusalem: Keter, 1974), p. 708; A. Lichtenstein, *The Seven Laws of Noah* (New York: Z. Berman Books, 1981).

21. Elon, *The Principles of Jewish Law*.

22. See A. D'Entreves, *Natural Law* (London: Hutchinson University Library, 1980).
23. Maimonides, *Laws of Kings* 9:1.
24. H. Hart, *Concept of Law* (Oxford: Oxford University Press, 1964), p. 188.
25. *Mekhilta Derabbi Yishmael, Masekhta Denezikin*, vol. 5, ed. H. Horowitz and I. Rabin, p. 263.
26. See B. Jackson, "The Concept of Religious Law in Judaism," *Aufsteig und Niedergang der Römischen Welt* 19(1979):33 for the significance of Divine sanctions in religious law.
27. *Turei Zahav, Shulhan Arukh, Yoreh Deah*, no. 158.
28. *Mekorei Ha-Rambam Le-Rashash, Laws of Kings* 9:4; *Or Sameah, Laws of Homicide* 4:3; *Mirkevet Hamishneh, Laws of Kings* 9:4; *Maaseh Rokeah, Laws of Kings* 9:4.
29. Maimonides, *Laws of Homicide* 4:9.
30. Maimonides, *Laws of Kings* 10:11.
31. *Responsa Iggrot Moshe, Yoreh Deah*, no. 36.
32. *Sanhedrin* 57b.
33. Exodus 21:22–23; Rashi, *Sanhedrin* 72b; Meiri, *Sanhedrin* 72b.
34. *Or Sameah, Laws of Forbidden Intercourse* 3:2; *Meshekh Hokhmah, Vayakhel* s.v. *shabbat shabbaton*.
35. *Sanhedrin* 59a, s.v. *mi ika*.
36. *Sanhedrin* 59a.
37. *Responsa Seridei Esh* 3, no. 127.
38. *Oholot* 7:6.
39. Rashi, *Sanhedrin* 72b; *Yad Remah, Sanhedrin* 72b.
40. Maimonides, *Laws of Homicide* 1:9.
41. *Sanhedrin* 72b, cf. *Jerusalem Talmud, Shabbat* 14:4.
42. See M. Stern, *Ha-Refuah le-Or ha-Halakhah* (Jerusalem: Institute for Research in Medicine and Halakhah, 5740), 1:1:8.
43. *Responsa Tzitz Eliezer* 13, no. 102; 14, no. 100.
44. R. Moses Feinstein, *"Bedin Harigat Ubar"–Sefer Zikaron le-Rabi Yehezkel Abramski* (Jerusalem: Moriah, 5737), p. 463.
45. See R. I. Y. Unterman, *Shevet Miyehuda*, 26; R. M. Y. Zweig, *Responsa Ohel Mosheh*, no. 16.
46. Y. Leibowitz, *Medicine and the Value of Human Life* (Tel Aviv: Sackler School of Medicine, Tel Aviv University, 1977).
47. See *Shulhan Arukh, Yoreh Deah* 339:1.
48. See *Encyclopedia Talmudit*, vol. 9, pp. 339–341.
49. Maimonides, *Guide for the Perplexed* 1:2.

CHAPTER 23

1. T. Thulborn, *Nature: Checking our Creationism*, 1990; 345:487.
2. L. Roth, *Spinoza, Descartes and Maimonides* (Oxford: the Clarendon Press, 1924).
3. H. Schulweis, *Moment* (Jan.–Feb. 1986): 60.
4. D. Hartman, *Crisis and Leadership. Epistles of Maimonides*, trans. and notes by A. Halkin (Philadelphia: Jewish Publication Society of America, 1985).
5. A. J. Heschel, *Maimonides: A Biography*, trans. by J. Neugroschel (New York: Farrar Straus Giroux, 1982).

6. J. Finkel, "Maimonides' Treatise on Resurrection: A Comparative Study," in S. W. Baron, ed., *Essays on Maimonides, an Octocentennial Volume* (New York: Columbia University Press, 1941).

7. *Emet Ve-Emunah* (New York: The Jewish Theological Seminary of America, The Rabbinical Assembly, and The United Synagogue of America, 1988).

8. S. M. Glick, "Sounding Board: Humanistic Medicine in a Modern Age," *New England Journal of Medicine* 304(1981):1036-38.

9. L. G. Oreopoulos, "The Meaning of Suffering," *Humane Medicine* 1(1986): 82-85.

10. Maimonides, *Pirké Moshe*, chap. 25.

11. A. Soffer, "The Devout Iconoclast," *Medica Judaica* 1:4.

12. M. Fox, *Interpreting Maimonides* (Chicago: The University of Chicago Press, 1990).

CHAPTER 24

1. According Ibn Abî Uṣaybī'a, *Uyûn al-Akhbâr,* Nizâr Riḍâ, ed. (Beirut, 1965), p. 577, Ibn Ǧumay'ʾs practice *(dukkân)* was situated in the *sûq al-qanâdil* in Fosṭâṭ, not far from Masīsa street, where according to al-Qifṭî *(Ikhbâr al-'ulamâ,* ed. Lippert, p. 318), Maimonides resided. However, in his *History of the Jews in Syria,* vol. 1 (Jerusalem, 1944), p. 297, Ashtor writes that Ibn Ǧumay' had a house in the Zuwayla quarter, i.e., in Cairo. Perhaps one can discern in this mutual silence an element of professional "discretion." Ibn Ǧumay' provoked the animosity of 'Alî ibn al-Munaǧǧim, who satirized him in his poetry, whereas, on the other hand, Yûsuf b. Hibat Allah b. Muslim eulogized him in his poetry.

2. *'Uyûn,* ed. Cairo, 2:112-15, and ed. Nizâr Ridâ (Beirut, 1965), pp. 576-79. See also H. Wüstenfeld, *Geschichte der arabischen Aerzte* (Göttingen, 1840), no. 183, p. 101; N. Leclerc, *Histoire de la médecine arabe,* vol. 2 (Paris, 1876) p. 53, and C. Brockelman, *Geschichte der arabischen Literatur,* vol. 1 (Leiden, 1942-3), p. 489 and *Supplementband* 1:892, and Ashtor, "Saladin and the Jews," *HUCA* 27(1956):310-31.

3. M. Steinschneider, *Arabischer Literatur der Juden,* (Frankfurt a. Main: J. Kauffmann, 1902), pp. 178-81, claims that the famous apostate Samuel Ibn 'Abbâs was also his pupil. The latter's teacher was in fact Hibat Allah Abû l-Barakât al-Baghdâdî. Cf. Samau'al al-Maghribî, *Ifhâm al-Yahûd,* M. Perlmann, ed., PAAJR 32(1964):76.

4. *Histoire des médecins juifs, anciens et modernes* (Brussels, 1844), no. XLII, pp. 55-56. Carmoly calls him Ebn-Djami.

5. On al-'Attar, see our article "Le *Minhâǧ ad-Dukkân* d'Abû l-Munä Da'ûd al-Isrâ'îlî: Contribution à l'histoire de la pharmacologie," *Revue de l'histoire de la médécine hébraïque* 115(1975):105-09.

6. Brockelman, *Supplementbd* 1:826.

7. "La Surveillance des professions médicales et para-médicales chez les Arabes," *Bulletin de l'Institut d'Égypte* 26(1944):119-34, p. 134. Reproduced in M. Meyerhof, *Studies in Medieval Arabic Medicine* (London, 1984), p. xi. Interestingly, in the present context, it can be pointed out that Meyerhof had previously mentioned Ibn Ǧumay' in a lecture on Jewish physicians in the Middle East, which he delivered in March 1936 at the Hebrew University, "Medieval Jewish Physicians in the Near East," *Isis* 28(1938):444-45. Reproduced in *Studies in Medieval Arabic Medicine,* VII.

8. "Sultan Saladin's Physician on the Transmission of Greek Medicine to the Arabs," *Bulletin of the History of Medicine* 18(1945):169-78. Reproduced in M. Meyerhof, *Studies in Medieval Arabic Medicine* (London, 1984), III. See also C. Rabin, "Ibn Jami' on the skeleton," *Science, Medicine and History: Essays in Honour of C. Singer*, vol. 1 (London, 1953), pp. 177-202.

9. V, no. 230 (25.5.43), 499-505 and no. 232 (8.6.43).

10. *Medicinalia Arabica. Studien über arabische medizinische Handschriften in Türkischen und syrischen Bibliotheken*, Abh. der Akad. der Wissensch. in Göttingen, Philol.-histor. Kl. III, 66 (Göttingen, 1966), p. 107. See also M. Ullmann, *Die Medezin im Islam* (Leiden/Köln, 1970), p. 164.

11. S. Jadon, "A Comparison of the Wealth, Prestige and Medical Works of the Physicians of Salâh ad-Dîn in Egypt and Syria," *Bulletin of the History of Medicine* 44:(1970):64-75.

12. Is he identical with the ra'îs 'Atiyyah (= Nathan) Dimasqî, mentioned by M. Steinschneider, *ZDMG* 47(1893):378?

13. The present writer has made a microfilm of his manuscript available in the Institute of Microfilmed Hebrew manuscripts of the Hebrew University. The manuscript is written in black ink on paper in an attractive Oriental cursive of twenty-one lines to a page. The text, interspersed with red punctuation and rubrics, more or less tallies with that published by Fähndrich, but occasionally there is a better reading where the editor was unable to decipher the Istanbul text, for example, for the poem on p. 31. However, Greek names are often corrupt, and a page is missing between folios 25b and 26a.

14. *Treatise to Salâh ad-Dîn on the Revival of the Art of Medicine by Ibn Gumay'*, ed. and trans. by Hartmut Fähndrich, *Abhandlungen für die Kunde des Morgenlandes*, vol. XLVI.3 (Wiesbaden, 1983), viii+ 50 + 50 pp. (Arabic text).

15. Incidentally, in volume XLVIII. 2 of the same series, Fähndrich has also recently edited and translated Qusta b. Luqa's *Treatise on Contagion: Abhandlung über die Ansteckung von Qustâ ibn Lûqâ* (Stuttgart, 1987).

16. *'Uyûn*, 1:15-109.

17. Cf. M. Meyerhof, "La fin de l'école d'Alexandrie d'après quelques auteurs arabes," *Archeion* 15(1933):1-15.

18. *Treatise*, p. 21.

19. Ibid., p. 22.

20. Ibid.

21. Ibid., p. 23.

22. Ibid., p. 27.

23. Ibid., p. 28.

24. M. Meyerhof, "Autobiographische Bruchstücke Galens aus arabischen Quellen," *Archiv f. Geschichte d. Medezin* 22(1929):72-86.

25. Perhaps Ibn Ǧumay' had in mind the Bimāristân an-Nâṣirî, which was founded by Saladin. The Andalusian, Ibn Ǧubayr, left a vivid description of it when he visited Egypt in 1182 at the time of our author. See A. Issa Bey, *Histoire des Bimaristans-hôpitaux à l'époque islamique* (Cairo, 1928), pp. 26-37.

26. Treatise, p. 29.

27. Ibid., p. 33.

28. Ibid., p. 34.

Index

Abortion, 202–205
Abraham Bar Hiyya, 86
Abraham ibn Daud, 146
Abravanel, 132–133
Action, mean and, 124
Afdal, al-, 10–11, 15, 16
Air, 9
Akabya, I. ben, 201
Akara, A., 176
Albee, G., 135–136
Albo, J., 153
Alcohol, religion and, 16–17
Allport, G., 135
Alroy, D., 183
Alshakar, M., 182
Altmann, A., 86
Amulets, causation and, 106–107, 111
Anatomy
    Maimonides' knowledge of, 60
    menstrual impurity and, 99
Anger, 139, 172
Animality, sexuality and, 36
Animals, religion and, 140–142
Aphorisms, 6–7, 16, 20, 22–23, 28, 44, 146–147

Architecture, 187–188
Aristarchus, 152, 160
Aristotle, 3, 14, 15, 19, 21, 25, 28, 53–55, 68, 69, 71, 76, 78–79, 80, 81, 91, 92, 93, 94, 95, 109, 119, 121–125, 145, 147, 148, 150, 153, 156, 158–159, 160, 161, 179, 195
Art, 187–188
Asaf the Sage, 15
Asthma, 8–9, 29, 30–31
    medical profession and, 193
    mental health and, 49
Astrology, 77–90
    Maimonides rejects, 84–90
    medieval science and, 77–84
Astronomy
    astrology and, 78, 83–84, 86, 89
    causation and, 109–110
    cosmology and, 159, 160–161
    formalistic/realistic approaches to, 95
    Jewish calendar and, 98–99
    medieval Jewish philosophy and, 72–73
Authoritarianism, Maimonides opposes, 207–213

Avicenna, 13, 14, 150
Azulai, C. J. D., 112, 182

Babad, J., 198
Bacher, W., 178
Baneth, 177
Bar Sela, A., 6, 11
Barukh of Sklov, 98
Barzel, U. S., 5, 59–63
Bioethics, Maimonides and, 205
Biological needs. *See* Needs
Bleich, J. D., 105–115
Bloch, S., 10
Blood vessels, medical treatment and, 60, 61
Body/soul dichotomy, perfection and, 28. *See also* Mind/body dichotomy
Boie, H. C., 180
Bone fracture, medical treatment of, 62
Bragman, L. J., 7, 10, 11
Broadie, A., 119–126
Bulka, R. P., 135–143
Butterworth, C. E., 11
Byzantium, 15

Calendar. *See* Jewish calendar
Capital punishment. *See* Death penalty
Carmoly, E., 217
Case history, Maimonides and, 41–48
Causation
  astrology and, 78–79
  cosmology and, 164
  dietary laws and, 129
  Maimonides on, 105–115
Chance, cosmology and, 161–162
Charlatanry, Arabic medicine and, 224–225
Chasles, M., 219
Christianity, Arabic medicine and, 221
City air, 9
Classification. *See* Nosology
Climate, asthma and, 9
Climatology, astrology and, 83–84
Clubbing of fingers, 7
Cohen of Dvinsk, M. S., 200–202, 203
Coincidence, cosmology and, 161–162
Conversion, authoritarianism and, 208

Copernicus, 152, 160
Cosmology, 151–165
  astrology and, 90
  chance/order, 161–162
  Kalàm and, 154–157
  Maimonides on, 161
  medieval Jewish philosophy and, 71–75
  primal cause, 157–161
  puzzle-solving, 151–152
  unifying intent, 163–165
Craftsmanship, medicine and, 18, 19
Creation
  astrology and, 90
  cosmology and, 162
  Gershom, Levi ben and, 91–92
  Maimonides on, 21–22
  mean and, 122
  medieval Jewish philosophy and, 71–75
  primal cause, 157–161
Crusades, 4
Culture, Greek influence on Jewish culture, 23–24
Cure-all book, 189–196

Daud, A. ibn, 146
Davidowitz, H. S., 177, 178
Death penalty, 52–53, 197–198
Decadence. *See* Vice
Depression. *See* Mental health
Descarte, R., 163, 164, 211
Determinism, astrology and, 86–87
Dethier, H., 151–165
Developmental factors
  mental health, 55–56
  psychology and, 140
Deviancy, psychology and, 135–136
Diabetes mellitus, 6–7
Diagnosis, case history, 43
Dienstag, J. I., 11, 185–188
Diet, 9, 10
Dietary laws
  causation and, 106
  Maimonides on, 127–133
  rabies, causation and, 107–108
Dietrich, A., 218
Dioscorides, 17

Index

Disease. *See also* Health; Mental health
  equilibrium and medical treatment, 60
  ethics and, 119–120
  prayer and, 112
Divorce, psychology and, 141
Doctrine of mean. *See* Mean
Dog bite, 9–10
Dohn, C. W., 180
Drugs (nonprescription), 10
Drugs (prescription), 11, 17
  medical treatment, 63
  nihilism and, 211
Duhem, P., 95

Edelman, Z. H., 181, 182
Edelstein, 149
Education, medical ethics and, 27
Efrâîm, Nethan'el ben, 215–229
Eisenman, D. J., 145–150
Eleazar, J. ben, 178
Emphysema, 7
Equilibrium, medical treatment and, 60
Eroticism, sexuality and, 37–39
Eruvin, geometry and, 100
Ethics
  bioethics, Maimonides and, 205
  feticide and abortion, 202–205
  Galen and, 27
  Hippocratic Oath, 23
  medical categories and, 119–126
  medicine and, 149, 150
  mental health and, 53–55
  mercy killing, 197–200
  sexuality and, 35
Euthanasia, homicide and, 112–113
Evil. *See* Good/evil dichotomy
Ezra, Abraham Ibn, 86, 178

Fadil, Al-Malik al-, 49, 57, 210
Fähndrich, H., 219
False. *See* True/false dichotomy
Farabi, Al-, 3, 28
Faris, E., 11
Fatalism, astrology and, 86–87
Febrile disease, medical treatment of, 62
Feinstein, M., 204
Fenton, P. B., 41, 215–229

Feticide, 202–205
Fichte, J. G., 164
Fits. *See* Seizures
Fox, M., 213
Fracture of bone, medical treatment and, 62
Frankl, V., 135
Frede, M., 149
Free will
  cosmology and, 155, 161
  good/evil dichotomy and, 137–138, 142–143
Freudenthal, G., 77–90
Friedenwald, H., 210
Fundamentalism
  authoritarianism and, 208–209
  messianism, 209–210

Galen, 3, 5, 6, 10, 14, 15, 16, 17, 18, 19, 20, 21, 22–23, 26, 27, 28, 29, 59, 61, 83, 91, 92, 94, 147, 148, 162, 176, 191, 192, 193, 194, 211, 221, 222, 226, 228
Gaon, S., 97
Gellman, Y., 189–196
Geometry, *halakhah* and, 100
Gershom, Levi ben
  astronomy and, 89–90
  creation and, 91–92
  Maimonides compared, 94–96
Gersonides. *See* Gershom, Levi ben
Ghazali, al-, 164
Gikatila, J., 177
Glick, S. M., 211
God. *See also* Religion; Theology
  apprehension of, 148
  Arabic medicine, 220
  Aristotle and, 68
  astrology and, 80, 90
  cosmology and, 162
  dichotomy and, 150
  good/evil dichotomy and, 137–138
  health and, 189–190
  hygiene and, 101
  Kalàm and, 154–157
  mean and, 122–123
  medieval Jewish philosophy and, 69, 73–74

God (*continued*)
  mental health and, 55–56, 171
  philosophy and, 153
  primal cause, 157–161
  progress and, 94
  pseudo-Maimonidean treatises, 175–179
  psychology and, 142–143
  science and, 100–101
  theory of attributes and, 95–96
Golden mean. *See* Mean
Good/evil dichotomy
  God and, 137–138, 142–143
  individual and, 194
  philosophy and, 136–137
  psychology and, 139
Goodman, L. E., 162, 163
Gordon, H. L., 11
Greek medicine. *See also* Hippocrates
  Arabic medicine and, 220–221
  Arabic works on, 14
  commentaries on Galen, 19
  Galen and, 15
  professionalization and, 18
Grossberg, M., 179
Čumayʻ, Ibn, 215–229
Guthrie, W. K. C., 145

Habib, Maharam ben, 111
Hacohen, M., 207
HaKohen of Lunel, Y., 98
Halakhah. *See also* Law
  causation and, 106, 111
  geometry and, 100
  mental health and, 50–52, 168–169
  progress and, 94
HaLevi, E., 98
Halevi, S. B. A., 208
Halevi, Y., 83
Hallucination, 189, 192, 194, 196
Hartman, D., 209
Harvey, W. Z., 33–39
Hasida, M. Z., 6
Haupt, P., 210
Health. *See also* Disease; Mental health
  current and future scholarship, 186–187
  dietary laws and, 127–133

  ethics and, 119–126
  God and, 189–190
  mental health, 167–172
  pseudo-Maimonidean treatises, 176, 179–180
  psychology and, 140
Hegel, G. F. W., 164
Hemorrhage, medical treatment of, 62
Hemorrhoids, 7–8
Hepatitis, 7
Heresh, Mattia ben, 107, 108
Herz, M., 175, 180
Heschel, A. J., 147, 209
Hillel, 125
Hippocrates, 3, 5–6, 10, 14–15, 18, 26, 28, 29, 81, 83, 148, 221, 227, 228
Hippocratic Oath, 23
Hiyya, Abraham Bar, 86
Hoff, H. E., 6, 11
Holistic approach, mental health, 167–168
Homicide
  euthanasia and, 112–113
  feticide and abortion, 202–205
  mercy killing, 197–200
  natural law and, 200–202
Hospitals, development of, 18
Humanism, Maimonides on, 24
Hume, D., 163, 164
Humor theory of disease
  astrology and, 81
  equilibrium and medical treatment, 60
  individual differences and, 81–82
Hygiene, 10, 101

Idolatry, psychology and, 142
Incantation, causation and, 107
Individual differences
  evil and, 194
  Maimonides on, 81–82
  Torah and medical profession, 190–191
Insanity. *See* Mental health
Insect stings, 9–10, 17
Intellect
  cosmology and, 159
  progression of life and, 140

psychology and, 139
religion and, 136–137
Intestines, medical treatment and, 61–62
Irony, 164
Isaacs, H. D., 41–48
Islam
  fundamentalism, 208–209
  medical profession and, 215–229
  religious medical precepts and, 16

Jacob of Kiev, Moshe ben, 182
Jaeger, W., 148, 149, 150
Jewish calendar, astronomy and, 98–99
Joseph ben Eleazar, 178

Kabbalism, pseudo-Maimonidean
    treatises, 177, 178, 181
Kahira, S., 212
Kalàm theologians, 70, 105, 154–157
Kant, I., 163–164
Kasher, H., 127–133
Kaufmann, D., 183
Kellner, M., 91–96
Kilayim, geometry and, 100
Kimhi, I., 146
Kluger, S., 112
Knowledge
  classification of, 145
  good/evil dichotomy and, 136–137
  theory of attributes and, 96
Kottek, S. S., 25–32
Kranzler, H. N., 49–57
Kraus, P., 218
Krieger, J. A., 181
Kroner, H., 7, 11, 180
Kuhn, T., 151, 152, 153–154

Landau, E., 198
Law. *See also* Halakhah
  authoritarianism and, 207–213
  feticide and abortion, 202–205
  homicide and natural law, 200–202
  mean and, 122–123
  mental health, halakhic perspective,
    50–52
  mercy killing, 197–200
  psychology and, 210–211
  science and, 93

Laymen, medical interest of, 16
Leibniz, G. W., 164
Leibowitz, J. O., xvii, 11
Levi, Y., 97–104
Levi ben Gershom. *See* Gershom, Levi
    ben
Liberality, health and, 120
Licentiousness. *See* Vice
Lieber, E., 13–24
Liver, hepatitis, 7
Logic, knowledge and, 145–146
Love, psychology and, 143
Lull, R., 179
Lung disease. *See* Pulmonary disease
Lust. *See* Vice

Maimon, J. L., 176
Maimonides
  birth of, 3
  death of, 5, 12
  education of, 3
  family life of, 4
  works of, 5
Marcus, S., 11
Margalith, D., 181
Marriage, psychology and, 140
Maslow, A. H., 140
Mattia ben Heresh, 107, 108
Mayerhof, Max, 11
Mean
  health and, 120
  mental health and, 53–55, 168–172
  psychology and, 138–140
  rabbinic quality of, 122
Medical ethics. *See* Ethics
Medical profession
  classification of sciences and,
    146–150
  development of, 17–18
  ethics and, 149–150
  God and, 189–190
  Islam and, 215–229
  superiority of, 130
  terminal illness, 197–200
  Torah and, 190
Medicine. *See* Health
Meiri, M., 197, 198
Menstrual impurity, anatomy and, 99

Mental health, 49–57, 167–172. *See also* Disease; Health; Psychology
  developmental perspective, 55–56
  ethical and philosophical perspective, 53–55
  halakhic perspective, 50–52
  historical perspective, 49–50
  holistic approach, 167–168
  law and, 210–211
  mean and, 168–172
  nosological perspective, 52–53
  physicians role and, 56–57
Mercy killing, terminal illness, 197–200
Messianism
  fundamentalism, 209–210
  pseudo-Maimonidean treatises, 182–183
Metaphysics
  Galen and, 191
  medicine and, 148–149
Meyerhof, M., 218
Mind/body dichotomy
  cosmology and, 163
  holism and, 167–168
  science and, 211
Minkin, J., 181
Miserliness, health and, 120
Mizrachi, E., 98
Modesty, perfection and, 30–31
Monotheism
  cosmology and, 156
  pseudo-Maimonidean treatises, 175–179
  psychology and, 142
Moshe ben Jacob of Kiev, 182
Mulk, Al-Said al, 211
Muntner, S., 6, 7–8, 9, 11, 180
Music, religion and, 16–17

Nachmanides, 110–111, 131, 132, 189
Narboni, Moshe, 81
Natural law
  homicide and, 200–202
  medical profession and, 192
  medieval Jewish philosophy and, 69, 74–75
Natural science
  medicine and, 17–18
  origin of knowledge and, 102–103
  Torah and, 102
Needs
  psychology and, 140
  sexuality and, 33–39
Nestorian school, 15
Nethan'el ben Efrâîm, 215–229
Neubauer, A., 182, 183
Neugebauer, O., 188
Newton, I., 164, 188
Nihilism, 164, 211
Noah, N., 219
Nosology
  medical profession, 146–150
  mental health, 52–53

Optics, *Sukkah* and, 99
Order, cosmology and, 161–162
Oreopoulos, L. G., 211
Oribasius, 222
Osler, W., 28

Paganism, medical knowledge and, 15, 21
Paradigm, cosmology and, 152
Parmenides, 159, 161
Passover, causation and, 106
Paulus of Aegina, 222
Perfection
  Arabic medicine, 220, 227–228
  body/soul dichotomy and, 28
  Greek notion of, 25
  Hebrew notion of, 26
  Maimonides/Galen compared, 27
  medical knowledge and, 26–27
  modesty and, 30–31
  pretense to, 29–30
  psychology and, 138
  science and, 101
  way of, 28–29
Perrault, C., 188
Philoponus, 162
Philosophy
  astrology and, 89
  causation and, 106
  classification and, 145–146
  current and future scholarship, 185–186

ethics and, 149
God and, 153
medicine and, 17–18
medieval Jewish, 67–68
mental health and, 53–55
primal cause, 157–161
psychology and, 136
science and, 69–75
Phlebotomy, medical treatment of, 63
Physics
cosmology and, 159
Maimonides on, 148
Pines, S., 86, 190, 193
Plato, 95, 147, 150, 156, 157, 164, 176
Poetry, cosmology and, 164
Poisons, 9–10, 17
Polak, G., 176
Prayer, disease and, 112
Pride, perfection, pretense to, 29–30
Primal cause, cosmology, 157–161
Probability theory, redemption of firstborn and, 99–100
Proclus, 159, 161
Professionalization. *See* Medical profession
Progress
Maimonides view of, 92–94
science and, 92
Provencali, Y., 97
Pseudo-Maimonidean treatises, 175–184
Pseudoscience, science contrasted, 105–115
Psychology, 135–143. *See also* Mental health
animals and, 140–142
free will and, 137–138
goals of, 135–136
law and, 210–211
love and, 143
mean and, 138–140
mental health, 167–172
Psychosomatic illness, asthma, 49
Ptolemy, 72, 95, 160
Pulmonary disease, 7
Pulse rate, case history, 43, 44

Rabbinowicz, I. M., 10
Rabies, causation and, 107–108, 114

Rabinovitch, N. L., 67–76
Rapoport, S., 176
Rashi (Shlomo Yitzhaqi), 189
Reason, science and, 152
Redemption of firstborn, probability theory and, 99–100
Regimen, 10–11, 16
medicine and, 149–150
mental health and, 49
sexuality and, 33
Reich, M., 167–172
Religion. *See also* God; Theology
Arabic medicine, 220
astrology and, 79–80
authoritarianism and, 207–213
current and future scholarship, 185–186
Galen and, 21
Kalàm and, 154–157
Maimonides introduces into medicine, 16, 21
mean and, 122–123
medieval Jewish philosophy and, 67–69
mental health and, 55–56, 171
progress and, 94
science and, 97–104
sexuality and, 36–39
theory of attributes and, 95–96
Repentance, mental health and, 170
Returnees, Torah and, 143
Revelation, cosmology and, 162
Rhazes of Persia, 3, 18, 19, 44, 226–227
Richard the Lion-Hearted, 4
Richler, B., 179
Rosenau, H., 188
Rosner, F., 3–12, 175–184
Rufus of Samaria, 14
Rules, puzzle-solving and, 152

Sabbath, geometry and, 100
Sages
rabies, causation and, 107–108
science and, 93
Saladin the Great, 4, 8, 10, 15, 209, 227
Samuel Ibn Tibbon. *See* Tibbon, Samuel Ibn
Sasoon, Musa ibn Alfadil Yusuf Ibn, 59

Savitz, H., 11
Schelling, F. W. J. von, 164
Schmiedl, A., 178
Science
   astrology, medieval science and, 77–84
   classifications of, 145–146
   cosmology and, 159
   current and future scholarship, 187
   God and, 100–101
   law and, 93
   Maimonides view of, 92–94
   medieval Jewish philosophy and, 69–75
   mind/body dichotomy and, 211
   origin of knowledge and, 102–103
   philosophy and, 153–154
   progress and, 92
   pseudoscience contrasted, 105–115
   reason and, 152
   religion and, 97–104
   self-perfection and, 101
   Torah and, 97
Scorpion stings, 17
Seizures, 11
Self-incrimination, 52–53
Self-perfection, science and, 101
Sexual intercourse, 8
Sexuality, 33–39, 172
Shalem, 26
Shilat, Y., 182
Sickness. *See* Disease
Sinclair, D. B., 197–205
Skoss, S. L., 11
Slaves, medical care provided by, 18
Snake bite, 9–10, 17
Socrates, 164
Sofer, C., 112
Soffer, A., 207–213
Sorcery. *See* Witchcraft
Soul
   astrology and, 81
   body/soul dichotomy, perfection and, 28
   dietary laws and, 127–133
   health and, 120
   mental health and, 55. *See also* Mental health

Spinoza, B., 163, 164
Steinschneider, M., 6, 10, 176, 178, 180
Stings, 9–10
Strauss, L., 150
Sukkah, optics and, 99

Tay-Sachs syndrome, 204
Teaching, doctrine of mean and, 122
Temperament. *See* Individual differences
Terminal illness, 197–200
Theology. *See also* God; Religion
   authoritarianism and, 212
   current and future scholarship, 185–186
   medical knowledge and, 15
Theory of attributes, religion and, 95–96
Thulborn, T., 207
Tibbon, Samuel Ibn, 4, 6, 10, 41, 108, 114, 115, 190
Torah
   dietary laws and, 127–133
   health and, 140
   medical profession and, 190–191
   psychology and, 141, 142
   returnees and, 143
   science and, 93, 97–104
Touati, C., 90
Treatment, 59–63
   case history, 43
   nonnatural remedies, 113
   psychology and, 138
   rabies, 107–108, 114
   religion and, 16–17
True/false dichotomy, philosophy and, 136–137

Urine, case history, 43–44
Uṣaybi'a, Ibn Abî, 216

Vajda, G., 177
Veil, L. de C. de, 188
Vice
   Arabic medicine, 219
   Aristotle and, 125
   dietary laws and, 131
   health and, 120, 121

Virtue
   dietary laws and, 129, 130–131
   mean and, 125–126

Waldenburg, E., 204
Weil, J., 188
Whitehead, A. N., 150
Winternitz, D., 10–11
Wischnitzer, R., 188
Witchcraft, Maimonides rejects, 111

Women, sexuality and, 35
Word strings, 190

Xenophon, 147

Yagal, A., 180
Yephet ha-Dayyan, 50

Zabara, 176
Zaks, 176
Zhur, Ibn, 3

About the Editors

Dr. Fred Rosner is a respected hematologist and renowned medical ethicist. He is director of the Department of Medicine at Mount Sinai Services at Queens Hospital Center, Jamaica, New York, and professor of medicine at the Mount Sinai School of Medicine, New York, New York. Dr. Rosner is the author, editor, or translator of many works, including *Medicine and Jewish Law*, *The Existence and Unity of God*, and *Six Treatises Attributed to Maimonides*.

Samuel S. Kottek is professor of the history of medicine at the Hebrew University–Hadassah Medical School, Jerusalem, as well as Secretary of the Israeli Society of the History of Medicine. The recipient of the 1989 Einhorn Prize for research in medical literature, Dr. Kottek has published over 160 papers. He was also the editor of acts of three symposia on medicine in the Bible and Talmud, and he is the associate editor of the journal *Korot*, devoted to the history of medicine and science, with special emphasis on Jewish aspects.